THE CARPET WARS

Christopher Kremmer

THE CARPET WARS

From Kabul to Baghdad:

A Ten-Year Journey

Along Ancient Trade Routes

An Imprint of HarperCollins*Publishers*

Permission to quote from *The Road to Oxiana* kindly granted by Peters Fraser Dunlop Group Limited on behalf of Robert Byron © copyright Robert Byron 1933; permission to quote from *Foundations of Islam* by Benjamin Walker kindly granted by Peter Owen Ltd, London; Permission to quote from *Central Asia,* edition 1 © copyright 1996, kindly granted by Lonely Planet Publications; permission to quote from *Oriental Carpets* by Volkmar Gantzhorn kindly granted by Volkmar Gantzhorn; permission to quote from *To the Frontier* by Geoffrey Moorhouse kindly granted by Gillon Aitken Associates; permission to quote from *Oriental Rugs: A Complete Guide* by Charles W. Jacobsen kindly granted by Charles E. Tuttle Co., Inc.

Internal carpet details generously provided by Bill Evans, Caspian Gallery,
    Sydney, Australia
Internal design by Katie Mitchell, HarperCollins Design Studio, Australia
Map design by Luke Causby, HarperCollins Design Studio, Australia
Internal photography (on stock) by George Fetting, Andrew Meares,
    Christopher Kremmer and Bill Evans

HarperCollins books may be purchased for educational, business, or sales promotional use. For information, please write: Special Markets Department, HarperCollins Publishers Inc., 10 East 53rd Street, New York, NY 10022.

First published in Australia in 2002 by HarperCollins Publishers Pty Limited.

FIRST AMERICAN EDITION

Printed on acid-free paper

Library of Congress Cataloging-in-Publication Data is available upon request.

ISBN 0-06-009732-9

02 03 04 05 06 ❖/QF 10 9 8 7 6 5 4 3 2 1

To Janaki

CONTENTS

Acknowledgments

Prior to this book even being conceived, I was indebted to a vast tribe of fellow writers, photojournalists, diplomats, aid workers, academics, United Nations staffers, officials of various governments, and, of course, carpet people. Serendipitous meetings produced many friendships and favours. Sadly not all of them can be acknowledged here, but I would like to express my gratitude to the following for their help, friendship and advice over the years: Syed Nasir Abbas Zaidi, Ghulam Rasoul Ahmadi, Ahmed Rashid, Jenny and David Housego, Brian Cloughley, Kathy Gannon, Khaled Mansour, Yolanda Hogencamp, Mike Sackett, Nancy Hatch Dupree, Gulam Nabi Butt, John Jennings, Steve Levine, Robert Adams, Tariq Zuberi, William Maley, Mufti Jamiluddin Ahmed, Masood Khalili, Mervyn Patterson, Ruth Harbinson-Gresham, Andrew Wilder, Mukhtar Ahmad, Robert Nickelsberg, Phil Goodwin, Ahmed Muslim, Fiaz Shah, Allan Brimalow, Jolyon Leslie, Hashmatullah Moslih, Geoff Kitney, Charles McFadden, Dinesh Kumar, Salah al-Mukhtar, Hossain Payghambary, David Windsor, Tim and Jan McGirk, Gordon Matthews, Milan Brezny and Bill Evans of Caspian Gallery in Sydney, Inderjit Singh Virdi, Rajdeep Sardesai and Sagarika Ghose, the late Bill Berquist, Cito and Lyn Cessna of Parkham Place Gallery in Sydney, Rupert and Sarah Colville, Geoff Brooks, Hillary Riggs, Sidney Petersen, Stephanie Bunker, Amanullah Khan, Hamish and Penny McDonald, Robin Jeffrey, James De Siun, Jonathan Harley, Dexter Filkins, Naseerullah Babar, Ian MacKinnon, Amitabh Mattoo, Ian Bulpitt, George Fetting, Christophe de Neuville, Rashid Qureshi, Ravi Nair, Saulat Raza, Andrew Meares, Rahimullah Yusufzai, Wahid Baman, Tim Hargreaves, Robert Marquand, Zahed Hussain, Zaheeruddin

Abdullah, Zaffar Abbas, Hannah Bloch, Cameron Barr, Gulam Rasull Khan, Robert Templer, Mirwais Umer Farooq, John Sharpe, Professor Hamid Algar, Earleen Fisher and Eric Fournier. To those others who for reasons of privacy cannot be named, your help is no less appreciated.

Sanjay Jha laboured conscientiously to transcribe hours of rambling dictaphone notations, and remained ever-energetic and cheerful. At HarperCollins my thanks goes in particular to publishing director Shona Martyn, as well as associate publisher Helen Littleton, senior editor Jesse Fink, senior designer Katie Mitchell, senior typesetter Graeme Jones, freelance typesetters Helen Beard, Rod Mercier and Kim Short, freelance proofreaders Rodney Stuart and Annabel Adair, freelance editor Devon Mills and freelance indexer Madeleine Davis. The professionalism and friendship of my agent Garth Nix was invaluable, as were the resources of several great libraries, including the State Library of New South Wales, the private collections of Krishen Bans, Maya Bahadur and Bill Evans, the Institute for Regional Studies in Islamabad, and the Carpet Museum in Tehran. Ludwig W. Adamec's *Historical Dictionary of Afghanistan* is an enduring treasure.

A portion of the royalties from this book go to the Society for the Preservation of Afghanistan's Cultural Heritage. Anyone wishing to support SPACH can contact them by writing to Nancy Hatch Dupree (ARIC), University Post Office Box 1084, Peshawar, Pakistan or email them at aric@brain.net.pk.

I especially wish to acknowledge a debt of gratitude owed to several friends and colleagues who paid the ultimate price for informing the world about the situation in Afghanistan. Natasha Singh, Mirwais Jalil, Azizullah Haideri and Sharon Herbaugh live eternal in our fond memory.

Finally to my wife Janaki, her family, and to Marlene, Ted and Melissa Kremmer, thanks for your support over the years of living, travelling and researching the 'wars'.

Author's Note

Long before 11 September 2001, when terrorism shook America, terror had been the lot of the people of Islamic West Asia. For more than two decades, war, dictatorship and economic hardship have stunted their lives, and the lives of their children. Generally the despots and militias responsible for this have been homegrown, but at various stages they have been aided and abetted by Western governments.

This book took shape over a decade of work in Afghanistan, Pakistan, Kashmir, Iran, Iraq, and the Central Asian republics, at a time when events in much of the region were of little concern to most people elsewhere. Since the attacks on New York and Washington, many have realised that a crisis, even in a remote corner of the world like Afghanistan, can precipitate disaster at home. Understanding the causes and effects of injustice in Muslim societies has become critical to the restoration of our own security. The carpet business might seem a curious place to seek such understanding, but as the region's largest export industry outside oil, those involved in the trade have borne the brunt of disorder. In any case, I present Muslim society here as I found it; it is a personal portrait of a different world in which many of my friends and interlocutors made or sold rugs. The encounters that provided the raw material for this book generally appear here in chronological order, albeit at times heavily compressed. In a few cases I have relocated a character or altered the sequence of events for narrative convenience. Where disclosure of any individual's identity might have posed a risk to them I have used pseudonyms and altered details which might identify them. The transliteration of foreign words — a source of much confusion and frustration — is based on personal preference, there being no general authority on the matter, and all dollar figures are in US dollars for consistency. Finally, adhering to the principle that a writer must protect his sources, the names of all the carpet dealers have been changed.

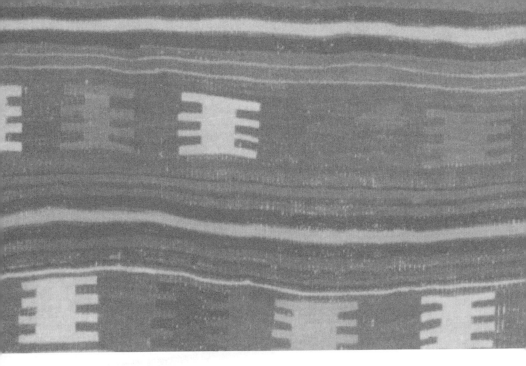

He who wars against the arts,
wars not against nations,
but against all mankind

— ARTHUR URBANE DILLEY

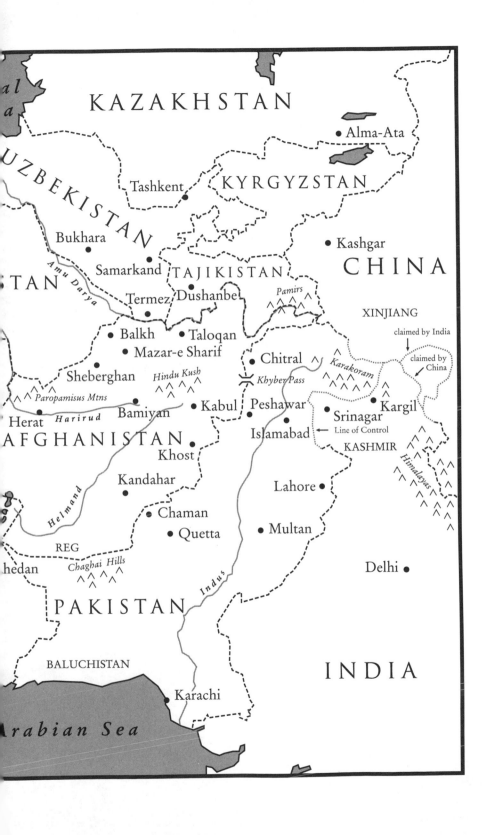

PART ONE

KABUL

1

✦

The Rug Merchant of Kabul

I will open thee a merchant's store, furnished with the costliest stuffs,
and thou shalt become famous amongst the folk, and take and give,
and buy and sell, and be well known in the city

— THE ARABIAN NIGHTS' ENTERTAINMENTS

'*As'salaam aleikum,*' he said — 'peace be upon you' — and there it was, in a country at war, in the musty air of Tariq Ahmed's humble shop. Peace.

'Come in, come in,' he beckoned, hand on his heart, a disembodied grin emerging from the gloom at the rear of the shop, followed by the eyes, which also smiled. 'This is your home.'

My 'home' was a feeble shopfront on Jade Idgah in Kabul's main rug bazaar. Assembled from matchstick timber and toffee glass, it looked ready to collapse with the sound of the next car horn. It was mid-afternoon in high summer, a sedate time of day. Running a meaty hand over his polished skull, Tariq stifled a yawn, smiling again, unable to credit it. There were so few customers these days. Seeing his stockinged feet, I slipped off my shoes and entered.

'You will take green tea,' he said, and before I could refuse produced an old, glazed teapot with gossamer cracks and held out a pair of finger cups and tiny carpet coasters. Hard green nuggets of tea tumbled from a brown paper bag, landing in the pot with a tinkle. The naked wires of the electric kettle flashed as he poked them into the power point, and a hissing sound soon filled the room. Rolled-up rugs lined the walls, insular and secret. But knowing them well, Tariq was more interested in unravelling me. What was my name? My country? Was I married? Did I have children? Satisfied with my answers, he rose from the floor and unfurled a rug, releasing a flurry of dust particles that danced in a narrow shaft of light streaming through a crack in the ceiling.

'Baluchi!' he declared, with a smile that said 'yes, it's true', adding, in case I didn't know, 'Made by nomad tribes. Desert people.'

The claret red and celestial blue wool hung lankly from Tariq's hands, presenting a galaxy of eight-pointed stars bordered by brilliant dots in ivory and yellow. Like a matador tempting a bull to charge, he turned the rug slightly left and right, highlighting its lustre.

'This is from my city, Herat,' he said, with a quick intake of breath. 'The nomad people come from the mountains to the bazaar, and sell these carpets there.'

Herat was a storied city of poets, architects and weavers, tucked beneath the wing of the Paropamisus Mountains, Afghanistan's defence against Central Asia's rampaging hordes. Still, the city had changed hands countless times over the centuries, falling to Genghis Khan and Russia's Red Army, instilling in its people a blend of Afghan honour and Persian charm. The history of the Baluchis was unwritten. Illiterate shepherds, legend claimed they came from the Taurus Mountains near the eastern Mediterranean, but had been shunted south-east from the Euphrates River by various conquerors until reaching the Indus River in about the fourteenth century. Unable to carve out a homeland for themselves, the six million-strong Baluchis were split between Iran, whose Persian language they spoke, and Afghanistan and Pakistan, whose Sunni Islam they shared. They occupied the arid regions between the Arabian Sea and Central Asia. I didn't know it then, but Baluchi was a label dealers gave to the weavings of a wide range of people in western Afghanistan, Iran and Pakistan.

Folding the rug and pressing it under his arm, Tariq demonstrated how the wool sprang back, eliminating the crease. Flipping it over, he ran a nail along its hard, ridged back, producing a scratching sound that put my teeth on edge, but which he appreciated like music. He could *hear* the knots, two hundred and forty to the square inch, he said, counting with the tip of his thumb amid a flutter of whispered computations. Turning it over again, he went down on all fours, poring through the pile as if searching for fleas on a dog, so absorbed that he quite forgot my presence. It was the provenance he was seeking, buried in the structure, not in its superficial design.

For the rest of that afternoon Tariq guided me through his nation of rugs. There were lush, silky carpets, sandpaper-stiff *kilims* and hermaphrodite combinations of both; Turkmens, Persians and Caucasians, some fringed in the finest wool, others in coarse goat hair. They came in a bewildering array of shapes and sizes, pillow-sized *mafrash,* long-distance runners, square *suzani* embroideries and thin flatweaves. The shepherd of this matted flock tutored me in the clarity and fidelity of dyes. Carpets, he said, were over four square metres, mats less than half that, and rugs were in between. But as the day wore on, the conversation broadened like a river of tea, coursing through the life and times of the rug merchant of Kabul.

At that time, Tariq Ahmed was in his late thirties, a Persian-speaking Tajik who, like most men in cosmopolitan Kabul, wore slacks and a business shirt, not the baggy pants and flowing overshirt known as *salwar kameez*. Although in a minority, the Tajiks formed the backbone of Afghanistan's small middle class, but Tariq had come up the hard way. The son of a cobbler, he was orphaned at an early age when his father drowned in the main river of western Afghanistan, the Hari Rud. His widowed mother was soon remarried to a confectioner who disdained his adopted son. One day, during the festival of *Eid ul-Fitr* marking the end of the fasting month of *Ramadan*, when demand for sweets is high, he had sent the boy to fetch a bag of rice from the market. Too young, and in the excitement of Eid and his first errand, Tariq lost the rice.

'He told my mother, "Your son has lost the rice", and he slapped her very hard,' Tariq recalled, suddenly bitter. 'He wanted money from her and she was crying, "How can I get you money?" So he opened a box of her clothes, took some pieces and said, "I will sell these to pay for the rice."'

Raised by his grandmother, who took in washing and shelled nuts to buy him pencils and books, Tariq sold fruit in the bazaar, where he discovered his true calling. At certain times of the year nomads would come into Herat from their camps in the mountains, their camels loaded down with carpets and trappings. They were loud, rough people, and the women bared their faces and sewed coins into their vividly coloured clothes. But their traditional weavings were popular with foreigners, who in those days would pass through Herat on overland tours, like gypsies themselves, travelling in camper vans and double-decker buses. One day, with the money he earned from his fruit basket, Tariq — not yet ten — bought a small *namak dan*, or salt bag, and sold it, using the profit he made to buy two more, and a *galeen firush*, or carpet seller, was born. An uncle later took him to Kabul where he sold door-to-door on commission. Conscripted into the army, he bribed his commander to let him continue trading in his spare time. Years passed and slowly Tariq accumulated enough money to buy the worst shop in the bazaar and to marry his cousin, Nazreen, who bore him two daughters. On the hill in Karte Parwan, overlooking Kabul, he had built a sprawling residence in stages as funds allowed, a potent symbol of his arrival as a merchant in the capital.

Reclining like a sultan, I had lost track of time, and the light outside was grey. I felt I should purchase something to make good for time wasted, but had little spare cash for souvenirs. It was 1991, and Kabul was besieged by Muslim rebels fighting the Moscow-backed government; it was also under economic embargo by the West. It wasn't as if I could pay by cheque, or at least I didn't think so.

'You don't like my carpets,' Tariq said, his smile crumbling, but when I explained the situation, it shone again. 'Ohhh, no problem,' he said. 'There are moneychangers in the bazaar with satellite telephones. They have accounts with Barclays Bank of London. They will accept your personal cheque and give me the money.'

'But what if the cheque bounced?' I asked, astonished by his trust.

'Our Prophet Mohammed, peace be upon him, said that even martyrdom will not atone for an unpaid debt.'

'But I'm not a Muslim.'

'No, but our God and your God are one. You are *ahl al-kitab* — people of the book. *Insh'allah*, God willing, you will not pay me with a bad cheque.'

In all the tossing and turning a dusky beauty had caught my eye, a small prayer rug that Tariq called a *Cowdani*. The Cowdani were a sub-tribe living in western Afghanistan. Their carpets were among the best weavings from the region around Herat, Tariq said, and old pieces were much sought after by collectors in the bazaar in Mashhad in neighbouring Iran, where most of their production sold. The centrepiece of Tariq's Cowdani was a ruthlessly geometric *mihrab*, the carpet equivalent of the niche in mosque walls facing Mecca. Like a fat paddle, this motif ran two-thirds of the rug's length, then jagged inwards at ninety degrees before continuing to the end. Inside it, the artisan had woven a 'tree of life', the ancient symbol which for Muslims represents the Garden of Paradise, but which for Jews and Christians is the Tree of the Knowledge of Good and Evil that bore the fruit consumed by Adam and Eve. Yet this tree was incredibly abstract with uniform leaves, thicker than its trunk, shaped like angular Maltese crosses and flanked by strange, crablike figures. Its singular design resembled a bold exclamation mark proclaiming 'One God'. The mihrab radiated outwards, amplified twenty times by borders of extreme intricacy separated by lines of white dots. The pile had been closely cropped to within a tenth of an inch and the knotting was so fine that the fabric crumpled like a handkerchief. Finally there were the colours: burgundy, burnt peach and, in the field, undyed camel wool glowing like dark olive oil.

I had been told that you must bargain — the vendors expected it and factored the markdown into their prices — but after a few awkward stabs I settled for a modest discount. Taking my cheque, Tariq handed me two receipts printed on pink tissue paper. One, to be presented to Customs, underestimated the price at $150. The other, to be shown to any future buyer, exaggerated it at $800. The rug merchant of Kabul had taught me my first trick of the trade. I had gone to the bazaar in search of gossip and ended up with a carpet instead.

Next day, I was supposed to be meeting the country's president, and I wanted to know what ordinary Kabulis thought of him. Mohammed Najibullah was the leader the departing Soviet Army had left behind, the last man standing between the *mujahideen* and Kabul.

'In Afghanistan we have a story about a man and a snake,' Tariq said slowly, as the kettle started to hiss again for one last pot of tea. 'The man is disturbed from his sleep, and when he wakes up he sees a snake leaving his bedroom, and escaping into the street. The next night he cannot sleep, and again the night after that. So, without sleep, he loses his health and his business is also finished. His friends ask, "Why you are not sleeping? The snake is gone from your house." But the man shakes his head and he tells the people, "How can I sleep? My house has become the road of the snake."'

His last tale told, Tariq began digging around in a small cupboard, emerging with a small box in his hand.

'Please accept this little present,' he said.

'*Tashakour*,' I heard myself reply.

It was a curio of beaten white metal, a *baz-o-band*, or octagonal box with two smaller metal tubes linked to it on either side. Afghans are fervent believers in charms, and these small boxes are used for keeping spells written on scraps of paper by descendants of the Prophet known as Sayyids.

'*Insh'allah*, you will come back to Kabul,' Tariq said. 'Some day, when the war is finished, I will show you God's country. The blue lakes of Band-e Amir, the Buddha statues of Bamiyan; maybe, if we have time, the Minaret of Jam.'

They were legendary places, the kind you remember from books. Limestone deposits over centuries had formed the lakes of Band-e Amir, and the Minaret of Jam, standing alone in a remote gorge near Chaghcharan, rivalled the famous Qutb Minar near Delhi. The Bamiyan statues were perhaps the most magnificent fusion of Asian and European art ever realised: Asian Buddhas draped in Greek robes carved in relief from a sandstone cliff face. They were the world's largest standing Buddhas, the tallest soaring fifty-five metres above the valley floor. When the fifth-century Chinese traveller Hsuan Tsang visited Bamiyan the stone megaliths were gilded and five thousand monks swarmed in the labyrinths. The big Buddhas had been calling me for years. Tariq and I shook hands on it.

Back home months later I opened the baz-o-band and found a small scrap of paper inside. Written on it was a message: 'I hope you will not forget me. Tariq.'

2

Elephant's Foot

In June 1987 I purchased my first Oriental carpet. The deal was done not in Istanbul's crowded *souk*, or Esfahan's covered bazaar, nor even in the riverside rug market of Kabul, but on a Hobart doorstep. In time and distance, Tasmania is a long way from the Old Silk Road. A former British penal colony, it is lashed by the Roaring Forties and its capital clings grimly to the skirts of Mount Wellington to avoid being blown clear across the ocean to South America. On an early winter's day, two Pakistani men knocked on the door of a brownstone terrace on Paternoster Row. Having just moved to the city — and not exactly besieged by guests — I let them in.

In *The Arabian Nights' Entertainments*, the merchant who sells Husayn the flying carpet is the prototype rug salesman.

> *O my lord, thinkest thou I price this carpet at too high a value? 'Tis true, O my lord, its properties are singular and marvellous. Whoever sitteth on this carpet and willeth in thought to be taken up and set down upon other site will, in the twinkling of an eye, be borne thither, be that place nearhand or distant many a day's journey and difficult to reach.[1]*

With similar elan, the itinerant merchants in my living room unrolled their treasures, revealing not just carpets, but an entire civilisation. Suddenly Central Asian warrior king Timur the Lame, or Tamerlane as he is more commonly known in the West, was charging across the living room, sabre in hand, severed heads lying in his wake and a trail of allure rising like dust behind him. Superlatives enriched the merchants' patter. Their floppy heirlooms were more than just rugs; they were handloomed pieces, of the highest quality; canny investments; items of cultural significance; arks of history. The rugs bore strange, spidery motifs — *guls* they called them, 'flowers' in Persian — and had grand titles like 'Princess Bukhara', so redolent of the Eastern khanates. The presence of these men and their wares filled my home with a spicy warmth on a blustery weekend. Yet I was torn, the curious Occidental wary of being gypped, and questioned the provenance of their wares. Unruffled, they produced with a flourish a 'Certificate of Authenticity' and announced a money-back guarantee. So we signed our treaty and off they went into the cold carrying a cheque for $500, a sum which approximated my bank balance at the time.

It took me years to realise that what I had purchased was not an old carpet but an old ruse. My 'Princess' turned out to be an ugly sister, a cheap new production from a Pakistani workshop where the dyes were as dreary as the working conditions and the designs were crude copies stolen from other cultures. The printed receipt made no false claims: the merchants had merely exploited my fantasies.

Walking towards the Presidential Secretariat in Kabul on a hot, sunny day, I remembered with nostalgia the rogues who had first got me interested in the age-old trade. But the man I would be meeting that morning was another kind of rogue entirely.

In 1979, three epochal events shattered the fragile peace of Islamic West Asia so profoundly that to this day the traditional carpet heartland has yet to fully recover. Islamic revolution swept away the monarchy in Iran, Saddam Hussein seized the presidency of Iraq, and Soviet troops invaded Afghanistan. I had come to Kabul to meet a man who had played, and still was playing, a pivotal role in the ongoing drama.

Mohammed Najibullah would not stand for any opposition to Afghanistan's communist regime. As head of the innocuously named State Information Service, otherwise known as the secret police, it was said he would personally conduct interrogations and if the suspects refused to co-operate, he would personally stomp them to death.[2] Although a graduate of medicine from Kabul University in 1975, he preferred killing to healing. When a leading Muslim cleric persisted in efforts to organise an exile movement against the regime, Najib ordered the murder of seventy-nine members of his family.

At that stage in my career I had not met many mass murderers, so a degree of trepidation was understandable. But Dr Najibullah turned out to be a perfect gentleman. Like many political leaders, his identity was malleable. As a young man he was a devout Muslim, but with communist influence in Afghanistan on the rise he discarded the Islamic suffix to his name, meaning 'of God', and Najibullah became 'Najib'. In the 1980s, with more than half a million Soviet troops in the country, it was a smart career move. The Russians had assassinated the president, installed a puppet and had all the main cities under their control. But as the war against the Islamic rebels dragged on, sapping Russian morale, Najib began to see a new role for himself as a healer who could bridge the gap between communists and holy warriors. Reverting to his old name, he found nationalism and became president. He changed the Soviet-style name of his People's Democratic Party of Afghanistan to the homegrown Watan, or Homeland, Party. When Soviet forces withdrew, his task was to persuade the Muslim rebels that Afghanistan was back in Afghan hands and that they should lay down their weapons.

After more than a decade of war, Kabul was no longer the freewheeling tourist capital which it once had been, yet it still had the same glorious location ringed by mountains which delighted the Moghul emperor Babur:

In one day, a man may go out of the town Kabul to where snow never falls, or he may go, in two hours, to where it never thaws . . . Fruits of hot and cold climates are to be had in the districts near the town. Among those of the cold climates . . . the grape, pomegranate, apricot, apple, quince, pear, peach, plum . . . almond and walnut . . . Of fruits of the hot climate . . . the orange, citron . . . sugar cane . . . jil-ghuza [pine nuts] and, from the hill-tracts, much honey.[3]

In the time of Babur, a descendant of both Genghis Khan and Timur the Lame, Kabul was a thriving trade centre where 'can be had the products of Khorasan [Iran], Rum [Turkey], Iraq and China; while it is Hindustan's own market'.[4] Now, marooned by fighting in the countryside and by political and economic sanctions imposed by the West, it could be reached only by military aircraft or irregularly scheduled flights from Moscow, New Delhi and a handful of other cities. Civilian aircraft approaching the city would plunge into a series of hard turns, corkscrewing down and throwing off flares to distract heat-seeking missiles fired by the mujahideen. From the deserted airport, with the letters K-A-B-U-L pushed to one corner of the terminal roof, a broad boulevard led into a sprawling town overlooked by the high battlements of the old citadel called Bala Hissar, and by the blue-domed mausoleum of Afghanistan's penultimate king, Nadir Shah. Driving down the poplar-lined boulevard to the Dar-al-Aman palace in the 1930s, the British adventurer-aesthete Robert Byron gasped:

In front of the poplars run streams confined by grass margins. Behind them are shady footwalks and a tangle of yellow and white roses, now in full flower and richly scented. And then at the end, O God, appears the turreted angle — not even the front — of a French municipal office, surrounded by a French municipal garden and entirely deserted.[5]

Now, less grandiose structures had sprung up in a jumble of neo-classical follies, gloomy socialist boxes and original mud-brick houses which clung to the hillsides, goats grazing on their flat roofs. Vast wall murals extolled government policy with smiling *mullahs* and barefaced women hailing family-planning programs, and steel shipping containers — dumped after carrying supplies in military convoys down the Salang Highway from the Soviet Union, and not valuable enough to risk the return trip — filled the gaps between buildings, merchants and tradespeople sitting inside with the metal doors flung open to catch the passing trade. Smuggling was an art form, its most exotic exponent being a man known only as 'The Chinaman', whose cornerstore bulged with Lipton's, Persil, Kleenex, and cartons of Heineken which spilled onto the street. Above all, the carpet trade still prospered, rugs lining the steep stone levee banks of the Kabul River until spring, when rising waters would force the traders to move them to higher ground.

The days when Afghans voted by dropping almonds into teapots bearing portraits of their favoured candidates were long gone. Forty years after his 1933 coronation in the Hall of Salutations, constitutional monarch King Zahir Shah had been sent into exile in Rome after a republican coup. Power now resided in a functional office block opposite the former royal palace.

Meeting the president, like getting a seat on the national airline Ariana Afghan Airlines, required little advance notice, and after a few formalities at the Foreign Ministry my appointment was confirmed. Arriving early, I found myself in a pleasant office where the president's secretary opened mail and made small talk. He was telling me how fortunate I was not to live in Afghanistan when a door swung open and a phalanx of square-shouldered, identically dressed men stormed through the room into an adjoining office.

'The president has come,' the secretary said.

Dr Najibullah was such a prime target for assassination that he was at all times protected by a human wall of burly, heavily armed lookalikes. In a society where honour is measured in proportion to revenge, he had made many enemies. Over a million people had died in the civil war and half the prewar population of fifteen million had been killed or displaced.[6] His fellow communists, meanwhile, were described by their own secret police as a pack of butchers. Najibullah had emerged from the maelstrom like a man leaving a public convenience: immaculately groomed but embarrassed by the mess he had left behind. Stripped of his human shield, the Afghan president sat waiting for me, dwarfed by his vast desk. He looked smaller in real life than in photos, and strangely pale, with a Stalinesque moustache. As I fiddled with my tape recorder, he reached out to shake hands, but before I could respond he withdrew his hand and started biting his fingernails. Cautiously extending it a second time, he fixed me with a smile that said, 'I know all your tricks, Western reporter.' He understood English, but for obscure political reasons would not converse in it.

'I hear that the president is a bodybuilder,' I said, starting with a softener.

'*Balay!*' he replied, holding his meaty hands on the table in front of him and smiling mischievously at the translator, who said, 'Yes.'

'Has he been lifting weights this morning?'

Stroking his knuckles, Najibullah pretended to require a translation, playing for time in which to analyse the political implications of the question. When the interpreter confirmed in Dari what he had already heard in English, a sly smile spread across his face and he began his response in a faint whisper, as if saying his prayers. It was a rambling, discursive answer, which the translator miraculously boiled down to six words.

'The president no longer pumps iron,' he said, feeling the heat of Najibullah's intense gaze. 'This morning, the President of Afghanistan completed one half hour of tennis and one hour of swimming.'

As the translator rendered these replies in an accent lifted straight from Voice of America, I noticed that Najib was distracted, listening to the drone of a military aircraft taking off from Kabul airport. Who was on that plane? his eyes seemed to ask. Where were they heading? Why hadn't he been informed? Then his smile returned. He knew.

By his own admission, Najibullah had been trained in the art of interviews by the KGB, and all questions about the war, his atrocious human rights record, and international isolation were parried as a matter of course. He spoke in a heavy wheeze, suggesting that access to the country's richest food, finest whisky and softest beds was counteracting his strenuous exercise regime. He laughed somewhat villainously at his own too-clever answers and urged the world to support him as a bulwark against Islamic terrorism. When I pointed out that his fast-paced modernisation had alienated his mujahideen opponents permanently, and that they now regarded him as a *kaffir*, or infidel, he looked at me with the sort of eyes that lie during confession.

'The President of Afghanistan has been born by Muslim parents. He believes in Islam,' the ponderous interpreter intoned. 'The holy religion of Islam is the religion of the people of Afghanistan, and every statesman, by taking into account the beliefs of the people, particularly in this respect, can successfully forge ahead.'

Marxism, communism and socialism were out. Nationalism, democracy and the rule of law were in. Najib was out. Syed Mohammed Najibullah Ahmadzai was in. But nobody was listening. Despite the largest airlift in Soviet military history to keep Kabul supplied with fuel and other essential commodities, the United States and Saudi Arabia were continuing to funnel weapons and money through Pakistan to the Islamist rebels who controlled most of the countryside beyond the lights of Kabul.[7] There was even talk that the old king, Zahir Shah, might return, but Najib had a communist's faith in dialectics.

'History cannot be reversed,' he replied when I asked about the king. 'I haven't seen such a miracle.'

At the conclusion of our meeting the president consented to having his photograph taken. As I rummaged in my bag for the camera, I noticed a beautiful carpet on the floor which covered the room. It was a dense sea of glossy, well-oiled wool the colour of darkest rose, its design an uncluttered composition of large octagons arranged with a blunt authority and containing trefoils. It was a substantial heirloom, and anywhere else it would have been heavily insured, but in Kabul such pieces were just part of the furniture, trodden on by paupers and potentates. When Timur the Lame was absent from his court, his throne carpet acted as deputy. Foreign emissaries were permitted to kiss and pay homage to it.

> *In the provincial capitals carpets symbolized the presence of the ruler, having at the same time the character of today's embassies — they were extraterritorial. The special protection of the owner was bestowed on refugees who succeeded in reaching the carpet. Even the red [!] carpet, which we today roll out when receiving visitors of state and stand on while listening to the national anthem, is our way of symbolically paying tribute to the authority of our guest.*[8]

Unable to resist expressing my admiration for the deep-piled beauty at my feet, I pointed to the floor and said, 'My, what a beautiful carpet.'

'Feel-*pai*,' the president replied with a throaty laugh, springing up and down on his toes on the masculine, sanguine 'Elephant's Foot', named after the fat symbols which stamped across the acme of Afghan rugs like the footprints of Babur's fighting jumbos. Moghul miniatures showed Babur holding court on a carpeted throne. When he ventured on military campaigns into the depths of the subcontinent, his tent was not complete without the finest carpets and tapestries to remind him of the pleasures of Kabul.

As he stood there on the *filpai*, his murderous feet trampling its gorgeous madder pile, mellowed and polished with the traffic of years, Najib no longer struck a self-serving pose. He was transparent at last, revealed as the heir of Babur, who lay entombed in a lovely garden named after him on the slopes of Sher Darwaza mountain overlooking the capital. This monumental carpet, with its balanced and spacious plan, was like a map of empire or a chessboard crowded with kings, as dramatic as Afghanistan itself, if more disciplined. Some trod lightly, others wiped their feet on it, defiling its beauty. But whoever stood on it ruled.

It would not be long before new, equally ruthless shahs would dislodge Najib from his knotted throne but for now he was the quintessential strongman. Wheezing like a tuneless accordion, he bent his hefty frame and stabbed his thumb into the luxurious pile near one of the large octagons.

'Feel-*pai!*' he boomed again, a true son of the Moghuls. Then, sensing my awe, he added mischievously, using English for the first time, 'Elephant's Foot!'

3

A Day in the Countryside

The driver was sixteen, an acne-faced teenaged conscript roused from his bed before dawn to prove to us that Najib had tamed the rebellious countryside. His callow, beardless face and shorn, scabby head protruded from the hatch in front of me, as if prepared for the antique Afghan torture in which a person is buried up to the neck, then has their head used as a football.

We had assembled at 4 a.m. at the capital's main garrison, where groggy mechanics bumbled for hours before getting the vehicle started. Still half asleep myself, I had forgotten my socks and shivered in the chilly night air, feeling as incompetent as the army which could provide neither a conveyance nor even a warming cup of tea. But then the sun leapt into the sky, ominously powerful so early in the morning, and the creaking armoured personnel carrier snorted flatulently to life. Soon, several tonnes of heavy metal were hurtling downhill, the bleary eyed teenager at the controls and me, suddenly wide-eyed, clinging to its shell. Past my cruelly deserted bed in the Continental Hotel we careered — the coffee that would make it all bearable undrunk — while this hideous youth, barely tall enough to see out of the hatch, pointed the gun barrel west. Our guide, seated atop the armoured car with the rest of us, was a five-star brigadier-general, no less. Abdul Halim Hamidi was a rotund man of alcoholic disposition, who would doze off and then awake in panic to regain his grip on the hull. Meanwhile, the gunner's black, padded helmet with cocker spaniel earflaps offered a dismal reminder that without a hat I would probably get sunstroke. We were sitting on top of the APC because, as the general explained, it was the best place to be if it struck an anti-tank mine.

'Not if you run into snipers!' said my companion, Robert Adams, the *Daily Telegraph*'s stringer, who had a repertoire of such unsettling information. He also had much better kit: fatigue pants with notebook pockets, photographer's vest with more pockets, a black-and-white-checked scarf (picked up on assignment in the Israeli-occupied territories) and marching boots. He looked more like a commando than a journalist.

'Do not worry,' the general barked, glancing covetously at Robert's chic outfit, 'the government is fully controlling these areas.'

It was difficult to obey the general's order not to worry. From the heights we could already see the city limits, and beyond them the barren, implacable mountains where the armed Muslim rebels ruled. If the general wanted to control something he might have started with our driver, whose heavy foot was propelling us at blistering speed towards an intersection at the bottom of the hill. The crossroad leading to Kote Sangi was congested in the morning rush with bicycles, jeeps, mules, handcarts and pedestrians. The troop carrier's eight tractor tyres thrummed with increasing urgency on the black tarmac, the tank-like vehicle bristling with antennae, spotlights and armour plating like a huge metal insect. If it had a horn I could not hear it, and the rubber tyres gave little warning to those caught in traffic ahead as we recklessly bore down on them. The boy driver was either oblivious to the crowd, or expected it to part like the Red Sea before Moses. Eventually our approach registered with an alarmed few, who began stampeding in panic. We were close enough to hear people calling out, those caught in the middle unable to escape. But still the driver pressed forward until we were almost on top of them, when at last he reacted. The air brakes gasped impotently against the momentum of the lumbering hulk, which ploughed across the intersection, scattering people and livestock. I saw something go under us in a flash and we were fifty metres past the crossing when the tank pulled irascibly to a halt.

Grimly, General Hamid dismounted from the vehicle, donning his cap as he walked back towards the intersection. Following him, I could see people gathering at a spot in the middle of the road, craning their necks over a huddled group in front of them. Striding into their midst, the general pushed forward until he was standing over the crumpled body of a young woman. The faces that pressed in around him were terrible, emaciated by something more than hunger. They were incredulous but silent, too fearful of the general's authority to voice an opinion, let alone grief or anger. At peak hour on a weekday morning, the busy crossing in Afghanistan's largest city was eerily silent. The Afghans looked on in despair, their spirit as crushed as the body of the girl on the road. Completing his cursory inspection, the general muttered something to a traffic cop, who had managed to hold on to his baton during the mêlée and now began using it to disperse the crowd. The general then turned and marched back to the armoured car. Unbelievably, we had encountered our first casualty of war even before leaving the safety of Kabul.

Anywhere else south of the Hindu Kush such an incident would have caused a riot. How many daily travesties had it taken to humble the proud, defiant Afghans?

The road to the garrison town of Maidan Shahr traversed a bucolic landscape dotted by willow trees. Wild grass and mimosa dusted the slopes and terraces in pistachio tones and there were groves of mulberry and walnut, most gone to seed, the villages depopulated. Caught between the army and the mujahideen, the rural population of Afghanistan had fled in their millions to Pakistan and Iran, robbing the rural economy of its industrious backbone. The mud-brick houses, their walls once as smooth as chipboard, had dribble-melted in the elements, or been pulverised by the army to deny the Muslim rebels their hiding places. Yet they were all around us, watching from the forbidding refuge of the mountains, Muslims from around the world who had come to fight Islam's version of the Spanish Civil War. The struggle against the communists had united the Muslims and forged a tactical alliance with the West. But occasionally there were remarkable examples of co-operation across the ideological divide. For a price, local mujahideen commanders could be persuaded to take a day off from the war, allowing the government to organise shambolic tours like ours.

The road continued west towards Bamiyan, its famous Buddhas separated from us by the single range of the Koh-e Baba. Past fields of lavender and poplar windbreaks we eventually reached a long *pul*, or bridge, over the Kabul River, fifteen kilometres from its source in the Sanglakh Range. The Kabul is the only Afghan river that reaches the sea, joining the mighty Indus at Attock in Pakistan. But here in its infancy, its flow reduced by mid summer, it looked unlikely ever to reach the Indian Ocean. Standing at both ends of the bridge were gunmen wearing turbans and waistcoats over their salwar kameez. They were Uzbeks and Turkmens from the northern province of Jowzjan. Feared everywhere as plunderers, they had supported the communists throughout the war. Hailing them like old friends, the general leapt off the armoured car and embraced the smiling Jowzjanis, whose gold teeth flashed in the sun. Sporting a jumble of Central Asian features, they spoke a Turkic dialect and there was an air of dissipation about them. With its ranks depleted by desertions, the Afghan Army needed the battle-hardened Jowzjanis to defend strategic locations like airports, dams, tunnels, forts and bridges. They were mercenaries who fought only for the right to loot, rape and murder. Ordinary Afghans called them *gilam jam*. In the north it referred to an Uzbek warlord who had gambled away everything he owned, even his carpets. In the south, it was an epithet reserved for the Uzbeks which meant 'carpet thieves'. Shod in curved Central Asian slippers, and with Kalashnikovs slung over their shoulders, the Jowzjanis were in absolute control of the area, and the village opposite the bridge seemed strangely deserted.

Further on, in a village called Taitimour, we were briefed by a barrel-chested Afghan Army officer called Colonel Saleem, who claimed to have defended the village from a recent rebel attack. A bulldog-faced man wearing a kind of green camouflage poncho and gaiters, he claimed to have killed hundreds of mujahideen in the operation, fifty of them where we stood under a stone house on a steep incline.

'They were firing machine guns and rocket-propelled grenades at a range of twenty metres,' Saleem said, the crump of distant artillery punctuating his spiel.

'Incoming or outgoing?' asked Robert, referring to the muffled explosions, as a smile played on his lips. Then, thinking aloud, he added, 'Outgoing, I think. Good. Now, when does the incoming start?'

Yet even with his military jargon, Robert could not talk up the danger. Traversing an area of intense rebel activity was all very well, but the battlefields in our immediate vicinity were silent. About the only danger we encountered came when, climbing a hill to get a better view, I heard a chorus of baleful voices from below. Turning, I saw all the soldiers frozen in attitudes of warning, some with their arms outstretched towards me.

'Land mines!' they were yelling.

Perspiring heavily, my feet feeling each step with awful intensity, I crept back down to the bottom of the hill. We had expected that our adventure with the Afghan Army might involve soldiers actually firing their weapons, but when I asked the general about it he said they were saving ammunition. 'We don't beat the mujahideen, but we teach them how to participate in a peaceful life,' Colonel Saleem explained. 'We hug them, rather than kill them.'

Travelling with the Afghan Army seemed more dangerous than fighting them. We had been driving for ten hours, slowly baking on the hot, exposed shell of the APC, without being given a drop of water. When the convoy became bogged in heavy bulldust, the soldiers rushed to a nearby river, splashing around like overgrown children. They drank their fill from its icy stream as the lily-livered, sunstroked foreigners enviously looked on. Eventually we reached a tent pitched on a scarified mountainside where the soldiers displayed freshly crated mortars, anti-tank mines and rockets, some with US and European markings, which they said they had captured from the rebels after teaching them the joys of a peaceful life.

On the long drive back to Kabul, the vacant peace of Taitimour haunted me. Separating myself from the rest of the party, I had walked alone around several of its buildings pockmarked with bullet holes. On the exterior wall of a house somebody had scrawled 'jihad' in the Pashto language beneath a clever likeness of Najibullah hanging from a gallows. In the refugee camps in Pakistan they wove similar images into their carpets.

4

Happy Fire

Ten dervishes can sleep under one blanket,
but two kings cannot find room in one clime

— BABUR-NAMA

The collapse of the Soviet Union brought a new government to power in Moscow which accepted defeat in the Cold War and halted military aid to Afghanistan. With Najibullah no longer able to dispense patronage, his allies defected to the mujahideen. Returning to his palatial residence inside the *Arg* one night, the president discovered that his security guard had been disarmed. At Kabul airport a United Nations aircraft was waiting to fly him to safety in exile, but as he rushed there he found the road blocked by the traitorous gilam jam militia. With no way out and in mortal fear for their lives, the president and his brother took refuge in the UN compound in the city.

In early 1992 there were no more escorted tours of the countryside, and the rival mujahideen commanders and their troops circling the capital were only a short taxi drive away. At Charikar, a town that sheltered under Judas trees at the foot of the Hindu Kush, the most famous guerilla leader of his time, Ahmad Shah Massoud, awaited his appointment with destiny. Alexander the Great, aged just twenty-six, had camped at Charikar in 329 BC before crossing the high passes into Central Asia in pursuit of Bessus and the remnants of the Achaemenid Empire, whose capital Persepolis he had ruined. After two years in the north, he returned to Charikar en route south to India, and people in the area still ascribe their fair skin and blue eyes to the thirty-two thousand-strong Greek Army who, forbidden by Alexander from loot and pillage, contented themselves with amorous pursuits. Massoud's ambitions were more modest, but his brilliance as a commander had been compared to that of Alexander, the last Western general to conquer Afghanistan.

One of the few mujahideen commanders to remain inside the country throughout the Soviet occupation, Massoud had joined the Islamists while a student of engineering at Kabul Polytechnic. The son of a Tajik general in the king's army, he was in the first wave of young Afghans who saw in Islam the unifying force that would drive the Russians out of their country, and he quickly attracted hundreds of followers willing to fight and die for the Islamist cause. After a failed coup in 1978, which reduced his group to fifteen men, he survived in the natural fortress of his native Panjshir Valley on little more than local knowledge and mulberries. He was almost captured again in 1984 when surrounded by Russian armour in the occupied Panjshir's fishbone network of ravines for five months. But by adapting the guerilla methods of Che Guevara, Mao Zedong and Ho Chi Minh to Afghan conditions, he hounded his enemies out of the valley and eventually out of the country. With the bulk of Saudi and American aid going to the Pakistan-based rebel leader Gulbuddin Hekmatyar, Massoud had financed his war by selling emeralds from the valley and lapis lazuli from mountainous Badakshan, once the prime supplier of the prized blue stone to Egypt's pharaohs. In a sparsely furnished room of a house on the southern outskirts of Charikar, the 'Lion of Panjshir' was now preparing for the final assault on Kabul, a city he had not seen for fifteen years.

Lean and catlike in appearance, his grizzled beard and long, hooked nose were balanced by almond-shaped eyes which still had the brightness of youth. Barely forty, he had been fighting for half his life, and gave the impression of being an essentially decent man, only doing what was necessary to defend his people. His 'people' were the Tajik minority. Massoud resented the Pakistan-based leaders of the Pashtun majority, who he felt had sat out the war while he did the fighting and were now descending like vultures to feast on the spoils. Sitting at one end of a lounge, with a few correspondents and acolytes crowding the floor at his feet, he began speaking with the whispered Islamic injunction '*Bismillah ar-Rahman ar-Rahim*' — In the name of Allah, the Compassionate, the Merciful — then conversed easily in Dari and French, a cultured warlord, holding his chin with long, crooked fingers, his answers peppered with *ouis* and *nons*.

'If we took Charikar and Bagram, it would be easy for us to go into Kabul. But we want to talk to other groups about it,' he said. 'I hope in these sensitive conditions all mujahideen factions will unite.'

Hekmatyar's Hizb-e Islami were already in Logar province only thirty-five kilometres from Kabul, but Massoud remained outwardly unconcerned

'If Hekmatyar had the ability, he would already be there,' he said, calling his rival a 'warmonger' for good measure.

It was a simple enough message, but a well-read warlord like Massoud knew his history. Almost six centuries earlier the court of Samarkand had sent an almost identical message to a son of Timur the Lame, who was at that time besieging them. 'Certainly you are the lawful heir and successor of Amir Timur,' they said, 'but fortune does not favour you, for if it did, you would be near the capital.'[9]

The warlords were now fighting over the same towns and forts, and even abusing each other in the same terms that their forefathers had. Only their weapons were more sophisticated.

As we left Charikar, individual mujahideen were wandering off into the fields, laying down their guns and spreading camel-coloured blankets for their afternoon prayers. In a golden light, they stood erect facing west towards Mecca with hands by their sides, then, cupping their hands to their faces, bore witness, uttering the *takbir* — '*Allahu Akbar*', God is great. Bending briefly with hands on knees, they stood and exclaimed again before kneeling and prostrating themselves with their foreheads touching the ground.

In their holy war against the kaffirs, each prayer could be their last. They had already given many *shaheed*, or martyrs. It was easy to believe this pious, righteous army of patriots might bring peace and order to Afghanistan.

Returning to Kabul that afternoon we passed a column of Massoud's men marching towards the capital. Then, at an army base on the outskirts of the city, near Dar-al-Aman palace — the core building in a new capital which King Amanullah had intended to build before tribal leaders backed by the mullahs brought about his fall in the 1920s — we came across some gunmen belonging to one of the militias who had taken over several silos containing gigantic Soviet-made SCUD-B surface-to-surface missiles. They were elated, like children who had just been given new toys, except these toys had a range of over two hundred and fifty kilometres. One of them said, 'If any group does not want peace in our country, we will use these missiles against them.' Fortunately the Russian technical advisors, who were the only people who knew how to operate the Scuds, had already left the country.

Kalashnikovs, not missiles, were still the weapon of choice for a guerilla army preparing to take a city. The AK-47 was a rifle so brutally efficient that it made short-range obliteration of human life about as complex as watering the garden. With such a weapon, an illiterate villager turned *jihadi* could lose himself for as long as there was ammunition.

In Afghan wars, momentum is everything, and now every other day a new city fell to the rebels. We marked them off on maps: Ghazni, Kandahar, Herat, Jalalabad, Gardez. Only Kabul remained, hanging like a big, ripe peach ready to fall off a tree. The river, now swollen with snowmelt, charged through the old *serai* of the capital as if hurrying to get out of the way of an impending tragedy. The city was under night curfew, and remnants of Najib's regime made daily appeals to the mujahideen to come and take over the government, but the rebels kept their distance.

Incredibly, it was still possible to find the odd communist in Kabul. Hard-drinking Marxists like Farid Mazdaq, boss of the central committee of the ruling Watan Party, were leaving their departure to the last moment as a final gesture of contempt for their enemies. At Mazdaq's flat in the Soviet-built Microrayon apartment complex for senior government officials, we were greeted by a small, scarred man with darkening stubble who opened his well-stocked liquor cabinet one last time. The ranking party member still at liberty in Kabul had done a deal with his old drinking buddy, the Uzbek leader Abdul Rashid Dostum, for safe passage. Najib had not been so lucky.

'Najib had a secret deal with the UN. He'd hand over power to a new government including the mujahideen, and in return the UN would help him escape to India,' said Mazdaq, throwing back a long shot, his face contorted with grim pleasure. 'But it didn't work. When we found out about it, Azimi changed the password that evening after the Cabinet meeting, and didn't tell Najib. So when he went to the airport, he couldn't get out!'

Mazdaq laughed from his belly and steadied his pouring arm for another round. The food came — rice, tender mutton, *nan*, nuts and plenty more liquor — prepared by a faithful servant. The work of a century, the modernisation of backward, unruly Afghanistan, drowned that night in a deluge of Russian vodka.

Ever since Emir Habibullah assumed the throne in 1901 and invited foreign technicians to build the country's first hydro-electric station at Jabal us-Saraj, the modernisers' efforts had been repeatedly stalled by jealous rivals, a reactionary clergy and their own corruption.

'Najib didn't have the password,' Mazdaq said again, his drink repeating on him. Although there were rumours of Mazdaq's corruption and ruthlessness, it was impossible to verify them. He would disappear from Kabul the following morning, popping up in Moscow a few months later. In a last act of kindness, he gave our driver the password for that night, enabling our small group to safely negotiate the blacked-out streets of the city.

At the Continental Hotel, perched on a ridge overlooking the city, the electricity and water had failed, and the only way of getting a shower was to buy cases of mineral water at inflated prices from The Chinaman on Chicken Street. Small generators provided a ghostly light in the corridors, and could power laptops and satellite telephones, while candles illuminated the rooms. It was not quite anarchy, but having slipped out of one order, Kabul had yet to be secured in another. In those final days the city drifted with a strangely pleasant lightness, free of anybody's control, and the imminence of change seemed as delightful as it was ominous.

On a cloudless morning in April, I woke up, went to the balcony of my hotel room, and saw the mujahideen trailing like ants along the mountain tops, following the ridges down into the capital. Below me, the hotel staff were raising a new flag of their own design, a plain green sheet which they hoped would save their post-communist necks. But the gunmen who at that very moment had entered the driveway, festooned with Kalashnikovs, grenades and rocket-launchers, had more practical concerns. After fourteen years in the hills, all Massoud unit commander Mohammed Ali wanted for himself and his men was a meal.

'We're tired and hungry,' the commander said, as several of his men got trapped in the revolving door which led into the lobby.

As they entered the 1960s-era hotel the younger rebels were slackjawed in wonder at what they saw. Like the North Vietnamese entering Saigon, most of them had never seen a modern city. Fussing over the commander, the hotel staff shepherded him downstairs into the staff canteen, so as not to unduly alarm the hotel's foreign guests.

Within hours, thousands of other armed guerillas were wandering the streets of Kabul with the same sense of wonder, now and then pausing to survey buildings which looked like they might make suitable headquarters for important members of any new government. In the south-western suburbs, Shia militiamen plastered the streets with posters of Iran's Ayatollah Khomeini, whose government had provided most of their weapons, while the neat, ideologically pure Pashtuns of Gulbuddin Hekmatyar's Hizb-e Islami quietly slipped into the Interior Ministry, which held large stocks of arms and ammunition and the files of Najibullah's secret police. Not until nightfall did the rival groups remember that they had won the great jihad. The time had come to celebrate.

In the house in Karte Parwan, not far from the hotel, Tariq Ahmed inspected the unglazed windows and bare brick walls of his unfinished dream, preoccupied with thoughts of house, family and carpets. His entire adult life, he realised, had been lived in the vast shadow cast by Afghanistan's cruel and turbulent history. Despite it all — the early poverty, conscription, the Soviet invasion and the holy war — he had not just survived but prospered, clawing his way up from urchin fruitseller in the Herat Bazaar to modestly wealthy and respectable merchant in the capital. Now everything he had worked for — the almost complete house, the small shop, his Toyota Corolla: the hard-won fruits of a productive life — suddenly lay in the path of destruction. Then there were the lives of his wife and daughters, more precious than his own. God, he prayed, would sort the righteous from the corrupt, the guilty from the innocent, and bring peace. The politicians and bureaucrats of the old order would surely run for their lives, but ordinary shopkeepers had nothing to fear. They had contributed to the war effort, giving food, money and information to the rebels' spy network. When Kabul radio had called the mujahideen 'bandits', they had tuned instead to Voice of

America, Radio Pakistan and the BBC, which called them 'freedom fighters'. The Kabulis, even the businessmen, had faith in their Muslim brothers, who had made many sacrifices for the country. Everyone longed for a return to the golden years of the 1960s, when foreign tourists flocked to Afghanistan and paid handsomely for their requirements and their souvenir carpets. There were, Tariq concluded, as many reasons to hope as to fear.

Standing on their rooftop that night, Tariq, his wife Nazreen and their daughters watched a phosphorous flare soar into the sky, hovering high over the city. Then, from the darkness below, streams of red tracer fire erupted from the guns of thousands of victorious mujahideen competing to knock the flare down. The thunder of the 'Happy Fire' frightened and exhilarated, its terrible beauty announcing the end of a civil war that had killed over a million people.

Watching the spectacle from my hotel room balcony, the prospect of peace in a country as beautiful and historic as Afghanistan began to sink in. There were excursions to plan, to the Bamiyan Buddhas and the blue lakes of Band-e Amir, and picnics at which Tariq and I would consume nothing but fresh fruit and swim in the invigorating rivers. There were alpine meadows to cross in Badakshan, all the way through the Wakhan Corridor to China, and carpet shopping in Mazar-e Sharif, where the *chaikhanas* looked like rug shops.

Earlier that day I had found Tariq's business card in my wallet — 'Tariq Ahmed Carpet Store. Verious Silk, Wiilen New and old Caprte and rugs' — and had gone to his shop on Jade Idgah, but found it locked. The following morning I was nudged from sleep by the distant sound of explosions echoing off the mountains which ringed Kabul. From the hotel, plumes of black smoke and grey dust could be seen rising from various points around the city.

It had begun with a dispute between Shias and Sunnis over control of the city's south-west and quickly spread, with Massoud's forces and Dostum's Uzbeks joining together to blast Hekmatyar's men from the positions they had occupied and push them out of town. The streets had emptied, women scuttling indoors in their *chaderis*, as the militias charged from battle to battle in tanks and trucks and even commandeered private cars and taxis. International intervention might possibly have brokered a truce, but the United States was preoccupied with the Balkans and Iraq. The Afghans were left to sort out their own problems the only way they knew.

Directed by local people pointing the way towards the *jang*, or war, I attached myself to a small group of foreign reporters scrambling between the skirmishes in hired taxis. Most of us had undergone some form of military training. One was a former US Marine, another had been conscripted into the Israeli Army, and a third wrote for the magazine *Soldier of Fortune*. But I was a complete novice. Hearing a commotion in the Shahr-e Now district, we went to an alley behind the Interior Ministry where, amid a terrible din of explosions and gunfire, Massoud's Jamiat militiamen were firing into the ministry through a gateway. The closer we got, the more laboured my breathing became, until my mouth felt as dry as if I had swallowed a cupful of sand.

'Where are we? What are we achieving here?' I asked the former Marine, who replied, 'I think we're trying to prove our manhood.'

About twenty metres from the ministry gateway the acrid odour of explosives laced the air and the noise was disorientating. Massoud's men were howling to each other in Dari, moving through the gateway under heavy fire. Occasionally one of the shooters would break away from the fight, moving back with his gun balanced rakishly over his shoulder as if he were on his way home from the office.

During one particularly heavy onslaught from Hekmatyar's forces lodged inside the Interior Ministry, several urchin boys gathered around me, laughing and playing war games in the midst of the actual war. Then a man approached, saying he had lived in Canada, and offered his services as a translator, but just as suddenly he disappeared in the next blast. The air around us had become thick with horrible whistles, whiplash sounds and cracks, and the quick *phut* heard only when a bullet passes you at lethally close range. I began to wonder how it might feel to be hit. Halfway down a long, straight alleyway I was stopped in my tracks by dead terror, unable to move my feet. All I wanted was to melt into the cornerstone of the deserted building in whose doorway I was cowering. When shame finally forced me to catch up with my friends, I found them sheltering in a concrete garage on the boundary wall, where a militiaman was using his rifle butt to crack open boxes of fresh ammunition. As smoke poured from a building nearby, we left the area after dusk with the battle for the Interior Ministry unresolved.

Trapped at home during that first week of Islamic 'rule', Tariq Ahmed stayed close to the radio, which informed him that all foreign embassies except Pakistan's had fled the capital, and that the Kabul Museum, repository of the nation's entire moveable cultural heritage, had been looted. Rumours passing from house to house told of a shortage of rope and twine in the villages on the way to Kabul: the city's 'liberators' were anticipating a big haul of booty. With no money to pay wages, the mujahideen commanders gave free rein to their men. The rebels first raided the armouries, then the garages, and then government offices, stealing guns, cars and valuables. They stole first, and decided later whether they needed the booty, selling the excess cheaply to locals. The Kabul Museum's priceless collection of Gandharan antiquities from the Indus Valley civilisation was decimated. A horde of thirty-five thousand ancient coins disappeared, and there were fears for the safety of the treasure of Telya Tepe, consisting of twenty thousand pieces of gold jewellery excavated by Russian archaeologists near the ancient city of Balkh in the 1970s. Twenty boxes of the most important antiquities sealed and stored by Najib's government were missing. Years later, antiquities looted from the Kabul Museum were still showing up in the markets of Peshawar and Europe.

Unknown to the looters, they were carrying on a venerable tradition. In 623 AD the Prophet Mohammed organised his first *razya*, or ambush, of a Meccan caravan.[10] On this and subsequent raids — some of which he personally led — the Prophet took one-fifth of the booty, a share stipulated in the Koran. Fourteen years later, when the desert-dwelling Arabs conquered the Persian city of Ctesiphon, they wandered awestruck among palaces and gardens 'which were as beautiful as paradise'.

> *In all the rooms were carpets the like of which they had never seen. One in particular covered the wall opposite the entrance into the immense banqueting hall and represented a garden. The ground was wrought in gold thread, the walks in silver, the verges studded with emeralds, the rivulets made of pearls, the trees and flowers of rubies, amethysts and other precious stones of variegated colours. Since all the booty was dealt out in certain fixed proportions, this fabulous carpet was cut up into small pieces and distributed along with the rest of the plunder.*[11]

In Chicken Street, home to the main carpet bazaar for tourists, I found the gilam jam. Barefoot and wearing checked turbans tied high on their shaved heads, they were jumping down from a truck as the driver slammed it into reverse and mounted the footpath, smashing in the door of a carpet and curio shop. The men were inflamed, forming a cordon around the truck. One of them even began raking a cross street with automatic gunfire as the others hauled out scores of rugs, throwing them into the truck. Looting with one hand, the shooter kept his rifle balanced on his hip with the other, scanning the street for any challenge. When the truck was full he slammed the tailgate shut, sprayed the street with a final burst of gunfire, climbed into the back, and then tore off towards the north.

Nothing was sacred to these holy warriors, whose enemies were other Muslims. Schools, mosques, even historical monuments like Nadir Shah's blue-domed mausoleum, which looked as if it had been used for target practice — all were blasted. Fires broke out at the Arg where rockets fell, and tanks rumbled through the old city blasting their way through private homes, sending thousands of terrified civilians fleeing through the narrow lanes. When there were no valuables left, the looting gunmen would steal people. Massoud's men started kidnapping for ransom and other groups followed suit. Even fundamental Islamic tenets, like respect for *purdah* (the seclusion of women), began breaking down. Women's quarters were the place most Afghan families stored their valuables, expecting even thieves to honour the traditional code. But purdah was routinely violated, along with the women themselves. And lest anyone forget that this was a holy war, there were occasional outbreaks of religious fervour: women abused for not wearing the full veil, cinemas showing licentious Indian films shut down, and cases of liquor taken off the shelves and smashed in the road. Yet these pious acts left Kabulis unimpressed. On a street corner I saw a woman, who had lost her family and possessions, fearlessly berating a group of armed mujahideen.

'You are animals,' she told them. 'Even the Russians were better Muslims than you cowards.'

Every day, crossing the city, I would look in to see if Tariq Ahmed's shop had reopened, but it never did. For me the shop became a source of personal resentment, as if the padlock was conspiring to deny me the slightest, most gentle reminder of Afghanistan's other side: the Persian manners and hospitality, and mastery of time. Confronted every day by the unpalatable aspects of the national character, I badly needed to see the old Afghan virtues of honesty, directness and honour which had been lost in a holy war-turned-ethnic bloodbath.

As the fighting worsened, and Hekmatyar's forces began indiscriminately rocketing the city from positions on the outskirts,

Tariq Ahmed had begun to consider his options. His cherished house no longer had electricity, phones were down and water supplies had evaporated. The situation then worsened when a government office adjacent to the house attracted the unwelcome attention of the Muslim 'freedom fighters'.

'They fight for freedom — freedom to loot,' Tariq told his family after the rebels stole two jeeps parked at the office next door. Then one day the rebels started banging on his door with their guns. They wanted food, of which there was barely enough for Tariq's own family, but he gave it to them. Returning the next day, they asked for hot water in which to bathe — so he gave them a few flasks. Soon Tariq realised that the men had occupied the adjacent building and were using his family as their personal attendants. Ensconced and increasingly comfortable, they began lounging on the second-floor balcony on warm evenings, scrutinising the activities in Tariq's rear garden. They paid particular attention to the women and girls, watching them with a slouching impudence. Finally, and inevitably, they demanded money. Thirty thousand *Afghanis*. Tariq gave them five thousand, then early the following morning moved his wife and daughters to a relative's house near the Pakistan Embassy. Returning to collect some valuables, he was spotted by the late-rising gunmen.

'Why, uncle, are you leaving this house?' their leader said. 'Somebody is telling you something wrong?'

'No. Thank you,' said Tariq, smiling. 'It's nice of you to be so concerned about me, very kind. But this is not my house, I live in a different place. I must go there.'

The immediate threat to the family eased but Tariq's life savings — his carpets — remained in jeopardy, protected by a mere padlock and shutter. With the gilam jam and other factions picking off the shops one by one, he needed urgently to move the rugs, numbering several hundred, to a place of greater safety. His relative and new host, Hajji Moosheer, had agreed to provide a haven for the carpets, so during a lull in the fighting Tariq had driven back and forth between the shop and the house, dodging the hijackers who roamed the streets stealing cars. At Hajji Moosheer's he selected a room with an extended alcove running along one side, folded the rugs and carefully stacked them in the recess. On more such furtive expeditions he braved gunfire and explosions to scour the neighbourhood for bricks, mortar and paint, taking whatever he found back to the house. When he had amassed sufficient materials he changed into his oldest clothes and began to build a wall to conceal his rugs, doing the job with such care that, after painting and some smudging, the new wall appeared to be part of the building's original structure.

After hanging on for fourteen years in a country at war, Tariq and his family were about to become refugees.

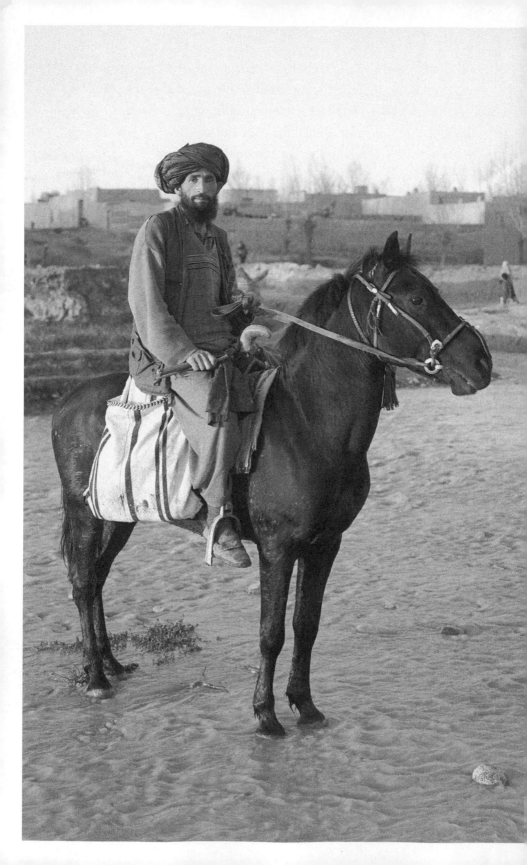

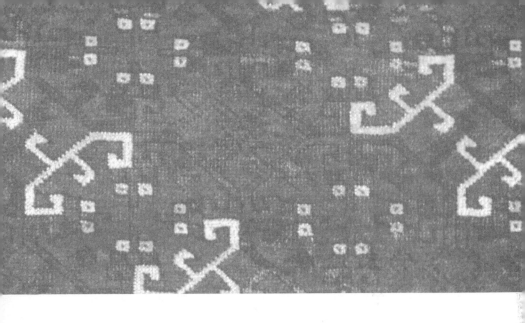

PART TWO

THE ROAD TO BALKH

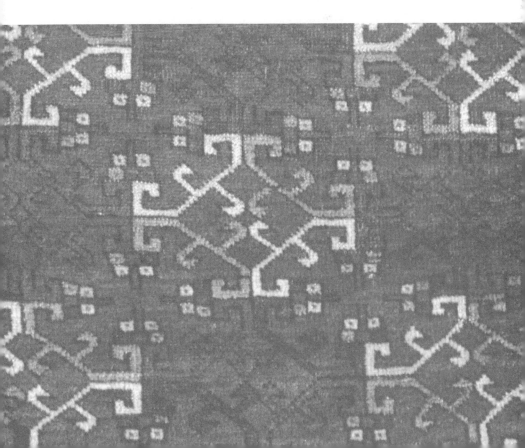

5

The Red Carpet

The early Muslims inhabited lands where people were born on carpets, prayed on them, and covered their tombs with them. For centuries, carpets have been a currency and an export, among the first commodities of a globalised trading system. Apart from trade, the main form of interaction between nations is war.

For most of the past two millennia the carpet heartlands have been in turmoil, raked by battles, invasions and migrations. In our own time, the most dramatic consequence has been the exodus of refugees, mainly Muslims, but also Jews, Christians, Sikhs, Buddhists, Zoroastrians and Hindus, from the lands where the earliest human civilisations blossomed. With their countries decimated, cultures pulverised and families scattered, they flee, carrying what is often the only portable asset they own — their carpets. For those who remain, the carpet business is one of the only functioning industries left, with shepherds, spinners, dyers, weavers, washers, transporters and traders increasingly dependent on the Muslim world's pre-eminent manufactured product for their survival. From the plummeting value of the *Afghani*, to the exodus of desert nomads from their traditional pastures, the Oriental carpet pervades the life of millions of people. And when the shooting stops, and the bazaar springs back to life as if nothing happened, you can lose yourself there, where carpet dealers recline on bolsters, retailing conversation outside time.

The fighting in Kabul had been going on since 1992, sending hundreds of thousands of civilians fleeing to the relative peace of the north. Forced out of the capital, Hizb-e Islami forces under Gulbuddin Hekmatyar had resorted to bombarding the city with thousands of rockets left over from the great jihad. But frustrated with Hekmatyar's failure to evict the Tajiks and Uzbeks from Kabul — a city they had ruled for almost three hundred years — the Pashtun majority turned to a new force composed of religious students under the leadership of a one-eyed mullah from Kandahar. The Taliban, as they would be known, were rapidly buying, proselytising and occasionally fighting their way towards the capital, and in September 1996 they forced the northern forces to abandon the city.

In the UN Special Mission Compound where he had been living with his brother for the past four years, former president Najibullah took the dramatic developments calmly. The Taliban were fellow Pashtuns, he told the UN security officer who visited him on the eve of the student militia's arrival. He was not afraid of them, and had turned down the Tajik Massoud's offer of safe passage. But entering Kabul that night, a small advance team of Talibs made a beeline for the compound and seized the former president. Acting on orders from their superiors, they beat him and his brother Shahpur unconscious, drove them to the Arg, castrated them, and dragged them half-alive behind a pickup truck several times around the former king's residence. When the battered and mutilated brothers could no longer sense pain, the Taliban assassins shot Najib dead and strangled Shahpur. Their bodies were then hoisted by the neck with steel cables from a police traffic control booth gaily painted like a barber's pole at a major crossroads, with cigarettes stuffed between their fingers as a symbol of their corruption. After daybreak word spread and curious Kabulis ventured out to inspect the ghastly sight of their former president, his torn, bloodied clothing hinting at the crude surgery to his groin. Young male dimwits amused themselves by pulling and pushing the corpses and stuffing cigarettes in their noses. Others, especially members of ethnic minorities, took the display as a sign of worse to come, and joined the exodus north towards Central Asia, most gravitating to Mazar-e Sharif, whose name means 'tomb of the noble'.

The blue-tiled fifteenth-century shrine which dominates the central square of Mazar arose, quite literally, from a dream. It is dedicated to Ali ibn Abi Talib, or Hazrat Ali, the Prophet Mohammed's son-in-law, and marks the spot where, according to legend, a white she-camel dropped dead after carrying the corpse of the murdered cleric all the way from Mesopotamia. Maps show Ali's actual burial place as Najaf in Iraq, but Mazar has remained a pilgrimage place since the twelfth century when the *caliph* appeared in the dream of a local mullah, personally confirming that he was indeed buried in Mazar. A grave was discovered, and work on the shrine began. Desecrated by Genghis Khan and repeatedly renovated, its profusion of blue tiles can be dazzling or dreary, depending on the light, but it still attracts thousands of pilgrims each day, as well as large flocks of white doves believed by the faithful to carry the souls of martyrs. Arriving at the shrine one spring morning, I found the doves famished, able to polish off the pound of grain I had brought for them within minutes.

The shrine of Hazrat Ali is holy for all Muslims, but the man it honours was pivotal in the schism which has divided Islam ever since his murder by religious rivals, an event which led the Shias to break away from the Sunni mainstream. Declaring Ali to be the first Imam, or spiritual successor of the Prophet, they denounced what they saw as the decadence of the orthodox Islamic leadership and determined to recognise only direct descendants of the Prophet as their leaders. The same year that Ali died, Muslim armies annexed the lands now known as Afghanistan,[1] spreading orthodox Islam in a country where Shias came to be a despised minority. In Afghanistan, most Shias are ethnic Hazaras, descendants of the Mongols who were enslaved by Pashtuns.

At a hotel restaurant not far from the shrine, the full extent of

Afghanistan's ethnic complexity was dramatically on show. Patrons lounged like lords on carpeted raised platforms: Uzbeks wearing padded jackets and heavily embroidered skullcaps, Tajiks in Western clothes and rolled woollen caps called *pakhool*, and Turkmens wearing black Karakul hats. Huddling in a corner under blankets were a small group of turbaned Pashtuns, who although they formed the majority south of the Hindu Kush, were outnumbered in the north.

Sitting quietly and alone at one table, I recognised a square-set young man dressed in blue denim who worked for a local aid agency. His thick beard was so meticulously groomed that it appeared stuck on, and he wore a silver ring set with a chunk of turquoise resembling an expensive knuckleduster.

'*As'salaam aleikum*,' I greeted Rasoul.

'*Waleikum as'salaam*,' he responded, taking a firm grip on my shoulders, and pressing his cheek against mine in the highly stylised kiss of salutation. 'Three times,' he whispered in my ear, hanging on grimly to subdue my mawkish tendency to disengage after the first kiss. At twenty-three, Rasoul was majoring in English Literature at the nearby Balkh University, but the slight bow, hand on heart and flutter of eyes were unmistakably Persian. His family were the ancestral leaders of Ali Chaupan, a village of high mud walls shaded by grape vines and almond trees on the outskirts of Mazar. But although of venerable status within their own community, the family were Hazaras. The *Hazare* were the unstoppable horde of Genghis Khan. Long since left behind, they now formed a 15 per cent minority in Afghanistan. In the downtrodden countenance of many Hazaras you could almost see the centuries of discrimination against them, but the blood of a long-lost ancestor had given Ghulam Rasoul Ahmadi the lofty bearing of a southern Pashtun, nicely complementing his graceful northern manners.

'Are you getting ready to welcome the Taliban?' I asked, anxious to gauge his feelings about the dramatic advances of the Pashtun militia in early 1997, the reason I had returned to the country.

Rasoul smiled like a student who opens an exam paper and sees the exact questions for which he has prepared.

'This is a very relevant issue,' he said, waving a hand at the assembled patrons. 'You see a few of those Pashtuns have beards. For personal reasons I also have one. But most men in the north are clean-shaven, or have a moustache. Do the Taliban think they can make these tough northern men grow beards?'

The answer was *balay*, yes.

'Well, they may think so,' he conceded, 'but we people of the north are different from southerners. Of course, like them, we are Muslims. But we are more influenced by Iran and Europe, even by Russia. Our young people like to wear Western clothes. Then there is the religious question for my own Hazara people. We are Shia, the minority in Islam, but they call us kaffirs and want to make us Sunnis like them. So do they expect us to roll out the red carpet for them? Remember, even the Soviet Army could not control the Hazarajat region of central Afghanistan.'

Rasoul's eyes narrowed with his smile.

Ever since the Aryans, or 'white race', had moved out of southern Russia through Persia to India in the second millennium BC, the region had been a melting pot of race and culture. Alexander the Great had married a Bactrian princess from Balkh, where Greek and Buddhist influences played freely in the fluted columns and robed Buddhas occasionally unearthed by archaeologists and grave robbers. This age-old multiculturalism had been supplemented by the recent arrival of refugees fleeing Taliban rule in Kabul. At the next table an old Turkmen gentleman in a striped *chapan*, or long coat, and hessian boots was mesmerised by the steam rising from his bowl of tea. Further along, the Uzbeks had kicked off their pointed *kalowsh* rubber clogs, good for walking in snow, and were picking their toes. In their corner, the Pashtuns stuck together, transparently scheming in collared overshirts, constantly adjusting their *puttoo* shoulder blankets. Their ancestors were troublemakers relocated to the north by the stormy nineteenth-century emir Abdur Rahman. Isolated and unwelcome in their new northern homes, they ironically became devoted agents of the Pashtun emir, relying on his help to survive the hostility directed at them. A few, like Rasoul's maternal forebears, intermarried.

Around us, waiters in soiled uniforms swaggered about with armfuls of bitter, oval-shaped nan. The cooks sweated over sizzling kebabs and steaming piles of *qabli pulao,* the staple food of the north, made from rice, mutton on the bone, onions, shredded carrots and raisins.

'There is something which may interest you,' said Rasoul, meticulously wiping a speck of rice from the corner of his mouth with a handkerchief. 'Tomorrow there will be a *buzkashi* tournament on the *maidan.* This game can tell you a lot about the character of the northern Afghan. I will find out the time and let you know when we meet at the university this afternoon.'

Taking leave of Rasoul with due ceremony, I headed out onto the streets of Mazar-e Sharif, a low-slung provincial capital with its back to the Hindu Kush on the verge of the vast Central Asian steppe. Women walked unveiled as traffic police dressed like toy grenadiers tried to clear paths for them between high-yoked, horse-drawn *droshkies* and shepherds herding flocks of fat-tailed sheep. Having accepted Soviet occupation, the city and its important shrine had been spared the damage inflicted on other cities during the Russian war. Passing the shrine, I was heading back to my guesthouse when a voice called out to me.

'You like to see carpet?'

Turning, I saw two young faces beaming at me from the doors of a rug shop opposite the shrine. Ten years since my first carpet purchase, I was no longer the callow victim of the predators who lurk in rug shops. On frequent visits to Afghanistan, I had whiled away many spare hours in search of small pieces, preferably tribal and not too expensive, building in the process a modest but cheerful collection. Curious, I entered Rafi and Asif's shop. They were refugees from Kabul, whose father had died carrying his rugs over the snowbound Hindu Kush after Massoud's men had blown up the Salang Tunnel, the main link between Mazar and the capital. Carrying on his business, the brothers Mohammed had supplemented their meagre inheritance with new work from the prodigious looms of the north.

As early as the sixth millennium BC, prehistoric peoples living near the Caspian Sea were spinning wool and plaiting it into crude mats, presumably to keep warm. In 1949, the Russian archaeologist Sergei Rudenko was excavating an ancient tomb locked in permafrost near Pazyryk in the Altai Mountains of southern Siberia when he unearthed the oldest carpet ever found. Buried among horse trappings, felt-applique work, Chinese silks, and flatwoven kilims, the Pazyryk Carpet measured a little under two metres square and was finely woven in wool on a red-ground chequerboard design, bordered with images of men, horses and deer. Carbon dating indicated its age to be around 2500 years. Speculation continues over who made it and where it was made, but the Pazyryk was indisputably the property of the Scythians, an equestrian Central Asian tribe who overran the Middle East in the seventh century.

The wares of the brothers Mohammed were not quite in that league, but they did possess a huge pile of carpets from the Turkmen villages that dominated weaving around Mazar. The unlettered Turkmen weavers had a saying — 'Unroll your carpets, and I shall see what is written in your heart' — and as Rafi unfurled a glossy, earth-brown Bukhara, it was clear he had a soft-spot for the bold work of the Tekke, the most famous of the clans. The rug was covered in guls, the complex, angular motifs believed by some to have served as tribal standards, and talismans against ill fortune. Before Genghis Khan, tent-dwelling Turkmen shepherds had marauded westwards in search of pasture under their chieftain Seljuk, conquering Persia and eventually settling in present-day Turkey. Visiting 'Turkomania' in the thirteenth century, Marco Polo declared that the 'best and handsomest carpets in the world are wrought here, and also silks of crimson and other rich colours'.[2] Wherever the restless Turkmens went, they left behind the echo of their language and the footprints of their guls. Imbued with the lawless spirit of the frontier, they were nevertheless devout Muslims, and it was Seljuk's capture of Jerusalem in the name of Islam in 1071 that provoked the First Crusade. Continuous pressure from the Mongols pushed successive waves of Turkmen people west, where their Ottoman descendants would establish a high culture, but the Turkmen heartland remained stubbornly tribal, organised in two confederations — the Black Sheep and the White Sheep — which were a constant thorn in the side of the Persian and Russian empires with their ceaseless raids on settled communities. By the seventeenth century the main Turkmen tribes were the Salor, Ersari, Yomud, Saryk, Chodor, Kizil Ayak and Tekke. They warred constantly with each other and specialised in hostage-taking for ransom or selling their prisoners into slavery. Each tribe had its own trademark gul — to use dealer's shorthand, the 'camel foot' of the Tekke, the 'fort' of the Salor and the 'dogs' of the Saryk. Only a colour united them - - red. The Turkmens made heavy use of wild perennial madder whose root, supplemented by poppy petals, cherry skins and rose roots, produced a rich palette of plum, terracotta, mahogany, tan, ox blood, violet, liver, bluish-brown and aubergine, and earned them their reputation as the 'Rembrandts' of weaving. Yet war was, perhaps, their greatest art, and the Tekke were better at it than the rest.

The Scottish anthropologist Ella Christie wrote: 'The Tekke tribes, the most savage of all the Turkomans, would not hesitate to sell into slavery the Prophet himself, did he fall into their hands.'[3]

Pursued by the Tekke, remnants of other tribes took refuge in northern Afghanistan where the Salor merged with the local population. As they overpowered other Turkmen tribes, so the Tekke's muscular gul replaced the others. But modernity was stalking even the Tekke, who met it head-on in the shape of the Imperial Russian Army which crushed them at Goek Tepe in 1881. The defeat of the rampaging Tekke permitted construction of the Central Asian Railway, which opened up the region's resources and projected the Tsar's power to the borders of British India, where his best spies vied with Britain's in what became known as 'The Great Game'. Turkmen weavers began using the new aniline dyes brought in by train. Although cheaper and easier to use, these never achieved the subtle patina of age acquired by vegetable-dyed woollen rugs. When the Soviets collectivised agriculture, imposing an economy which had no room for nomads, the tribal system was further debased, and religious persecution by the Bolsheviks sent more conservative Turkmen Sunni Muslims fleeing across the Amu Darya into Afghanistan. In 1917, Turkestan was annexed and later split into five ethnically based Soviet Socialist Republics. A new state enterprise, the Argus Trading Company, acquired a monopoly on production and marketing of Turkmen carpets, pioneering some dodgy business practices which afflict the trade to this day:

> The new Russian trading company Argus found it was difficult to sell tribal rugs, but easy to sell rugs which were reputed to have come out of the palaces. The public's innate snobbery saw and heard what it wanted to, and perfectly ordinary, good tribal rugs pompously re-entitled Princess Bukhara, and Royal Bukhara, sold in large numbers. These ridiculous and inaccurate terms have now also been ... adopted by many undiscerning and ignorant dealers.[4]

Having undermined the nomadic economy and culture, the Russians carried off the spoils, shipping huge quantities of antique rugs on the train to Moscow. Fine pieces were cut up and used to upholster chairs, while the best of the royal and private collections were later confiscated by the Soviet state, which dumped them on the European and North American markets in the 1920s when money was needed to fund an early five-year plan. Well-meaning Russian anthropologists of the Soviet period like V. G. Moshkova, an intrepid woman who undertook six field trips into West Turkestan, studied what was left of Turkmen culture, but by then it was too late. Lamented one Russian observer: 'Like the breath of the Hydra our culture exhales a withering and deadly influence. Traditional art, traditional influence and traditional meaning are no longer able to withstand the seduction of materialist values.'[5]

Fossicking through a pile of rugs slumped against the wall, Rafi came up with an older piece less than a metre square, which I recognised as a Tekke with Saryk guls. Dyed to a clear, deep claret, it was quite alluring, but revived painful memories of an earlier brush with the Turkmens. In the now defunct Dean's Hotel in Peshawar, I had chanced upon an opulent matching pair of antiques from a Turkmen loom. They were the genuine article, with a spacious layout of six guls pointing to a venerable ancestry, possibly nineteenth century. The proprietor of the shop called them 'wedding rugs'. On the threshold of matrimony myself, visions of an Eastern potentate and his princess spending their first night on these very mats enticed me, and the merchant's limited but precise English had an answer for every question.

'Are these true vegetable dyes?' I asked.

'Yes!'

'The rugs are definitely handmade?'

'Yes!'

'So, on the wedding night, the man and the woman would sleep next to each other, on this pair of carpets?'

'Yes!'

'They would make children there?'

'Yes! Yes! Yes!'

Courts, in their wisdom, allow no such leading questions. Had I asked, 'Do these rugs sing? Do they dance? Do they do household chores?' the answers would have been the same because, apart from 'rugs' and 'wedding', 'yes' was undoubtedly the only English word in the merchant's vocabulary. For years, I retold the story of the wedding rugs, first to my fiancée, to whom they were gifted, and then to friends and family, only to be humiliated when informed by an expert that they were actually *juval*, the rectangular storage bags with plain kilim backing which, along with the smaller *torbas* and mafrash, are nowadays stuffed to form cushions. What the merchant had tried to explain was that such items were woven by young Turkmen women as part of their wedding dowries. And not only juval: children's rugs called *salachak*; tassled arches called *kapunuk*; woollen doors called *engsi*; *ok bash*, which covered the pointed ends of tent poles; *asmalyk*, trappings which graced the flanks of camels; *kese*, wallets or moneybags; and *namazlyk*, prayer rugs. They even made pentagonal covers to decorate the knees of camels taking part in wedding parties. Few of these survive from the eighteenth century because they were used until they fell apart; when new ones were woven, the designs passed down the generations.

With their men out jousting in chainmail and curing leather and skins, Turkmen women were hard at work producing the spectacular weavings their culture is most remembered for. They worked on crude horizontal frame looms, the techniques passed from mother to daughter in a chain of knowledge which spanned centuries. Girls learned the language of the loom before they could speak. Weaving was something young women took seriously, simply because their marriage prospects depended on it. When you unearth a matching pair of opulent Turkmen juval, you behold the passion of a young woman's dreams.

In the 1960s the American textiles writer Charles Jacobsen boldly declared, 'There are many who do not appreciate Oriental Rugs, nor can they appreciate the great paintings of Rubens, Rembrandt, and Michelangelo.'[6] But what Michelangelo did for the ceiling of the Sistine Chapel, tribal women had done long before for the floors of their tents. The art of the illiterates was more walked upon than studied, their beautiful things disciplined by use as storage vessels or furnishings in nomadic societies. All the men did was sell or steal them. Or, in my case, buy them. Adopting a variety of stern expressions designed to dissuade Rafi from wasting my time, I bludgeoned down his price and bought the Saryk.

Afghanistan has always been a curious mixture of medieval custom and bold stabs at reform. In most homes, women eat little, and last, consuming the leftovers of husbands and children. Male land mine victims always get preference in the distribution of prostheses, and in the villages an eloping girl will occasionally meet a grisly end, buried up to her neck and shot in the head by a male relative. But the country exists simultaneously in several eras. In 1928, King Amanullah scandalised conservatives by removing compulsory purdah, the physical isolation of women from men other than relatives, and the head-to-foot veil, or chaderi. A counterattack by the mullahs succeeded, forcing Amanullah to abdicate, but thirty years later a progressive prime minister, Mohammed Daoud, tried again, appearing on a reviewing stand with the bare-faced wives of his entire Cabinet. Daoud challenged the mullahs to find Koranic chapters that contradicted the action and jailed them when they failed to do so. Under a new Constitution women voted and ran for office for the first time in 1965, and in the cities women wore Western skirts and blouses, and worked as teachers, doctors and administrators, although the vast majority of women still did not graduate from high school. Now, the Taliban had come, and women were being forced out of their jobs and locked out of schools and universities. They were whipped if found in the company of men other than relatives, and widows — banned from supporting themselves — had no option but to beg in the street, terrorised by religious police who routinely accused them of whoring.

Mazar was still free of all that. At the leafy campus of Balkh University, where 40 per cent of the students were women, Rasoul had promised to introduce me to one of them.

Zhala Najrabi was a model of precociousness, if not a model student. She was twenty-one, had a petite figure, and green eyes that flashed boldly whenever she said something outrageous, which was quite often. When I asked if she was married, intended to marry or even wanted to marry, she flicked her auburn ponytail coquettishly.

'I am happy to be free,' she said. 'Anyway, I have my exams to finish.'

Hearing this, her friends who had gathered round us like footballers in a huddle, exploded into laughter. Zhala's long, painted fingernails were the only thing she studied assiduously. She was passing — barely — and was smart and pretty enough to get away with it, amusing and scandalising the entire campus with her blue jeans and independent attitudes. As she bustled off, leaving me engulfed in a heady veil of perfume, I cried out for an interview, which she granted.

'You may come to my home tomorrow morning,' she said, waving me off.

It was a bright spring morning when I arrived at the Najrabi household on Saraqi Mahbus (Prison Road), a few hundred metres away from Mazar jail, to find Zhala impatient, almost grumpy. She had, it transpired, been up all night.

'Were you unwell?' I inquired solicitously, cowed immediately by her imperious manner.

'Ill? Of course not!' she scolded me. 'No, I was watching television.'

I had noticed the family's improvised satellite dish on my way into the house, a huge colander-like hoop-and-wire affair. But this rude signal-catcher was not trained on any Western frequency. Zhala had been spellbound by something closer to home: the spicy, gyrating melodies of Bollywood movies broadcast in Hindi from India.

'Bollywood is best in our culture,' she said. 'But we dance better than those Indian girls.'

Zhala was wickedly cheeky, but that in itself was nothing new to Mazar. Not far from her house was the tomb of Rabi'a Balkhi, the sister of a tenth-century ruler of Balkh and said to be the first woman to compose poetry in both Arabic and Persian. Rabi'a gained immortality when her brother, after discovering love letters she had written to a Turkish slave boy, threw her into a *hamam*, or steam bath, and had her veins slashed.

As her life ebbed away, the legend says, she wrote a poem in blood and Persian on the wall of the hamam:

> *I knew not when I rode the high-blooded steed*
> *The harder I pulled its reins the less it would heed.*
> *Love is an ocean with such a vast space*
> *No wise man can swim it in any place.*
> *A true lover should be faithful till the end*
> *And face life's reprobated trend.*
> *When see things hideous, fancy them neat*
> *Eat poison, but taste sugar sweet.*[7]

Zhala's eight-year-old sister carried an electric fan into the room, plugged it in, switched it on, adjusted the direction, then flopped down onto the floor to enjoy the novelty of having a guest in the house, while brother Mazdaq, in his early teens, brought pale green tea and ice cream. The family were refugees from the fighting in Kabul and couldn't afford much; the floors were covered in cheap kilims and the roof was made of baked mud and straw, packed between round wooden beams. But Afghan hospitality is a loaves and fishes miracle in which, it is said, even an onion can be given graciously. Zhala's mother had died of an illness twelve years earlier. Her youngest brother, whose saucer eyes and chubby cheeks still brightened the family portrait, was also dead, the victim of one of the thousands of rockets fired at Kabul by the mujahideen. Zhala's widower father had been an officer in the Afghan Army under President Babrak Karmal. In those days the family had been well off, even owning a car.

Revived by her tea, Zhala seemed ready to engage me. Lounging on carpet bolsters in an eye-catching red dress with a gold embroidered breastplate, she reeled off a list of her competencies: diploma in personal computing, comfortable in WordPerfect, Lotus and Excel, fluent in English and Dari. In her spare time she worked as a nurse at a Tajik refugee camp run by Médecins Sans Frontières. She was trying to impress me, and it was working. Accomplished and pretty, all pale skin and wayward audacity, Zhala was sure to drive some young man insane, which raised the issue of dowry. Was she required, like a Turkmen girl, to provide a suite of woven wool goods? Had she ever woven a carpet? A pair of crimson juval? Kneeguards for ceremonial camels?

There is a famous photograph which once made the cover of *National Geographic* of a young Afghan girl with piercing eyes of jade, wearing a tattered, dirt-red scarf. It is a haunting image, the face of a child whose expression seems both traumatised and indignant. Her eyes warn, and challenge, and resent. It was with such eyes that Zhala fixed me.

'Woven carpets?' she snorted. 'You must be joking!'

6

Great Game

A word said is a shot fired

— UZBEK SAYING[8]

In March 1980 fifty Russian soldiers were invited to the outskirts of Mazar-e Sharif to watch a game of buzkashi. The venue was desolate open ground verging on desert where the Russians had built wheat silos as a gift to the Afghan government. A few years later the Soviet Army occupied the country and the silos supplied their soldiers, while the Afghans went hungry. Surprised but delighted by the unexpected invitation to join the festivities, the Russian troops watched amazed as local *chapandaz* whipped their horses into a frenzy and tussled for control of a headless calf, one or two riders occasionally breaking free from the mêlée to score a 'goal' by dropping the carcass inside the *halal*, or circle of justice, chalked on the ground in lime. But as the Russians watched the game, the Afghans were watching the Russians and when their guests were entirely engrossed, fell upon them, beating and trampling them to death.[9]

On the field where the killings had taken place years before, Rasoul and I took our seats under an aluminium sky, nervously eyeing the crowd for any sign of a repeat performance. 'Buzkashi' was an Uzbek word which meant 'goat grabbing', but the 'buz' —

which fell apart too easily in the tussle — was replaced by the sturdier carcass of a calf which had been gutted, filled with sand and soaked overnight. Weighing about fifty kilograms, its hoofs were removed to make it more difficult to pick up. The game had apparently evolved from an earlier version, devised by the warrior-aesthete Timur the Lame, played with the decapitated corpses of enemy soldiers.

Before us several dozen mounted horsemen were perched on carpeted saddles and shod in knee-high riding boots with four-inch heels. They had converged over the buz, which lay inside the circle in front of us, and were fiercely lashing their mounts — and sometimes each other — pressing towards the centre of the pack and bending low to get hold of the dead calf. It was a grim, scrappy struggle until one of them got a grip and took off at a gallop towards a pennant planted near the silos five hundred metres away, pursued by a dust-raising mob.

Short and stocky, with a low centre of gravity, the horses were every bit as ornery as their riders, biting and butting each other whenever possible. Their equine ancestors had been known to form their own riderless raiding parties, storming nomad camps to kill the stallions and abscond with the mares.[10] Breeding would eventually produce the Akhal-Tekke, renowned for its stamina and speed, whose most famous offspring was Bucephalus, the steed ridden by Alexander the Great when he defeated the Parthians.[11] It could take up to five years to build up the horses' inherent bad temper and aggression sufficiently to make good buzkashi ponies. Fed on barley, eggs, salt, melons and butter, their careers could extend over thirty years, and the best became national celebrities.

An emerging thunder which made the ground tremble signalled the return of the pack, hoofs clashing as they reared up and almost toppled into the front row of seats in the grandstand. The riders, holding their whips in their teeth, wore the same crazed expressions as their horses, and the blustery air was thick with the sounds of whinnying horses and cracking whips. There were, supposedly, two teams, but without uniforms it was difficult to tell them apart and rumours swept the bleachers around us of sneak defections mid-game, much as the various Muslim militias kept switching sides in the civil war. In the midst of it all a ragged, howling figure began dancing dementedly on the open ground in front of the stands. The jester, who in better times would have been outlandishly dressed, had to lavish praise on the victorious riders or risk a flogging from the proud horsemen. He also had to be funny. Bad things had happened to dull ones.

In the stands the spectators were all men. Wrapped in blankets they looked as cutthroat, if not as manic, as the riders and their massed faces formed a tableau of long-eyed Mongols and Uzbeks, and olive-skinned Turks and Arabs. They were variously sage, excitable, pugilistic, suspicious and beaten. The goat-grabbing game of life was tougher than anything happening on the field, yet somehow the elderly managed to achieve a physical eminence which contrasted vividly with the dumb clay of nearby youths, who amused themselves with that other great game — egg-cracking. Take two men, give each a hardboiled egg, and then watch as they tap-tap-tap the eggs together. The one whose egg cracks first is the loser. Millions of *Afghanis* change hands this way.

Finally, when all the pulling, grabbing, tugging, tearing and pushing had torn the buz apart, a torrid argument erupted over who held the largest remnant and was therefore the winner of the cash prize. As the crowd began streaming away, their pockets full of broken eggs, Rasoul — whose name means 'messenger', and who was a fount of interesting facts — informed me that the horse that had won the most prize-money was owned by a certain Talook Hariddar.

'I should like to point out here,' he said, in his uniquely stilted cadence, 'that Talook Hariddar is a Hazara. The rider is Hazara too.'

'Is the horse also a Hazara?' I asked.

'Maybe,' Rasoul said, warming to the idea. 'Yes, I think the horse is also from Hazarajat.'

'And the calf?'

'No.' Definitely, the calf is Pashtun.'

Ethnic team spirit notwithstanding, the Uzbeks were generally acknowledged as the masters of buzkashi. Descended from the Mongol chieftain Uzbeg Khan, they were remnants of Genghis Khan's Golden Horde which stormed into the heart of Asia in the sixteenth century, seizing its great cities of Samarkand, Bukhara and Tashkent; however their empire later broke up into to principalities. Uzbek weaving reflected this turbulent history, their jazz-lightning tie-dye embroidered textiles evoking what one writer called 'a barbaric quality [which] sums up all our romantic notions of Tartar savagery'.[12]

The leader of the Afghan Uzbeks and the notorious gilam jam was Abdul Rashid Dostum. A portrait of the bull-necked general, who had risen from security guard and gasfields driller to lead an army of thirty thousand men, greeted arrivals at Mazar airport. Dostum represented many interests, but mainly his own. His northern fiefdom was being propped up financially by Iran, Uzbekistan and Russia, all of which saw a divided Afghanistan as less of a threat than a united one. They saw the hard-drinking, buzkashi-playing Dostum as an effective bulwark against the spread of Taliban-style fundamentalism. His mere laughter was said to have caused the deaths of several people.

Behind the rammed earth ramparts of Dostum's nineteenth-century Qila-e Jangi, a short drive south of Mazar-e Sharif, terrors were commonplace and little reported. A correspondent visiting the 'Fortress of War' on one occasion reported seeing fresh pieces of flesh littering the courtyard. Inquiring of the guards whether a goat had just been slaughtered, he was told that an hour earlier Dostum had punished a soldier for stealing by having a tank driven over him.[13] The general was killing off potential rivals for the Uzbek leadership, and the blood feuds were becoming unmanageable. The Taliban, meanwhile, had begun referring to him as a 'blood-sucking former communist' and everyone knew that if the Talibs made it to Mazar, Dostum had an early appointment with a lamppost.

At the gates of Qila-e Jangi gruesome Uzbek troops dressed in woollen greatcoats, blue fur hats and regulation moustaches stood guard with automatic weapons. Inside the fort, the presence of a bulletproofed black Cadillac stretch limousine indicated that the general was in residence. Around the fort's interior walls were portraits of some of the ten thousand men who had died fighting for Dostum since he assumed command of the northern forces. In the courtyard, turbaned petitioners and uniformed officers milled around awaiting an audience, losing their place in the queue to the small group of foreign reporters who were ushered inside by officials. We found him ensconced in a surprisingly small upstairs office with the curtains drawn. In this bunker-like atmosphere the physically imposing Uzbek leader forced a smile and bade us to sit down. With chairs in short supply, I sat on the edge of his carpet, an old sign of deference, or fear.

General Dostum's woollen shirt was as thick as a rug, and festooned with four-star epaulettes. Luxurious eyebrows converged above his nose, his hair was greying and his moustache bristled. There was none of the normally effusive Afghan hospitality, and from the outset it was clear that the general was uncomfortable answering difficult questions but tolerated journalists because unlike his terrified courtiers they would at least offer unvarnished accounts of the situation outside the fort. In his gruff Turkic dialect, one word intruded into most sentences — 'Toli-*bon*'. Sketching battlefields on the back of an envelope, the general elaborated his plans for the defence of the north. With Kabul and

Herat firmly under their control and bolstered by volunteers from neighbouring Pakistan, the Taliban had broken through the last mountain pass in the west, but were held up by the spring rains which had turned the sandy wastes between Herat and Mazar into a vast bog. Reports of the Talibs' imminent offensive had, nevertheless, persuaded many of Dostum's best generals to flee to Uzbekistan. Morale was low, panic gripped the local money market and his troops hadn't been paid for months. Still, the Uzbek leader tried his best to sound positive.

'Those who wanted to escape have already escaped,' he said, dropping his pen and working his worry beads with vigour. 'Those generals beside General Dostum now are the ones who love their country, who want to work, who want to serve their people. They are not scared of any killing, or any dying, or anything. They're ready to lose their lives.'

As he spoke Dostum swivelled in his chair, so that eventually the only part of his body still facing us was his left shoulder. He was holed up in his fort, and talking to his worry beads.

'I have constructed the best *madrassas* and mosques for the people to read and learn the Holy Koran and Islamic activities,' he said, aggrieved by his ungrateful subjects. 'Thousands of families have been given gas by me.'

Dostum bore more than a passing resemblance to the psychotic Orientals of numerous old fictions. The black-hearted Serdar in James Morier's *The Adventures of Hajji Baba of Ispahan* came to mind: 'No law, human or divine, ever stood in the way of his sensuality; and when his passions were roused, he put no bounds to his violence and cruelty.' But like the Serdar, Dostum had several qualities which attracted his followers to him. He too was liberal and enterprising, and had 'so much quickness and penetration, and acted so politically towards the Shah and his government, that he was always treated with the greatest confidence and consideration'. He too 'lived in princely magnificence; was remarkable for his hospitality, and making no mystery of his irregularity as a Mussulman, was frank and open in his demeanour, affable to his inferiors, and the very best companion to those who shared his debaucheries'.[14]

His reputation for generosity included the practice of gifting rugs and saddlebags to his visitors. But times were tough — journalistic ethics also — and we left Qila-e Jangi empty-handed.

7

The Mother of Cities

Afghanistan is a stark beauty, vicious and seductive. A certain type of person will brave any difficulty to get there, then having arrived, continuously pinch themselves to ensure they are not dreaming. A landscape might be denuded, a human settlement abandoned or lost, but always, just beneath the ground, lies history of preposterous grandeur. Chance encounters hold unexpected charms; perhaps an old man wearing a set of spectacles made up from several different pairs, or a burnt-cheeked street kid with more sass than a tonight show host. They are everywhere, these individuals of undaunted humankind, irrepressibly optimistic and proud.

'Here at last,' wrote Robert Byron, arriving in Herat to find not a single shop selling alcohol, 'is Asia without an inferiority complex.'[15]

Like prophets, travel writers are inspired by the journals of their predecessors, and leave their own revelations for those who come later. Following in their footsteps is a pilgrim's odyssey. In Afghanistan you can stand before a citadel which still controls the city below it, and know that little has changed since Byron, Bruce Chatwin or Nancy Hatch Dupree stood there, looking at the very same thing. In the early 1990s you could still hitch free rides on United Nations aircraft to the remotest parts of the country. In the small jets you got to know your pilots, often young Scandinavians who'd taken the jobs to boost their flying hours.

Heading for Herat on one occasion, one of them agreed to overfly Bamiyan, and from fifteen thousand feet we stared in awe at the colossal Buddhas carved into the honey-coloured sandstone cliffs overlooking the city, followed by a three hundred and sixty-degree loop over the blue lakes of Band-e Amir with the surrounding mountains mirrored in their still waters.

I found Chatwin in Herat, in spirit at least, smitten by 'men in mountainous turbans, strolling hand in hand, with roses in their mouths and rifles wrapped in flowered chintz'.[16] Even after the Russians had flattened most of the city and riddled the ruins with land mines, people still walked that way. In the early 1990s, Heratis were trickling home from the refugee camps in Iran, happy simply to have their city back. At his hole-in-the-wall shop on the Street of Goldsmiths, Haider Kebabi was turning the skewers again, fanning the charcoal brazier and shielding his eyes from its greasy smoke. James A. Michener had been a regular there while researching *Caravans*, or so the *kebabchi* said, as shafts of light streamed down through the smoke holes in the ceiling. You could measure the proprietor's joy simply by estimating the number of kebabs he could make in a day, and multiplying it by the remaining days of his life. He was slipping bonus fat kebabs in between the mutton ones.

In Herat, anything still standing was heroic. On the outskirts of town, five fifteenth-century minarets soared thirty metres high, the remnants of a dozen such towers which once graced the capital of an empire stretching from China to the Tigris. In the 1800s, an Irish artillery officer on leave from the East India Company, Eldridge Pottinger, had arranged to have several of the minarets demolished to provide a clear field of fire should the Russians invade. Pottinger was ahead of his time. When, a century later, the Russians finally arrived, they holed several of the surviving minarets with rockets. Wartime felling of trees — which had protected the monuments from the '120 day' winds that rake the plains every summer — saw their protective cladding of cerulean blue tiles literally blown away. Children brought up during the war studied maths from books containing such exercises as 'One [picture of a hand-grenade] plus one [picture of a hand-grenade] equals two [picture of two hand-grenades]'. Nearby were glass-topped graves containing the skeletons of some thousands of civilians massacred by the Russians after a demonstration against their occupation in 1979.

The city was nothing if not resilient. Its vines still boasted seventeen varieties of grapes, including 'The Bride's Little Finger', renowned for its sweetness. Walking in the street one day I saw a man sitting on a rug. When I asked half-jokingly whether he might sell it, he leapt to his feet and began beating it so furiously that we were soon enveloped in a billowing cloud of dust. A modest but colourful piece, it cost $20 and came with a priceless memory. In a cluttered shop behind the grand mosque where Sultan Ghiyasuddin, builder of the Minaret of Jam lies buried, lake-blue goblets made by Herat's last traditional glassblower were on sale. Museums in the West had planned to send experts to Herat to preserve the craft, but before they could do so, civil war engulfed the city again.

When Byron passed through Herat in the 1930s, he was heading for northern Afghanistan. Inspired by a photograph he had seen of a Seljuk tomb-tower on the Turkestan plain, his quest to find the roots of Islamic architecture eventually took him to the ancient city of Balkh, a twenty-minute drive west of Mazar-e Sharif.

Almost seventy years later a gas pipeline led the way across a timeless landscape of sickle-wielding farmers and camel drivers wrapped in shawls to avoid the sting of a sandstorm. Across the road, Turkmen shepherds led flocks of black Karakul lambs, the lucrative gift of spring flying like black bullets through the storm, while bored soldiers manning tanks and gun turrets looked on. At one point, the road itself entered the portals of a vast walled enclosure, and I thought we had reached Balkh, but on closer inspection it was clearly of more recent vintage. In the 1920s, when the Russians invaded in support of the dethroned King Amanullah, a small detachment of Russians had been besieged inside Dehdadi Fort by Turkmens. According to Byron, they survived a 'wretched fight' by dragging their guns from one side of the fort to the other.

The legend of Balkh is based mainly on the historic figures who lived or passed through there. Six hundred years before Christ, Zoroaster arrived in the cool, fragrant climate of the Amu Darya Valley, then under Persian rule. Preaching a new faith which incorporated old Aryan rituals like fire worship and the drinking of a fermented sacramental liquid called ambrosia, Zoroaster converted King Vishtaspa of Balkh to his teaching that after death the soul would be judged according to a person's thoughts, words and acts. Zoroaster himself would die in Balkh, murdered by a Turk from north of the Amu Darya, or Oxus as it was known to the Greeks, but Zoroastrianism would dominate Persia until the coming of Islam twelve hundred years later. Known to the Arabs as the 'mother of cities', Balkh kept on assimilating new influences. Alexander the Great's conquests ushered in five hundred years of Greek influence, blended with the teachings of Buddhism then emerging from India. Nestorian Christians found a refuge in Balkh and vigorous debates on religious questions, and the study of medicine and science, enlivened its universities.

Around the first century AD, Balkh became an important staging post on the Silk Road, selling and trans-shipping raw silk from China to Persia and eventually Europe. The city spawned many imitators, among them Samarkand, Marakanda, Bukhara, Khiva, Merv, Tus, Ravy and Qom. After Muslim Arab armies arrived in 663 AD an Islamic renaissance flowered in its thriving bazaars, bathhouses and barrel-vaulted palaces. By the eighth century the military prowess, artistic refinement and scientific achievements of the Islamic world had far surpassed the Christian West. Thinkers, poets and mathematicians thrived in Balkh, among them the Persian free-thinker Omar Khayyam, who spent his formative years there. In 1207, the city gave birth to another wild man, the poet Jalal-ud-Din Balkhi, also known as Rumi, who held that music and poetry could facilitate direct and ecstatic experience of God, and founded the Sufi Muslim order of whirling dervishes.

Twenty kilometres west of Mazar a low line of weathered ramparts appeared on the horizon — the walls of ancient Balkh. In May 1934 Byron had passed through the same gap I now entered. The sandstorm had drained the sky of every colour except grey, against which a few isolated trees denuded of their leaves posed like ghastly skeletons. Here and there nameless mounds of melted earth rose up, the secret of their original purpose eroded away. It was as Byron had described it:

> . . . *worn grey-white shapes of a bygone architecture, mounds, furrowed and bleached by the rain and sun, wearier than any human works I ever saw; a twisted pyramid, a tapering platform, a clump of battlements, a crouching beast, all familiars of the Bactrian Greeks and of Marco Polo after them. They ought to have vanished. But the very impact of the sun, calling out the obstinacy of their ashen clay, has conserved some inextinguishable spark of form, a spark such as a Roman earthwork or a grass-grown barrow has not, which still flickers on against a world brighter than itself, tired as only a suicide frustrated can be tired.*[17]

In the early thirteenth century a holocaust, the like of which had never been seen before, engulfed the 'mother of cities'. An obscure Mongol chieftain had written to Khwarizm Shah, then Muslim ruler of mighty Balkh, suggesting a treaty between them.

'I am the sovereign of the sunrise,' the letter pompously declared, 'and thou the sovereign of the sunset. Let there be a firm treaty of friendship, amity, and peace.'

When the chieftain, later to become known as Genghis Khan, received no reply from the haughty Khwarizm, he despatched messengers who were sent back with their beards singed. It was not the first insult Genghis had suffered at the hands of Muslim princes.

Invited to sit on a carpet in the comfortable camp of a Turkmen army, he discovered a pit had been dug beneath it. The arrogance of the world's leading civilisation at the time inspired in Genghis a pitiless wrath which reduced the great Islamic cities to deserts. The sacking of Nishapur, Merv, Herat, Balkh and Samarkand saw displaced Muslims flood into Delhi, contributing to its cultural epiphany in the thirteenth and fourteenth centuries.[18] Driven all the way to Konya, in today's Turkey, Rumi spoke for the refugees:

A man goes to sleep in the town
where he has always lived,
and he dreams he's living
in another town.
In the dream, he doesn't remember
the town he's sleeping in . . .
He believes
the reality of the dream town.
The world is that kind of sleep.
The dust of many crumbled cities
settles over us like a forgetful doze,
but we are older than those cities.[19]

The collapse of the great Islamic centres of the time was not entirely due to the Mongol war of steppe against city. The strength of Muslim society, and its ability to resist assaults of the kind Genghis inflicted, had already been undermined by the growing power of fundamentalist clerics, who insisted that the arts, sciences and philosophy submit to theology. The twelfth-century orthodox Islamic theologian Abu Hamid Al-Ghazali held that all fields of inquiry must conform to religious doctrine. Asked by his students which subjects they should disregard, he nominated medicine, astronomy and poetry. When in the twelfth century the great scientist Abu Raihan al-Biruni invented an instrument for calculating dates on the Muslim calendar, he was denounced as an infidel.

By about the end of the thirteenth century it was clear that the Muslim initiative in almost every branch of learning, including science, medicine and philosophy, had virtually come to an end, and was passing by slow degrees to the West. This was due mainly to the increasing hold exerted on all Islamic studies by religion, which discouraged such 'foreign' pursuits as hostile to Islam, the study of science being regarded as particularly 'accursed'.[20]

Squatting on a plain so bare that the curvature of the earth seemed visible was Byron's 'crouching beast', a faceless sphinx. Before being massacred in their thousands the good citizens of Balkh had buried their fortunes, and now in this cratered, unearthly landscape small bands of grave robbers went about their spadework. The scavengers were picking over mounds that appeared to have already been excavated. Beyond a ploughed field awaiting seed, the land rose up, playing strange tricks with the horizon, as if the plain had been churned up and dumped there. When I bothered a dough-faced Uzbek digger with a sack slung over his shoulder, he showed me his haul for the day — a fragment of pottery which could have been made the previous week or a millennium ago. The takings must have been thin, otherwise half of Balkh province would have been there shovelling with him. Or perhaps the people of the fallen city still had some respect for their noble past, and preferred not to hang around these depressing burrows and tailings heaps, like crows around carrion.

In a cubbyhole office in neighbouring Pakistan, the dowager queen of Afghanophiles, Nancy Hatch Depree, looked on from a distance at the rape of her favourite country. At seventy-two she was still working diligently at the Afghan Resource and Information Centre in Peshawar, the archive she had established at a time when invasion and war threatened to obliterate the history, as well as the man-made heritage, of the country. She was telling me she had seen people in Balkh carting off fluted columns from the ancient mounds to prop up their houses. Interrupted by a young Pakistani staffer, she took delivery of her mail. Opening the very first letter, she froze.

'This is what I was afraid of,' she moaned as she read its contents.

It was the latest report on the state of the colossal Buddha statues in Bamiyan, and the news was not good. It confirmed more artillery shell damage to the larger of the two stone Buddhas, which stood more than fifty metres high. Wrapped in a green woollen scarf, with thick, black-rimmed spectacles perched on her flat koala-like nose, she thanked the messenger with a weary 'tashakour'. Since being posted to Kabul with the US Embassy in 1962 she had lived sixteen years in Afghanistan, and travelled its length and breadth with her late anthropologist husband Louis on his field trips. In 1978 they were expelled by the communists, but moved to Peshawar and joined the large community of Afghan-watchers based there. For twenty years she had been lovingly assembling her archive, hoping to transfer it to Kabul when peace returned. In the meantime, she regularly sent steel boxes full of books — 'box libraries' she called them — to the war-ravaged villages, probably doing more to promote literacy than the entire Afghan government.

First recorded in 400 AD by the Chinese Buddhist pilgrim Fa Hsien, the Bamiyan Buddhas were so large they had survived centuries of Muslim vandalism, which had erased their faces and damaged their flowing stone robes. More than two hundred years after Fa Hsien, when another Chinese pilgrim, Hsuan Tsang, visited Bamiyan, the 'marvellous valley' was still a haven for pilgrims, scholars and traders plying the Silk Road. During the latest civil war, the monks' cells, carved from the cliff face behind the colossi and decorated with glorious frescoes, accommodated militiamen and explosives were stored at the feet of the Buddhas. On 16 April

1997 a Taliban commander besieging Bamiyan threatened to blow up the statues once his troops succeeded in taking the city. Strict Muslims consider any image of the human form to be idolatrous. Amid international outrage, the Taliban leadership in Kandahar issued a statement denying any intention of harming the statues. As a stalwart of the Society for the Preservation of Afghanistan's Cultural Heritage (SPACH), Nancy had nagged the Taliban into promising to safeguard the megaliths. Despite their promises, some damage occurred as the area changed hands between militia groups. SPACH had persuaded one of the groups to remove a gun emplacement that troops had positioned on the head of one Buddha, which was attracting enemy fire. But Nancy felt she was fighting a losing battle against scavengers, as well as iconoclasts, all over the country.

'They don't care about pottery shards,' she scoffed. 'At Ai Khanoum they've got bulldozers and they're looking for Greek columns. It was the easternmost Greek city on earth, and there were gymnasiums and theatres. You've got people building their shops inside the old Buddhist monastic caves in Pul-i-Kumri. The Minaret of Jam is being undermined by the river in Ghor.'

She loved Kabul, where she'd met her husband, and Kishim where, during a field trip, she'd lived in a mosque for three months.

'Oh and then there's Tashkurghan, of course,' she said with a faraway look. 'I weep for Tashkurghan.'

Some sixty kilometres east of Mazar, in the ancient town of Tashkurghan, stood the Tim Bazaar. Built in 1845 by a local *beg*, or tribal leader, and run on guild lines, it was one of the last traditional covered markets in Afghanistan. In the nineteenth century the town was one of a series of predatory city-states on the Turkestan plain, sheltering inside five-kilometre-long city walls (Tashkurghan means 'stone walls') as it levied tribute from caravans travelling between India and Bukhara. Writers down the centuries had praised the town, now known as Khulm, for its shady arbours, and on a hot and dusty afternoon in the early 1960s the peripatetic English author Bruce Chatwin had stopped there. 'I really did stumble on melons as I passed and had green thoughts in a green shade,' he fondly recalled.[21]

Just prior to the Soviet invasion the town was a virtual orchard fed by irrigating channels which ran through the streets. The bazaar sold everything from sheep and cattle to silk from India. The heart of the bazaar was the intersection of two covered alleys under a mud-brick cupola decorated with floral frescoes. Antique Chinese plates preserved from the Silk Road days were inset in the stucco, with the largest plate crowning the summit of the dome. Sixteen shops housed in niches cut into the walls below specialised in embroidered *kola,* the caps around which turbans are twisted. Armed only with a cherished copy of Nancy's *An Historical Guide to Afghanistan,* I had set out to find it.

Heading east from Mazar, the Salang Highway cut across a saltpan desert dotted with hardy tamarisk trees, sage bush and the occasional rusting hulk of a Russian tank. Prayer flags fluttered over graves, and Dostum's artillery guns were dug into dried-mud redoubts. The Russians had built the highway, linking northern and southern Afghanistan, and then used it for the invasion. It was still the best road in the country, but now Iran paid local labourers to maintain it should Tehran ever need to make a rapid forced entry. Less than an hour's drive from Mazar, the distant mountains suddenly closed in on the road and I got my first glimpse of the fabled township, set at the mouth of a dramatic gorge and awash with cherry blossom.

The governor of the mainly Tajik district was a crusty old gentleman with an officious-looking folder and a creased Karakul hat. Abdul Masay greeted me warmly on Kochi Abdar, the Street of

Water, and led me on a tour of some imaginary irrigation works he was doing with foreign aid. Then, at my request, he deputed a young man with a rifle to take me to the heart of old Tashkurghan, the covered Tim Bazaar. The downy-faced gunman carried two large pink roses; one, in his hand, in which he occasionally buried his nose, and the other sprouting from the barrel of the rifle slung on a strap over his shoulder. As he led me along an avenue of fruit trees I imagined the dark, winding alleys of the bazaar, with its roof of felt and animal hides and tiny keyhole shops in niches. My book contained a small black-and-white photograph of it which was everyone's Eastern fantasy come to life. Twenty years of war had left the town completely isolated, untrampled by tour groups or backpackers. I would have it entirely to myself. Marching up an incline we passed through a ruined quarter where roofless mud houses had been abandoned since the jihad against the Russians. Reaching a flat open area slightly above the surrounding ruins, the boy stood and turned. From where we stood, a panorama of devastation stretched out in all directions, hardly a building left habitable.

'Which way to Tim Bazaar?' I asked in Dari.

The boy's face radiated with a huge smile, seemingly enchanted at understanding the question in his own language and overjoyed at knowing the answer.

'*Maw rasi dim* (We have arrived),' he declared.

'But I see no buildings,' I said, groping for the right words to lead us out of this wilderness and into the musty confines of the bazaar. But all I could do was repeat the question, and all he could do was repeat his answer.

'*Injast. Maw injastim!* (It's here. We are here!)'

The more I insisted we had not arrived, the more warmly he assured me that we had. Amused beyond endurance, he seemed to think I was teasing him, making him out to be some sort of tricky joker. The more abjectly I protested, the more he giggled, like a child unable to bear a tickle. Definitely we had arrived. Undoubtedly we had arrived. No, there was nowhere else to go. But where was the bazaar?

Finally, deducing that my poor Dari was responsible for the farce, he broke into halting English.

'This Tim Bazaar,' he said, his voice hollow with wonder. 'This murder bazaar.'

As he shoved his nose triumphantly into the heart of his rose and inhaled lustily, the depressing reality sank in. It was like reaching Mecca and finding no mosque. There was no longer a Tim Bazaar. It had been destroyed in the war. Stunned, I was looking blankly at the ruins when a toothless, turbaned old man appeared and asked us to follow him.

A short distance away, we came upon a pair of bullet-riddled wooden doors leading into a small, dilapidated compound. Through more doors we entered what appeared to be a fragment of a mosque, a single gallery of a once larger structure. It had lost its minaret, but inside, the vaulted, whitewashed ceilings and blind arcades of cusped, tapering arches were pristinely preserved, and the quiet voices of a few Afghans who were inspecting the sanctuary echoed softly in the chamber. Preserved intact on the western wall, was the mihrab, or prayer niche.

That was all that remained of Tashkurghan's 'murdered' bazaar.

8

The Taliban Cometh

Beyond Balkh lay carpet country, the Turkmen towns of Aqcha and Andkhoi and Uzbek-dominated Maimana, famous for its kilims. Along the way was Sheberghan, Dostum's hometown, where the warlord-general lived in a fort.

Every year, when the mountain passes cleared and the boggy roads of spring became motorably hard in northern Afghanistan, the fighting season began. But in 1997, the season started not with an offensive, but a rebellion. The assassination in May of a senior Uzbek commander, Abdur Rahman Haqqani — allegedly carried out on Dostum's orders — convulsed the north. At Haqqani's home in Mazar-e Sharif, the thick red pile of Turkmen rugs had absorbed the blood of the commander, who had been shot ten times with a Makarov pistol by a guest as they were having tea. But the fragile alliance of Uzbek clans which kept Dostum in power could not absorb the political shock. In Maimana, the thirty-five-year-old scion of a prominent Uzbek family, Abdul Malik Palawan, who feared he might be next on the hit list, declared open rebellion against Dostum and threw in his lot with the Taliban. The whereabouts of the general himself were a mystery.

Rapidly mobilised in informal fighting units called *lashkars,* the Taliban were speeding towards Sheberghan as fast as their Japanese pickup trucks would carry them. Lashkars received no pay but found profitable activities in newly conquered areas; car stealing was a favourite. The southern Pashtuns were storming into the north with Malik's consent, gathering weapons and searching for Dostum along the way. Camped in Mazar-e Sharif, I lamented the absence of Robert Adams, with all his informed military patter of 'outgoing' and 'incoming'. Discussing options with a few other colleagues, we decided not to wait for the incoming Taliban, but to be outgoing ourselves, and meet them halfway in Sheberghan.

Heat haze stampeded across the desert road leading to Dostum's home base. After driving for about two hours, we ended up at a steel archway supporting a portrait of the general, where police stopped the car and radioed ahead for instructions. As we waited in the stifling heat, a towheaded young conscript approached the car, pointed at the portrait of his leader and gave a thumbs down.

'Dostum,' he said with a grimace.

After the harsh, open light of the desert, Sheberghan's neat, tree-lined avenues were a pleasant oasis. Dostum had lavished money on showpiece buildings and gardens, and the stores in Ittefaq Market bulged with television sets and posters featuring Bollywood actresses, like Madhuri Dixit. But with troops under the Taliban flag massing on the western approaches, an exodus had begun. At the main bus station men were bundling live sheep and cattle into the luggage bins of an intercity bus headed for Mazar. Tanks rolled west along the main street towards the frontline. Ambulances came the other way. Suddenly, our decision to form a welcoming party for the Taliban seemed foolhardy, and I was almost relieved when Dostum's men rounded us up, escorted us back to the steel gate where Sheberghan surrenders to the desert, and pointed us towards Mazar.

As we drove east, less than two hours ahead of the advancing rebels, Dostum's fiefdom unravelled before me like a video played backwards at double speed. At a military airbase just outside the town his MiG fighter planes were scrambling, as his Pashtun fighter pilots flew to Kabul to deliver their planes to the Taliban. Past camel trains and martyrs' graves we swept into Aqcha, a mixed Turkmen and Uzbek town famed for its weekly carpet market where Karavoyan, Charkush and Kizilayak villagers would come from distant villages to show their work. Bales of wool in old rose colour dried on the town's flat rooftops, but predictably enough the rug bazaar was closed. Seated outside on a charpoy cot covered with a striped kilim, a man was playing chess with a friend and pouring tea from a blue enamel pot. The intricacies of Afghan politics have been compared to chess, except that chess has rules and the pieces don't continuously change colour, nor are they likely at any moment to explode in your hand.

Writing a thousand years ago, Omar Khayyam saw life itself as little more than a doomed struggle to avoid checkmate:

> *Tis all a chequerboard of Nights and Days,*
> *Where Destiny with Men for pieces plays,*
> *Hither and thither moves, and mates, and slays,*
> *And one by one back in the closet lays.*[22]

The Afghan tea drinking ceremony is eternal, but it would be the last game of chess played in Aqcha for some time. The Taliban had banned the game, believing that kings, queens, bishops and rooks violated Koranic injunctions against images of living things. Asked if he would be augmenting his moustache with a beard to convince the Taliban that he was a 'good' Muslim, the man, Wahidullah, simply shrugged good-naturedly and continued his game.

Closer to Mazar, people were not so philosophical. At a checkpoint near Balkh the car was mobbed by Dostum troops who had lost contact with Sheberghan. Hearing our news, they hurriedly began gathering their possessions to flee, while our driver — fearing for his wife and children — begged to return immediately to Mazar. The next checkpoint was controlled by Balkh Pashtuns, surly men who carefully checked our car and papers and whose presence meant Dostum no longer controlled the road between his two main centres of power. Finally, entering

Mazar at three o'clock that afternoon, we found crowds running aimlessly in the streets, snatching at anything they could grab from others and smashing shop windows in order to loot. Dostum portraits were being torn down and ripped up in the street and soldiers were seizing cars at gunpoint to make their getaway. Then it became quiet, an unearthly quiet in a city of several hundred thousand people, as the citizenry bolted their doors and awaited whatever might come.

Towards dusk, Malik's mutineers sped into town in tanks and jeeps, firing their AK-47s into the air and shouting 'Allahu Akbar' — probably, as a departing Dostum official noted bitterly, for the first time in their lives. One of their first acts was to release all the prisoners from Mazar jail, including sundry murderers and rapists along with genuine political prisoners. The rebel leader Malik, a babyfaced warlord with no hope of a beard, took up residence in a bungalow where the ultimate symbol of power and legitimacy — Dostum's now bullet-riddled Cadillac — stood parked in the drive. When the Taliban blazed into Mazar the following afternoon, it was in attack Toyotas, several thousand armed men seated in sixes and sevens with machine guns mounted in the back. They had driven four hundred kilometres from Badgis, many having spontaneously joined up with the victorious convoy as it swept through towns along the way. Suddenly they were all 'holy warriors of Islam, trees in the garden of valour'.[23] A young man, who called himself Mullah Gul Mohammad from Sar-e Pul, stood beside his truck near the shrine of Hazrat Ali, allowing his lieutenants to thump pushy onlookers with their rifle butts.

'Everything which is against Islam we will stop,' he said, announcing that with immediate effect thieves would have their hands amputated, music was banned and all men had to grow beards. Women found outside the home in anything other than full chaderi would be flogged on the spot. With the Taliban's white flag fluttering over the shrine of Hazrat Ali, members of the student army began smashing stocks of videotape at the local television station and stringing the contents of the cassettes around gates and lampposts. At the mosque, loudspeakers began broadcasting the new regulations. The number of turbaned, unshaven, sandal-wearing Talibs carrying quivers of rocket-propelled grenades grew steadily, bolstered by planeloads of Pakistani volunteers flown in from Kandahar. On the scorched streets, women who days before had walked confidently in skirts and blouses now sailed past in veils.

At the Sultan Raziah School on Mormul Street, the hollow sound of the *adhan*, the *muezzin's* call to prayer, floated across a deserted playground as doves scattered under the draught of a low-flying chopper. The flower beds were neatly planted and colourful wall murals depicted the school's namesake, an enlightened female governor of Mazar in times past, wearing a headscarf and holding a book. Rather than challenging me, a guard dog appealed for affection, and the lone human guard was an old, grey-bearded man who said the school had been looted and was now closed. But unable to suppress his innate Afghan hospitality, he let me in. In what must have been the admin office, the school's records, including a box full of passport-sized photographs of the pupils, had been flung across the room. Hundreds of smiling faces looked up from the floor, their heads swathed in scarfs. It was a girls' school. Amid the contents of drawers and cupboards strewn on the floor was a page of a child's essay which began: 'You, lady teacher, by your knowledge a society can benefit.'

Islam is not a misogynistic religion, but it has been influenced by the cultural prejudices of the environment that produced and nurtured it. Mohammed was a poor seventh-century Arab man whose life was transformed not only by God but also by a rich, twice-widowed mother of three children called Khadija, who gave him a job managing her trading enterprises and later married him.

Until her death twenty-four years later she was his most reliable advocate, advisor and supporter, and her grave above the valley of Mecca is still visited by pilgrims. Mohammed said of her: 'When I was poor she shared her wealth with me. When I was rejected she believed in me. She declared I spoke the truth, when others called me a liar. And through her Allah granted me children, while withholding those of other women.'[24]

After Khadija's death, Mohammed would take many wives, receiving revelations which exempted him personally from the rule limiting Muslim men to four partners.[25] Like the Book of Genesis, sacred to Christians and Jews, which quotes God telling Eve, 'Your desire shall be for your husband and he shall rule over you',[26] the Koran says:

Men have authority over women because Allah has made the one superior to the other, and because they spend their wealth to maintain them. Good women are obedient. They guard their unseen parts because Allah has guarded them. As for those from whom you fear disobedience, admonish them and send them to beds apart and beat them.[27]

Despite this, the Koran lays down the legal rights of Muslim women in regard to marriage and, in particular, inheritance rights, which for centuries were far ahead of those enjoyed by women in other faiths. The Koran stipulates only that the Prophet's wives wear the veil, and its application to women in general varies from country to country, and region to region. It is more commonly seen in villages than in cities, and it was from the villages that the Taliban emerged.

The spectre of the veil now hung over Mazar. A few days before, still in her Western gear, Zhala Najrabi had gone to Balkh University to find all the classrooms deserted and nobody around to explain why. Returning home, she found her father burying the family's satellite dish. When I went to her house, accompanied by Rasoul the day after the Taliban entered the city, she was sitting cross-legged on a mattress, staring at the stumps of her nails. By meeting us unveiled she was risking a flogging.

'Everything is finished,' she said, 'life is finished.'

She may not have been the perfect student, but she had passed her exams three years running and was only four months short of collecting her degree. But Balkh University would not be issuing any more degrees to female students. It was impossible to believe that only a few hours earlier in the mosque, her future had been declared null and void. Zhala's plight had stunned her brother into weepy silence as he stood at the doorway listening.

'How can I stay in the home?' she asked with a bitter, crooked smile. 'I'd rather leave the country, although I love my country. But to stay at home means to die.'

The family's possessions were packed in jute bags for the moment when the Salang Tunnel reopened so they could once again take to the road as refugees, probably to Pakistan where Zhala's grandmother lived. None of the neighbouring Muslim countries restricted women's access to work or education, yet young Pakistani men were flocking to Afghanistan to help build the Muslim paradise, forcing westernised Afghans to seek sanctuary in Pakistan. It was a strange traffic indeed.

'Why should a boy who has lower grades than me get a place in university?' Zhala demanded that I explain. 'I wanted to be a good translator, but unfortunately I have to be a good housewife. Why have the Taliban done this?'

All over the city, teenage girls, working women and even musicians, whose livelihood also had become suddenly illegal, were asking the same question. Why?

'Because these Taliban have no mothers,' Zhala answered herself, choking on the abusive Afghan expression. 'They think they are good Muslims and that we are not.'

There was not much Mazar's women could do about the new dispensation, but one group was not giving up without a fight. In the village of Ali Chaupan, a short drive south of the city, the Shia Hazaras were preparing to defend themselves. Rasoul had spent the previous few days there with his family but returned to Mazar because, as he put it, to leave a foreigner like me in a strange city at such a time would simply not be the Afghan thing to do.

'The Shias are extremely nervous,' he said, explaining that the Taliban planned to disarm the population and then forcibly convert the minority Shias to Sunni Islam. 'At first the people thought life would not be disturbed because Malik was there, but now they are saying it's a Taliban takeover.'

Indeed, Malik was himself having second thoughts about his decision to invite the Taliban to Mazar. Contrary to his expectations, he had been appointed a deputy minister in the Taliban government, a lower position than he held under Dostum.

Afghanistan is a shooter's paradise in which most families have guns. Whenever they conquered an area the Taliban were careful to disarm the population, forestalling any further resistance. In the Pashtun south, the policy had been welcomed as a way of re-establishing law and order. But in the north, minorities like the Shias saw it as a way of putting them at the Pashtuns' mercy. People were handing over some of their weapons but secretly burying the balance.

That afternoon two Talibs who had gone to the predominantly Shia locality of Syedabad — the Streets of the Saints — to disarm the population had been shot dead. Rushing there we found no bodies, just several armed Shias clustered around a shot-up jeep, anxiously preparing for the inevitable reprisals.

'The Taliban should not come here,' shouted Mohammed Ibrahim, brandishing his weapon as if trying to reassure himself. 'We don't need their security, we have our own. Mazar will become the graveyard of the Taliban.'

It was the moment of truth for Mazar-e Sharif. As the Talibs massed men, tanks and weaponry on Prison Road, within sight of Zhala's house, ordinary Shia men were accepting their wives' blessings, gathering their weapons and taking up positions in their localities. At Ali Chaupan, Rasoul's brother Amir Yaqub, who belonged to a Shia militia outfit called Harakat-e Islami-yi Afghanistan, the Islamic Movement of Afghanistan, and who was the traditional head of the Hazara community there, organised the village's defences. In Mazar, rumours spread of sightings of Imami Zaman, the twelfth or 'Hidden' Imam, who Shias believe will usher in Judgment Day. Outside the high mud walls of Mazar jail a siege had developed. A tank was parked outside, its gun pointing towards a group of Shias holed up in a compound further along the road. A young Talib from Herat, who was guarding the rear of the tank, chatted garrulously in between sending bursts of clearing fire in the direction of an alleyway opposite, the bullets raising dust and piercing steel doors.

'We will hang all these damned Shias,' he said, laughing and joking with his brothers-in-arms. Hearing him, Rasoul and I fell back along the road towards the city in order to watch the situation from a safer distance. Men were crawling in stealth across the rooftops, quivers of rocket-propelled grenades on their backs like modern-day archers. They were Malik's men, and at first I thought they were there to provide cover in case of a Taliban retreat. But if they were reinforcements, why the need for stealth?

Suddenly a great din broke out from beyond the prison. A civilian walking nonchalantly among the Taliban units besieging the Shias had produced an automatic rifle from under his coat and started spraying the Pashtuns with bullets. With the Talibs scattering in all directions the Shias poured out of their boltholes, turning the tables and pursuing their opponents through the back lanes. Unfamiliar with the area, the young Talibs fell back along Prison Road, where they were hit from behind by rockets fired by Malik's snipers, a Shakespearean stab in the back as the evening call to prayer began drifting across the rooftops. Running for our lives into a side street, Rasoul and I sought shelter in an open doorway, which led into a typical mud-brick family home arranged around an open courtyard. Inside, four generations cowered. Shaking his head and muttering about the insanity of it all, Syedi Mohammed asked his unveiled wife to make green tea for us, which we sipped for comfort and courage as the building shuddered with the force of explosions outside and flying ordnance whistled over the open courtyard. Among the family there was no panic, just a resigned foreboding and silent prayers that this lowering night should pass safely. During a lull in the firing the old man opened the door a crack and called out, 'Look, it's a Talib!'

'What's he doing?' asked one of his sons, incredulous, following his father out into the lane. Malik's snipers had hit a Taliban jeep, and being loaded with ammunition the vehicle had exploded in flames. Three Talibs had been incinerated, but one who had been thrown clear crawled to the neighbourhood mosque, where Syedi Mohammed, a Shia Hazara, went to comfort him. The family received the son's report with wide-eyed disbelief, but were driven back inside by the boom of an exploding grenade and the spatter of Kalashnikov fire.

As the sky above the courtyard darkened, and the air thickened with the smell of gunpowder, Rasoul and I weighed our options: spend the night trapped in Syedabad, the epicentre of the fighting, or try to reach the United Nations compound before nightfall. Our hosts were obliging, and leaving would involve a hazardous journey on foot across town, with no guarantee of safety when we got there. If, however, the Sunni extremist Taliban got the upper hand, a Shia house was not the place to be, so we thanked our hosts and headed off, Rasoul leading the way through the back streets cautiously, sprinting across main roads, staying close to walls and pausing at intersections, accompanied all the way by the terrible soundtrack of warfare. Just as we reached the sky blue iron gates of the UN, a tank standing opposite the compound began firing a series of shattering volleys towards the shrine. For the longest time we stood there, banging and shouting to make ourselves heard over the whooshing blast of the tank, but to no effect. Either they couldn't hear us or they were unwilling to leave the building to open the gate. We were about to hightail it when the door opened, and I realised that Rasoul had probably saved my life.

Inside the airless basement of the UN guesthouse the few expatriates still in the city huddled in terror. For the next eighteen hours, as the battle for the city raged outside, we stayed there as gunfire shattered the upstairs windows and the building next door caught fire, flooding the basement with noxious fumes. Without electricity, we huddled around a single gas lantern for a simple dinner of stale nan, canned fish, and coffee heated on a small camp stove on the floor. The UN security officer, Isireli Dugu, spoke reassuringly about New York's awareness of our situation, adding that the wheels of a rescue plan were probably already in motion.

As the only Afghan among us, Rasoul's exclusion from any evacuation plan was as understood as it was unspoken. He was pacing restlessly, and I realised he was worried about his family. Although he didn't know it, Ali Chaupan was at that moment under attack from the retreating Talibs, who had escaped south of the city and were looking for a place to dig in. Several times Rasoul went upstairs to 'check the situation', despite Dugu's prophetic warnings of the dangers of leaving the basement. Sure enough, standing at a screen door on the top floor later that night, Rasoul was hit by a tiny piece of shrapnel which passed through his forearm. The wound was small but descending the stairs, cradling his arm, he was in shock. His brother had been paralysed by a similar injury, and although there was barely a drop of blood issuing from the entry point, he was losing feeling in the arm. Several times that night I had to dissuade him from leaving the compound, so anxious was he to seek medical treatment, despite the continuous churning of heavy machine guns on the street outside.

It was noon the following day before we were able to leave the building. In the May sunshine the population of Mazar-e Sharif had begun to emerge like tortoises from their shells. They walked in twos and threes, surveying the damage and pointing out the more egregious examples of destruction. At the hospital Rasoul was able to get his arm dressed while interpreting for my interview with one of the doctors. Along Prison Road the bodies of the Taliban lay where they had fallen, their faces frozen in expressions of surprise. The 'seekers of religious knowledge' had found the ultimate religious truth. There were at least three hundred dead, thousands had been captured, and all remaining Talibs had fled the city any way they could. The Shias and Uzbeks had triumphed.

As I walked along the road counting bodies and taking notes, a pickup truck bearing Red Cross markings pulled up and two young foreign men got down and began loading bodies into the truck. After they'd lifted a few, one of them — who bore a resemblance to Frans Hals's 'Laughing Cavalier', complete with impish beard and floppy hat — harangued me in a thick European accent.

'Ay, zhornalist!' he called to me. 'Wot are yer doing wiz yer notebook? Elp us carry zeez bah-deez.'

I tried ignoring him, continuing to count the dead Talibs.

'Allo, yer,' he persisted. 'Meester Notebook! Meester Zhornalist! Wot eez yer prob-lum?'

'No problem,' I said.

'Well? Are yer going to elp?'

There was no point explaining that I had a job to do.

'Allez!' the Laughing Cavalier said, tugging at the shirt of his colleague and staring at me with his head cocked. 'Yer see ziz guy? Eez too bee-zee to elp us. Pah! Zhornalists!'

Later I heard that one young Talib had survived by playing dead among a pile of his lifeless comrades, maintaining the ruse long enough to be picked up and transported to safety by International Red Cross workers, who reacted with shock as the cadaver rose and hurriedly made off.

9

Across the Amu Darya

'Why are you leaving?' Rasoul asked, as if only a lunatic would want to escape the madhouse. It was a sunny morning, and Rasoul and I were standing once more outside the UN compound's gates, which were now peppered with bullet holes. He was back from the village and his family were alive and well, but he said he had personally helped bury seventy people who had died defending Ali Chaupan as the Taliban fell back through the villages near Mazar. All UN and aid agency premises had been bombarded or looted and there were signs of worse to come. As he bubbled with heroic tales, Rasoul could see the white off-road vehicles with UN markings lining up outside the compound and foreigners streaming out to dump their belongings in the trucks. Belatedly realising that an evacuation was underway, he looked at me and said, 'You don't think the Taliban will return, do you?'

The UN evacuation would be the last bus out of Mazar for some time. Anyone not on board was welcome to stay, but Afghans were not invited. Around us, hundreds of locals had gathered, sitting on fences, cars and the burnt-out shell of a military vehicle, their conversations creating a sombre, murmuring hum. The appointed time of departure had passed, as officials awaited the return of a British television crew who had gone out early to shoot some final footage and to search for cameras stolen by Shia militias during the fighting. At 8.30 a.m., when they had not returned, the ranking UN official made the decision to leave them behind and ordered that the evacuation begin. With no more time for questions or farewells, Rasoul solemnly proffered his cheek. I climbed into the truck and the convoy began moving.

Standing by the road, Rasoul noticed a sudden change in the mood of the crowd. Around him, people were blaming the UN for cooking up the original alliance between Malik and the Taliban. Now that the scheme had failed, they were saying, the foreigners were abandoning Mazar. With the departure of each vehicle, their anger grew, and when the last car in the convoy moved off, it was surrounded by the mob which stoned it and dragged its occupants out onto the road. Gazing from the window of one of the lead cars as it passed the jail, into which Malik's men were herding Taliban prisoners, I was shaken from my thoughts by a thick, urgent stream of call signs on our Codan high frequency radio.

'Sierra Thirty-one Anthony calling Oscar Bravo. Do you read me? Over.'

It was Isireli Dugu, the UN security officer, whose car had been bringing up the rear. In a frightened voice, struggling to be heard above an uproar, he was ordering the convoy to proceed.

'Do not turn back,' he was shouting. 'Repeat. Do *not* turn back!'

Inside each of the dozen or so vehicles in the convoy, the awful message produced a stunned silence. As his voice faded out Dugu maintained his insistence that the evacuation proceed. As the suburbs gave way to the desert, the job of abandoning him was completed in grim silence. We were all sitting comfortably in our cars, except for our guilt. As we moved steadily through a dusty cheddar landscape, another voice on the radio was urgently trying to raise Sierra Thirty-one Anthony. But there was no response and the lonely caller trailed off like mission control hopelessly calling some astronaut lost on the moon. Turning to look back, I saw the Turkmen rug I had bought in Mazar, my trophy rolled and rocking on top of other luggage behind the back seat, and felt a burning shame.

Dugu, it turned out, was lucky. He had escaped the mob and taken refuge back at the UN guesthouse. Soon other guests would arrive. The British TV crew had finally turned up just as the mayhem was erupting. As they struggled to turn their car around, the mob set upon them, plundering their aluminium cases containing hundreds of thousands of pounds' worth of monitors, mixers, lighting and audio gear, and satellite telephones, and even ripping the backpack off one foreigner. Seeing the pandemonium ahead, the crew travelling in a second vehicle escaped to a nearby government office to seek the intervention of General Majid Ruzie, commander of the northern army's Eighteenth Division with special responsibility for security in Mazar-e Sharif. Ruzie was a hard but reasonable man, whose daughter studied medicine at Balkh University. In the recent upheavals he had sided with Malik and, by extension, with the Taliban. But now, confronted by a threat to the peace so recently restored in Mazar, and by an affront to his personal honour, Ruzie vowed to find the culprits who had stolen the TV crew's equipment. On General Ruzie's orders two teenage boys who had been caught carrying away some of the equipment were taken to the UN compound. As the horrified television crew appealed for clemency, the thieves were shot dead with two quick bursts from an AK-47. 'It was over so quickly,' said Vladimir Lozinsky, a member of the TV crew. 'The alleged thieves were just kids, really. They had that weak, pleading look as if they knew they were going to die.' With order restored and Ruzie's honour satisfied, Dugu and the crew were freed to join the exodus.

The road to Hairatan on the ancient Amu Darya bordering Uzbekistan was littered with the detritus of a fleeing army and its general. A truck carrying a 122mm artillery piece stood beside the road, abandoned because there was no time to fix a puncture. As the Taliban moved towards Hairatan, the Uzbek authorities had dumped hundreds of tonnes of concrete blocks, steel anti-tank barriers and razor wire on the bridge to deter further northern movement, and by the time General Dostum had reached the border in a luxury four-wheel-drive jeep, the 'Friendship Bridge' across the river had been closed. Dressed in his commander's uniform and accompanied by a retinue of one hundred and twenty people, Dostum had been forced to get down and walk, having been relieved of his valuables by his own security guards, who stayed behind. They spared his life, however, and he flew off soon afterwards from Uzbekistan to claim political asylum in Turkey.

Now it was our turn to flee. Below the two hundred metre-long white-painted steel bridge, the river water roiled in brown eddies. Uzbek helicopter gunships hovered overhead, as an eagle swooped into the reed beds, while downriver the cranes of Hairatan port towered on the horizon like prehistoric birds. In 1979, four motorised rifle divisions of the Soviet Army had crossed the river at the same point on pontoon bridges, the beginning of an ill-starred adventure. The adventure would end nine years and forty-nine days later, in February 1989, when Lieutenant-General Boris V. Gromov walked back across the bridge heading north, and declared that, 'In spite of our sacrifices and losses, we have totally fulfilled our internationalist duty.' Gromov was welcomed home in the border town of Termez and his troops — minus the fifteen thousand who had died — were presented with wristwatches.[28] America had lost three times as many of its soldiers in Vietnam and had survived as a superpower. But for the Soviet Union, the humiliation was fatal. The newly independent country of Uzbekistan that we could see just across the river was proof enough of that.

After waiting several hours outside a fence, then passing through extraordinary security checks, I carried my luggage and my carpet across the bridge. Beyond a sign that read 'Welcome to Uzbekistan' we were met by a group of bottle-blonde ethnic Russian women wearing lipstick, makeup and figure-hugging uniforms who staffed the Uzbek Immigration post. Ahead of us, perhaps only five or six hours' drive away, lay Samarkand, where Timur the Lame had sat on a carpeted throne, and beyond it, Bukhara, a cradle of Islamic civilisation. They seemed like perfect places to get a little rest and restore a little faith. It came as a rude shock to realise we were not welcome in Uzbekistan.

'Better you go back to New Delhi and apply for a visa there,' said a mysterious official with a thick Russian accent.

'But I have a visa. They just stamped it.'

'Yes I know, but the situation now is not suitable. For the journalist there should be program.'

Fortunately, the UN flight to Pakistan that day had been cancelled, so with permission to stay one night in Uzbekistan, I flagged down a local taxi and headed for Termez.

Barren, dun-coloured Afghanistan gave way to electric green Uzbekistan, a landscape transformed by immense irrigation works which exploited the vast annual snowmelt of the Pamirs. By intercepting water in immense quantities to irrigate its cotton farms, Uzbekistan had destroyed the Aral Sea in the north-west, where docks now stood in the desert. The road to Termez, however, was one long oasis, albeit a heavily militarised one. With a red alert in force, there was frenetic activity inside large observation bunkers dug into the hillsides facing the river, where uniformed officers walked briskly about carrying files and clipboards. A few kilometres behind this scene of military efficiency, hundreds of brutish-looking tanks stood parked in rows.

Termez was an ancient town, but had been redesigned during Soviet times along grand socialist lines and boasted a dead heart of vast public squares. The devil was in the socialist detail of tortured plumbing and dismal lighting at the Surkhan Hotel, but it hardly mattered. Lowering myself onto the single mattress in my room, I felt for the first time the accumulated stress of the previous week. My feet, wrists, back and face all ached and I was sticky with leftover sweat, but of nasty memories of stinking corpses and flying metal, there were none. My mind was a blank, and I fell into a bottomless sleep.

That summer, three thousand Taliban and a similar number of their opponents were killed or wounded in the fighting in Afghanistan's north. An additional two hundred and fifty Pakistani Taliban volunteers were killed and more than five hundred taken prisoner. In the chaos, which continued for over a year, General Dostum would return from Turkey, flush with money to rebuild his alliances. To undermine the feckless Malik, he uncovered twenty mass graves in the Dasht-e Layli desert near Sheberghan, said to contain the bodies of some two thousand of the captured Taliban. According to the United Nations, they had been tortured before being killed. In the intense heat of summer on the Turkestan plain, hundreds of them had been locked in steel shipping containers until they suffocated and baked to a crisp. Others were thrown down wells, followed by live hand-grenades, or shot ten at a time in front of trenches. It took six days to kill all of them.

The Prophet Mohammed had once witnessed a similar massacre. After besieging the Jews of Korayza in 627 AD, Mohammed watched as a trench was dug in the marketplace and more than eight hundred captives, with their hands tied behind them, were led to the edge in groups of five. There, they were beheaded, and their bodies pushed into the trench.[29] At Dasht-e Layli, though, there was an important difference; instead of Muslim massacring Jew, it was Muslim killing Muslim.

Despite the debacle, the Taliban refused to give up. On 8 August 1998, after several unsuccessful attempts, the Sunni Muslim militia, led by Pashtun sympathisers from Balkh, entered Mazar-e Sharif. They found the city abandoned by the Uzbek and Shia militias that had been resisting their advances. According to numerous testimonials collected from survivors by UN agencies, anyone standing in the street, including unarmed civilians, was mown down by machine gun fire. Witnesses said the loudspeakers of all the mosques were calling on all Shias to convert to Sunni Islam or be shot on the spot. The following day Sunni zealots went door to door, demanding that male residents say their prayers. Those who didn't know the Sunni form were executed. Some people were merely stopped on the street by armed Pashtuns and shot if they answered questions in Dari, the local dialect of Persian. The Iranian consulate, which was the main conduit for Iranian assistance to the northern militias, was a prime target. The last moments of eight diplomats and a journalist from the Iranian news agency IRNA were heard in Tehran, as they made frantic satellite telephone calls for help. Teams of cleaners later toiled for a full day to remove all traces of blood from the building's basement, supposedly protected by diplomatic immunity, where the Iranians were executed. For months afterwards the Taliban blocked efforts by independent observers to visit the city.

I had lost contact with Rasoul, but some time later I received a letter bearing an Islamabad postmark and covered with colourful stamps featuring Mohammad Ali Jinnah and the Government College in Lahore. It was from Zhala, and began

I don't know how to start. The trouble of Afghan people, especially women, is too much that I can't write it down ... We had to move to another city in north part of Afghanistan. That city was controlled by another party. I got a job. I was a teacher for eight months then the Taliban captured all Afghanistan, so that we had to move toward Pakistan and left our poor but lovely country. It's about nine months that I live in Pakistan. We are disappointed. There's nothing for us in our own country or other countries. No one helps us ... I am very sorry about style of my writing. Sometimes I consider you as a good friend sometime very formal and also after a long time I am writing because there's no need for us to write (and read). We aren't to be considered as a part of society. We are the miserable sex. We are woman. I am really very sorry.

PART THREE

KANDAHAR

10

Habib is Habib

At the foot of the Khyber Pass, where a gateless border post teems with travellers, traders and refugees, barrows, bicycles, cars and minibuses, a simple sign marks the territorial limit of Afghanistan. Amid the din of honking horns and barking vendors, and the shambles of bales and jerrycans, it is a testament to the folly that borders can be. In 1998, large black letters on a white concrete signpost spelt out the word 'PAKISTAN', but closer inspection revealed evidence of an earlier sign, more deeply etched, but painted over. It read, 'INDIA'.

Perhaps the signwriters in 1947 were too busy erecting new signs elsewhere to pull down the last post of the former British Raj. At the foot of the Margalla Hills further east, they would eventually erect a capital, Islamabad, a city of wide boulevards and monumental buildings, meant to signify the unity and thrusting confidence of the 'Land of the Pure'. The Shah Faisal Mosque, supposedly the world's largest, is typical, built in aggressively angular Gulf emirate-style. Modern, soulless and empty, Islamabad denies the earthy reality of the country it was built to govern. When the rug of life became threadbare, as it often did in Islamabad, I would gravitate towards the arboreal kilim hanging like a flag of hope outside an establishment named Caravan Carpits.[1] Lurking under its canopy sat the proprietor, regarding the passing traffic with sceptical, hooded eyes and a set mouth, his chin resting in the palm of his hand. He was boldly drawn with an aquiline nose and big jaw, and his rangy frame was draped in a cool, collared salwar kameez, the whole ensemble as affectedly careless as a spider in a web. When he saw you approaching, a blazing smile would part Habib's lips and a trumpeting, elephantine roar would rock the capital.

'OHHH, you've come,' he cried one day when I turned up, as if he had been waiting for me. 'How is your wife? How is your family? Your body? How is it feeling? Your parents? Fine? OHHH, come in. COME IN!'

You couldn't buy a welcome like Habib's. Like a fine Caucasian rug, he had a lot going on but was never too busy.

'Nothing we are selling, but we are happy too much!' he said, defeating the problem. 'If I show a Pakistani an old car-pit, he becomes insulted. He says, "Was I born only for slapping?" His temperature becomes very high. He will say, "Do you think I am poor? Shitty on your mouth! Even my mother I don't like, because she is old. I have a new house, why do I want an old car-pit?" In-credible customer. In-credible!'

For a long time I assumed that Habib was himself a Pakistani, and puzzled over these unremitting attacks on his countrymen. Then one day after I became a regular visitor — if not a regular customer — he took me into his confidence.

'Promise me you will tell nobody,' he said, drawing me into the conspiracy. 'You want to know why Habib knows so much about Afghan car-pit, eh? Surely, there is a reason. Habib, himself, is like this Afghan car-pit. Habib is Afghan!'

Not only Afghan, he was a Pashtun belonging to the fierce tribe split between Pakistan and Afghanistan by the Durand Line, the borderline drawn by the British in the late nineteenth century. A hated symbol of imperialism ever since, it had not only divided the Pashtuns, but denied landlocked Afghanistan access to the Indus

River. To mollify them, the Pashtuns were allowed free movement across the line, and it was understood that they would always rule in Kabul. In Pakistan's tribal areas, federal laws pertained only to the roads, with the rest governed by *pashtunwali*, the tribal code which allows kidnapping, honour killings, and free rein on unlicensed weapons ranging from antique carbines to Stinger missiles. Armed and quick to take offence, the Pashtuns had dealt Genghis Khan a few hard blows. Despite their excessive courage and inadequate discipline, they were idealised by the British as the backbone of a martial race, and later by the Americans as the freedom-loving mujahideen capable even of defeating the Soviet superpower. Then, when the Soviet Union collapsed and the Taliban came on the scene, Pashtun culture was abruptly recast as barbaric, misogynist and evil. But I was proud to have a Pashtun friend.

Habib had spent twenty years in Pakistan as a refugee. He had fair skin, brown hair, and long sideburns like an Afghan Elvis. When he was twelve his father had taken him in a horse-drawn tonga to a village where a man was selling a carpet. After protracted negotiations a price was agreed, but as his father counted out thousands of *Afghanis*, Habib, who had never seen such a large amount of money, panicked and began to weep. Patiently his father whispered that he could sell the carpet for a higher price than he was paying, but his son was inconsolable.

'Don't buy it,' Habib cried, 'you're spending all our family's money.'

Even the seller tried to reassure the boy, who remained implacable.

'You're lying,' he lashed out. 'Return our money!'

It continued for hours, the worst tantrum the village had ever seen.

Eventually the father overcame his son's objections, and on that day in Logar a carpet *wallah* was born. He had learned his English in the trade, and our lengthy discussions about our rugs, loves and politics were regularly interspersed with apologies for what he feared was his poor grammar.

'Of every two words, one is not right,' he lamented. 'You are just guessing about my words. I have BROKEN THE LEG OF ENGLISH! Ninety per cent is broken. Ten per cent is in the emergency ward!'

But if our meetings were extended affairs it was not due to any language difficulty. Habib distilled the wisdom of the common man so incisively that he had me taking notes. Aware that his insights were invaluable, he rationed them, fitting me in between the time-wasting customers, itinerant hawkers, persistent beggars, bribe seekers, people asking directions, and phone calls from overseas buyers and the rug-addict diplomats of the capital. The fax machine rang constantly, spluttering out messages many pages in length bearing half-tone images of carpet designs. A Singaporean buyer, who clearly trusted Habib's taste, had deposited $5000 in his bank account and ordered him to send more rugs.

The Pashtuns are not traditionally weavers, but in the upheaval of war some had developed their knowledge of rugs to survive. As my own interest in carpets had slowly developed over the years, Habib had freed me from many delusions. The best rugs did not gravitate to the top of the pile, by virtue of being more frequently considered, nor were they hidden at the bottom. Bigger pieces, he explained, went below because they provided a firmer footing for the stack. He claimed the ability to determine a rug's provenance on the basis of its smell alone. Spending time with him also cured me of my early guilt about forcing carpet sellers to constantly unroll their wares. It is all that saves them from lives of complete lassitude. In fact, one should never feel *any* pity whatsoever for *any* carpet dealer. It is the customer who should be pitied.

The Singaporean buyer wanted Chinese carpets, and fax in hand, Habib began picking out old pastel pieces that had trickled down the Karakoram Highway which links Gilgit in Pakistan's Northern Areas with China's western Xinjiang province. They were from Xinjiang, the home of Uighur Muslims who blended Persian knots and Chinese symbols representing dragons, ducks, bats and deer.

Habib's pieces, from the Khotan oasis in the desert of East Turkestan, came in cool hues of lemon, olive green, pink and sky blue. They bore fret panels of interlocking swastikas, the Chinese symbol for happiness.

'Old is gold,' he hummed, happy as a swastika himself, setting aside several rolls.

'What about the one on the wall?' I suggested, pointing at a superb 'pomegranate' carpet that I had long coveted, hoping this expression of interest might save it from the unseen buyer. But my concern was misplaced.

'Not everything is for selling,' Habib said, the collector prevailing over the seller in him. 'I like to see something for myself. When I see this, my heart jumps on the car-pit. I never want to be separated from it.'

Checking his watch, worn facing in, he disappeared briefly, returning with some newspaper, cold drinks and a plate of oily mutton samosas. Spreading the newspaper on the floor and fetching a toilet roll for napkins, he arranged the food, then kicked off his *chappals* under a desk, threw the towel from around his neck over the back of a chair, and eased himself onto the floor. In the Afghan way, all joking and bluster — in fact all conversation — came to an abrupt end and we ate in complete silence. Somehow the food, which was sordidly good, seemed not to agree with him and he motioned to my notebook, preparing me for dictation.

'Believe me,' he began, 'I am ashamed to be Afghan. All good people have left. Only the rubbish is remain. I hate Afghan people now. They have no sense. Why you beat yourself? It's very cruel. For Eid they send prisoners cut up in pieces. Gulbuddin — that shit man — he is the devil, with two mouths always fighting each other. He fights with his mouth.'

His fair skin was now flushed with the oily food and his mouth pouted bitterly. Embarrassment and regret permeated the air.

'Nobody is in Logar now. Only my servant is still in Logar looking after the wheat,' he said, pushing an alumina basin towards me and pouring water over my hands from a ewer.

Then, holding up one of the deeply fried, meat-filled samosas, he exhibited it with unconcealed disgust.

'I'm twenty-five, and I'm looking like too much more. Twenty years from twenty-five I have been away from my country. My grandfather, he was born in the car-pit. He die in the car-pit. But day by day *I* am becoming Punjabi!'

To Pashtuns, Punjabis represented the antithesis of pashtunwali. Where honour demanded violent conflict, the Punjabis would choose wheedling compromise, Habib contended. He would not listen when I tried to tell him about all the fine Punjabis I had known. The fact was, he said, that they'd grabbed the country's best irrigated agricultural land after Partition, and that their heavy, ghee-drenched foods and rambunctious *bhangra* music were all but Indian. With them in charge, how could Pakistan possibly live up to its name?

'What about Benazir Bhutto?' I piped up hopefully. 'She's not a Punjabi . . . she's from Sindh.' But Habib had no time for anyone.

'The she-donkey is no better than the he-donkey,' he sighed. 'They're all thieves. Taliban should come and cut off their looter hands! Taliban are good people, respecting people. Not like these Punjabis and "Dollar" Afghans.'

To prove his point he got up and switched on the radio, betting there would be a new corruption scandal on the news. Instead, the Urdu voice that followed the boisterous, old-fashioned news theme of Radio Pakistan brought scandal of a different order. Massive bombs had exploded outside the American embassies in Nairobi and Dar es Salaam. Hundreds of people were dead, thousands injured, and commentators were already blaming the massacre on a Saudi-born Islamic radical by the name of Osama bin Laden. Bin Laden was living in Afghanistan, and the United States wanted the Taliban to hand him over for trial.

'Listen,' said Habib, pointing again at my notebook. 'Taliban will never give up Osama. This is not the Pashtun way. In our culture, we have a system — it's called *nanawati*. Even if a murderer comes to my house, I must give shelter to him, give food to him, make sure he is comfortable, everything nice for him, for three days. Even a murderer!'

'What about a rapist?'

'Anybody!'

'But what if the guest commits a crime in your home?'

'Then I take revenge on him, and his family. That is the Pashtun way.'

A man of his word, Habib had recently given nanawati himself to a Western woman who had taken refuge in his shop after a traffic accident. He had even turned away police who had tried to question the woman.

'Even Osama, if he is coming through my door, into my car-pit shop, now, immediately I will rescue him. American CIA and army cannot snatch him from Habib.'

'Why's that?'

'Because my friend, religion is religion, politics is politics, true is true. And HABIB IS HABIB!'

Alas, the chances of Osama bin Laden walking into Habib's carpet store anytime soon were rather limited. If he was to be found at all, it was in the southern city of Kandahar where he was reportedly living. But when I asked Habib if he knew anyone there, he flew into a tizz.

'You can't go there!' he moaned. 'You don't have a beard. I could give you some medicine to make it grow, but it would take time. Believe me, Afghanistan is a fully dangerous country. You shouldn't go there. Once is okay, but going, going, going? No!'

It took fully half an hour to convince Habib of the necessity of visiting Kandahar.

'Then, if you are in Kandahar you should meet Hajji Kandahari,' he said, suddenly reconciled to the idea. 'He is also in this car-pit business. Say Habib wishes him long life. And give him this money for me.'

Stuffing five one-hundred dollar notes in my hand, Habib grasped me by the shoulders and said he knew a way of ensuring my safety in Afghanistan. All I had to do was recite the *shahadet*.

'Repeat after Habib,' he said. 'I testify.'

'I testify ...'

'That there is no God but Allah.'

'That there is no God but Allah ...'

'And Mohammed is His Prophet!'

11

Heroes and Villains

Kandahar, Afghanistan's second-largest city, had the feel of one of those fly-clotted, stagecoach towns from the Wild West, complete with tumbleweeds, but no saloons. Decades of fighting had chewed up all the roads to a fine, lung-clogging powder which was constantly being raised by trucks piled high and swaying with second-hand television sets en route to Pakistan, where it was still legal to watch them. The Taliban had made beards compulsory for men and had banned music, all representations of the human form, and even kite-flying, which they felt might disturb the pious at prayer. Women were confined to the veil and not permitted to venture outside their homes unless accompanied by a male relative, let alone to drive a car, work, or attend school or college. The Taliban had abrogated all previous laws, and made the Holy Koran the Constitution of Afghanistan. Kandahar was indisputably their capital, and an early crucible for the movement's Islamic experiments.

Arriving early for my first-ever meeting with a Talib, I had paused to look in at a domed shrine opposite the governor's office. It was the mausoleum of Ahmad Shah Durrani, the Pashtun warlord who in 1747 had gouged the new nation of Afghanistan from the declining empires of the Persians and Moghuls. He too had made Kandahar his capital, and high on the interior walls of the shrine, under its soaring dome, a scrolling Arabic inscription read:

'When Ahmad Shah raises his sword, thousands of heads are bowed. From far and wide, the sound of Ahmad Shah's sword strikes fear in the hearts of his enemies.'

The instruments of this fear — a brass helmet engraved with Koranic verses, a forearm sheath, chainmail gloves, and a steel spike and silver scabbard — were laid out in a glass display case. The floors were covered in Turkmen carpets. The riches of Khorasan, including the Koh-i-Noor (Mountain of Light) diamond, now in the Tower of London, had once accumulated at this ancient crossroads between India and Central Asia, but the shrine was a modest affair brutishly decorated with cheap chandeliers and crude tiling. Wrenching his kingdom together — leaving aside decorating it — appeared to have occupied most of Ahmad Shah's time, but he rested in peace now under a raised tomb set to one side, where men bowed to the *qibla* wall facing Mecca. Seated on a mattress near the door, two hawkish men had been regarding me with obvious suspicion from the moment I entered.

'What is your religion?' one asked in Pashto, as I left. 'Do you believe in God? Do you know the Hadith?'

Across an open courtyard stood a smaller building, more expertly tiled and faced with subtle green Lashkar Gah marble resembling onyx, but unfortunately it was closed. Inside it was kept a cloak said to have belonged to the Prophet Mohammed, gifted to Ahmad Shah by the Emir of Bukhara in 1768 to seal a border treaty. The cloak was not publicly displayed, except at times of most critical national emergency.

In 1994 Afghanistan was in the depths of just such a crisis and in need of a miracle. The curse of the mujahideen had reduced Kabul to ruins and in Kandahar vicious infighting between rival warlords had pulverised Ahmad Shah's well-designed city, stripping it of every lootable asset right down to the powerlines. The old land-owning Pashtun families, who had dominated for centuries, were swept aside and without their protection Kandaharis were plundered mercilessly, with children of both sexes kidnapped and killed for the sexual pleasure of the 'freedom fighters'. The outside world — which had seen Afghanistan's war against Soviet invasion as a *cause célèbre* — was no longer interested in Afghan problems, so it was left to conservative village mullahs to do something about it. In a small village just off the highway between Kandahar and Herat, a thirty-five-year-old Pashtun villager, Mohammed Omar, had been a guerilla as well as a priest, and had lost his right eye fighting Najibullah's communist-backed forces. He was running a mosque and school in Singesar village, when neighbours complained that a local commander had abducted several teenage girls and was holding them at his camp nearby. The girls' heads had been shaved to make them look more like the young boys preferred by the warlord, and they had been raped repeatedly. Calling for volunteers, Mullah Omar gathered fifteen students, or *talibs*, collected some weapons and attacked the warlord's base, freeing the girls, hanging the commander from the barrel of a tank and dismantling a checkpoint which for years had been used to extort money from travellers along the highway.

The legend of Mullah Omar is disputed by many Afghans, who believe he is not even one of them, but a Pakistani. But as his power grew and word of his exploits spread, hundreds and then thousands of young Pashtuns, including many refugees from Pakistan, began swarming into Kandahar to support the new army of *Taliban*, or religious students. The Taliban's next target was the main Pashtun leader, Gulbuddin Hekmatyar, who had failed to retake Kabul from the northern forces. The Pakistan government of Benazir Bhutto withdrew Islamabad's backing for Hekmatyar and threw its support behind the new fundamentalist movement. With money, fuel and weapons acquired with Pakistan's help, military victories soon followed, swelling Mullah Omar's reputation and his sense of destiny.

'We took up arms to achieve the aims of the Afghan jihad and save our people from further suffering at the hands of the so-called mujahideen,' he would later say.[2]

In the loose, non-hierarchical structure of Sunni Islam in Afghanistan, mullahs are often part-time, barely literate preachers whose main tasks — like priests everywhere — are to provide religious sanction to births, deaths and marriages. Mullah Omar was very much in that mould but two years later his meteoric rise was crowned as he stood on the roof of a building overlooking the city's main square, hailed by a grateful populace and draped in the cloak of the Prophet. Chosen as Emir-ul Mohmineen — Commander of the Faithful — by a grand *jirga*, or council of more than a thousand religious leaders, he had removed the cloak from its shrine for the first time since 1935, when its protection against a cholera epidemic had been invoked. By the time Taliban troops seized Kabul, the rebirth of Kandahar as a slapdash rural trading post was already well underway. The city's tallest building, the six-storey Kandahar Hotel, was a bombed-out shell but the Bank of Afghanistan was open again, its entrance provided by the steel doors of a shipping container. Sheep and goats mustered by shepherds circled the Shah-e Danu Chowk, a small memorial to martyrs of Afghanistan's many wars including the three against Britain, and barrows bulged with fruits from the Arghandab River orchards.

At the Governorate, meeting Mullah Omar was out of the question as he refused to see non-Muslims.[3] He had only once been photographed — without his permission — and radio stations had been asked to stop using recordings of his voice. Tall, well built and turbaned, the young leader was purported to spend his days sitting on a bed dispensing authorisation 'chits', and *Afghanis* and American dollars from a metal safe, to petitioners.[4] In an adjacent office sat Mullah Hassan Rehmani, another of the original fifteen gunmen who formed the Taliban and one of Mullah Omar's oldest and most trusted confidants.

Entering the cavernous government offices, I was led to a curtained empty room and told to wait. Soon the curtains parted and a one-legged, black-bearded giant with a gentle face hobbled into the room and bade me a deferential welcome. Mullah Hassan belonged to what has been called the world's most disabled leadership. His leader's lost eye had been stitched over; he'd lost his own right leg to a bullet fired by Soviet troops near Kandahar in the late 1980s; and shrapnel had torn off part of the little finger of his right hand. Originally from poverty-stricken Oruzgan province, he had gone to Pakistan as a refugee, returning regularly to fight as a *mujahid*. Now, in his early forties, he was governor of Kandahar and was widely seen as Mullah Omar's right-hand man, a member of the inner circle whose policies had made the Taliban a global pariah and cost them Afghanistan's seat in the United Nations. Mullah Hassan apologised for keeping me waiting, uttered a quick '*Bismillah ar-Rahman ar-Rahim*' and served tea and cake.

'We were worried about our country,' he said, handing me a cup. 'During the years of war a terrible situation had developed. Our people had lost sight of God. Many were acting without conscience. The society was in chaos, so we introduced these rules simply to guide the people back to a good way of living, for the benefit of everyone.'

As he spoke, Mullah Hassan massaged his leg just above the stump, whether to allay pain or boost circulation I wasn't sure. These visible scars were powerful symbols of the Talibs' self-sacrifice, but there was psychological damage as well. Mullah Hassan, probably the most avuncular of all the Taliban leaders, had been known to throw tables and chairs when the pressure of being nice to infidels became too much, and one United Nations official had narrowly avoided a throttling. But then the Taliban were not politicians, skilled in the art of compromise. They were village mullahs, schooled in a literalist interpretation of the Koran. Like Christian tele-evangelists, they believed fervently in 'the far-spread terrors of Judgment Day'. After capturing Kandahar one of their first acts had been to raise chains across the main roads five times a day, forcing motorists from their cars and into the mosques to pray.

'When we came here, we just wanted to bring attention to the need to pray,' Mullah Hassan explained, almost apologetically. 'Now people know themselves to pray, so we don't need the chains.'

Adulterers, however, could not be trusted to repent and were still being lashed, and homosexuals, of whom there were many in Pashtun areas, were having stone walls bulldozed on top of them, a punishment derived from the Old Testament story of Sodom and Gomorrah, in which the walls of sinful cities are toppled. Mullah Hassan, with his laconic, humble manner, did not seem like the sort of man who would enjoy such a spectacle. His big black turban was wound unevenly round his head, giving him a shambolic charm, and his chocolate brown eyes were warm with humour.

'Yes, we have imposed the *Shari'at*. It is our law,' he said, adding mischievously, 'It is also the law in Saudi Arabia, which has good relations with the United States.'

With one of his nine beefy fingers Mullah Hassan brushed at a delicate mole beneath his left eye, as if wiping away a tear. A plastic foot disappeared into a slip-on shoe. The curls in his beard tangled with a woollen vest, required even in summer to combat the permanent chill in the lofty halls of the Governorate. Mullah Hassan chuckled like a well-loved, big-boned uncle.

'We are controlling the majority of the territory. Isn't it our right to have the recognition of the world?' he asked.

Emerging from the cool quiet of the Governorate into the glare, noise and breathless heat of midday, I hailed a motorised rickshaw which took me shuddering and honking across town, past a sea of hirsute faces. Half the adult population had beards, and the absence of visible women accentuated the overall hairiness of Kandahar. Men pulled at their beards, stroked them, scratched them and even pointed with them, as they bargained, played for time, worried, thought and gave directions. Many of them wanted to shave, and resented the imposition of the beard, but it could have been worse. In Tsarist Russia, Peter the Great had taxed beards. The local newspaper *Tolo-e Afghan* ('Rise of the Afghan') carried interesting reports about the fighting against Massoud's forces at Bagram, the Chechen uprising, and an official notification that *Afghanis* should be used in all transactions, not Pakistani rupees. But not a single picture or illustration of a living thing did it contain: only dull photos of buildings, tanks and other inanimate objects. In the Koran, Mohammed puts a curse on men who paint or draw men or animals,[5] and in the Hadith the Prophet calls makers of figurative images 'the worst of men'. According to Sir Richard Burton, all Muslims except those of the Maliki school traditionally believe that makers of images will be commanded on Judgment Day to animate them, and if they fail to, will be sent to the Fire.

> *This severity arose apparently from the necessity of putting down idol-worship, and, perhaps for the same reason, the Greek Church admits pictures but not statues. Of course the command has been honoured with extensive breaching: for instance, all the Sultans of Stambul have had their portraits drawn and painted.*[6]

The Book of Exodus also denounces 'graven images, or any likeness of anything that is in Heaven above, or that is in the earth beneath, or that is in the water under the earth'. Buddha, too, preferred no images to be made of himself. In other words, all the major religions except Hinduism have at some time had a quarrel with the figurative arts. But Islam's generally greater antagonism towards them 'brought picture painting practically to extinction'[7] in the Muslim world. Not surprisingly, the main painting schools in Persia and the Moghul Empire specialised in easily concealed miniatures.

It was, therefore, somewhat of a surprise to find the Kandahar Photo Studio open for business. The film stock was fresh, although they did no processing. Instead, people were sending their film to Pakistan, a few hours' drive away.

Traders were among the first to see the potential of the student army that became the Taliban. By removing the proliferating checkpoints set up by rapacious local militias the Talibs had reopened the lucrative trade routes across western Afghanistan from Turkmenistan and Iran to Pakistan. In return, the smugglers shared their profits with the militia. Tightening UN sanctions on air services and financial dealings between Afghanistan and the outside world — which applied even to Mullah Omar's personal bank accounts — appeared not to have affected the thriving trade, which relied mainly on corrupt Customs officials in neighbouring countries. In the early days of the Taliban every family had been forced to volunteer a son to join the religious army. Now, with their increased turnover, Kandahari businessmen were able to pay the going rate to bribe officials — $2000 per son — to get exempted from military service. The old family business tradition, disrupted by war for a generation, was reviving, if at a sedate pace. Out of the sun, in the arched galleries of Kandahar's old Sarposha Bazaar, men of enormous girth presided over carpets and enormous piles of elfin leather slippers. Taking directions, I headed off in search of Habib's pal, Hajji Kandahari.

Flanking the entrance to the arcade, two beards sat on the raised *masturbah* of a keyhole carpet shop. They were silver, with the shaved upper lip of pious Muslims, one beard impenetrably thick, the other thin with age. Hajji Kandahari was busy sorting through a pile of Taimani weavings sold to him by a trader from Farah in the far west of Afghanistan. His father sat impassively kneading yellow worry beads on the stone sill above the pavement, contemplating the passing trade with a steady gaze that withheld its verdict on the masses. But his son, who had undertaken the *hajj*, or pilgrimage to Mecca, hustled like a man making up for lost time. Inviting me to climb into his cavernous cell, the Hajji continued folding his lively pieces, which were part kilim, part piled and knotted carpet, and part weft-wrapped *soumak*. They came in odd shapes, typical of nomads' looms, brimming with human, animal and vegetable life forms. Pomegranate trees sprouted, camels jogged and peacocks preened. Some featured battle scenes in which mujahideen shouldered missile-launchers to bring down Russian helicopters. The 'war rugs' were part of the country's folk history, and it was obvious that the Taliban's edict on images had yet to fully penetrate the bazaar. Nomads have always woven playful representations of life around them, presenting Islamic theologians with a dilemma. Their solution was the tortured theological justification that 'images of life-forms are specifically allowed on carpets and pillows, since stepping, sitting, or leaning on them are deprecatory acts'.[8] Indeed, some experts argued that Islamic decorative and abstract arts had only achieved their epiphany because of the discipline imposed by the taboo.[9]

As the muezzin's call echoed through the bazaar, the Hajji began closing up shop, assuring me that I could continue browsing after lunch. Walking towards Char Suq (Four Bazaars) he inquired about Habib's health and I handed him the money, the proceeds of some rugs Habib had sold for him on consignment. 'With this money, Insh'allah, I will return to Mecca,' he said, fondly recalling his earlier pilgrimage. Negotiating the narrow streets, we came to a lane which bore the scars of its former status as a frontline between the city's warring commanders. Every wall, lamppost and awning was perforated or pockmarked with what must have been apocalyptic gunfire between the forces of Hekmatyar and Dostum. Through a lime-green door we entered a capacious room painted in temperate shades of lemon and blue, with a lofty, whitewashed dome ceiling. On the floor a massive orange kilim from Maimana was laid out.

'I have a garden in the desert. If it was Friday I would take you there,' the Hajji said, removing his lace prayer cap to reveal silver stubble, and handing me a wet towelette sachet. We were sitting on cushions around a U-shaped 'table' formed by long, gaily printed plastic sheets laid out on the floor, waited on by the Hajji's youngest son who distributed plates of mutton kebabs, stewed chicken, lady's fingers, curd and nan. It was an overwhelming spread deserving the praise of an Arab bard, not my meagre gratitude. Having weathered the storm of war, the Hajji was determined to enjoy life and give thanks and praise.

'Just one shirt I had,' he said. 'One shirt left, and my life. They took so many carpets. Pieces left to us by my grandmother and grandfather. But I don't care so much. I'm just happy I still have my sons.'

Only the help of a Hindu moneylender had allowed the Hajji to get back on his feet. The small Hindu community in Afghanistan had survived for centuries, like the Jews and Sikhs, specialising in businesses like moneylending that Muslims were prevented by their religion from running. But now the old traditions were breaking down, and amid the growing intolerance, the minorities were finding it difficult to function, and family by family, were leaving. Crafty Muslim merchants, whose wealth found ways around religious injunctions, exploited the difficult position of their Jewish, Hindu and Christian competitors, buying them out cheaply. On a previous visit to Char Suq I had met one of the last Hindu moneylenders, Rajesh Sham Lal, who was considering leaving. As a Hindu he was granted special exemption from the Taliban's 1998 decree on beards and wore only a small moustache; nor was he required to close his shop during prayer times. Now, the Taliban had announced that all Hindus would be required to wear large yellow stars on their clothing. The idea had a precedent in Persia, where from the ninth century to the nineteenth century Jews were required to wear a yellow ribbon. The Taliban said that their own move was a well-meaning effort to protect minorities from harassment by police and others who wrongly expected them to live according to Islamic practices. The reaction of the minorities, however, was predictable: a new exodus. Having rescued Hajji Kandahari from destitution, the Hindu moneylender was now selling out to the Hajji's son.

'Maybe one day, if the situation changes and he comes back, we can return the many kindnesses that man has done,' the Hajji said.

12

The Lost Tribe

The first mosque I ever entered was in Alexandria, set high above the Corniche overlooking the Mediterranean Sea. It was a cool, calm place of refuge from the heat and bustle outside. Giant carpets worn thin by generations of knees covered the vast stone floors. Since that first pleasing brush with Islam, those positive impressions of a calm and simple piety without bells and whistles have remained with me.

Instead of ten commandments, Muslims have five, and not all of them are compulsory. A good Muslim should believe in the god of Abraham, Moses and Jesus Christ, known in Islam as Allah; pray five times a day wherever is convenient; give alms to the poor; fast during the day throughout the holy month of Ramadan; and, if possible, undertake the hajj at least once in his or her lifetime. All other Islamic laws are the result of interpretation of the Koran and the sayings and acts of the Prophet Mohammed, which are known collectively as the Hadith, and these differ from place to place. This combination of simplicity and flexibility — and the galvanising effect the new faith had on its first Arab followers and their armies — accounts for the rapid spread of Islam in the years immediately after the Prophet received his revelations in 610–613 AD. The god of the Muslims is compassionate and merciful, and their Prophet inveighed against compulsion and extremism in matters of religion,[10] although the Koran, like the Old and New Testaments, warns of hellfire for all who do not accept its message. Yet because it sees Mohammed's revelations as a refinement of earlier prophecy, it is ambivalent towards the pre-existing religions of Zoroastrianism, Judaism and Christianity, while completely intolerant of other faiths, such as Hinduism and Buddhism. Its critique of Christianity centres on the question of the divinity of Jesus Christ, something Manichean Christians also doubted.

'Those who say:"The Lord of Mercy has begotten a son", preach a monstrous falsehood,' says the Koran, which also rejects the Holy Spirit and Holy Trinity as contrary to the oneness of God, and disputes Jesus's miracles. Jews, Christians and Zoroastrians, for their part, see Mohammed as at best misguided, and at worst a charlatan. Certainly, there has never been much willingness to consider the challenge that Islam — which literally means 'submission' — poses to their faiths.

At the start of the twenty-first century, the breach between the monotheistic faiths is arguably greater than at any time since Pope Urban II declared the First Crusade at Clermont Cathedral in 1095. The decline of the Ottoman Empire and Western colonisation of countries with large Muslim populations gave birth to modern pan-Islamic nationalism. At the end of World War II, with decolonisation in full swing, the creation of the state of Israel and its forcible occupation of Palestinian territories in 1948 gave renewed impetus to violent Islamic reaction. The Cold War exacerbated the problem, with the United States and Soviet Union vying for control of Middle Eastern governments, the 1953 US-instigated Iran coup and 1979 Soviet invasion of Afghanistan being the prime examples.

In Afghanistan, as the West sided with Islamists against communists, it found itself allied to various groups and individuals whose long-term goal was the elimination of all Western influence in the region. Among them was a willowy Arab veteran of the Afghan wars, Osama bin Laden.

Born in 1957 in Saudi Arabia, bin Laden was the seventeenth of some fifty children sired by a Yemeni construction magnate whose firm had renovated the holy sites at Mecca and Medina. With his inherited fortune, the young bin Laden had sponsored some fifteen thousand Arab volunteers who took part in the Afghan jihad. For most of the 1980s he had led his 'Afghans' in daring attacks on the Soviet occupying forces. Near the eastern Afghan city of Khost he had helped build a fortified complex of tunnels, armouries, training facilities and hospitals for the rebels, funded by the CIA. But bin Laden fell out with Washington during the Gulf War, when US forces were deployed in Saudi Arabia to defend the kingdom against the threat of Iraqi attack. Bin Laden believed that like the segregated species in an Islamic garden, Christians and Muslims should not mix. 'In our religion, it is not permissible for any non-Muslim to stay in our country,' he once said. He also considered the presence of US forces to be an act of desecration of the land of Mecca and Medina.[11] Launching his own personal holy war, his money and experience would henceforth be devoted to attacking American interests wherever they were vulnerable.

Having based himself in Sudan for several years, bin Laden was hounded out by pressure from Western governments and moderate Arab regimes, and in May 1996 was forced to take refuge in southern Afghanistan. It was the time when the Taliban were gathering force, and soon he was pitching in with money and advice to help the cause of his Sunni fundamentalist brothers. His backing had a direct personal motive as well: with the Saudi government withdrawing his citizenship and the Americans putting a bounty of $5 million on his head, he desperately needed the refuge a like-minded Muslim government could offer. While keeping his hosts happy, the millionaire militant set about cultivating an international cadre of like-minded Muslims, inspiring them with hatred towards non-Muslims, and encouraging violent acts against them. Several thousand Egyptians, Chechens, Sudanese, Bangladeshis, Uzbeks, Filipinos,

Pakistanis, Algerians and Kashmiris joined the ranks of his organisation, Al-Qa'ida (The Military Base), and began training at some of the facilities he had built in the hills around Khost, Jalalabad and elsewhere. Afghanistan, bin Laden said, was 'a land in which I can breathe a pure, free air to perform my duty in enjoining what is right and forbidding what is wrong'. Living there for one day, he said, was 'like a thousand days of praying in an ordinary mosque'.[12]

Even before moving to Afghanistan, the Americans believed, bin Laden had instigated deadly attacks on American troops in Saudi Arabia and Somalia. More worryingly, he was also suspected of making efforts to obtain chemical, biological and nuclear weapons, and was alleged to control as many as five thousand Muslim militants in fifty countries. Implicated in the bombings of the two US embassies in Africa in 1998, bin Laden was described by President Bill Clinton as the 'pre-eminent organiser and financier of international terrorism'.

It was not common in Kandahar to see six-foot-five Arabs walking on the street, but bin Laden's presence was palpable. Camped with his four wives, numerous children and an entourage of some one hundred and sixty people thirty kilometres away near Kandahar airport, he had undertaken numerous civic works to assist in the restoration of the war-ravaged city. On a large block of land on the Herat road, the largest construction project seen in the city for years was nearing completion. A mini-village of modern townhouses protected by barbed wire and floodlights, and garishly decorated with Islamic scriptures and crown symbols, was bin Laden's gift to Mullah Omar, who took up residence behind its high walls as soon as it was completed. Bin Laden's bulldozers were also helping repair Kandahar's roads, and his money was paying for pilgrimages to Mecca by senior officials. He had been seen inspecting his good works, alighting from a gleaming new Japanese four-wheel-drive vehicle with the aid of a walking stick. The same car had been spotted in a long convoy which left the city each

Friday headed for Arghandab village, where bin Laden and Mullah Omar were said to enjoy a spot of fishing with hand-grenades. Reclining on the cool riverbank, they would chat for hours, a couple of veterans recalling old wars, and perhaps preparing for new ones. There were unconfirmed rumours that the friendship had been buttressed by intermarriage. The rumours, alas, would have to remain unconfirmed, because after an interview bin Laden had given to a Western television crew a few months earlier, the Taliban had banned him from talking to Western visitors.

When I had asked Mullah Hassan about bin Laden, the table between us had shifted suddenly several centimetres to the right. For a moment I thought an earth tremor had shaken Kandahar, but it was only Mullah Hassan's restless peg-leg pushing it away. He smiled patiently.

'He is an extremely sober and calm person,' he replied. 'He has good ideas. He respects us. Remember, he was already in Afghanistan before we captured the area where he was living, around Jalalabad. Many of his people died fighting for the freedom of Afghans. He even helped the United States. He was the cause of them becoming supreme.'

'But if you don't hand him over, the rest of the world will isolate you,' I reminded my host.

'Yes, they can do that if they choose. But he has not broken any law of our Islamic emirate. He has human rights just like anybody. There is no legal agreement between Afghanistan and the United States for exchange of prisoners. We are accountable before God, and if we gave him up to his enemies in violation of law, it would be against our conscience. Now they have some dispute between them, but that is not our concern. We are Pashtuns, and we must ensure the safety of our guests.'

So other-worldly was this response that I could only conclude that the Taliban were exactly what they appeared to be: barely educated, war-wounded mullahs from Pashtun villages where ordinary families lived in mud forts protected by gun turrets, and the word for compromise — *gibran* — translated as 'surrender'.

Despite the enormous gulf in their respective world view, most UN and non-government aid workers were willing to give the Taliban a chance. One night in Kandahar, I was invited to dine with an American aid worker, Bill Berquist, and some of his colleagues based in the city. They were housed in a spartan but comfortable suburban house, where satellite television, imported videotapes and even the odd case of beer eased the strain of living under the Taliban's puritanical regime. Over dinner that night there was only one subject on the agenda: the Taliban. As the agronomists, mine-clearers, engineers and hydrologists let off steam over a few illicit drinks, their target was neither the student army nor the Pashtuns, nor politicians or aid bureaucrats. The enemy was the media.

'The Taliban are like a lost tribe. You know, we've found them, and now everybody wants us to eliminate them. Why can't we just study them for a while like good ol' anthropologists?' said Berquist, a burnished, wiry man who smoked a pipe. 'Sure, they're weird, but so for heaven's sake are the Europeans! They don't floss and they don't use non-sexist language, but this is not the evil empire.'

Berquist, who headed an acronym which stood for the Office for the Co-ordination of Humanitarian Assistance, believed sensational reporting stripped of context was creating a hostile mood in donor countries, making it increasingly difficult to aid one of the world's poorest countries. He cited initiatives like home schools for girls and the dismantling of the infamous 'Tower of Babel', where television sets and tape from disembowelled videotapes were strung up as a public example, as proof of a gradual relaxation by the militia. The Western media was telling the truth, but not the whole truth about the Taliban.

'You can't bully Afghans. To change them you have to talk to them. But right now it's edict against edict. The Taliban leaders don't need us. They're stronger if we're not here. It's the ordinary Afghan who needs us,' Berquist said, fiddling irritably with his pipe.

'What about the shuttlecocks?' I asked, using aid worker parlance for women draped in the head-to-foot veil.

'Well, they're gettin' hit around by both sides,' Berquist replied. 'Go ask them if they want to be used as pawns on the chessboard of a bunch of well-fed femocrats in New York. Go ask those abused girls at Singesar what they think of the Taliban.'

In Peshawar, Nancy Hatch Dupree had said similar things about the issue of women.

'All this hard-nosed Western feminism is doing a disservice to Afghan women,' she'd told me, clutching her head as if the whole issue gave her a migraine. 'Honour is at the heart of Pashtun culture, and the Pashtun's honour code is based on protecting women. These are pretty wild places and over the centuries that's led to women not having so much freedom of movement. But it's not just the Taliban or the Pashtuns. You go into Turkmen or Tajik villages and most of the women there are still in purdah too. In New York they know fiddle-dee-dee about it.'

There was no point telling the aid workers that they didn't understand the politics of the big picture. They understood it fine; they just didn't agree with it. For Bill Berquist, dealing with the Taliban was a daily routine. He'd even met Mullah Omar once, in the early days, when foreigners could still find themselves in the same room with the now-reclusive Emir-ul Mohmineen.

'He's just a very simple man. Doesn't know much about the outside world, but knows Afghanistan's in one hell of a mess and thinks his way'll improve things,' Bill said. 'He's got a sense of humour — reckons he was a great shot against the Soviets. Heck, we were on the same side in those days! Now he's being demonised, of course, but for Pete's sake, the guy is just a village mullah. But take my word for it, Islam is not the problem. The problem is religious intolerance and fundamentalism, and that's a global phenomenon. We've got Christian fundos beaming in here on the short-wave radio, Jewish fundos wreaking havoc in the Holy Land, Hindu fundos knocking down mosques. They all feed off each other.'

The practical difficulties involved in helping the Taliban were, however, significant. In the course of a campaign to reduce high levels of malaria in and around Kandahar, a foreign aid agency found that many Afghans did not know that mosquitoes caused the illness. Deciding that a pamphlet should be produced to explain the link, the agency thought that, because most Afghans were illiterate, a line drawing of a mosquito biting a human arm would probably be the most effective way of getting the message across. Soon after the pamphlet began circulating, the agency got a visit from a Taliban official who informed them that they had violated the law against images of life forms. Eager to conform, the agency staff offered to remove the picture of the human arm, but the official was not placated. The mosquito also was a living thing, he said, and although he understood the need to warn people that mosquitoes carried malaria, the image must be removed. Eventually, much to the relief of all concerned, the issue was resolved. After much discussion, new pamphlets depicting the mosquito impaled on a bowie knife were issued.

13

Capital Punishment

'**P**rayer is better than sleeping,' wailed a voice like the cry of Tarzan in the dead of night. It was shrill and discordant, guttural and punctuated by a hacking cough. Not since the first muezzin, Bilal, had bellowed the adhan, had the call to prayer been so decisively murdered. Woken from a deep slumber at 2 a.m., I very much doubted many Kandaharis would be taking up the muezzin's kind offer.

My attempts to secure meetings with Mullah Omar and Osama bin Laden had drawn a complete blank, as had requests to visit Bamiyan, Mazar and even Herat. The only place left to go was Kabul. On the bus to the airport, violence broke out when the airline staff hijacked the vehicle, landing kicks and punches to force the passengers off, and leaving them stranded in the desert. The employees — who claimed it was a staff bus — allowed me to stay on board, as a guest of Afghanistan. At Kandahar airport, an incongruous Pop folly of billowing white concrete sails built with American aid in the 1960s, the terminal had been stripped bare and no longer possessed a single chair, and sand blew in through the shattered windows. A group of lithe, dark-skinned young men wearing Palestinian-style scarves, or *kuffiya*, got offended when I asked if they were Sudanese and whether they had met bin Laden. Lacking the usual airport distractions, I climbed a narrow staircase to the control tower, where several turbaned men slouched listlessly listening to Radio Shari'a. They told me it was dangerous to fly Ariana Afghan, which had already lost two planes that year, both crashing into mountains on the route from Kandahar to Kabul with many casualties.

Mullah Omar had visited Kabul only once in the three years since his forces seized the capital, and then in secret. The official line was that he would move to Kabul when the war ended and the country was reunited, but I imagined fear of flying and an aversion to the bone-jarring two-day drive via Ghazni had more to do with it. Ariana made more money selling overflight rights to foreign airlines than it did selling tickets on its planes. On board the ageing Boeing 727 half the seats had been removed to make room for cargo, including several crates containing goats. The barely serviceable plane laboured along the runway, past cannibalised fuselages of former aircraft, and hung ludicrously low in the sky all the way to Kabul.

It had been six years since my last visit to the Afghan capital, and I was unprepared for what awaited me. Once lively and industrious, it had become a demoralised, desperately poor city. The ruins of its buildings stretched for blocks and people with dead eyes roamed about in tatters. Most people had not eaten meat for months and the desperate unemployed gathered on street corners to fight among themselves over the few day-labouring jobs on offer from passing contractors. Humiliated men sat on the roadsides begging with one hand out and another covering their face. The only reason anyone was still in Kabul was if they were too sick or too poor to make the day trip to become refugees in Pakistan. The Continental Hotel was full of ghosts, and I had it all to myself, the only paying guest in a three hundred-room hotel. Groping my way downstairs to the dining room during a power cut one night, I came upon a young man kneeling on the floor, his hands cupped in rapturous prayer. Taking a table, I watched him across the darkened room, his face illuminated in the flickering light of a candle. When he was done he stood up, folded his mat and took my order. The evening curfew was still in place, with a new password issued nightly by the Interior Ministry, and the ceaseless drone of military aircraft carrying volunteers and weapons to the northern frontlines lulled me to sleep each night.

In the city below, the streets were daubed in official slogans: 'Sister, your veil is your fortress', 'Throw reason to the wind — it stinks of corruption'. Scores of men who had committed the crime of trimming their beards languished in Pul-e Charki jail and widows, banned like all women from working, begged in the bazaar. Tribes of orphans roamed the streets: urchin boys and girls with burnt cheeks, shaved heads and a cocky, badgering humour which was the only sign of hope anywhere. Squad cars of the General Department for Prevention of Vice and the Promotion of Virtue — the religious police — cruised the streets in four-wheel-drive vehicles with darkened windscreens, arresting and beating people for minor infractions and picking up women they accused of immodesty. Although music was banned, the vehicles of these moral dog-catchers broadcast unaccompanied singing of Koranic verses, adding to the sombre mood. Kabulis suffered the habitual violence and intolerance of their new overlords as a mutt suffers a callous master.

With traditional entertainments including the city's sixteen cinemas shut down, Kabul people had by 1998 turned to the brutish, Taliban-approved alternative of public executions, amputations and floggings. Tens of thousands of spectators would crowd into the National Stadium most Fridays to watch convicted murderers like Wali Mohammed from Khost being executed. The pre-execution entertainment consisted of two young men being flogged for drinking whisky. With his hands tied and his feet in chains, Wali Mohammed was made to kneel as his victim's brother shot him three times with a Kalashnikov. As the gunshots rang out the crowd surged out of the stands, eager for a closer look at the dead man, his blood oozing into the thick turf of the football field. Taliban gunmen fired into the air to restore order.

By the early twentieth century, Shari'a punishments had virtually disappeared in Islamic societies under the influence of modernising tendencies, but they were revived when the Saudi princes unified the Arabian Peninsula. The Wahabi sect, founded by Abdul Wahab in the eighteenth century, used the lash and the axe to cleanse Arab society of what the sect saw as Sufism's corrupting influence. Officially, the Shari'at had ceased to be law in Afghanistan in the 1920s, but in Kandahar Bill Berquist recalled having seen a beheading in the early 1970s. Under the Pashtun Taliban, *qisas* — the right of revenge — was once again the law. Announced on Radio Shari'a on Thursday nights, public executions were carried out on Fridays, with people travelling from neighbouring provinces to witness the spectacle. One day at the stadium, I found bitterly disappointed spectators streaming away following the sudden cancellation of one such event. Some, like Babur Khan, a businessman who had travelled by bus from Logar province to see the show, had brought their young sons. He thought the government should pay the bus fares of those who had attended the cancelled event.

'After all,' he said, 'if nobody comes, what is the reason for having the executions?'

Initially the introduction of Islamic punishments saw a decline in theft, but gradually the deterrent wore off. Mohammed Yaqub was among six thieves, including several Talibs, who underwent amputations one Friday in January 1999 before a crowd of several thousand spectators. His left foot was lopped off for stealing three carpets worth about $200. He was already missing his right hand, amputated six months earlier for another heist. With his foot removed, Mohammed was made to hop a circuit of the stadium, exhibiting the stump of his wrist to the crowd. After the amputations that day, several hands and feet belonging to Mohammed and the five other thieves were seen hanging from a tree in the New Town district, presumably strung up as a warning to others. That same month, wall-toppling for homosexuals made its debut in the capital. An eighty-four-year-old man accused of sexually assaulting a boy was buried under such a wall and reported dead by an international news agency. But the reporter must have left early. Had he waited, he would have witnessed the amazing sight of Shuma Khan dusting himself off as he emerged from the rubble innocent before God, and even the Taliban, who interpreted his survival as a sign of Allah's will. Taken to hospital instead of the cemetery, the old man said later that he had confessed under torture.[13]

Taliban justice was a mixture of Shari'a law with Afghan characteristics, a throwback to the days of the Pashtun emir, Abdur Rahman. The emir was described by the British Viceroy of India, Lord Curzon, as 'a patriot and a monster' who executed thousands of rebels and rivals by blinding them with quick lime, blowing them out of guns, throwing them down wells or freezing them alive. When one of his harem girls was found pregnant — presumably one he had neglected — the emir had her tied up in a sack and brought into the Durbar hall, where he ran her through with a sword. Two men discussing some forbidden subject had their lips stitched together and dissidents, identified by spies who roamed the bazaars, had their tongues torn out by the roots. En route to Kabul, Curzon passed an iron cage swinging from a tall pole in which rattled the bleaching bones of a robber left to die. Abdur Rahman defended his methods, claiming they were the only way to deal with a race 'so treacherous and criminally inclined'. Curzon liked the emir despite his 'at times insupportable truculence', concluding that he was probably compelled to behave in such a manner 'for the sake of appearances with his own people'.

'This man of blood loved scents and colours and gardens and singing birds and flowers,' the approving viceroy cooed after meeting him.[14] Others concluded that the Iron Emir suffered from a mental or metabolic disorder.

In Islam's collective memory, eighth-century Baghdad was the perfect state where spiritual and temporal authority resided in the person of the caliph Haroun al-Rashid. Haroun was renowned for disguising himself as a peasant and roaming the souks to see for himself the plight of the citizenry. One day in the bazaar, he heard the story of a merchant who, about to embark on the pilgrimage to Mecca, left a jar of olives with a friend for safekeeping, concealing within the jar a fortune in gold coins. Years passed and the jar lay undisturbed in the cellar, but one night the friend's wife found she was out of olives, and thinking no harm would come of it, opened the jar. The olives were excellent and over the next few weeks the couple finished them, discovering the gold. Seven years later the traveller returned to find his olives perfectly preserved, but his money missing. Arguing with his friend, who denied all knowledge of the jar's contents, he took him before a *qazi,* but was unable to prove any wrongdoing and lost the case.

Cruising the souk, Haroun al-Rashid had stumbled upon a group of children holding a mock retrial of the case. Olives, a junior defence attorney was pointing out, lasted only three years. After seven years, the contents of the jar should have been mouldy. Clearly, the jar had been disturbed. Armed with the wisdom of a streetwise kid, the caliph summoned the accused, extracted a confession, and sentenced him to death.[15]

Somewhere in Kabul lay Tariq Ahmed's rugs, mouldering behind their false wall, entrusted to what he hoped was a true friend. But where was Tariq, I wondered. Far away in America, not caring for the carpets he no longer needed? Stranded in a refugee camp somewhere in Pakistan? Or was he here, somewhere in this tragedy? His name was still painted on the thin glass panes of his shop on Jade Idgah but a couple of men there knew nothing of his whereabouts and the shelves were empty apart from some tarnished trinkets. The buildings along Kabul's other road of rugs — Chicken Street — were largely unscathed, but their once-great treasures had been looted or spirited away, and the shopping street of Jade Maiwan resembled Dresden after World War II. If carpets were a parallel currency, then Afghanistan's economy was in the red, the dark red of the filpais hanging over the steel fence of Kabul's small central park, a red whose shade seemed to have deepened over the years, reflecting the general depression. Like the new flag of the Islamic emirate — a black Koranic verse on a white background which read, 'There is no God other than Allah and Mohammed is His Messenger' — Kabul's palette had been reduced to a monotone.

Walking in Chicken Street one morning, I felt a sudden tug on my shirt and, before I knew what was happening, found myself being dragged inside one of the shops, where a gnomish man in a threadbare jacket introduced himself as Abdul Razzaque, one of the Shia Hazaras despised by the Taliban.

'Have you heard the news?' he asked, wiping his brow from his exertions. 'It was on BBC this morning. All non-Muslims must leave Afghanistan!'

'What? Why?' I spluttered. 'Did Mullah Omar say that?'

'Not Mullah Omar — the United States. The radio is saying that America is getting ready to attack Afghanistan. You must leave immediately, but first, please buy a carpet. I think it is the last chance for you!'

The idea that the United States would send troops into Afghanistan was simply too preposterous to believe and, convinced that Abdul had misheard, I paused to browse.

Unlike the arrogant filpais and proud Baluchis, his rugs spoke of poverty and cultural rupture. Some of the designs had gone horribly wrong, as if the weaver had suffered a stroke midway through. Borders gyrated like seismographs in an earthquake, or weaved drunkenly. Instead of lying flat they undulated. Idiosyncracies, even mistakes, are prized in carpets. The most commonly appreciated flaw is an *abrash*, a sudden change in depth of colour caused by unevenly dyed wool. The weary mother who steals a moment from her loom to suckle her child and loses her place in the design, or becomes a refugee and resumes the half-finished rug in another country with different wool, often creates a unique artwork. Her peasant's 'diary' will be traded and stolen and traded again, at ever-increasing prices, until finally it ends up endowing the polished marble floor of an affluent residence with 'character'. Devout Muslims will often make a deliberate mistake, rather than challenge the perfection of Allah. But Abdul's rugs were an abomination. The Shroud of Turin was in better condition. They were faded instead of mellowed, impoverished rather than enriched. Some were moulting, others completely bald, and others emitted a dank odour as if they had recently been disinterred. It wasn't that the heavy traffic of the Bactrians, or Genghis Khan and the Timurids, had worn them bare. They were no good in the first place. I refrained from asking their age because I already knew the answer: they were too old.

Rooting around in his disorderly pile, his every action mimicked by his young son, Abdul emerged holding two small pieces: one an unusually colourful Turkmen Saryk in a pole-diamond segmented design with *topra gol* named after the last Afghan king, Zahir Shah; the other a vivid blue Dokhtar-e Qazi.

'Old antique pieces,' Abdul ventured. 'At least sixty years old.'

The Zahir Shahi was an interesting piece, extremely fine at four hundred knots to the square inch, but incorrect tension on the warps at one end of the loom had created a gathering effect which could only be mended temporarily by stretching. The blue rug was in better shape, but the unhealthy vigour of its palette suggested the use of synthetic dyes.

In nomadic societies the master dyer was the wise man of the tribe; his recipes, based on natural mineral and vegetable extracts, were kept a closely guarded secret. Natural dyes took a month or more of soaking to imbue wool with their subtle shades, compared to boiling the wool for two hours in chemicals, but the investment paid off with colours that were mellow and long-lasting.

'Take cinnabar, indigo and alum, grind and sift lighter than light dust of the high hills,' began the instructions followed by a dyer from Tabriz for making Birbul's Blue. 'Soak for ten hours, keep stirring it, put in the wool and soak for many hours. Boil for three hours, wash in kurd water, water in which kurds and whey have been well beaten up, leave for three hours, then wash again and beat in water.' Ingredients included 'root of Spurge, skin of Onion, St John's Wort, leaves of Tanner's Sumach, berries of Buckthorn, flowers of Camomile, stigma of Saffron, stem of Sage and all of Bastard Hemp'.[16] Onion skins, weld, vine and autumnal apple leaves, pomegranate skins and saffron crocuses are still used to produce gold and yellow colours. Walnut husks and iron oxide made black for outlines, but rugs dyed with iron solution actually corrode. Crushed leaves of indigo, a native plant of southern Asia, are powdered and fermented in a vat with potash, slaked lime and grape sugar to produce blue, the Persian colour of *behesht*, or Paradise. Requiring an alkaline liquid in which to brew, indigo is sometimes fermented in urine, sealed in jars and left in the sun for up to eight weeks.

Before I could reconsider the merits of the blue Dokhtar-e Qazi, Abdul thrust a lustreless, dried-out Turkmen on me. The finest quality wool used for carpets is clipped from the neck, shoulders and flanks of lambs reared at higher altitudes. Rich in natural oils, it is known as *kurk*. But this suicidal Turkmen, whose pile surrendered to the touch in fluffy balls, suggested *tabachi* from the opposite end of the life cycle. It could only have been made from the wool of a dead sheep.

'Good price. Very cheap price,' said Abdul, dismayed by my apparent disgust.

The inspection reached its nadir when the merchant dived into a dark corner and produced an armful of torn end borders and corners of destroyed rugs which he must have scavenged from bombed-out buildings. Someone had obviously told Abdul about fragments, the latest trend in the trade. At the London sales, collectors were paying tens of thousands of pounds for swatches of antique Persians. High prices were tempting owners to tear to shreds valuable antiques which would be even more valuable if sold in instalments. Intrepid collectors could then experience the joy of tracking down the scattered fragments and piecing them back together again at double the price. Commenting on London's October 1998 'Islamic Week' Market, at which a fragment of a seventeenth-century garden carpet once owned by the great German-born collector Robert von Hirsch sold for £56 500, the trade journal *Hali* noted:

> *These results indicate there are buyers to whom art is more important than decoration, a gift to the imagination more important than tactile quality. Even so, some experienced traditional carpet dealers were shaking their heads in disbelief at the prices made for these 'scraps'.*[17]

Writing in the same journal, Penny Oakley reported that although the scale and concept of the original carpet had been made more accessible by piecing it back together, 'sadly, soon after its sale it was again split into four, each fragment entering a different private collection'.

As I flipped listlessly through Abdul's remnants, he followed my body language like a hawk: the pinched nose, the heavy sighs, the sadly shaking head and, worst of all, the complete absence of questions or even comments about his wares. The atmosphere in the shop grew heavy with anticipation, panic and despair. Reports from Mazar spoke of massacres and the forced conversion of Shias to Sunni Islam. In Kabul, Abdul Razzaque had to close his shop to attend prayers at one, four and six o'clock every afternoon, and it was illegal to invite a foreigner to his home. Shia Hazaras — whose distinctive features made them easy targets — were being prevented from boarding buses which could take them to exile in Pakistan, and the anxiety of living in fear was etched in Abdul's face. How would he feed the beautiful boy in the little salwar who played at being a carpet dealer on the floor as we browsed? This was Abdul's last stand.

'Sir, tell me honestly, what do you think? Make an offer, please.'

'There's nothing I like,' I said, unable to marry my sympathy for his plight with the business of carpet buying.

'Nothing? But sir, what about the Turkmen? The blue. This is old indigo, natural colour. Very cheap price. Very blue.'

'No, no. Not blue,' I said with an involuntary shudder. 'I don't like the colour.'

Kabul was dying, and I didn't like the colour. At the limit of his endurance, Abdul addressed me in a sad but steady voice.

'Sir! You see my son here?'

'Yes, Abdul.'

'There is no school for him except Taliban school, where they teach him to kill his father. So he is coming with me to the shop every day, last three months. And he asks me, "Father, what do you do? Are you doctor? Are you teacher? Are you driving the fire engine?" And I tell him, "No, my darling son. I am none of these things. Your father is a carpet dealer. He sells carpets to foreigners, and that way he gets the money to feed you, my darling, and your brother and sisters, and your dear mother, and your grandparents and your aunty, and your cousins." So my son, he thinks about this, and then he asks me, "But Baba-jan, why do Afghan people not buy any carpets?" And I tell him that it's because Afghan people are fighting. Too much fighting! They have no money for carpets. But the foreigner, he has some money, and so he buys. So, my son, he is very happy for this, and he is telling the other children, "Oh, my father is a businessman. He has a shop. He is selling carpets to the foreigners." And he is coming with me, and he is waiting with me, and I am telling him about the carpets, and how we do this business, and how, when he grows up, he can become a carpet seller and have his own shop. But after two weeks, three weeks, no customer is coming to this shop. So then my boy, he is asking me, over and over, many times, again and again, "Baba-jan! Where is the foreigner? Why he is not coming? How will we make the money to buy food for our mother, and for the cousins?" And I say to my son, "Don't worry, my darling. Allah is merciful. He will provide for us. He protects us. Have faith, my dear. Everything will be fine. Everything will be okay."'

A compressed silence filled the stale, dejected store. Abdul Razzaque looked me straight in the eye, smiled what I feared might be his last smile, and said, 'Sir. Please accept my apologies for kidnapping you into my shop. You are my first customer for three months. Please buy something, anything, so that my son can see what his father is.'

I had been hoping to meet Maulvi Ahmad Jan, a former carpet merchant who had joined the Taliban and was now Minister for Industries. But in a country with virtually no functioning industries, he was inexplicably busy. In fact, finding anyone in the administration at their desk was peculiarly difficult. Instead of being in meetings, ministers were often said to be 'praying' or away on the hajj. Others would conduct business in the morning and head off to the northern frontlines to fight Massoud's forces in the afternoon; the governor of the State Bank, Mullah Ehsanullah Ehsan, had died fighting in Mazar. But the most common response to any request to meet a minister was 'He's in Kandahar'. The Taliban had in fact moved the capital there but, typically, had neglected to announce it. After many rejections I resorted to raiding ministers' homes, only to find that they rarely spent more than one night in any one house, fearing opposition hit squads or, more likely, leadership rivals. The bleary eyed men who provided security at their houses had little to do except sleep and drink endless pots of green tea. At the Finance Ministry, the clocks had all stopped but the minister was at least at his desk. My glee was soon tempered, however, when he declined to be interviewed without giving any reason. Asked if he might change his mind if I came back later, his secretary informed me that 'a Talib never changes his mind'. This strident, faceless government treasured its privacy.

Eventually a breakthrough came. At the grand offices of Da Afghanistan Bank, the country's central reserve, I blustered my way up a sweeping staircase, entering an immense room flanked by colossal pillars, its floor covered with the largest carpet I had ever seen. At a glance it must have rivalled what was at the time said to be the world's biggest, a seventy square metre piece woven in the 1950s by Turkmen women which decorated the Bolshoi Theatre in Moscow. Of course, none of these modern monsters were a patch on the largest carpet ever made, the legendary 'Spring of Chosroes', discovered by Byzantine invaders entering the Sassanian palace of the Persian King Chosroes II at Dastagerd in 628 AD. The carpet, or tapestry according to some experts, measured about nine hundred square metres and boasted silver and gold thread, pearls and precious stones. Alas, as so often happened to the treasures of Central Asia, it was cut up as booty by invaders who looted the palace.[18] How this 'Spring of Kabul', a tan filpai with a stately patina, had ever survived the mujahideen's plunder was a complete mystery. Probably its huge bulk prevented them getting it out the door.

The Taliban claimed that political parties were not permitted by the Koran. Government was a voluntary activity, for which officials received an allowance of about $7 a month for food and clothing, while soldiers were given only their guns and their keep. This was how they ran a country of twenty-four million people, and at Da Afghanistan Bank it showed. Seated awkwardly behind a vast desk in a massive office was Mullah Syed Mahmoodullah, the second deputy governor of the bank. He was twenty-five, an illiterate from Zabol province with a thin, feline face and a dark green turban.

On the wall behind him a calendar depicted a Kalashnikov being thrust over the globe by a fist. We were introduced to each other by a dapper, elderly man in a pin-striped suit who described himself as an advisor, and who had been with the bank since before the deputy governor was born. His untrimmed beard was heavily streaked with grey, contrasting with the minister's jet black growth.

Talibs like Mullah Mahmoodullah, educated exclusively in the recitation of the Koran, could not find their way around their offices, let alone a bank ledger or the national accounts. Much as they resented it, they relied on officials from former regimes to stave off the complete collapse of their ministries. There were many dangers for the old-timers — informers denouncing them as communist spies, perhaps a bullet in the head from an enraged boss — and they survived on salaries of less than $10 per month. But they were so desperate they were willing to take the risk. Once extremely important people who attended conferences abroad, they now clung grimly to their positions, hoping one day to wake up and find that the past two decades had all been a terrible dream. In the meantime they read files to the violent, unlettered peasants from Kandahar, Zabol, Helmand and Oruzgan who now ruled, their beards growing greyer by the month. As we spoke, the deputy minister searched sullenly for something in his desk drawers. In the course of the search he extracted a hand gun and several boxes of ammunition, dumping them on the desk and putting them back when he'd found what he wanted. Hacking into a spittoon, he wiped his mouth and regarded me with not much more affection than the contents of the receptacle. He had consented to be interviewed for one reason only: he wanted to harangue the West for not recognising the Taliban administration.

'We're struggling to make a pure Islamic country here. If they don't want relations with us, too bad. We'll never accept interference. We rely only on God,' he mumbled.

The economic management of Afghanistan was complicated by the existence of at least three separate currencies, none of which were recognised by all the warring factions. There were Taliban *Afghanis*, Massoud *Afghanis*, and even a few Dostum *Afghanis* still lying around. Counterfeiting by opposing factions was a huge problem, and in northern areas conquered by the Taliban the demonetisation of all opposing currencies had wiped out the life savings of ordinary people. How, I wondered, did the government plan to compensate those affected?

'Our policy is to say it is not a registered banknote. We will never accept it,' Mullah Mahmoodullah said through his secretary.

'But people are destitute. They have lost their life savings. Even your own soldiers haven't been paid for months,' I said.

'As for the people with savings in Dostum or Massoud *Afghanis*, we cannot help them. But it is not true about the salaries. Even today we distributed money.'

'How much?'

'I don't know.'

'What about the overall money supply? What is the bank's estimate of the amount of money in circulation?'

'That's a secret,' Mullah Mahmoodullah shot back vehemently, tucking his stockinged feet underneath him in the chair.

'What about counterfeit *Afghanis*?' Did the mullah have any idea of how much forged money was in circulation?

'No, I have no idea.'

'What about prices? With the war, inflation must be very high. I've heard figures of 240 per cent. True?'

The deputy governor looked at his advisor, they exchanged words, and then he said, 'We don't have that information at the moment.'

The armed priest was hardly a mine of interesting information but he did know the exchange rate — 70 000 *Afghanis* to the US dollar. It had been forty-five to the dollar before the war. I was on my way out when the minister muttered something in Pashto to his official.

'My minister would like to say something,' said Grey Beard.

Black Beard cleared his throat, then in the cadence of a mullah calling from a minaret, he half-declaimed, half-sang, 'I want to complain to the world that since the Taliban have come to power, other countries refuse to see the improvements. I ask you, the journalist, in your holy vocation, not to propagate lies and distortions, and to convey a clear picture to the world against these negative things. We are proud as Muslims, even if we are poor. Soon we will make a pure Islamic government. We won't bend to any pressure. The Islamic Emirate of Afghanistan demands international recognition by UNO!'

'UNO?' I asked Grey Beard.

'U-N-O,' the official said, explaining the antique terminology. 'The United Nations Organisation.'

'*Insh'allah*, without exaggeration the collapse of the United States will begin from here in Afghanistan,' the minister concluded, 'because the Prophet — peace be upon Him — said, "You can have a shared government with a pagan but not with an oppressor."'

The interview was over. I knew that, because the minister brought his fist down so hard on his vast desk that his tea cup jumped.

There may have been chronic malnutrition in the city, but when lunchtime came any Talib worth his salt headed for the best restaurant in town, 'The Herat' in the New Town district. Around noon, parking spaces would evaporate in the street outside, taken by twin-cab off-road pickups with the roll bars and spotlights preferred by Talib commanders. Clearing a path through the black-shrouded widows who gathered each lunchtime to beg outside, they piled into the restaurant, bearing arms. After washing and checking their look in the mirrors, they were shown by blue-uniformed waiters to an elevated section of the restaurant, where they lounged on bolsters and watched the rest of us sitting on chairs at the tables below. Over bowls of *yakhni* and plates of *pulao*, washed down with imported cola and a milk-rice confection with pistachio nuts, you heard snatches of conversation in Urdu, Hindustani, Punjabi and Arabic, the languages of several thousand foreign volunteers from Pakistan and Arab countries who had joined the Taliban's summer offensive. Some of them were Sunni extremists sheltering in Afghanistan after committing atrocities against the Shias in Pakistan.

Lunching at The Herat, I joined a table of interpreters from the Foreign Ministry who shocked me by confirming Abdul's story about the evacuation of non-Muslims. The United States government had chartered a DC-10 to speed up the removal of its citizens from neighbouring Pakistan in response to what Ambassador Thomas W. Simons Jr described as a 'pattern of threats' from Muslim groups. Islamabad was reported as tense, security was being tightened around the American, Egyptian and Iranian embassies, and foreigners had been told to exercise caution while moving around. Off the record, US officials were talking about a 'viper's nest' of terrorists in neighbouring Afghanistan and the 'instant gratification' an attack on them might provide. Informed that a United Nations plane was due to depart soon carrying evacuees, I rushed to the UN, and from there to the airport.

Passing through the murky corridors of the terminal building and descending onto the apron, I was relieved to see the UN plane taxiing to a standstill. Waiting to farewell several of the passengers was a silver-haired European man in an extraordinary full-dress military uniform. He was Lieutenant-Colonel Carmine Calo, an Italian air force officer who had arrived recently in Kabul to take up his duties as a UN military observer. His colleagues had told me about him; his lively humour and warmth had quickly endeared him to everybody, especially the local staff.

'You're staying?' I asked, suspecting he would need to be there to monitor the fallout if the United States retaliated for the embassy bombings.

'Yes, yes,' he responded jocularly, as the sun flashed off the fancy braid on his uniform. 'We don't know what the threat is exactly. We've just been told to evacuate non-essential staff. But somebody has to keep an eye on things.'

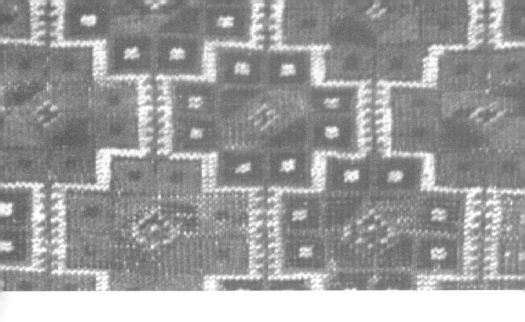

PART FOUR

PESHAWAR

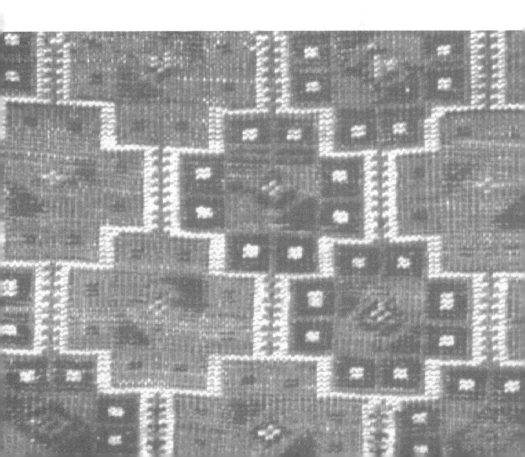

14

Cruise Control

On a late summer's night in August 1998, Maaz Ali was settling down to dinner under a sky illuminated by shooting stars in eastern Afghanistan. The conversation around the camp was the usual awkward mixture of grand plans and homesick recollections, but the mood was relaxed. The Punjabi volunteers had been at the Zhawar Kili camp for almost three years now, apart from occasional forays to northern Afghanistan, where they had participated in some of the Taliban's battles against the Tajiks, the Uzbeks and the hated Shia Hazaras. A nineteen-year-old Pakistani from Bahawalpur on the Sutlej River, Maaz was expecting to soon embark on the biggest challenge of his life: a difficult and dangerous mission to Kashmir to join the fight against Indian rule. His best friend Khaled, from the smaller town of Sahiwal, was coming too. As it happened, they didn't need to go that far for a dangerous adventure. That night, sitting around the camp stove, one hundred and fifty kilometres south of Kabul, the hi-tech 'war of the future' came to them.

At about ten o'clock, as he was about to turn in, Maaz heard what he thought was a jet flying low overhead. A split second later everyone heard it, but before they could even stand up the dormitories and common rooms of the camp were convulsed by the impact of several enormous explosions. In the mayhem that followed, Khaled collapsed on the ground, blood spurting from the right side of his head. His clothing was torn in several places, where dark red patches were quickly spreading. Nobody knew exactly what was going on. The surprise attack had struck with overwhelming force, destroying the mosque where hours earlier almost the entire student body was assembled in prayer.

'There was panic for a few hours,' said Maaz, tears of rage frozen in his eyes. Although he had been sitting only a few metres from Khaled during the attack, he was completely unscathed. 'We knew we were under attack and we wanted to hit back, but we could do nothing. Eventually we collected the injured and took them to the hospital.'

As his comrades began piling up the bodies of the dead, Maaz Ali tended to Khaled's wounds. What he'd thought were 'planes' were in fact Tomahawk cruise missiles: pilotless, jet-propelled rockets six metres long and guided by computers with Global Positioning Systems (GPS). US Navy destroyers and submarines cruising the Arabian Sea off the coast of Pakistan had fired about seventy of them — more than the number used during the entire 1991 Gulf War. They had set a terrain-hugging course, flying over the Chaghai Hills along Pakistan's border with Afghanistan to deliver their payloads of bomblets and anti-personnel weapons. The missiles were moving at over eight hundred kilometres per hour when they slammed into the dormitories, mosques, lecture halls and armouries of six camps around the Afghan town of Khost, including the Al-Badr facility funded and managed by Osama bin Laden.[1] It had been an awesome demonstration of America's power to exercise lethal force by remote control. Twenty-one people were dead.

Two days earlier, as I flew into Islamabad airport from Kabul, the skies had been dotted with nothing more threatening than brightly coloured paper kites. But in Pakistan even children's kites carry a hidden menace, their strings coated with finely ground glass capable of cutting other kites' strings in dogfights. As our eighteen-seat aircraft descended, the volume of plywood, string and paper thrust up into the sky increased, like flak in a children's version of an air defence exercise. The airport terminal teemed with pilgrims returning from Saudi Arabia, and the luggage carousel was crowded with plastic jerrycans of saltish water from the well of Zam Zam, the Muslim equivalent of Lourdes. After collecting their jerrycans and pausing for a brief prayer on mats in the arrival hall's mini-mosque, the pilgrims headed into the city, passing hundreds of Americans being evacuated from Islamabad the same day. Also arriving in Pakistan were casualties from the US missile strikes on Khost. Doctors there had been unable to cope with the number of injured, and advised Maaz to take his friend to Rawalpindi, Islamabad's twin city.

As he lay in his bed at the civil hospital, the injured young man could barely speak and was in great pain from burns to his arms and legs. Dressed in striped hospital pyjamas, he groaned, interrupting Maaz, who would pause in his story, reach for a glass and try to feed water through his friend's burnt lips. Khaled's head was heavily bandaged and he had lost all the toes on his right foot.

The American assault had been timed to coincide with bin Laden's presence at the camps, but a meeting the Saudi millionaire was due to attend there had been cancelled at the last minute, and the Taliban had confirmed that he was alive and unharmed at an undisclosed 'safer place'. In his own statement, delivered in London and Peshawar, bin Laden declared that 'the battle has not started yet', and promised to respond to the missile attacks 'with deeds, not words'.

At Khost, Maaz Ali had been learning to use a gun. Laying land mines, firing rocket-propelled grenades, detonating Claymore anti-tank mines and setting bombs and booby traps were also part of his tuition. In 1995 his group, the Harakat ul-Ansar, had kidnapped and held five young Westerners holidaying in Kashmir and beheaded one of them, a Norwegian, Hans Christian Ostro. Many of the bomb blasts they had set off in the Kashmir Valley had killed civilians. Yet, like the volunteers who went to fight for the Republicans in Franco's Spain, Maaz and Khaled were idealists as well as soldiers.

'We are not terrorists. We are just fighting for our religion,' Maaz said. If innocent bystanders were hurt, he reasoned, it was regrettable but unavoidable. As he spoke, Maaz's voice was constricted by a swelling sense of injury and injustice. He told of the inhumane nature of the Tomahawk missiles, how they had released thousands of smaller bombs designed to kill and maim people. This soldier of Islam seemed surprised to discover that his enemy had the same propensity for violence as he did. As he spoke, the doctor on duty, Mohammed Imdad, dropped by to check on Khaled's condition.

'We removed a lot of shrapnel from this boy's head. His injuries must have been caused by some kind of anti-personnel weapon, probably a cluster bomb,' he said, then, suddenly turning from diagnosis to analysis, added, 'The Jews have turned the Christians against the Muslims, but the price for America and its allies will be high.'

The doctor was an educated man, but the sight of fellow Pakistani Muslims injured by American Christian missiles had provoked a 'tribal' reaction. At Friday prayers the next day preachers at Islamabad's Abpara Mosque issued a *fatwa* endorsing revenge attacks on Americans, whether civilian or military. 'It is permissible now, as far as Islam is concerned, to kill Americans,' they cried, voices distorted by anger and the cheap public address system. Suitably stirred, young worshippers spilled out onto the streets, their righteous, adolescent anger channelled harmlessly against unreachable foes. But in Kabul, an easier target was in reach.

The morning after the missile strikes, Carmine Calo, the forty-two-year-old UN military observer I had met at Kabul airport, was driving a colleague, French diplomat Eric Lavertu, around the city when their car was blocked by a Taliban pickup truck bearing Defence Ministry markings. A man aged in his thirties with a wispy beard and wearing salwar kameez and a brown turban stepped from the vehicle, loaded a Kalashnikov assault rifle, and opened fire on the UN off-roader. He fired methodically, shot by shot, rather than spraying the car and its occupants, before driving off. Inside the UN car, Lavertu had received superficial wounds to his neck, but Calo was bleeding profusely from a wound to his abdomen and his arm had been broken by a bullet. Rushed to the Red Cross hospital at Wazir Akbar Khan, he was operated on and spent the night there. Before turning in, his spirits were lifted by a conversation with a fellow Italian UN staffer, Dr Eric Donelli, and the news that doctors believed he would make a full recovery. But the following morning his condition suddenly deteriorated, and he died from internal bleeding at around ten o'clock. His body, draped in the sky blue flag of the United Nations, was flown to Islamabad that afternoon. Two Pakistani men were later arrested and charged with Calo's murder.

Months later a Taliban judge convicted the two Pakistani Talibs of Colonel Calo's murder and invited his family to send a close male relative to cut off the killers' heads, an invitation which appalled Calo's grieving widow.

'I'd like to see them dead,' Maria Pepe told the Milan daily *Il Giornale*, 'but I wouldn't have the courage to give the order to take their lives. We do not want revenge, but justice.'

The American missiles had evaded Pakistani radar, and although they had gone nowhere near Islamabad, Habib claimed to have seen them flashing across the night sky over Badshah Market.

'They were long — VAAIRRY LONG,' Habib grinned. 'And on one side somebody was writing "Love, Monica. Kiss. Kiss. Kiss".'

As I arrived, the telephone rang and Habib bounded towards his desk. Picking up the handset he made a long, looping movement with his hand, indicating that the call was long distance, then covered the mouthpiece and whispered, 'Clinton calling!'

Fortunately the president, who was being accused of ordering the missile strikes to distract attention from an embarrassing affair with a White House intern, spoke fluent Hindustani and their conversation flowed with innumerable *tik-taks*, *acchas* and *bilco teek-hais*. Call ended, Habib returned to the couch, raised an open palm and whipped it into mine, the Muslim 'High Five', or *baiya*, with which Mohammed himself would seal oaths.[2]

'My every word must be joking,' he said, in his croaky, rasping voice. 'Joke is my life! If Clinton give me dollars, but no joke, I DON'T TAKE IT!'

Then, drawing me in with a sideways glance and an absurd leer, he confessed to a secret passion.

'Habib love Monica. TRUE!' he said. 'In Islam, a man can have two, three, four wives. WHY NOT? Another, another, another. No forcing. Men are like this, and Clinton he like it. But his religion is Christian, so im-possible! He see panty. Suddenly he become too crazy for Monica. Allah gives and forgives. Man gets and forgets.'

As Minister for Joking in Habib's car-pit Cabinet I was obliged to laugh, but I did not like the turn the conversation had taken. We were drifting inexorably towards the one subject you should never, ever discuss with a Muslim man: women. Did my wife 'know' other men before our marriage, he inquired. If so, how could I accept it? Western society was irretrievably corrupt. He had seen music television, with naked black people dancing. Is this reasonable, he asked.

'In Afghanistan, if a man look once at a girl, she will ask him, "Do you have a mother? Do you have a sister?" If he look two times at this girl, her brother will not ask anything. Just kill. Habib have three sisters, so maybe he must kill also. But in your country — OH MY GOD — you are having too much divorce. No family for little childrens. You got AIDS, everybody dying. You got old women dressing like young women, body hanging out.'

The Koran was explicit: men had authority over women because Allah had made one superior to the other and because men financially supported women. As I was a Western man, Habib felt the independent behaviour of Western women was a dishonour to me personally. Pressured to justify this state of affairs, I stumbled into a rambling discourse on the unmanageable nature of human sexuality, the pointlessness of puritanical injunctions, and the victimless nature of certain crimes.

'No, no, no. NO!' he protested, scratching his balls. 'Habib is old-fashion man!'

My sex-crazed culture, he predicted, was doomed to drown in a pool of depravity. Surely the Islamic system was superior, he said, standing over me, citing chapter and verse of the scriptures, when over his shoulder I noticed the most extraordinary sight. Behind him two extremely comely young women with high cheekbones and full bosoms had stealthily entered the shop and were choking in silent laughter as they snuck up behind him. They were wearing flashy jewellery, and their lurid saris displayed gorgeous fat rolls at the waist as they playfully wrestled for the right to surprise Habib. Pressing her bosom hard into his back, one of them cupped her bejewelled hands over his eyes and growled 'Guess who?' in guttural Punjabi. Smiling like Ray Charles, Habib sniffed for clues in her perfume and then, grabbing her arms, spun around, beaming expectantly. Suddenly he shrieked as if he'd seen a ghost.

'*BITAAAHH*!' he remonstrated. 'What are YOU doing here?'

Smoothing creases from her sari, she pouted. 'What's eating you today?' she said, poking a finger coyly in her cheek and curling her tongue across her top lip.

'*CHALO BIBI*! *CHALO*!' Habib barked.

As Habib began pushing the girl out the door, she caught hold of her girlfriend and suggested with her eyes that I might like to meet them in the godown, the cellar where Habib kept his choicest pieces. Yet she was not remotely interested in carpets.

'We're hot! Let us cool down in your godown,' she appealed to Habib, raising an eyebrow and waggling her head. Then she turned vicious, bawling, 'You'll regret it if you're not nice to us. God will take away what you don't use.'

It was strange behaviour for Pakistani women. Belatedly, I realised they were not Pakistani women at all. They were Pakistani men, *hijras*, or transsexuals. As I began to laugh, Habib cast a harried look over his shoulder. He was blushing.

'What for you laughing at?' he moaned. 'These crazy people. CRAZY!'

'I think she wants to go down in the godown, Habib.'

'No, not that. Always they are coming for money to me.'

'And what do they give in return?'

Instead of answering, he shot me a murderous look; then, with a huge effort, bundled the hijras out the door, like a pair of unwanted rugs.

'You mind the shop. I will bring lunch,' he yelled, herding the hijras away.

In the now-deserted shop, the mute silence of the carpets encouraged reflection. Perusing the rugs, which stood rolled in various sizes like organ pipes in a cathedral, it was easy to see why the early Christians had assigned them sacred functions, laying out the bodies of their deceased popes and bishops on them, or using them as altar covers long before Islam existed. The Moorish invasion of Iberia in the eighth century brought the carpet loom to Europe in significant numbers for the first time, and carpets were among the booty carried home by the Crusaders. But reverence for rugs would survive centuries of religious rivalry. When England's King Henry VIII died in 1547, his inventories listed over four hundred Turkish carpets. In Venice on feast days, or when the Doge and the Senate paraded on St Mark's Square, the people would hang out their rugs as a sign of respect.[3] European artists drawn to rich palettes and designs further popularised the Oriental rug, with examples featured in the works of Hans Holbein the Younger, Vermeer, Mantegna, Carpaccio, Giotto, Lotto and Terborch. Henri Matisse was a collector. Eventually imports placed such a burden on the exchequers that European kings and queens decided to encourage weaving within their realms,

In 1608, Pierre Dupont opened a workshop in the basement of the Louvre, and France's famous Aubusson and Savonnerie looms were later rivalled by England's Axminster.

In 1932, Arthur Urbane Dilley formed the Hajji Baba Society in the United States, and collecting became organised. To Dilley, Oriental carpets recorded national personalities, documenting 'a vast drama, whose every thread is woven into the art of rugs'.[4] They were 'a beautiful subject, limitless as a sunset'.[5] Two years earlier, and rather less romantically, *Fortune* magazine had declared:

> *Persian rugs are not only collector's objects: they are the greatest of all collector's objects. They provide the amateur with every possible thrill. Their value is very high: somewhere between the square foot price of New York real estate and the square foot price of [Thomas Gainsborough's] The Blue Boy . . . They are, as a class, the rarest of all seriously collectible works of great art . . . And as for the lore of the Persian rug — there is a body of erudition into which the specialist can disappear from the vulgar eye like a porpoise plumping into a bed of kelp. There never was so deep a sea of learning.[6]*

Lacking an army, a fortune, or significant expertise, my quest for carpet glory was wholly quixotic. Locked out of the investment market, where the prices start at $10 000, I bargain-hunted at the bottom of the pile, hoping my travels to far-flung places would turn up rare rugs for a pittance. As I sat minding Habib's shop, the telephone rang. It was Chaudhury Akhtar calling to say that some Afghan refugees had come to him with several old Turkmen pieces, and wanting to know if he should send them over.

'Fine,' I said. 'But make it by four.'

Then a Pakistani man arrived wanting prices on Mori Bukhara runners. His relative in the States thought there might be a market for them in California. What was my best price? Unrolling a few of the hall carpets, I gave some estimates, which he dutifully noted down in his diary, promising to return. Two other men followed, asking if I had any Senna kilims — which I did — and after inspecting them offered twenty dollars each.

'Im-possible,' I said, refusing to budge. They left.

Returning with two plates of chicken *biryani*, Habib seemed pleased with my executive decision-making.

'*BISMILLAH*! We are business partners now,' he crowed, laying his newspaper tablecloth on the floor.

'What about your other partners?'

'What? Them? Those crazy people? You know me. You KNOW me,' he said, glancing at the door and leaning towards me with a worldly air.

'You know, when you go to the sea, you can see every kind of animal. Fish, crocodile, and too many kind of things you can see in the river or sea. But you cannot imagine everything that is on the land.'

We chewed on that for a while, Habib's big jawbone gnawing the food, his furrowed brow nodding ponderously with the truth of it. It wasn't exactly a power lunch. Habib had no inside information about prime ministerial corruption or the whereabouts of Osama bin Laden. In fact, most of what he said was pure nonsense. But I was comfortable in his company, with the quiet newspaper lunches and the childish, bombastic comedy which prevailed the rest of the time. Despite our differences in religion and culture, we knew and liked each other. It wasn't such a small achievement. Yet were we rivals, or partners, in the thicket of deception, commerce and romance that was the battleground of the carpet wars? I needed to know. Would he, I asked, share with me the secrets of the trade?

'Look, I will tell to you,' he said after a long pause. 'Knotting is not everything. The car-pit should lay flatly. Front and back should be same colour. Repairs you can see more clearly if you look at the underside.'

'That's it?'

'That's it.'

Since the missile strikes, the expatriate presence in Pakistan had noticeably thinned, especially in Peshawar, capital of the North-West Frontier Province, where Pashtuns and Afghans dominated. Informed that I was heading there to see the situation for myself, Habib, as always, was against it.

'Oh, Peshawar,' he said. 'If you don't know it, your life is very happy.'

Still he gave me a couple of contacts in the bazaar there.

After lunch we descended into the godown, where his premium collection stood in stacks three metres high.

'This Baluchi. Aina gul, one hundred years old. This is car-pit car-pit. Better than gold. Wall use. This Hatchlu, two thousand eight hundred dollars. Yomud Ersari, one hundred and sixty years old, three thousand six hundred dollars. This is carefully work, definitely vegetable dye. You cannot find this. Before, people buy vegetable for dye, now they buy for food. Yomud Chubash, wood colour, mixed guls, eight hundred. This camel wool, CAMEL WOOL! He got it, he spin it by hand.'

The longish red and blue 'Aina Kotshak' Baluchi with the abrash at one end was a stately work, and I wanted it badly. But the price was prohibitive.

'What's the matter, my friend?' Habib asked. 'Oh, you win my heart. I want to see you smiling, happy. Don't pay anything! Take this car-pit back to your country.'

As the shadows outside began lengthening he walked me along the open arcade, where the other rug merchants sat awaiting their prey. When one of them made a show of inviting me to view his wares, Habib grabbed my hand and told the interloper, 'No, no, no, no! He doesn't want to buy your car-pits.' Winking theatrically at me, he said, 'I never want to lose you!'

15

Khyber Bazaar

The walls that once defended Peshawar, Pakistan's carpet capital, had long since fallen, their historic fabric put to more practical uses like building new houses. Separated by the Khyber Pass from the Afghan border fifty kilometres away, its name meant 'frontier town'. But Qissa Khawani, the 'Street of Storytellers', had been invaded by refugees. The Afghans had taken over.

Among growling trishaw engines and blasting truck horns, they plied their trade from horse-drawn tongas and ageing pickups, axles groaning under rug loads. The art deco Rose Hotel and Ayub Mansions, smart getaways under the Raj, now functioned as clearing houses for the looms of nations. They sparked with an energy so electric it could have run their fans, lights and air-conditioners. All the haggling power of Kabul, Herat and Mazar-e Sharif had been swept up, mounting with gathering force into a tidal wave which had crashed over Peshawar. Commuters leapt on and off reckless buses, skittling children who ran haywire between them. Mobile crews of Customs police dressed in SWAT team uniforms roamed the bazaar in 4x4s with guns cocked, shouting as they chased down the vehicles of suspected smugglers. Here, where the mule vied with the minibus, and bird-sellers, coppersmiths and mercers chased the ever-elusive rupee, the rug lords ruled.

Knotting carpets is an industry much older than Pakistan itself, having been introduced into the region in the eleventh century by the Ghaznavids. The Moghul emperors Jehangir and Shah Jahan commissioned some of the finest carpets ever made. Because rug making was not indigenous to the Indus region, the designs were of necessity copied from elsewhere. Although anathema to collectors, copying has been around as long as carpets themselves. In the eighth century Oriental motifs showed up in the illuminated manuscripts of the Book of Lindisfarne. Chinese cloudbands could appear on rugs made in Persia and Spain, and the designs of the Mamluks, the Balkan slaves who in the fifteenth century conquered Egypt, have been compared to the mandalas of Tibet. Pakistani weavers drew their inspiration from Persia and Turkestan. Their 'Royal Bukhara' was, in fact, a Tekke.

But in 1930 an unfortunate incident blackened the name of the subcontinent's rugs. Enterprising Punjabi craftsmen had begun copying Turkmen designs in finely knotted pieces which sold for good prices abroad. But to the dismay of their new owners, these rugs rapidly disintegrated due to a defect in the wool. The yarn, it transpired, had been obtained from discarded British Army socks.[7]

After Partition, when many Muslim weavers migrated from India to Pakistan, the government of independent Pakistan subsidised new carpet factories. When he wasn't creating a new nation, the founder of Pakistan, Mohammed Ali Jinnah, was collecting carpets. At the time of his death, the Quaid-e Azam owned 153 carpets, including many Persian pieces over a century old. After Jinnah's death, they fell into disrepair, until a retired government servant called Azher Samdani took to restoring them. 'I could not bear the idea that a personal collection of our beloved leader should wither away like that,' Samdani said.[8] Half a century on, the country produced four million square metres of hand-knotted carpets every year and it was said that in some villages in Punjab every second home had a loom. Big players like Badshah Group, Abbas Corp, Latif Enterprises, Shalimar Carpet, and Imran Brothers dominated an export industry worth $300 million a year which employed one and a half million people. With such high stakes, the Pakistan Carpet Manufacturers and Exporters' Association was an anthill of intrigue, with charges of election-rigging occasionally surfacing in the press. The Karachi-based newspaper *Dawn* reported the complaints of one manufacturer, who requested that his name be withheld for 'fear of reprisals from those with money to lose'.

> *They are not exporting quality carpets now. Our values are not being maintained. All they want is money, money money ... We, the true carpet makers and dealers, are in the same position as Van Gogh; no one will appreciate us until we and our art are dead and gone ... These people are not making carpet, they are making money.*[9]

Ironically, exports to the United States had been stagnant since 1979, the year the Soviet Union invaded Afghanistan. In those days, Peshawar ran on CIA money bound for the mujahideen. Nowadays, the country's economy was being undermined by a slow slide towards fundamentalist and sectarian violence, discouraging investment and foreign tourists, who chose less troubled destinations. Nuclear tests had done little to help the situation.

Still, Pakistan, like its arch-enemy India, remained one of the world's largest exporters of new handmade rugs. Alas, a typical 'Mori Bukhara' from Pakistan is a rug of no consequence. No matter how detailed the design, how fine the knotting, how lustrous the wool, they are usually quite ugly, with dreary colours and robotic execution. The vital element of cultural continuity is missing, swept away by politics, urbanisation and modern methods of production. Yet the Mori Bukhara is one of the world's most popular styles, sold at clearance sales everywhere.

Hajji Hazrat Shah Market, also known as Balkh Market, was built like a small fortress, dug in behind Peshawar's posh new Park Inn Hotel. It was run by Multani Pashtuns, but there wasn't much Pashtun hospitality there. The three-storey beehive formed a grimy central courtyard, where young men with cold jade eyes and bobbed, shoulder-length hair lounged insolently on string charpoys covered with Maimana kilims. When I gave them the name of a merchant Habib had recommended, they laughed contemptuously.

'He's gone to Kabul,' said one; then another corrected, 'No, no. To America,' which got an even bigger laugh. They were so funny I could have smacked them, but not wanting to unleash a chain of honour killings I swallowed my pride instead. The British had salted their lands, destroyed their fruit trees, blockaded them, and when nothing worked, given them titles like *Malik*. But they never controlled the Pashtuns. Arrogant and cussed, this was their place. It stank of horse manure and the tea was the colour of urine.

Exploring the open gallery on the market's first floor, I came to an iron balustrade overlooking a greasy backstreet full of mechanics working on car engines. Its filth compelling, I had been gazing into the alley for some time when, from the corner of my eye, I noticed a man bending low to unlock a steel shutter, which he lifted to reveal a carpet stall of destitute paucity. There was something perplexing about him, perhaps his cleanliness against the general squalor. His beard was neatly trimmed, his salwar kameez flawlessly laundered and his white cotton skullcap pristine. When he noticed me staring, he stared back with a confused smile.

It was Tariq. Gone were the slacks and business shirt, replaced by the traditional overshirt and vest, and the smile that once shone under a rakish moustache was now buried in a beard. It had been seven years and another country, four regimes in Kabul and a lot of fighting since we'd drunk tea in the small shop on Jade Idgah. Frankly, I don't think he remembered me — just one of thousands of customers who had passed through his shop — but I had never forgotten the rug merchant of Kabul and had seen through the beard he had been forced to grow for his rare forays back to the Afghan capital.

'It's a long time. What brings you to Pakistan?' he asked, raising his hands around him as if to apologise for his surroundings. His slight smile was struggling to enliven his jaded visage, and he appeared wary and ill at ease. His stall was a nameless cell, damp patches exposed on the concrete walls. There were some old kilims cut up to make cushion covers, and a Taimani flatweave from Chaghcharan, near the leaning Minaret of Jam, but nowhere to make tea, and instead of offering some Tariq said he had just stopped by to collect some rugs for washing. Barely pausing to shoulder a few pieces, he was locking up again and bidding me goodbye, even before we had exchanged addresses. The Tariq of memory had been gracious and generous with his time. The Tariq of reality seemed preoccupied and busy.

'Tariq! Wait . . .' I said, as he turned to leave.

'Yes?'

'Those carpets. They need washing?'

'Of course. They just came from Afghanistan.'

'Where do you wash them? In a laundry?'

'No. It's a special place where they do this kind of washing.'

'Is it far?'

'Not very far. Maybe fifteen minutes by rickshaw.'

'Can I come with you?'

A bemused double-take stalled him. He looked at me carefully, then the old, slow smile shone through the beard.

'Sure,' he said. 'Why not?'

Tariq's story was told in the back seat of a motorised rickshaw, whose driver exercised unfettered hostility in his relations with the rest of the traffic. Straining to be heard over incessant quacking horns, Tariq recalled his decision to leave Afghanistan as if it were an unhealed wound.

'That was the most difficult decision in my life,' he said. 'I had just bought the bathroom tiles for my new house. Then a rocket fell on our bazaar. I thought to myself, "The situation is getting too bad. I must take my family and go to Pakistan."'

To abandon his house was to betray a life's ambition, the symbol of his rise from street orphan to conscript soldier, and finally to prosperous trader in the capital. With his carpets safely hidden in their secret cache, he had gathered a few basic possessions, some blankets and pillows and a pressure cooker, and set out from Kabul with his wife and three daughters in the back of a truck to Pakistan, a country he had never seen. But on the outskirts of Jalalabad, halfway to Peshawar, the truck was stopped at a checkpoint.

'They said, "You are not allowed to go to Pakistan. The border is closed." We thought, "Oh! They are mujahideen. They are truthful." But actually they wanted money. They said, "You are from Herat. What are you doing here?" They were Pashtuns who thought we were Shias and should go to Iran. They said, "You must go to Herat. Why you are going to Pakistan?" We said, "This is closer. Why should we go to Herat? This is all Afghanistan." But their leader refused. For two weeks we had to stay there, just beside the road. Pashtun people were allowed through, but when we asked, they said we had to pay fifty thousand *Afghanis*. I bargained with them and finally they agreed to accept thirty thousand. Their leader was called Malem — it means teacher. In Afghanistan we had many professors, engineers, teachers. But our life was very bad.'

Several times Tariq had returned to Kabul but, although it was only ten hours' drive away, infighting and economic collapse had made it virtually uninhabitable. After a rocket fell just metres from his carpet vault he'd decided his rugs were no longer safe there. Entrusting all three hundred of them, weighing over a tonne, to a Herati truck driver, he sold his prized Corolla for a third of its value and left his house and shop in the care of relatives.

'All through the Russian war we were hearing about refugees. We couldn't understand why they went to Pakistan and Iran.

In Kabul, everything was fine. Even with the communist government. When the mujahideen came, we were also happy. We thought, "They are good people. The war is over." We couldn't believe it when they continued fighting, and we ourselves became refugees.'

For a time after the Taliban entered Kabul the situation improved, but the twin scourges of hijacking of cars and kidnapping soon returned and his occasional trips to check on his house became hedged again with risk. If he stayed more than a day, and word filtered out that a merchant was in town, the threat of being kidnapped for ransom was real. In Peshawar, meanwhile, the diaspora had turned every second Afghan into a rug merchant. Competition was fierce, and the countless daily failures, humiliations and obstacles encountered by a refugee had taken their toll on Tariq. His sentences were peppered with fatalistic *Insh'allahs*, his hands knotted. His three children had become five, all daughters, a heavy burden for an Afghan father who must see them all married off and secure. With no son to help cushion his old age he had become an anxious man.

Fifteen minutes from Khyber Bazaar, our rickshaw squealed to a halt at the blue steel gates of a high-walled compound on Dauwra Road, where dozens of men purposefully carried carpets to and fro and the air was rank with chlorine. One man wielding a flame-thrower was scorching Maimana and Senna kilims to remove the small, loose fibres which betray cheap, new production. After firing, the kilims were loaded into an industrial-size tumble drier to remove the charred odour. After that, they were carried to several concrete vats, where they were doused in a solution of acetic acid which bleached new rugs, softening their vivid colours and producing a silky sheen. After soaking in this lye for forty-eight hours, the rugs were dumped on a concrete area where two men shampooed and rinsed them, pushing off the suds with long-handled squeegees and buckets of water. They were then hung out over the compound's brick walls to dry for a day or two, or left baking in the sun for a month or more, a process known as 'sun washing', which further faded them. Slumped over the walls were prematurely aged Baluchi, Kashan and Afghan rugs. Magentas had mellowed to plum, browns to wheatish tan, their pile remaining dark at the roots, like a bottle blonde's hair. The whole process — scorching, shaking, washing and drying — cost a dollar a metre and, by weakening the carpet's fibre, shortened its life. But it steeply increased the price a gullible buyer might pay.

There were some sixty washeries in Peshawar profiting from the mysterious Western fetish for antiques, or failing that, fakes. The workers on Dauwra Road had no idea why they were ruining perfectly good rugs with flame-throwers and acid baths, but like the Afghan villagers who spread new rugs on the highway to be worn by passing traffic, they knew damaged goods fetched higher prices than new ones. Other techniques included burial to encourage the growth of corrosive mildew, scraping on rocks until holes appeared, and rubbing with iron filings, dirt or coffee grounds to produce those valuable earthy tones. There simply were not enough real antiques to go around — hadn't been for decades.

> By 1905 the supply of antique and semi-antique rugs, or in other words, rugs with soft colors, was already becoming scarce. A way had to be found to get soft colored rugs overnight. To accomplish this, plants were set up in and around New York City for chemical bleaching of these rugs after they arrived in this country. The final result was that not only were the rugs bleached, but in most cases the rugs were retouched by a painting process, then waxed and run through hot rolls to give the rug a high glossy finish.[10]

The chemical runoff from the Peshawar washeries ran untreated into the city's gutters and eventually into the Kabul and Indus rivers. In August 1999 the government of the North-West Frontier Province had set a deadline for shifting all carpet-washing and -weaving units from the city, on the grounds that they caused 'environmental degradation and adversely affect[ed] the city's

Carpets are perishable items, and few of the earliest examples survive. Fortunately, affluent sixteenth-century European merchants like Georg Gisze (*pictured*) developed a taste for Anatolian rugs, which decorated their portraits, this one painted by Hans Holbein the Younger (1497–1543). Such was Holbein's contribution to recording early carpet designs that one of the main Turkmen *guls*, or motifs, is named after him.

'An emerging thunder which made the ground tremble signalled the return of the pack, hoofs clashing as they reared up and almost toppled into the front row of seats in the grandstand.' In northern Afghanistan, *buzkashi* separates the men from the boys. In this most Afghan of sports, the unruly competitors compete for possession of a dead calf.

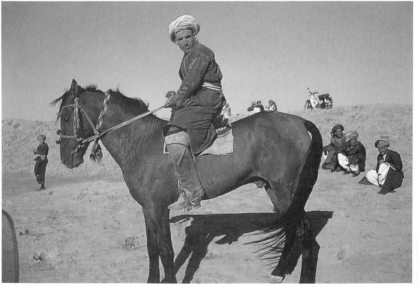

A *chapandaz*, or buzkashi rider, mounted on his steed. Buzkashi ponies are fed on barley, melons, eggs, and butter, to give strength just before a contest. Their careers can extend over thirty years, and the best become national heroes.

'... from fifteen thousand feet we stared in awe at the colossal Buddhas carved into the honey-coloured sandstone cliffs overlooking the city, followed by a three hundred and sixty-degree loop over the blue lakes of Band-e Amir with the surrounding mountains mirrored in their still waters.' Before the civil war, the lakes of Band-e Amir were a major tourist attraction of central Afghanistan, along with the Bamiyan Buddhas.

Fifty-three kilometres long, the narrow, winding Khyber Pass presents a forbidding entrance to Afghanistan. But much of history's traffic — from the Aryans to Alexander the Great — came from the opposite direction, using the Khyber as the gateway to India. The pass now links Afghanistan to Pakistan's Federally Administered Tribal Areas.

CHRISTOPHER KREMMER

In parts of Afghanistan, the carpet industry is the only one that has survived decades of war. In Sarposha Bazaar, in the southern city of Kandahar, the carpet business is handed down from father to son, sustaining the former royal capital in times of violent disorder.

CHRISTOPHER KREMMER

'Among growling trishaw engines and blasting truck horns, they plied their trade from horse-drawn tongas and ageing pickups, axles groaning under rug loads.' Khyber Bazaar in Peshawar, the capital of Pakistan's North-West Frontier Province, is a major wholesale market for Afghan rugs.

Defying efforts to eliminate it, child labour remains an important part of Pakistan's carpet industry. Many child labourers, like this twelve-year-old Afghan boy at work on a loom in Peshawar, are the children of refugees, posing a dilemma for social activists, who free the children at the risk of impoverishing their desperate families.

'There were lush, silky carpets, sandpaper-stiff *kilims* and hermaphrodite combinations of both; Turkmens, Persians and Caucasians, some fringed in the finest wool, others in coarse goat hair. They came in a bewildering array of shapes and sizes.' Afghan refugees sell rugs in neighbouring Pakistan.

Northern militiamen, Sar-e Pul, Afghanistan, 1997. Like soldiers over the centuries, Afghan militiamen are often unpaid, but are free to loot in conquered territories. They also earn a lucrative living from road tolls levied on passing traffic at unofficial checkpoints.

CHRISTOPHER KREMMER

A negotiated surrender of the northern Afghan city of Mazar-e Sharif in May 1997 turned into a bloodbath when a rebellion by the city's Shia population forced the Sunni Muslim Taliban to flee. Here, a Taliban fighter carries a dead comrade away from the scene of the fighting in which some three hundred Talibs were killed in a seventeen-hour battle.

ROBERT NICKELSBERG

The Shrine of Hazrat Ali, Mazar-e Sharif. The shrine marks the spot where Afghans believe the son-in-law of the Prophet Mohammed is buried. Most scholars believe Shia Islam's first Imam lies buried in Najaf, Iraq, but Mazar has remained a pilgrimage place since the twelfth century. Visitors feed the pigeons, believing they carry the souls of martyrs.

Kabul, Afghanistan, 1996. Throughout the decade-long Soviet occupation, the Afghan capital remained immune from the devastation visited on the countryside, where the Red Army fought a losing battle to subdue the Afghan *mujahideen*. But when the victorious Muslim rebels finally seized Kabul in 1992, they turned their guns on each other, destroying much of the city in the process.

Long before the Taliban, women in many parts of Afghanistan lived cloistered lives, confined to the all-enveloping *chaderi*, or veil. In 1999 on the outskirts of Farkhar, Takhar province, in the Hindu Kush, local women were beyond the reach of the Taliban, but the veil still ruled.

drainage system'. 'We want to encourage the carpet business but not at the cost of people's health,' it said.[11]

But most of the washeries were still there.

Having dumped Tariq's rugs for 'washing' we returned to Khyber Bazaar where he led the way past an angry tangle of powerlines outside Sadat ('Lucky') Market and into the Shan Hotel. At the front desk, receptionist Dawood Khan sat reading an Urdu newspaper beneath a tariff board which offered 'Single room with carpet Rs. 90' and 'Double room with carpet Rs. 190'. Some rooms had dozens of carpets and cost nothing, functioning as full-time carpet shops. In fact the entire building was a vast rug repository. All day and into the night young boys carried trays of tea and plates of kebab through the murky corridors, the snacks fuelling the trade. Steel kebab skewers, plastic Chinese plates, gnawed carrot pieces, squeezed lemons and cigarette butts littered the halls, and discarded shoes formed hillocks at the open doors of shops like Abdul Istalifi's Baluch Carpet House, Noorani Carpets, and Uzbek Oriental Carpets and Kilims. Choosing a room at random on the fourth floor, I found Hajji Chooli from Andkhoi, whose entire stock had been bagged and stacked in a container-size pile awaiting the shipping agent. The agents were the middlemen who controlled the bulk export trade. For each container shipped they received a subsidy of about $20000 from the government and a freight fee of $5000 from the carpet dealer, who was not permitted to export in bulk on his own. Sale of the agency licences was itself a lucrative business. In Hajji Chooli, I found for the first time a carpet dealer with no time.

'If you want to buy, I'll talk,' he said, looking as if neither prospect much pleased him, 'but if you just want to talk, I'm busy. And there's nothing left to sell anyway.'

Leading the retreat, Tariq took me across the hall to shop number fifty-six.

'This was my shop when I first came from Kabul,' he said, explaining that he had moved out when the rent got too high.

Cross-legged on the floor sat the current occupant, a kindly man called Amir Jan who was repairing rugs with a needle and yarn. In all of the Khyber Bazaar no one could match him in this venerable art, as old as carpets themselves. Half buried under an antique Iranian Kashan, he welcomed us but kept working. With his bushy grey hair and black eyebrows and beard he looked like an exotically marked bear in a cave, and his deft fingers ceaselessly pushed a heavy needle back and forth through the rug's central medallion. It was intricate, relentless work, re-piling, colour-matching and replicating the original design. Sometimes the rugs he was given to restore were little more than a mass of threads. As he chatted with Tariq he kept a short length of yarn in the corner of his mouth, ready for the next stitch. Nobody knew how much the moth-eaten Kashan had cost the owner in a tourist shop in Sadar Bazaar, but he was paying twenty thousand rupees to have new knots added where the old ones had been eaten away.

Amir Jan — his real name was Malem Jan Mohammad — had been a teacher in a village outside Kabul until the night a Massoud soldier came into his home asking for money, and then shot dead his eldest son. An educated man, he had never touched a carpet before arriving in Peshawar, where rug repair work was all he could find. Now he toiled twelve to fifteen hours a day, obsessively re-piling damaged pieces and napping on the floor when weariness overcame him. The Kashan had taken two months so far, with Amir Jan and his surviving son Najib working on it simultaneously, the vintage beauty protectively covering the legs of both father and son. Gently lifting the rug and placing it on the floor beside him, the older man dropped a cassette into a tape player and the voice of the long-dead Ustad Sarahung, a favourite of the old king, filled the air. As we drank green tea a young boy snipped away with shears at an unclipped rug, and slowly its vases filled with blossoms appeared like a developing Polaroid. A dramatic Caucasian motif could assert itself through the thickest pile, but detailed floral design needed the closest possible shave. With the nostalgic voice of Ustad Sarahung lilting in the background, Amir Jan took a rolled carpet from behind him and opened it on the floor between us. It was a superb Bakhtiari of playful geometry in grape blue and terracotta, teeming with scarabs and beasties within borders of scrolling vines.

'We had to replace the entire border at one end,' he said, beaming at his handiwork. 'If you can pick which end is the repair, you can have the rug.'

The repair had taken the patient Amir Jan months to complete and cost many thousands of rupees. The exquisite piece did not even belong to him, yet such was his pride in it that he was willing to gamble all on the precision of his work. With only two borders to choose from, we were even-money to win. Before I could decline, Tariq had fallen to the floor and was poring over the Bakhtiari like a sniffer dog: looking at it back and front, running his hand over the knots, smelling it; he did everything except lick or listen to it — a human gold detector.

'How many chances do we get?' he asked the repairer.

'One,' said the mellow restorer, amused by our desperation.

We took our chance, opting for the border with the darker blue. Amir Jan kept his carpet.

In the three months after the cruise missile strikes and the evacuation of most expatriates, Peshawar's hotels were still empty. I could have had a room anywhere, but Tariq — whose mood had lightened during the day — would not hear of me staying anywhere else but with his family in their rented house in the Afghan suburb of Hayatabad, near the airport.

The taxi took us past green wheatfields and mud-brick houses to Hayatabad's main street, whose smooth, divided road and underground power supply were the envy of Peshawar. It was not how you expected a refugee settlement to look. Turning off, we passed through the local market, pulling up outside a modest terrace house. The iron gate was opened by a pretty young girl with dark rings under her eyes, Tariq's third daughter, Fatima, who seemed greatly fascinated by me and immediately assigned herself the role of maid. Crossing a small courtyard, I removed my shoes and was taken to a simple but clean upstairs room covered in rugs, with a stack of freshly laundered bedding on a floor mattress. After washing off the day's dust I went downstairs to a living room decorated with a laminated poster of pilgrims swirling in long, blurred streaks around the *Kaaba*, the central stone structure within the Great Mosque in Mecca. With great solemnity Tariq introduced his wife, Nazreen, a handsome woman in her late thirties, dressed in a tailored checked suit with a black *dupatta*, or scarf, covering her hair. But no sooner had we been introduced than Nazreen disappeared immediately into another room, from which issued the sound of screaming children and elderly in-laws. In the formal emptiness of the living room Tariq and I sat in isolation, interrupted only briefly when Fatima, now changed into a pretty red dress with a moon-and-stars print, served tea.

We dined that evening on *aushak*, delicious Afghan ravioli filled with leek and beef and covered in lentils and hard yoghurt. Fatima served the food, replaced the soap in the bathroom and brought hand towels when we were finished. When we had eaten and washed she appeared coyly at the doorway with a school exercise book labelled 'English Language'. Her work was neat and accurate and she remembered most of it when I tested her.

'She's the smart one in the family,' said Tariq with obvious pride.

Instead of taking a post-repast stroll, Tariq led us up a narrow staircase to the roof where a child's bicycle was propped up against a wall. Leaping onto the bike, Fatima rode round and round in circles, basking so thoroughly in my approval that I feared the distraction might drive her off the roof, but she remained in control in the confined space. Tariq said he had bought the bicycle for her in Dubai on one of his rug forays, but that in the conservative Afghan neighbourhood of Hayatabad it was not wise for a girl to ride a bicycle on the streets. It began to rain, and we took shelter inside, where I fell asleep to the patter of the rain and dreamt that Fatima — still dressed in her pretty dress with the moon and stars — was lost in the jungle and being stalked by tigers. The tigers all rode bicycles and they were spinning around her at dizzying speed, riding so fast they became a blur and actually melted into a ring-shaped pool of butter, over which Fatima daintily stepped as she went on her way.

Tariq had spoken of fine Chechen pieces turning up in Peshawar, defying gravity in a market where the best is almost magnetically drawn by high prices to the West, so the following day we went in search of them. Caucasians are renowned for their barbarously bold designs and huge arachnid guls. I had visited the Caucasus in the early 1980s, when the region was still part of the Soviet Union. For eight hundred years it had been a battlefield for Armenians, Georgians, Russians, Persians, Kurds, Arabs, Ossets, Azeris, Tartars, Mongols and Turks, and between Christianity and Islam; a history as dramatic as its rugs. The itinerary framed by the state organisation Intourist emphasised palaces of culture and monuments to the Great October Revolution, rather than rugs. We drove from Yerevan, past Lake Sevan and the mountains of Nagorno-Karabakh, to oil-rich Baku basking on the shores of the Caspian Sea; we savoured the alcoholic fruits of Georgia's vines and marvelled at the soaring twin peaks of Mount Ararat, the legendary site where Noah's Ark came to rest after the Great Flood; we toured the Caspian oil rigs, ate in an old *caravanserai* converted into a restaurant, and wondered if the train still went to Tehran, by then firmly under Ayatollah Khomeini's control. Yet in one of the world's great weaving regions, Kazaks, Shirvans and Karabakhs were invisible. In the entire week not a single hand-knotted carpet did we see. It was as if the visceral pleasure of a rug such as the Karachop was an embarrassment or threat, to be hushed up and hidden away.

Now, with Tariq leading the way, we turned out of Khyber Bazaar and climbed the stairs of the Kamran Hotel, another once-grand establishment now turned carpet warehouse, opposite Sadat Market. In a long, large room we found Azerbaijan Carpets, where the staff were almost as numerous as the rugs. There must have been a dozen young men, all sporting overshirts and stubble, flipping and touting pieces from a region of such genetic, cultural and religious diversity that it was once called Jabal-al Alsun, the Mountain of Languages.[12] On a Daghestan runner, a jagged, abstract dragon flew across a field of cochineal and Prussian blue, bordered by zigzagging Zs. An 'Eagle Kazak' from Karabakh exploded with angular sunbursts, throwing off dangerous, pronged rays, while an emerald green Shirvan sang with joyous colours and contrast. Tariq stood over a brusque Chechen with a single large pashali gul which resembled a Formula One racing car viewed from above.

'They never show *us* these things,' he whispered, eyes wide with amazement at the treasures the presence of a 'rich' foreigner could reveal. But then, when he heard the prices the boys were quoting, he succumbed to a fit of contradictory pique.

'These things you can get anywhere,' he said.

In fact, they were eminently collectible, their vitality capable of fetching top prices at auction. All of which made their presence here in low-priced Peshawar inexplicable, until one of the boys mentioned the war in Chechnya.

'The Russians are behaving like wild dogs in Chechnya, just like they did in Afghanistan,' he said, his moon face insisting it was true. 'The freedom fighters bring these carpets from Chechnya, we buy them, and with this money they go for training in Afghanistan to fight against the Russians.'

Before the revolution in Iran, students had carried rugs when they went abroad to fund their studies in the West, and Afghan feminists from the Revolutionary Association of the Women of Afghanistan still carried carpets on trips abroad to raise funds.

Carpets were war by other means, and all sides were using them.

At the newspaper stall in Hayatabad Market, Afghan men stood looking at pictures of themselves in decades-old brochures which once sold to tourists heading to Afghanistan but were now bought by homesick refugees. Around them, donkeys brayed and car horns beeped, while at a sidewalk bakery, boys kneaded dough into balls and plastered them onto the inner walls of *tandoor* ovens. The cooked nan, extracted with long rods held like tweezers, was wrapped in newspaper and sold across a counter covered with the threadbare remnant of an old rug. Peshawar was not that different from Afghanistan, but as the tourist brochures illustrated, Afghanistan itself had changed. One read:

Visitors to Afghanistan are entitled to duty-free export of thirty square metres of carpets, ten skins — excluding Karakul — cut and polished precious stones, including lapis lazuli, handicrafts and a limited variety of antiques. Hotels in Bamiyan and Mazar offer high-class yurt accommodation, and in Kabul don't miss the Marco Polo Night Club.

'Why do you always read these things?' one refugee at the newsstand chided another. 'By the third page your heart is broken.'

In the living room of Tariq's house, long plastic dining sheets covered the floor in preparation for the arrival of an important guest. Soon the doorbell rang and a man of regal bearing with a Santa Claus-length silver beard and pinstripe waistcoat popped his head through the door curtains.

'Samad Jamalzadah, immigration attorney,' he declared, extending a fine-boned hand. 'The Europeans are tightening entry requirements again. Praise Allah, it is a crime to be Afghan these days.'

Jamalzadah, it turned out, was helping Tariq in his efforts to find asylum in a third country. This involved submitting volleys of applications to foreign embassies and the United Nations High Commissioner for Refugees, even though Tariq had not formally registered as a refugee in Pakistan itself. From the way Tariq was fussing over him, calling for tea and special sweets, it was clear he possessed considerable powers, if only those required to read the complex application forms which those seeking asylum abroad must fill in. Jamalzadah had obtained asylum for his own wife in the Netherlands, where she now lived with their daughter — proof of his skills. Honey-coloured skin and a wet smile gave him a doctoral air and he stroked his beard as he dispensed morsels of information about migration trends and policies around the world.

'Hajji Jumma Khan from Herat has been deported from India,' he told Tariq. 'He renewed his visa in Faridabad but in Delhi they said it was not valid, so he had to fly to Dubai, then from Dubai to Pakistan. He had taken so many carpets, fifty thousand dollars' worth, but Customs impounded them. After four months his nephew cleared them and sold them, but only for about half their true value.'

Lowering himself stiffly onto the cushion-covered floor, he briefly studied my face as his long, bony fingers reached out to accept a pile of Tariq's documents.

'In the Western country, I feel I am less than a human being. This is not life, actually,' he said. 'Everywhere we go we feel discrimination. Any person you call in Europe, he's busy, except the weekend. Then he is washing his car. He wants marijuana, he wants opium. He has no right even to listen to music a little bit loud. We Afghans are always shouting, this is our culture, but in your countries it's not allowed. They think life is only there, but I think life is here, in the East. Best weather is here. Best fruit is here. Best agricultural produce here. The beautiful girl is here. No whisky from Scotland, but hashish, opium, all these things we can get here.'

As he spoke, his eye glanced across the pages of birth and marriage certificates, statutory declarations, health clearances and completed application forms Tariq had handed him. The immigration agent's tone suddenly became formal.

'Tariq, as I have already told you, you must know somebody in the host country. He must be a citizen from, say, America, Canada, Britain, Australia — some such country. This man, he must agree to be your sponsor. Like that, you have forty per cent chance. Better if he should also write a letter to the member of parliament, or the Cabinet, saying, "I know this man. He is a good man. He is a family man. But he has five daughters, so how can he live with this Taliban?" That way you have ninety per cent chance. Have you made such a contact?'

Tariq shook his head sheepishly.

'So what can be done?' Jamalzadah said. 'You don't realise, my friend, you are dealing with the rulers of this godless world. Just like in the ocean, big fish eats small fish. America watches like an eagle! Where is the best bite? Now, oil is the best bite. So they take Saudi Arabia and Kuwait.'

Leaning uncomfortably on his arm, Tariq sprang forward and refilled the glass of his friend, who appeared to know plenty about the failings of Western countries but not quite enough to help Tariq get into them. Perhaps it was just his way of softening the blow of rejection that the majority of his clients were fated to suffer.

'The West likes to talk about human rights, but it's only words,' he said. 'Whenever Muslims try to build their country, Western countries intervene and destroy everything. Look at what they did to Indonesia. Destroy a big Muslim country to make a small Christian one like East Timor. And, of course, there is no justice in the Western country for Muslim refugees. As the wise man has said, "He who has the most gold, has the most justice."'

'But Mr Jamalzadah,' I said, 'if Western countries are so terrible, and if they treat Muslims so badly, why are you helping Muslims emigrate to those countries?'

Jamalzadah's cup stopped just short of his lips and he looked at Tariq and smiled, as if the question was a lapse in hospitality which might still be excused. Then he looked at me as if to say, 'You must be joking.' Tariq's face was plastered with a hideously weak smile, as if someone had just defecated on the floor.

'Which is your country?' asked Jamalzadah.

I told him it was of no consequence.

'Correct!' he said. 'Afghans are of no consequence also. Where Afghans go is of no consequence. We would prefer to stay in our own beautiful country, but it is *kaput*. Now we go anywhere to survive.'

'But why not go to Muslim countries if you feel discriminated against in the West?'

'Muslim countries are poor. They have no facilities.'

'Saudi Arabia is not poor. Kuwait has facilities.'

'Yes, but if they allow it, soon they will be flooded with Afghans.'

'But that's the same excuse Western countries use to say no.'

Jamalzadah smiled a pinched smile and made an elaborate business of getting to his feet.

'Where is the bathroom?' he asked Tariq, who led him out.

Alone, I could ponder the consequences of my intemperate words. I had disgraced my Afghan host before an important guest. It was unforgivable. I felt I should leave. But to my amazement, when Tariq returned he wore a naughty, boyish smile. Refilling my cup, he explained that Jamalzadah had recently failed in a bid to sneak into Canada, which had cost him more than ten thousand dollars.

'He has that kind of money?'

'Sure. Why not? The migration business is better than the carpet business.'

Returning to the room Jamalzadah pointedly remained standing, an imperious presence drawing us to our feet.

'Here in Eastern countries there is no self-responsibility among the people,' he said, placing a woollen cap over his sparse, silvery dome. 'A German who sees a piece of litter on the street will pick it up and put in the bin. But if a Pakistani sees one piece of paper on the street he will tear it up and make it two pieces.'

Then, turning to me and extending his hand as if to be kissed, he departed.

This gracious exit left me dumb with admiration. The cunning old rogue had rolled up the moral high ground like a carpet and taken it with him.

Later that night, I telephoned home and received a message from a friend of Rasoul's. For more than a year I had been attempting to find him through foreign aid agencies working in Afghanistan. The message was from a woman, Ruth Harbinson-Gresham, who had worked with him at a Christian aid agency in Mazar. She knew what had happened to him after the Taliban finally conquered the city.

'I understand he just fled. His mother told him to,' her e-mail said.

He was hiding in the town of Attock, near the Indus River, a ninety-minute drive east of Peshawar.

16

Violence by Degree

Driver Wajed Ali was with me through thick and thin, a close-shave specialist in hairy situations who had just escaped Afghanistan by a whisker. Regarded as not sufficiently hirsute, he'd been subjected to a hounding by the trichogenous Taliban.

'Taliban are *baaad* people,' he said, holding a flat, upturned palm at his waist, then stroking a non-existent beard from his cheeks to his navel. 'They come Afghanistan, I go Pakistan. They come Pakistan, I go India.'

A Jalalabad Pashtun, Wajed was a stubble guy. He had stubble on his stubble, darkening with every kilometre. A brush with those cheeks could cause severe abrasions. Rather than avail himself of the insulation that nature provided, Wajed preferred to wrap up in layer after layer of woollen apparel — *kurta*, vest, jacket and blanket — as he guided his tiny 'Khyber' through the ice fog that had enveloped Peshawar on the morning of our departure. We were headed for Attock, the old fortress town on the east bank of the Indus where Rasoul had taken refuge. On the way I planned to make a call on Pakistan's largest and oldest religious seminary at Akora Khattak. Nose pressed to the windscreen, Wajed muttered obscure oaths at the dense shroud that enveloped a road barely illuminated by an insipid winter sun. Objects and people loomed like wraiths from the ghastly, oyster-coloured haze: blinkered horses, police in gas masks, camels, tractors from hell, snotty nosed children, brick kilns, buffaloes, gum trees sagging in silhouette, mangy dogs, brass pots and more men in blankets.

As if too much fog was not enough, local people worked hard to produce more by boiling kettles, grilling kebabs over smouldering fires, breathing, and urinating, which created steaming puddles. The fog had grounded aircraft, delayed train and bus services and caused the cancellation of a major cricket match that Wajed had his heart set on watching. The screen of the Khyber's mini-TV remained a foggy blank, despite his occasional wiping. For what seemed like hours we were stuck behind a hideous three-wheeler with copper filigree mudguards and a mural of a heart driven through with a dagger. Sometimes Wajed would panic, stabbing at the brakes until whatever phantom that had disturbed him abated. On the outskirts of the city the thick vapour lifted somewhat, revealing mountains of vegetable peelings and garbage which lined the Grand Trunk Road. With the scent of freedom flaring his nostrils, Wajed floored the accelerator and boldly claimed the full width of the road.

'Sahib is a nervous passenger. Better eyes *bund hai*,' he said, plunging us headlong into oblivion.

Because Pakistan is a young nation it is easy to forget that the region it occupies was home to one of the world's first civilisations. As early as 4000 BC primitive farmers were cultivating vegetables and grains along the banks of the Indus River and by 2700 BC two major cities, Harappa and Mohenjodaro, and numerous smaller towns had emerged. However, around 1500 BC the Indus civilisation was smashed by Aryan invaders from the north, who brought fire worship and a strict caste system to keep themselves separate from local people in the lands they occupied, including India. By the early eighth century, the Indus Valley was dominated by Hinduism and Buddhism, but when an Arab sailing *dhow* was snatched by pirates in the Arabian Sea off the coast of Sindh, Islam seized the opportunity. Dispatched to make an example of the unruly Sindhis, a teenage

Arab commander called Mohammad bin Qasim drove deep into the interior, and by 724 AD Arab rule extended as far as Multan. Although the Arabs would eventually be forced out, Islam stayed and prospered over the centuries. In 1947, when a war-weary Britain decided it could no longer maintain its Raj on the subcontinent, Muslims staked their claim to a separate state. The Karachi lawyer and independence leader Mohammed Ali Jinnah, arguing for Partition, declared confidently of Hindus and Muslims that 'we are different beings ... our names, our clothes, our foods ... we challenge each other at every point of the compass'.[13] Persuaded that a holocaust would ensue if Hindus and Muslims were forced to live together, or possibly just eager to be rid of its one-time jewel in the crown, the departing British consented to Jinnah's plan for a separate Pakistan, in which culturally distinct Punjabis, Sindhis, Baluchis, Bengalis and Pashtuns would form a nation united by a common religion.

Over half a century later, Pakistan is one of only three 'Islamic Republics' in the world, the others being Iran and Afghanistan. Its flag is white and Islamic green, with a crescent and star. Yet several factors have conspired against the development of a vigorously anti-Western Islamic state: the British colonial past; a well-heeled, Oxbridge-educated Anglophile local elite; a Cold War alliance with the United States against the Soviet Union and India; the diverse religious and cultural identity of the regions forming Pakistan; and perhaps even cricket. In 1968 the Chinese supreme leader Mao Zedong, receiving the Pakistan foreign minister, asked with characteristic bluntness, 'What is the difference between you and Indians? You look the same to me. Aren't you only temporarily separated from the Indians?' In 1971, Pakistan's eastern provinces broke away to form Bangladesh, demolishing the 'Two Nation' theory on which Pakistan was founded, prompting writers like Tariq Ali to pose the question: Can Pakistan survive? With the loss of its east wing, Islamabad turned towards the Arab world for inspiration and financial support, especially Saudi Arabia.

As Pakistan's search for security and national renewal accelerated, Islamisation became the panacea. In the 1970s, Prime Minister Zulfikar Ali Bhutto banned consumption of alcohol; then the man who toppled him and had him executed, General Zia ul-Haq, intensified the process, introducing limited Shari'a law.

Before leaving Islamabad I had told Habib that I would be visiting Akora Khattak, a crucible of the latest drive for a more Islamic Pakistan. Given his constant efforts to convert me, I thought he would approve, but as ever his reaction defied expectations.

'One thing I will tell you,' he said, casting a furtive glance at the shop's front door. 'These mullahs are garbage people. All he is getting is money, money. Nobody in Pakistan is liking these mullahs people, but they are giving to him because they want to be the best Muslims, even better than an Arab.'

Another source had given his advice on the sensitive issue of religion. 'The Gopher' was about the best-connected, most experienced Western diplomat in the capital, a man so astute that his opinion was crucial on any important issue, but who always insisted on complete anonymity. Over coffee and cookies in his office one morning, he had confessed his deepest fears about the direction in which Pakistan was heading.

'What really strikes me these days is the beards,' he said, his own small and orderly moustache twitching. 'The number of beards is terrifying.'

The Gopher was no trichophobe, but he saw in the proliferation of facial hair evidence of the growing popularity of what the academic Edward W. Said called 'a hazy fantasy of seventh-century Mecca as a panacea for numerous ills in today's Muslim world'.[14]

'Shari'a in this country is not codified,' The Gopher went on. 'Iranian mullahs are educated, well-informed people. They attend college in Qom, study history, theology, philosophy, language, maths and science. To be an ayatollah you need a degree — several degrees if you look at Iraq or Iran. Many clerics in those places have served abroad and speak several languages. But here, three mosques all say prayers at different times. There's no central authority you can appeal to for an ultimate decision on things like that. If they try to introduce Shari'a here, I promise you, it will be chaos.'

With our Khyber demonstrating all the speed of a Mercedes but none of the safety features, I decided to give Wajed Ali a calming tea break. Halfway to Akora Khattak we turned into an anonymous compound where a smiling, gap-toothed man in a houndstooth vest was plotting the course of the Islamic revolution. Although we had never met, Professor Mohammed Ibrahim Khan, president of Jama'at-e Islami, or Party of Islam, in the North-West Frontier Province, greeted me like an old friend, ushering me upstairs to a cosy first-floor office where a copy of Pakistan's Constitution — not the Koran — took pride of place on his desk. The Jama'at were first-generation Islamists who had backed the Afghan mujahideen and were now in danger of being marginalised by younger, more radical groups like the Lashkar-e Taiba, which backed the Taliban. Professor Khan was the antithesis of the prototype scowling fundamentalist. A former journalism teacher who had also studied law, he advocated a minimalist approach to cleaning up the nation's politics. The Jama'at-e Islami believed constitutional change was unnecessary to achieve an Islamic state.

'We already have an Islamic Constitution. We just don't implement it, like our democracy which always ends up being run by the army,' Khan-*saheb* said, reaching for his 'holy book'. 'It's all here in Articles 62 and 63 of the Constitution. Any candidate for election must be "a Muslim of good character and not commonly known as one who violates Islamic injunctions". Now, I ask you, how many members of our National Assembly or Senate meet that qualification?'

Samuel P. Huntington compared the Islamic resurgence to the Roman Catholic Reformation, calling both 'reactions to the stagnation and corruption of existing institutions'.[15] Professor Khan built a compelling critique along similar lines. After half a century of independence, he said, two out of every three Pakistanis could not read or write. Less than one in ten spoke the official language, Urdu. Civil infrastructure was crumbling, and the average salary was three thousand rupees or about $50 a month. Even a can of ghee cost nine hundred rupees. Muslim organisations were assuming responsibility for social welfare, law enforcement, and education, areas in which the government had abdicated its role. High birth rates meant that half the population was under twenty-five, with only 4 per cent over sixty-five. The country had a nuclear bomb in one hand and a begging bowl in the other. People were turning to religion and mosque attendance was up, while the prosperous — instead of fighting to defend and reform the parliamentary system — ransacked the public purse and got their children educated and domiciled abroad. The prime minister's own family had bought four apartments in London's Park Lane. The system could not provide justice, employment, education or security.

'All the systems have been tried in this country. Now the people are ready and want to have an experience of the religious system,' he said. 'We are securing a land wherein we will have an experiment of Islam.'

In fact, the Jama'at had opposed the creation of Pakistan in the first place, believing all Muslim societies should unite in one nation. This stance had affected its popularity among ordinary Pakistanis, who had constantly rejected it at the polls. The Jama'at performed so badly in the 1986 elections that it had avoided fielding candidates ever since. Its real support was untested, as was its grand vision of pure Islamic politics. But the professor's logic was airtight and circular. If it wasn't working, it wasn't Islamic. The perfect system had not been tried yet.

Rejoining Wajed and driving on, I mulled over the professor's arguments, which seemed to hark back to the days before the Magna Carta, when the vote in England was confined to nobles, and parliament was made up exclusively of bishops, knights and barons. Restricting the franchise seemed a recipe for corruption and Pakistan already had enough of that. Where would they find these 'good Muslims'? Who would decide who they were? Above all, how would they avoid the violent sectarianism that had afflicted Afghanistan?

Along the Grand Trunk Road, women struggled past in ice-blue chadors whipped by the draught of passing vehicles, whose drivers — all men — were locked in a maniacal quest for martyrdom. Some fifteen kilometres west of Attock, at Akora Khattak, stood a cluster of rough-and-ready buildings housing the Dar-ul-Uloom Haqqania, dubbed the 'Islamic Harvard', a Taliban factory with a one-item syllabus of jihad. The mullahs' traditional control of education in most Islamic countries is one of the main engines of contemporary Islamic fundamentalism, and this school was the alma mater of at least eight ministers in the Taliban's government and of numerous governors and senior officials, including the governor of Kandahar, Mullah Hassan, and the Afghan ambassador to Pakistan. On several occasions during major Taliban offensives the school's principal, Maulana Sami ul-Haq, had allegedly shut down the campus and ordered students to go to Afghanistan to fight. The Prophet Mohammed, unlike pacifist religious leaders like Buddha and Jesus Christ, was also a military leader, and it was this aspect of his life that inspired the jihadis. In Islamic societies the traditional purpose of schools was the propagation of the faith, and private institutions rather than governments tended to control curricula. With the twentieth century came modern Western methods of teaching, but as a third of Pakistan's federal budget was spent on the military, and even more on servicing debt, little had remained for education. An estimated forty thousand privately funded schools had sprung up to fill the void, most of them unregistered.

Driving into the sprawling forty-acre campus at Akora Khattak, Wajed guided the Khyber sheepishly through a flock of students in white cotton prayer caps whose ages ranged from seven to forty. The three thousand students came from as far afield as Uzbekistan and China. The school promoted the conservative Deobandi Islamic tradition, a movement which originated in northern India in the nineteenth century when Muslim traditionalists influenced by Muhammad ibn Abdul Wahab of Arabia rebelled against the progressive ideas emanating from Aligarh, India's main centre of Islamic scholarship.

Arriving unannounced, I found the *maulana* away on business but one of his sons, twenty-seven-year-old Rashid ul-Haq, took me on an escorted tour. The dormitories were daubed with wall murals of automatic weapons and Koranic verses, and filled with students from Afghanistan, Tajikistan, Chechnya and Kashmir, as well as Pakistan. The Arabic Hadith, translated into Pashto, Urdu and Uzbeki, was their main subject, although science and maths were also taught. In the classrooms boys droned like worker bees at low wooden benches. Singling out one boy of about twelve, Rashid told him to recite the Koran for us.

'Which part of the Koran is he reciting?' I asked, unfamiliar with Arabic.

'All of it,' replied Rashid. 'He's a *hafiz*. He knows all 114 *suras* by heart.'

As I stood smiling and shaking my head at the boy's mental prowess, he continued chanting phlegmatically.

Refugee children, who were given a monthly stipend of a hundred rupees, or about $2, worked in the school's vegetable garden, and followed a heavy daily program of study beginning with prayers at 3 a.m. But compared to the violence and dislocation of life in Afghanistan, the madrassas provided a secure, relatively normal boarding school life, with good discipline and a strong sense of identity and purpose — the right atmosphere for producing achievers.

But when I asked the boys what they wanted to do when they grew up, the only answer was 'be an Islamic scholar'. The campus was clearly expanding rapidly and unfinished concrete structures abounded. Steel reinforcing rods sprouted like sugarcane from the rooftops, urging the builders to aim higher. A convention centre with a planned capacity of twenty-five thousand people was planned and new dormitories, libraries and other facilities were in various stages of completion. But already the names of thousands of graduates were chiselled in regimented columns along the walls. Hermetically sealed in a self-perpetuating, theocratic hive, the boys were not being trained to excel in society. They were being moulded as soldiers in what one newspaper called 'an empire of soft-voiced, sandal-wearing followers that makes generals and bureaucrats quake in their boots'.[16] In a difficult job market, they would have few of the skills required to build productive, happy lives, only anger and an implacable conviction that Islam must prevail around the globe. Students from Pakistani madrassas had begun showing up on battlefields from Chechnya to Mindanao, fighting on the side of Muslim separatists. But Rashid insisted that no military training was given at Akora Khattak.

'If any Pakistani student goes to Afghanistan without our permission, it is just to keep company with his friends and sightsee,' he said feebly, drawing suppressed giggles from some of the older boys hanging around his office.

There were no girls at the Haqqania madrassa. Yet Pakistanis had twice elected a woman prime minister. In Pakistan's cities women generally were free to work, be educated, drive, and smoke if they wished, although it took a determined woman to do all four. Immodest dress was still frowned upon, but the veil and even the dupatta were not mandatory. Even Rashid's father Sami ul-Haq's position on women was liberal. He'd reportedly been caught once in a *ménage à trois* in a hotel and ever since had been colloquially known as 'Sami the Sandwich'. His son, however, was toeing the company line.

'The people are demanding that Pakistan adopt Taliban policies,' he said, his voice echoing inside a new but as yet unused auditorium. 'Islam is the biggest respecter of women. Their role should be to look after their husbands and children and make their sons into perfect men for their society.'

A cold wind penetrated the broken windows of the college's computer room, where students were glued to the Arabic edition of Windows 95. They were logging on to Muslim websites featuring 'agony aunts' like Shaykh Abdul Aziz bin Abdullah bin Baz, who advised his readers to treat 'with hatred and animosity' friends who did not fast or say their prayers. They also visited the homepages of various jihadi groups, like the Lashkar-e Taiba, whose enemies included Pakistan's Shia Muslim minority as well as the Indian forces in Kashmir. The students were taking the Prophet's injunction to fight unending holy war literally, although other Muslims prefer to interpret the term jihad — which translates literally as 'striving' — as the endless quest for self-improvement.

'The Islamic revolution in Pakistan is not far away,' Rashid assured me, as if predicting something as benign as a sunny day. But while it might be cathartic, perhaps even inevitable, like all desperate remedies it was fraught with risk. As with their Afghan counterparts, the Pakistani Taliban seemed more immediately hostile to other Muslims than towards the Satanic West. Not just the Shias, but even other fundamentalists, like the Jama'at's leader, Qazi Hussain Ahmed, needed to watch their backs.

'Qazi is a good Muslim,' said Rashid, walking me to my car. 'But he is ineffective. His ideas and power are imaginary. He thinks he can use Islam, but Islam will use him, and everyone like him, to establish its dominance.'

17

The Siege of Attock Fort

To Alexander the Great the Indus River at Attock was a river too far. When he departed Macedonia in 334 BC his army numbered thirty-seven thousand. But as he stood on the west bank of the Indus, where pale blue waters from the Himalayas blend with the turbid brown Kabul River ice melt from the Hindu Kush, he had lost two-thirds of his men and carried a serious shoulder wound from a battle in Swat. He named the river Nil Ab, after the Nile, and could have left it at that, turned back to Europe and been welcomed home as the greatest adventurer of all time. But at Attock, Alexander crossed the Rubicon, intending to conquer India. He would never see his homeland again. Skirting the Himalayan foothills, the weary Greek armies moved south-east into India. At Amritsar the troops mutinied and there began the long and treacherous retreat that ended with Alexander's death in Babylon.

About eighty kilometres east of Peshawar the Grand Trunk Road switched abruptly southwards, crossed the Kabul River, then turned east again and bridged the Indus, leaving the North-West Frontier Province and entering Punjab. The original road was built by the Moghul emperor Akbar, who in the 1580s surveyed the high eastern bank of the Indus and decided to build a large fort there above the river's sweeping bend. Writer Geoffrey Moorhouse, who crossed the river in the summer of 1983, gave a memorable description of the fort in *To the Frontier*:

> *It was a splendid piece of military architecture, thoughtfully situated with a rocky ridge protecting its rear. The outer battlements were the most arresting thing about it, ruddy brown castellated walls which flowed down a hillside and along the river bank before climbing uphill again. Turrets punctuated them at intervals, and so did large gun ports, while a barbican protruded massively at the water's edge. So extensively did those walls ramble unbroken along the contours of the ground, a couple of miles at least, that it was like looking at the fortifications of a town in medieval Spain after the Moors had been there.*[17]

Akbar built the fort to defend the north-west frontier of his Indian empire from rampaging Afghans, but as Wajed turned our car off the highway and into Attock town he made an observation that would have had Akbar turning in his mausoleum.

'This Attock. More Afghans than Pakistanis living here,' he said.

The sun had emerged from its foggy hangover and the streets were alive with colour and movement. Unlike most Pakistani towns, Attock was neatly tended, with flowerbeds planted in traffic roundabouts, and the people's brightly coloured clothing contrasted vividly with the drab greys, blues and browns preferred by the locals. They were Turkmens mainly, with a sprinkling of Hazaras, some fifty thousand altogether, who had fled the fighting in northern Afghanistan. Some had walked overland for more than a month to reach here. So numerous were the new arrivals that local Pakistanis had staged a general strike in protest at the threat they posed to jobs and the pressure they exerted on local services.

Like fugitive dyes running from a bad rug, the two and a half million Afghans living in exile held the record for being the world's largest single group of refugees and had done for the previous twenty years. Every twist and turn in the conflict was accompanied by a new exodus or influx: Pashtuns shifting to and from Pakistan, Tajiks crossing the mountains on their way north, Shia Hazaras falling back into the Central Highlands. My old friend Ghulam Rasoul Ahmadi's story was one of thousands of lives thrown like chaff to the wind. I had not forgotten his abandoned expression in the confusion and violence surrounding the evacuation from Mazar. When the Taliban finally succeeded in capturing the city for the third time, I feared the worst, knowing that the Shias would be singled out for revenge. Then, when the message arrived that he was alive and living in Pakistan, euphoria followed. But information pieced together from the Christian aid group helping him, and a brief telephone conversation with Rasoul himself, indicated the reality of exile was not so simple. He was wanted by the Taliban for mass murder.

'There is a warrant out for the arrest of all the brothers from that family. It's probably just to get a hold of Amir Yaqub, Rasoul's oldest brother. He was a "commander" and had many men,' Ruth Harbinson-Gresham had informed me in an e-mail. 'Regardless of the truth about Yaqub's actual involvement in the massacre of the Taliban troops last year in the Dasht-e Layli desert, the Taliban obviously hold him responsible and want him and therefore all his brothers. Does this clarify anything? Hope you do get to see Rasoul face to face. Happy hunting, Ruth.'

Over a faltering telephone connection from Attock, Rasoul had told me harrowing tales of cousins killed or tortured and conveyed his anxiety over his mother and sisters, left behind with no male relative to protect them. His brothers Yaqub and Yusuf were also in Pakistan but they had been shocked to find that the Taliban's long arm could grab them even there. A cousin, captured and tortured by the student army, had revealed their whereabouts, and Taliban sympathisers and plain clothes Pakistani police, who they suspected of being from Inter-Services Intelligence, began harassing them as part of a campaign to cleanse Peshawar of anti-Taliban elements.

The massacre of Taliban prisoners in Dasht-e Layli was being used to target opponents, with anyone opposed to the Taliban being accused of involvement. Fleeing Peshawar, the brothers Ahmadi were hiding in Attock.

Rasoul was sitting on the boundary wall of a dusty sports field, watching a group of unemployed Afghan youths playing soccer, when I arrived. In a brown leather jacket with epaulettes and aviator sunglasses, he looked like some kind of spook. His beard was trimmed and he had grown stockier, perhaps due to a lack of activity in hiding. But his stiff gait and formal cheek presses with the whispered 'three times' were the same. So was his handshake, warm on the coldest day.

'I have missed you,' he said, words measured and spaced like bricks in a wall. 'See the street leading away from the park over there? Walk to the top and go into the last house on the left. They're expecting you. You can leave your car here. I'll join you soon. I should tell my friends that you were a stranger asking directions. Sorry.'

I was heading off when he called me back.

'By the way,' he said, 'where did you get this driver? He's Pashtun, I think.'

'Don't worry,' I replied. 'Wajed is a leading critic of the Taliban.'

At the house, I was ushered into a courtyard where I removed my shoes in the Muslim manner and was shown through a curtained doorway into a sparse, spotless room, empty except for carpets and bolsters, a typical Afghan reception parlour. A wall calendar reminded the occupants that 'The heart retains its scars longer than most parts of the body'.

Soon the curtains parted and Rasoul bustled in, smiling and apologising for the subterfuge.

'We have to be slightly careful,' he said, peeling off his jacket and shades. 'Who knows how long we will have to stay? I was washing some clothes the other day, here in the bathroom, and I heard some shooting from outside. Would you believe that sound made me homesick? Our mother and sisters are in Mazar. Some Pashtuns are still keeping Hazaras safe, but the security is really only good for

Pashtuns living there. There was much killing in the early days. The governor has changed since then; it's quieter, but you never know.'

Rolling up one of the sleeves of his blue denim shirt, he showed me a small, pale scar on his inner left arm, the exit hole of the piece of shrapnel that had struck him on that long night in Mazar eighteen months before. It was completely healed, almost vanished, but as the wall calendar said, there were other wounds.

The door curtain rustled again and Rasoul's elder half-brother, Yaqub, entered the room. I had come to associate a certain macho bravura with Afghan warriors, but Yaqub presented an altogether different aspect. His skin was puffy and pallid and he greeted me with a slightly fevered smile and a clinging grip. He had a straggly, greying beard, a dishevelled salwar kameez, and bare feet. He was startled briefly when the doorbell rang and remained wide-eyed until assured by another brother that it was just a cousin arriving. Apart from a chunky gold watch, he had few of the trappings of power one might associate with a regional political leader. He sat on the floor, kneading his pudgy calves and looking totally fed up.

'I had no involvement in what happened at Dasht-e Layli,' he said, speaking Dari with Rasoul translating. 'It was Malik and his people. The Taliban wanted Malik to go to Kabul to join the government. They agreed to stop sending reinforcements to the north, but they insisted that he personally move to Kabul. He knew he would be their hostage there, so when the Shia uprising began, Malik and the others decided to hit the Taliban as hard and as fast as possible, so that they would never come back to the north.'

As Yaqub spoke, the others sat in silence stroking their beards, like a tableau of wise Mongols. A little girl peeked at me from her hiding place in the folds of the door curtain. After a lunch of pulao and grilled lamb served on an edible plate of nan, we discussed the possibility of the brothers finding asylum in a third country. But the timing could hardly have been worse. There were so many refugees, and so few countries willing to take them. Desperate Afghans and

Iraqis were risking their lives and life's savings on hazardous sea journeys organised by 'people smugglers'. The black joke among the beleaguered staff of the UN High Commissioner for Refugees was that in order to prove a well-founded fear of persecution, an Afghan needed to be dead already.

I wanted to help Rasoul, who I knew and trusted, but his brother's case was far more complicated. It was Yaqub's fate as the eldest male in his family to be their protector. Fate, too, had decided that his family should be the ancestral leaders of the Shias of Ali Chaupan. As the local leader of a Shia party in a village under attack by Pashtuns, he must have taken up arms to defend his family and community. But deeper, darker ghosts lurked in the disused wells and abandoned shipping containers in the desert outside Sheberghan. Rightly or wrongly, the Taliban's accusations against Yaqub had besmirched his reputation. Atrocities having been perpetrated by all sides, it was difficult to believe the protestations of innocence of any of the combatants.

As I prepared to leave, Yaqub disappeared from the room for a moment, returning with a pair of new Turkmen donkey bags. Bowing, he presented them with a formality that made me blush redder than their crimson hue, and he physically prevented me from leaving until I accepted them.

As Rasoul walked me back to the car that afternoon I asked him how the Afghans in Attock were supporting themselves.

'Why, of course, by weaving carpets,' he replied. 'Would you like to see?'

A short drive away we came to an open-sided shed, behind which some Afghan boys with shaved heads sat at tall vertical looms arranged in rows. The large looms, suspended from the iron crossbeams that supported the shed roof, were capable of producing room-size carpets. The place was run by a Pakistani policeman, Nasir Khan, to whom Rasoul introduced me as a foreign buyer. Thinking me to be a potential business partner, Nasir freely explained the financial bottom line. He operated two hundred looms spread around the district, sixty in Attock alone, and sold over four hundred square metres of carpet a month. The young weavers were paid seventeen hundred Pakistan rupees, about $35, per square metre of rug knotted. Nasir would then sell the carpet for two and a half thousand rupees per metre to exporters in Lahore, who in turn would sell it for four thousand to British and American buyers. The rugs were Persian medallion designs of a kind commonly found in major rug emporiums from Sydney to London to New York. The icing on the cake was the 4 per cent bonus on all sales paid to him by the Pakistan government, despite the fact that the rugs were made by children, of whom a hundred and fifty were living under his 'care'.

Among them was twelve-year-old Bashir, who had recently arrived from Istalif, one of Afghanistan's most beautiful villages set in the Koh Daman, a valley ringed by barren hills north of Kabul. Istalif was famed for its orchards and blue-green pottery, and even the Moghul emperor Babur had written lovingly of its fast-flowing stream, 'with waters needing no ice'. But as a mainly Tajik village in an area controlled by the Taliban, Istalif had witnessed the anger of the Pashtuns. Accompanied by Arabs and Pakistani volunteers, they had locked people inside their homes, then burnt the village. The orchards were then cut down and the irrigation channels blown up. Bashir's family had fled to Kabul, and they had sent the boy to Pakistan, where he was safer and could earn money to support him.

Absorbed in his intricate work Bashir was seated facing a harp-like array of warps suspended on the loom. He used a hooked steel spike to tie two warp strings together, forming a knot and cutting the wool with the sharp edge of the spike. He worked fast, tying a knot every second or two as he moved horizontally along the face of the tautly strung loom. The warps made a thrumming sound as he plucked them, his lips pursed with concentration, following the design sketched on a piece of graph paper on the bench beside him. Balls of wool dyed in charcoal, orange, almond and green — the weaver's palette — hung from the loom within reach above his head. A quick calculation revealed that he was tying about twenty thousand knots a day, working from seven until six, seven days a week. When a line of knots was completed he would take a heavy steel comb as big as his hand and pound them down onto the adjacent row, then weave a line of woollen weft above them and begin tying another layer of knots on top of that. A metre of carpet, its shaggy pile unshorn, disappeared below him and up the back of the loom.

There were thousands of boys like Bashir in Pakistan. Generally they were paid a pittance, and poorly fed. It was quite common for the children to injure themselves by catching the pointed end of their knot-cutters in their noses or eyes, but their employers usually refused to pay their medical costs. In big workshops child weavers — mainly orphans, stolen children and those from debt-ridden families — were driven at an inhuman pace, with foremen calling out colour changes over loudspeakers. Liberated child labourers told of beatings meted out to children who could not keep pace, their tiny bodies being strung up on their looms in carpet crucifixions. In one extreme case, a boy weaver of Bashir's age, Iqbal Mashi, was murdered in mysterious circumstances in Pakistan in 1985. Aid agencies claimed that the boy, who had featured in anti-child labour campaigns, was killed by the carpet mafia. At one point the South Asian Coalition On Child Servitude had called for an international boycott of rugs made in the subcontinent, and introduced the 'Rugmark' certification scheme, guaranteeing child labour-free carpets. With exports threatened by the bad publicity, Pakistan made efforts to rehabilitate some twenty-five thousand child weavers and adopted the Rugmark scheme. But in November 1998 a joint Pakistan Government–International Labour Organisation survey found that some 3.6 million children were still working, many of them as carpet weavers.

Bashir was the only member of his family with a job. He had started his rug with several centimetres of woven, unknotted kilim, then added a few lines of knots in a cross-hatch pattern, then another band of sand-coloured flatweave before beginning the pile. It was a nice piece. Methodical and quiet, he set his own pace and I wondered whether weaving had helped him forget the trauma of the attack on Istalif. His wage of six rupees per row of knots, or about $3 a day, was being sent to Kabul. The loom was his only school and his family's only support, but if he continued weaving throughout his adolescence, his growing fingers would become deformed, his eyesight damaged and his intellect stunted.

'The sky is the limit for this business,' Nasir told me, leading the way into what, by Attock standards, was a palatial home. 'All we need are these Afghan people — I feed them three times a day and provide them with all facilities, and in return they spin gold. We're running out of land for new workshops, so that's why last year we set up this one next door to our home.'

'You see,' said Rasoul in a whisper, when Nasir Khan was making a phone call, 'the Afghan war makes us good workers for the Pakistanis.'

As Nasir served soft drinks in his living room, I inspected the family photo gallery on his mantelpiece. He was twenty-one and unmarried, the middle brother of three, one of whom was in Saudi Arabia. They were keen horsemen and had filled display cases with their silver trophies inscribed in Urdu.

'Can I visit your country?' Nasir suddenly asked. 'I very much would like to travel abroad. Can you help me?'

You could just imagine the visa application: 'Profession: Slave driver.'

Bidding Nasir Khan goodbye, and promising to place our order for a million square metres of rugs soon, we headed away from Attock and back to the Grand Trunk Road. Amid a chorus of trumpeting trucks and the cries of touts spruiking fifty-rupee bus rides to Peshawar, we embraced.

'*Khudar Hafiz*,' Rasoul said. 'Farewell'.

As Wajed sped me towards Islamabad, the difficulties of doing anything to help Rasoul seemed to increase with the passing milestones. The authorities required references, sponsorships and numbered forms, and the number of different categories for refugee, special humanitarian and jeopardy cases seemed designed to be an impenetrable maze. As a 'proposer' I would be obligated to financially guarantee his first few months abroad and possibly have to pay for his airfares and accommodation. It usually took at least eighteen months just to process an application, and many applications were in limbo for much longer than that. But that night, after dinner, as the swirling sounds of a Pakistani TV soap opera drifted up through the stairwell of my guesthouse, I switched on my computer and began typing a letter.

To Whom It May Concern

This is to draw your urgent attention to the case of Afghan refugee Mr GHULAM RASOUL AHMADI, currently living in Pakistan, whose safety is in serious jeopardy . . .

PART FIVE

BAGHDAD

18

Late for the War

Oh, for a world without visas! Obtaining them can require guile and persistence, a creative approach to the truth, and in extreme cases — so I am told — bribery. Having been obtained, the hard-won stamp, sticker or piece of paper will often lay wasted beyond its validity date. Then you apply for another one. In Afghanistan, a certificate of authenticity from a box of chocolates had been known to impress border guards. But Iraq was another matter.

The military attack by the United States and Britain, codenamed 'Operation Desert Fox', was entering its fourth night when my Royal Jordanian Airlines plane landed in Amman and I raced to the offices of the Eagle Taxi Company, opposite Abdili bus station, where drivers between jobs nodded off to the sound of television coverage of the bombing of Baghdad, a ten-hour drive away. Slapping a hundred and thirty *dinars* on the counter, I was soon ensconced in a 1980 Chevrolet Caprice, the kind once used as police cars in the States, with a carpeted dashboard and a Palestinian Arab called Karim at the wheel.

The streets of Amman were alive with Muslims breaking the Ramadan fast in sweetshops bathed in gaslight. We had stocked up with kebab sandwiches and bottled water, had a spare tyre mounted on the roof, and were accompanied by swooning Arabic songs from the tape deck. With Karim's worry beads swaying hypnotically from the rearview mirror we climbed eastwards out of Amman towards Jordan's eastern plateau, under a sky clotted with stars. As we drove towards the border, long lines of fuel tankers passed us coming the other way, bringing Iraqi oil into resource-poor Jordan. At wayside stalls men in red-checked scarves huddled over oil stoves, drinking sweet tea to fend off the dry, brittle cold. After several hours a brilliantly lit array of buildings, arches, tollgates and parking bays, glowing like an alien space station, came into sight across the black basalt desert. It was the Iraqi border.

'Coming for the war?' said the Jordanian officer, handing back my passport and pointing across a no man's land of towering Saddam images. 'You're welcome!'

A gridlock of GM Suburbans, Buicks and Cadillacs made the place look like the car park of an American shopping mall. One thing the Iraqis and their enemies had in common was a lust for oil, and as the gas guzzlers clogging the drive-through Customs bays at Trebil made clear, Iraqi oil was cheap. Wearing the plastic badge issued to me by a Baghdad-approved doctor after I had tested HIV-negative in New Delhi, I was wandering alone in a confused state, trying to remember my five words of Arabic which might determine where the formalities began, when I was approached by a diminutive Iraqi wearing a soiled yellow corduroy jacket, who relieved me of my bags.

'That Clinton is a bastard. But you are welcome!' he said, charging $10 for some undefined service he had rendered, and pointing me towards one of several poorly marked buildings.

With a state of hostilities in progress, restrictions applied to laptop computers, cameras, satellite telephones; in short, any equipment that might have been adapted to aid the Allied war effort. The computer and camera I was carrying were sealed, not to be opened again until I reached the Information Ministry in Baghdad. Men with rubber stamps 'fined' me for not having a letter of invitation from an Iraqi government agency, about which the Iraqi Embassy in New Delhi had said nothing. Finally, a doctor from Iraqi's Health Department stationed at Trebil denied all knowledge of the Indian doctor who had issued my health badge and, insisting that he be allowed to draw blood, produced a gargantuan syringe of uncertain provenance and a length of nylon strap.

'Iraq has no medicine. If you are not healthy you die!' he roared to gales of laughter from the assembled bribe-seekers. 'Due to sanctions we cannot even send your body home to your family. We'll bury you in Baghdad.'

Everybody knew I was late for the war, so when inevitably one of the officials took me aside and whispered that payment of another 'fine' might preclude the need for a jab, the dollars and dinars began to flow. Assured there was only one further formality to undergo, I strode to the final hut, waving to Karim to be ready for a quick departure. It was warm inside the hut, and the Customs officials were huddled around a two-bar electric radiator, listening so intently to a crackling radio that they declined to accept my proffered passport. The radio was emitting a stream of urgent Arabic, punctuated with words like 'Ar-mair-ee-KAR', 'But-LAR' and 'KROOZE'. Finally, with a huge shrug, one of them sidled up, took my passport and stamped it with a brutal finality.

'War is finish,' he said with a leer. 'Iraqi people have win a great victory!'

After four nights of bombing, the United States had announced the suspension of Operation Desert Fox. The reason given was a desire not to offend Muslims by bombing during Ramadan. No longer late for the war, I had missed it altogether. My long and expensive odyssey had left me marooned without a purpose. Baghdad was almost five hundred kilometres away across the desert, Amman more than three hundred kilometres back the other way. There was nothing but sand between Trebil and Ramadi on the Euphrates River. Then it struck me: peace. Peace was the story. Shooting stars rather than missiles flashed across the sky as Karim cranked up the Chevy and I settled into a deep slumber in the velour-covered back seat. If he hurried we might reach Baghdad in time to file something with the appropriate dateline.

Iraq was once, like the United States today, a country of firsts. Sedentary society emerged in Mesopotamia around 5000 BC when people learned to plant, irrigate and harvest crops. Three thousand years before Christ, writing based on abstract symbols was invented to label the fruits of agricultural surplus. When a potter's wheel was turned on its side and hitched to a horse, modern transportation was born. It was where time was first carved into sixty minutes, and circles into three hundred and sixty degrees. When in the ninth century the Arab caliph Haroun al-Rashid wanted to demonstrate his society's superiority over Europe, he sent Charlemagne a clock. Haroun's palace in Baghdad boasted twenty-two thousand carpets, a collection managed by the 'Office of the Carpet Inspector'. Since the coming of Islam, the region's fortunes had been determined by battles for control of the new religion. After the death of Mohammed, his successors shifted their capitals from Arabia to Iraq, and then Syria. In their rug-lined palaces in Damascus, the Ummayad caliphs had grown despotic and corrupt. But in 749 AD, descendants of the Prophet's uncle Abbas overthrew the Ummayads. Thirteen years later, the caliph Abu Jafar al-Mansur engaged Khalid ibn Barmak, a descendant of Buddhist high priests from an ancient monastery in Balkh, to choose a site for his new capital of Baghdad. Barmak chose the west bank of the Tigris, and decided its orientation according to cosmological and geomantric principles. Baghdad would remain the centre of the Muslim world for five hundred years, its bejewelled mosques, bathhouses and bazaars immortalised in the *The Arabian Nights' Entertainments*. In 1258, Hulagu Khan, a grandson of Genghis Khan, overthrew the last Abbasid caliph and, according to Muslim historians, destroyed the city. But Marco Polo, who claimed to have visited Baghdad under Mongol rule, reported that 'Mahometan law is here regularly studied, as well as magic, physics, astronomy, geomancy, and physiognomy. It is the noblest and most extensive city to be found in this part of the world.'[1] The first Mongol Il-khans, in fact, were Buddhists, generally tolerant in religious matters. If Islam suffered, 'it was by being deposed from its traditionally privileged position'.[2] Baghdad, nevertheless, entered a steady decline as power shifted to the Persians, Turks and Timurids. By 1638, when the Ottoman Turks conquered Baghdad, the city's population was a meagre fourteen thousand, having once been two million. It was not until the twentieth century that a magic potion revived its splendour. The elixir was oil.

During World War I, British troops fighting the Turks occupied the city, then still part of the Ottoman Empire. The British campaign, starring T. E. Lawrence, better known as 'Lawrence of Arabia', was partly aimed at protecting the investments of British companies in the recently discovered oil fields. The British declared Iraq a protectorate and installed the Hashemite Bedouin *sharifs* of Mecca and Medina as the new rulers. The new king of Iraq, Faisal I, had been driven out of Syria by the French but was now given the throne in Baghdad, while the British also picked up his brother Abdullah, who they made Emir of Transjordan. Hashemite rule over Iraq would last less than fifty years, but the basic character of Western involvement in the region — the use of force to determine who rules, based on oil interests — endures to this day.

Oil money and thousands of guest workers from the Muslim world built the grand highway along which Karim and I sped that night. It was a pristine multi-lane divided road, marred only by occasional skidmarks and buckled guard rails where drivers had nodded off into eternity. It was indeed a good sleeping road, but some time after dozing off I was jolted awake by a violent bucking motion, the force of which held me down. In the front seat I could see Karim locked in mortal battle with the steering wheel, the car swerving rapidly amid the screech of tyres.

Fatigue had almost been the death of us. Karim had fallen asleep and almost lost control, waking just in time to avoid colliding with the guard rail at high speed. Exhausted by the shock of the sudden emergency, he limply guided the vehicle to the side of the road, pulled the handbrake on, and declared he must sleep. We stood beside the car in a dark desert, ruffled by a stiff, cold breeze, struggling to communicate in a clumsy mixture of English, Arabic and sign language. Forcing him to continue would have been suicidal, but I was in the grip of dateline fever, and had convinced myself that nothing in the world was so important as our reaching Baghdad by the morning. Amid much palming and smiling, I took possession of the keys, bustled Karim into the Chevy's back seat, and positioned myself behind the steering wheel of the enormous vehicle. We moved off, cautiously at first, then with gathering speed, and soon Karim was snoring.

Traversing the desert is like crossing the Arab soul. On moonlit nights like this the traditional Bedouin would gather around campfires telling stories and drinking coffee, or head out to hunt nocturnal prey. The desert's starry canopy guided their travels, and inspired Arab folklore, poetry and ballads sung to the moon. Yet kilometre after kilometre on this modern highway, I saw not a living thing. Amid surreal desolation, I drove through the night until the stars dimmed, the dunes and *wadis* slowly materialised, and dawn imparted a blush to the high, wispy clouds of a fine day. In the sunlight I noticed the march of the powerlines, rising and falling so rhythmically beside the road that they made me giddy.

A few kilometres before Ramadi, Karim awoke, squinting blearily into the rising sun, and we encountered our next problem. Wartime rationing was in force and all the petrol stations along the highway were shut. As the Chevy's fuel gauge began to dip, my hopes focused increasingly on Ramadi. With Karim back at the wheel, we drove into the sprawling river port city as the sound of an air-raid siren slowly unwound. Troops guarded all government buildings, and truck-mounted anti-aircraft guns were parked at several places with their barrels pointed expectantly towards the sky. Stopped for precious minutes by police asking questions, we found several bowsers, only to be turned away. Others were locked and deserted. I was starting to get desperate and began nagging Karim, who in turn got into a raging argument with a bowser boy, dragging him to a locked petrol pump and insisting that he open it. Suddenly, several young men in leather jackets appeared from nowhere, confronting Karim and shouting at him to release the boy. Their scar-faced leader began to circle Karim menacingly, ready to pounce and give him a good beating or worse. Stunned at first, Karim let the boy go and backed with extreme caution towards the car; then, in a lightning movement, he leapt into the driver's seat and skidded out of the drive amid a hail of insults and kicks at the rear bumper. Humiliated and angry, he hurtled past the police checkpoint and back onto the highway. Our search for fuel was over.

We still had about a hundred kilometres to go to Baghdad, but Karim decided — *Insh'allah* — to go for it. Blasting over the broad, reed-fringed reach of the Euphrates, we hurtled across the bridge — rebuilt since the Gulf War and mercifully unscathed by the current hostilities — and sped across a pancake-flat plain towards the capital. As we approached the outskirts, the Baghdad skyline loomed on the horizon and billboard-size images of the most famous moustache since Joseph Stalin's began crowding the roadside. There was Sheikh Saddam in Arab headgear, Soldier Saddam in general's uniform, Suave Saddam grinning cheesily in a business suit, Jazzy Saddam in a white suit, and Saint Saddam kissing the open pages of the Koran. This multi-skilled leader was variously mounted on a stallion, thoughtful at his desk, and stepping into the cockpit of a jet fighter in goggles and leathers. Sweating every kilometre, my anxieties began to colour these ubiquitous images. Was he smiling or gritting his teeth? Was he raising his hand to silence applause, or requesting permission to go to the bathroom? One huge portrait had him gazing into a small coffee cup, the man of destiny analysing the dregs for his fortune. But the most unforgettable image was a silhouette of

Saddam dressed in a Bogart trenchcoat and holding a smouldering cigarette. The billboards suggested the Iraqi leader was omnipresent and omniscient, but I feared the overall effect was to portray him as a chameleon-like master of disguises, a man of a million faces. Which one was the real Saddam Hussein?

It was Sunday morning and isolated plumes of black smoke rose from bombed buildings, but hardly enough to smudge the burning blue sky or taint the cool morning air. We glided the final few kilometres into the city on a sea of asphalt, past turquoise blue mosque domes, palaces topped with ack-ack guns, and the rising sun framed in an arch formed by massive crossed scimitars held by two fists modelled on Saddam's own hands. Here and there, between the buildings and date palm groves, I caught glimpses of the placid, sparkling Tigris, curving between the city's eastern and western banks like a diamond necklace between a woman's breasts, the river's channels marked by orange buoys. The LA of the East, Baghdad dazzled the hapless wanderer with a glorious history and glamorous modernity.

At the Al-Rashid Hotel, hit a few years earlier by an American cruise missile but now fully functioning, I trampled the face of George Bush, strategically located as a floor mosaic at the main entrance, skirted a Christmas tree on which staff were hanging fairy lights, and checked in.

19

Tyranny, Hypocrisy, Bastardry and Confusion

'What did I do to America?' asked Jassim Zuweiby, lying with his head bandaged in Yarmouk hospital after an American bomb fell on him.[3] It was over seven years since the Gulf War and the mantra that the United States had 'no quarrel with the Iraqi people' provided little consolation to this civilian resident of Baghdad. He could not know that his injuries, and the more serious ones sustained by his daughter, as well as the damage to his property, were purely 'collateral'. When American servicemen scrawled 'Hold On To Yer Butt', 'Die You Magets' and 'This Is Gunna Hurt' on the bomb casings, they probably thought their messages would be read by 'The Beast of Baghdad' only, and perhaps a few evil lieutenants.[4] Yet Saddam hadn't suffered a scratch and Zuweiby was bleeding from his head.

For most of the 1990s Iraq had been providing America with target practice, and the world with an object lesson in what Samuel P. Huntington called the West's 'superiority in applying organised violence'. The boffins called it 'asymmetric' warfare; others just called it amoral. Since the hi-tech Gulf War — when somebody had the bright idea of fitting bombs with television cameras — we have been fixated by images of Iraq's destruction. We had front-row seats at the Pentagon briefings, and were there in the cockpit with our modern-day knights on their winged chargers. And like them, the unequal battle made us all a bit less human, capable of experiencing the adrenalin rush of killing, without fear or feeling.

By 1990 Saddam Hussein's Iraq had a one million-strong army and had been the world's biggest arms purchaser for five years running.[5] Concerned that low oil prices were limiting his ability to quickly rebuild Iraq after its debilitating eight-year war against Iran, Saddam accused neighbouring Kuwait of conspiring with the West to keep prices low by overproduction. Demanding that Kuwait immediately pay him $10 billion in compensation, he moved two hundred thousand Iraqi soldiers to the border and, when the money was not forthcoming, invaded and annexed Kuwait in August 1990. After the failure of diplomatic efforts to reach a settlement, the UN set a six-week deadline for Iraq to withdraw, mobilising four hundred and twenty-five thousand troops from over thirty nations, including Arab Muslim countries, in the largest military operation since World War II. But the Iraqi leader ignored the ultimatum, and on 17 January 1991 the bombing started.

Both Saddam and President Bush were prepared to gamble their careers, and the lives of their countrymen, on victory. With Kuwait in its grasp, Iraq controlled 20 per cent of global reserves, and if the Iraqis conquered neighbouring Saudi Arabia that share would rise to 40 per cent. With his goal of making Iraq a new Arab superpower within reach, Saddam toughed out the Allied air campaign, believing his opponents did not have the stomach for the casualties likely to be inflicted on them in a ground war. The reward for defeat, he knew, was probably death at the hands of his own people. As the leader of a nervous democracy Bush was old enough to remember the fate of the last US president humiliated by a Middle Eastern nation — Jimmy Carter — and was prepared to take enormous risks to avoid it. Despite the awesome firepower he had assembled, some of the weaponry, like Tomahawk cruise missiles and Stealth bombers, had never before been used in conflict. Public opinion in the United States was sensitive, not only to the loss of US soldiers but also to Iraqi civilian casualties. Should Iraqi Scud missile attacks on Israel draw the Jewish state into the war, the allied coalition of nations would lose its Arab and Islamic members.

To defeat Iraq, Bush deployed three-quarters of his nation's active tactical aircraft, almost half its modern battle tanks and aircraft carriers, and over one-third of its army personnel.[6] Yet the ground war, which began in February 1991, would last only one hundred hours. Three-quarters of Iraq's troops chose to surrender rather than fight. They were shown kissing the hands of US Marines and begging for their lives. American F-15 fighter planes chased retreating Iraqi soldiers and civilians, killing and maiming hundreds of them on what became known as the 'Highway of Death'. In the triumphal aftermath President Bush declared the dawn of a 'New World Order'. But despite spending $61 billion, he had failed to remove Saddam.

Having lined up a return fare to Amman, Karim had put me in the capable hands of Hussain, another satisfied Chevrolet owner, whose car boasted white-wall tyres on spoked wheels, six television-size rear brake lights, Arabic plates and a pink plastic Bugs Bunny which waved 'Hi' from the dashboard. Having been sent on an errand to change money, Hussain proved himself by returning with wads of dinars bundled and stamped in English and Arabic with the words 'In God We Trust'. Even in the middle of a war all sides seemed to have kept their sense of humour. In the car park of the Al-Rashid Hotel that morning, the taxi drivers had greeted each other with so much kissing and high praise that it must have been a competition to see who laughed first, despite having spent four nights in the bomb shelters.

Operation Desert Fox had lasted seventy hours, cost $500 million, and involved an allied coalition comprising only the United States and Britain. The onslaught had killed sixty-two Iraqi soldiers and destroyed or severely damaged over a hundred buildings, including the offices of Iraqi military intelligence, the Special Security Organisation, and the palace of Saddam's daughter in his hometown of Tikrit. But in a city spread over six hundred and fifty square kilometres, which had been levelled by Mongols, Persians and Turkmens among others, the physical and psychological impact was minimal. Telephone, electricity and water services were all functioning normally. Shops were open, the roads hummed with traffic, and wedding parties posed for photographs in sunny Zawra Park. Even contestants in the Second Um al-Ma'aik Teams Chess Championship at Sadeer Hotel had played on during the bombing.

The attacks were justified on the grounds that Saddam was developing weapons of mass destruction, and had blocked efforts by UN inspectors to monitor such programs. Later it was revealed that suspected chemical weapons plants were not targeted, because hitting them might unleash plumes of poisonous gas.

'We're not going to take a chance and try to target any facility that would release any kind of horrific damage to innocent people,' US defense secretary William Cohen told the *Today* program on NBC. If chemical, biological and nuclear facilities in Baghdad were officially off-limits to US bombers, surely Saddam had found the perfect hiding place. Western analysts, if not governments, conceded that the Pentagon's initial assertions of significant damage were 'an awkward combination of propaganda and complete rubbish'.[7] Operation Desert Fox demonstrated, above all else, the limited effectiveness of war from the skies alone.

As Hussain and I cruised the palm-fringed boulevards of Baghdad on a bright winter's afternoon, we were accompanied by a guide-interpreter assigned by the Ministry of Information, the modern-day equivalent of the *dragoman* that Islamic societies have for centuries used to watch over nosy foreigners. Books, it used to be said, were written in Cairo, printed in Beirut and read in Baghdad. But knowledge, however sophisticated it was in Arab, Turkish and Persian cultures, was not intended to be shared with outsiders. For centuries the Persians had enriched their empire by manufacturing silk, the secret of which they had wheedled out of the Chinese, then denied to Europe. In modern times, official secrecy redoubled as Arab countries failed to develop democratic institutions. The Arabs considered themselves too innately open for their own good, and had to work hard to develop discretion. My dragoman was a matronly woman called Elham, whose job was to ensure that shocking stories and images of civilian casualties and defiant Iraqis swearing allegiance to Saddam Hussein reached the West, in order to undermine support for the regime's continued isolation. Stories about Saddam's ruthless reign, or military posture, were to be prevented.

With this in mind, Elham directed Hussain across the sweeping 'July Fourteen bridge' to the shattered façade of Iraq's largest hospital. The 1200-bed, eleven-storey Saddam Medical City stood opposite a group of public buildings which dated back to Ottoman rule. Several cruise missiles had crashed into the old Defence Ministry building, built during the Hashemite period of the early twentieth century. Chill winds whipped us as we stood looking at the toppled columns of the ministry and the damage to the hospital, where three patients had died of cardiac arrest from the shock of the explosions. The war, it seemed, was no respecter of cultural heritage or human life. The hospital was barely two hundred metres from the hospital, and the slightest error in targeting could have turned the medical centre into a mausoleum. As I stared in silence at the defaced hospital, my feelings must have been obvious.

'See the arrogance of the American *superpower*,' Elham said, the last word coated in contempt.

The largest military action against Iraq since the Gulf War had been triggered by a dispute over inspections designed to dismantle Iraq's capability for producing chemical and biological weapons. The United Nations Special Commission, UNSCOM, had been working in Iraq since the Gulf War, but in 1998 disputes had arisen over the aggressive style of the inspectors. Called to adjudicate on the issue, the UNSCOM chairman, a former Australian diplomat,

Richard Butler, had reported to the UN Security Council that Baghdad had failed to fully co-operate with the inspectors. What was not publicly known at that time was the fact that, far from being a fully independent UN commission, UNSCOM had since 1992 been co-operating covertly with Western intelligence agencies and Israeli intelligence to collect information about Iraq. In 1995, the then chief inspector, a former US Marine intelligence officer, Scott Ritter, travelled to Israel and persuaded Mossad to provide sophisticated scanners and recording equipment to eavesdrop on Iraqi security forces as they moved weapons and materials around the country to avoid detection. When Ritter resigned in August 1998 he went public, charging that UNSCOM had allowed itself to become a conduit for US intelligence gathering and that Butler had acted under directions from the US government. In his book about his period as UNSCOM chairman, Butler denied acting under such direction. He admitted he 'accepted help from the intelligence branches of some UN member states' in order to 'breach the Iraqi wall of deceit', but said that if some countries took advantage of UNSCOM for their own intelligence-gathering purposes, it was 'without my knowledge or approval'.[8] The dispute with Ritter, however, was soon overshadowed by Butler's report that Iraq had not co-operated with UN weapons inspections. Again, Butler was at odds with senior colleagues. His own political advisor, French diplomat Eric Fournier, was diametrically opposed to the report sent by Butler to the Security Council on 15 December 1998, in which the UNSCOM chairman said Iraq had imposed new restrictions on the inspectors' work, thereby ensuring that 'no progress was able to be made in either disarmament or accounting for its prohibited weapons programmes'.[9] After submitting his report, Butler ordered the evacuation of UNSCOM staff from Iraq. The following day, the bombing began.

Ritter, too, would later write a book and both he and Butler hit the talkshow circuit to promote their differing versions of events.

But Fournier kept a low profile, returning to the Foreign Ministry in Paris, which posted him to India. When I met him at his office on New Delhi's Shantipath — 'Peace Street' — over a year later, the wounds of the UNSCOM debacle were still fresh in his mind.

'Why did the bombings occur in December 1998? Well, because Richard Butler reported that the Iraqis had not co-operated with inspections, even though more than three hundred had taken place in a few weeks and only a handful had been a problem. Three out of three hundred did not go perfectly smoothly. Yet Butler's report was very critical. The report did not say, "On the whole, the trial has gone smoothly for three months." It said Iraq has never ever co-operated with us. It went back to 1991. This report, drafted like that, was a good excuse for some members of the Security Council to take action. But the co-operation of Iraq in that period was better than ever,' he said.

Like the stylish embassy building in which he worked, Fournier was suave and sophisticated, arguing cogently — even in a foreign language like English — about the demerits of the policy towards Iraq. As he saw it, the question came down to the purpose of the inspections.

'We had been able to account for and destroy 817 of 819 imported operational missiles of proscribed range over five hundred kilometres. We got all the mobile launchers for Al-Hussein-modified Scud missiles, and we destroyed seventy-three of seventy-five chemical and biological warheads. We had a permanent team of less than thirty inspectors and could build up quickly to a hundred. Some people felt a good team needed seven hundred people to cover Iraq, but it depends on the target. If the target is to find everything about the past, even seventy thousand inspectors would not make a perfect picture.'

He paused, then went on: 'This is Iraq, not Germany. They don't have paperwork accounts for everything. People have been killed, moved, threatened. There had been strong political pressure, so people were not sure what to say. We wanted to know where were the shells imported from, say, Spain in 1974. Where was the list? We wanted the chequebook stubs, and the documents in which orders were given to truck drivers. Can you imagine? A truck driver meets these weird people who ask the question, "Where were you ten years ago at three in the morning?" He will say, "I'm not sure." The problem was there was no political solution envisaged. It was more comfortable to keep looking than to decide what to do with Iraq. In December 1998 that's exactly what took place.'

With Ritter's admission that he had maintained secret contacts with Israeli intelligence, UNSCOM's credibility suffered a mortal blow. Within the UN, Butler became the focus of discontent that his actions had served US interests, not those of the United Nations. According to Fournier, Butler had come under intense pressure from the Clinton Administration to stay aggressive on Iraq. In June 1998, after a visit to Baghdad, Butler had flown to Bahrain where he addressed a news conference. Fournier was with him.

'After the press conference at which he had been positive about closing the whole disarmament issue, Richard received a call from Washington or New York, and from his responses I could gather that there was a very highly placed person at the State Department on the other end, and that they were not very happy at the prospect of any positive outcome for Iraq. The moment we showed too much confidence, we had too many people coming out of the darkness saying, "You fools!"'

Later at a meeting of about twenty people, Fournier went public with his concerns.

'I told Richard Butler directly in the presence of those people that I did not agree with the conclusions of the report. I said that if we are to compare the results of all the inspections which were organised during this period, on the whole, the co-operation extended to us was satisfactory. My personal view was that there was a distortion ... the aim of the report was not to give a statement on those seven years, but on the co-operation extended by the Iraqi authorities in November 1998.'

All the players ended up bruised, but the main casualty of Operation Desert Fox turned out to be UNSCOM, the world's main instrument in containing Iraq's efforts to acquire weapons of mass destruction.

UNSCOM's offices in Baghdad were deserted now, the inspectors home with their families for Christmas and unlikely to be returning to Iraq under their existing mandate. All non-essential staff of other UN agencies had been evacuated before the bombing, but at the UN Children's Fund (UNICEF) office the chief representative, Philippe Heffinck, was happily pottering about like one of those lonely types who prefer the office on weekends.

'The Saddam Medical Centre? Yes, it's in a bad state,' Heffinck said. 'I'm sending a team down there to assess the damage. We should have contractors carrying out repairs within a few days.'

It seemed extraordinary that one UN agency should trigger a bombing campaign while another cleaned up the mess, but Philippe had neatly compartmentalised the issues in his own mind, and probably avoided a turf war within the UN.

'There's a pressing humanitarian need which has been created and which we intend to address,' was all he would say. Other UN officials had been unable to reconcile their position, and had resigned in protest over sanctions against Baghdad. Elham could quote their resignation letters word for word.

'Sanctions are starving six thousand Iraqi infants to death every month. The UN officials themselves say this is genocide,' she said, suggesting we visit another site nearby where civilians had been injured. 'My children are also Iraqi children. I had to sell my jewellery, some furniture, even books, but now there is nothing left to sell and the situation is becoming critical.'

Passing the imposing gates of the presidential palace, which fronted the Tigris on 'Mother of Our Bones' Boulevard, I asked Elham how long the anti-aircraft guns had been on top of the gates. 'Guns?' she said, still absorbed in her own thoughts. 'Oh those. Well, you know, we are not allowed to discuss military questions.'

Iraq's moderate form of Islam had once endeared it to both Washington and Moscow. Iraqi women could show their faces, be educated and work, romance with their boyfriends in public parks or amuse themselves with television, music and chess. Since the eleventh century, Iraqi mullahs had developed doctrines of public law which mitigated the punishments of the Shari'a, creating space in which religious minorities could survive, and civil society and the liberal arts could prosper. When in 1980 Saddam declared war on Iran, his regime portrayed the action as a crusade against the 'sickness' of religious fundamentalism.

'We are defending the values of the modern world against a barbaric onslaught,' his Undersecretary of Information, Abdul Gabbar Mohsen, told a correspondent in Baghdad in 1982. 'And we are confident that the future will prevail over bygone days.'[10]

But as his regime became more isolated, Saddam began to acquire an interest in religion, adding the words 'God is Great' to the Iraqi flag. Iraqi historians were soon hard at work tracing their leader's ancestral links to the Prophet Mohammed. Iraq remained the most naturally secular country in the Middle East, although the hardships and suffering of Saddam's ceaseless conflicts were contributing to increased mosque attendances and fasting during Ramadan, which had begun the day before my arrival.

During the ninth month of the Muslim lunar calendar devout Muslims are supposed to abstain from food, drink and sex between sunrise and sunset. Non-Muslims are free to eat, but out of courtesy should not do so in the presence of those fasting. Not having had a proper meal in days, and tormented by hunger pangs, I finally raised the issue of lunch with Elham.

'Yes of course,' she replied, clearly delighted, and on her recommendation Hussain drove us along Al-Karrada Street towards the swank district of Arasat, Baghdad's Beverly Hills, where the rich browse in boutiques, galleries and well-stocked supermarkets. It turned out Elham was feeling unwell — although slightly peckish — and so qualified for an exemption from the fast. The Gumar Al-Zaman Restaurant on Al-Hendia Street was a haven of luxury with Persian rugs, a white baby grand piano, and piped Julio Iglesias music. Wine glasses hung by their stems over the bar, not a legal drop in them since Saddam found Allah during the war. The place had been patronised by the dreaded UNSCOM weapons inspectors until their expulsion, but was now deserted. Despite the absence of other customers, appetiser chef Mohammed Kasim agreed to make us a meal and wait at table. Clad in white jeans and designer stubble, the well-built twenty-six-year-old economics student told us he was working to pay his way through university. He had been at home on the second night of the air strikes when the windows of his family's apartment were blown in.

'It's foolish. It doesn't benefit anyone,' he said, setting the table with crisp white linen and polished cutlery. Kasim was writing to foreign universities with the aim of continuing his education abroad. The brain drain, which had started with the overthrow of the Hashemite monarchy in the 1950s, was now a haemorrhage.

My morning had been a rather grim exercise in bearing the brunt of Iraqi anger and desperation. At the university intelligent young men and women in Western dress had railed against Western policy, blaming it for their lack of opportunities. Old men and young children selling cigarettes on street corners had told harrowing tales of personal tragedy and financial crisis. And now, as we settled at our table next to the window overlooking Al-Hendia Street, Elham embarked on a long recitation of her financial difficulties. She looked quite prosperous, a tight black skirt hugging her ample hips and her neck graced by a modicum of tasteful jewellery. To get a job dealing with foreign reporters she must have had connections. Through mouthfuls of grilled lamb, rice with almonds and raisins, and Coca-Cola, she kept up a relentless monologue of woe, the lament of the previously well-off, not the cry of the destitute, until I could no longer listen, and focused instead on the mannequins that pouted at us from a boutique across the street.

With cardamom-spiced coffee lingering on our palates, we left the restaurant, passing the art galleries, gymnasiums and furniture stores that still cater to Iraq's privileged. On Al-Karada Street, road gangs had plugged a burst water main and were shovelling dirt into a gaping crater where a bomb had fallen. An old three-storey building had given up the ghost after the impact, collapsing into a pile of rubble on the pavement. Rapid reconstruction was emblematic of Saddam's defiance. All the bridges destroyed in 1991 had been rebuilt, and Baghdad's damaged telephone tower had risen again, taller than before, and even surpassing a similar tower in London. A ritzy restaurant where a meal cost several months of an average person's salary now crowned the 106 metre-tall Saddam International Tower.

Turning into Sa'adoun Street, we stopped at a small carpet shop whose mundane façade hid a minor Aladdin's cave of Kurdish and Turkmen pieces at absurdly low prices. A small antique Tekke in Van Dyke brown caught my fancy. It was like Iraq: very old and worn down, but built on excellent foundations. The piece was so finely knotted that, like the silk Hereke prayer rug made by the Turkish master weaver Zareh Penyamin, it could almost be folded up like a handkerchief and put in your pocket. Asked for his price, the vendor arrived at what he clearly believed was an outrageous sum of $150. Why I didn't snap it up right then without bargaining I don't know; probably sheer perversity, or an evil desire to exploit the prevailing poverty. I decided to shop around.

Now Elham was studying me, as if the brief foray into the rug shop had revealed some unforeseen potential. Her attempt to prevent me from speaking to some soldiers near the hospital that morning, and her persistent refusal to talk about anything even remotely related to military matters, had created tension between us. But as Hussain deposited me back at the hotel she became friendly, walking with me into the lobby and admiring the Christmas tree on display.

'I'm sorry you couldn't talk to the soldiers this morning,' she said, with a rare smile. 'I have a relative who is in the army. Maybe we can meet him socially. Would that interest you?'

Of course it would, I said.

'You would not be permitted to discuss military matters. It would be strictly a social meeting.'

That was fine, I replied.

'All right, then. I will talk with him tonight and fix a time for tomorrow evening.'

We parted at the elevator, and as the lift carried me to the seventh floor, my opinion of Elham — and sympathy for her — began to rise.

20

The Sheikh with One Million Camels

It was after breakfast already. Hussain was not in the car park, Elham had not arrived and I was furious. A meeting with the editor of the English-language *Baghdad Observer* — the only appointment I had made so far — wasn't until the evening, and the day's potential was evaporating before my eyes. Being stuck in my hotel room waiting for the car was achieving nothing, and I was heading off to the Information Ministry press centre when the telephone rang. A male voice introduced himself as Salar, my new assistant. Elham, he said, had suddenly been taken ill and would not be working with me any more. The finality of the 'any more' — as if she had suddenly developed cancer — aroused my suspicions. Elham had been perfectly well, apart from the feigned illness that allowed her to eat a hearty lunch during Ramadan, and I knew it would take much more than a cold to keep her away from her job. After blustering briefly Salar buckled, confessing that, yes, Elham had been removed from my case. Badgered for the reason, he said she had met that morning with her boss and informed him about her plan to introduce me to her relative, the soldier.

'The ministry feels that a woman is not strong enough to control a male correspondent,' Salar said, adding that he was busy with other work and could not join me until the following day.

'You should tell me now what you want to do tomorrow,' he said, more as an order than a suggestion. 'Is there anywhere you wish to go?'

The rules stipulated that I wasn't permitted to work in Baghdad without a government minder. Now my minder had been taken away and her replacement was busy. Was I being punished? Was there any point in staying? Stuck for an answer, I said the first thing that came to mind.

'Babylon,' I told Salar. 'Take me to Babylon.'

In the car park, Hussain had arrived, confirming he had spent the morning with Elham as she shuttled between various government offices, refusing to accept her fate or allow him to return to the hotel. Eventually he had fled, he told me, tapping his head to convey Elham's state of mind. Grounded for the rest of the day, we embarked on an unofficial tour of Baghdad.

Two rivers bordered the city's sprawling souk: the stately Tigris, and the river of cars that stalls and banks up along the street of the caliph al-Rashid. The commercial hub of Rusafa district was clogged with scarred car flesh, the drivers making brief, hopeless stabs at their horns, turning off their engines and beseeching traffic police to clear the obstacles. But the main obstacle was Rashid Street itself, a varicose relic built before cars and so resigned to its maladies that there was talk of turning it into a pedestrian mall. Barrowpushers squeezed through the gridlock, watched by men lounging on for-sale sofas. Intense young spivs leant against colonnades, old men leant on walking sticks, and demobbed soldiers leant on prostheses. Children sold cigarettes and matches, and grandmothers knitted and shelled peas on the wrought iron and timber balconies overlooking it all. Where the street opened out around the three hundred-year-old brown brick Marjan Mosque, traffic began moving again and the drivers leant out to navigate, unable to see through the cracked and shattered windshields that were the leitmotiv of sanctions.

Once the world's second-largest oil producer, Iraq had become poorer than Bangladesh, its oil production down to one-third of prewar levels. Lack of spare parts meant its wells and refineries could produce only half the $10 billion worth of oil a year allowed under the Oil For Food program, the largest aid effort in UN history, which provided every Iraqi a basic monthly ration of flour, cooking oil, tea, salt, sugar, rice, dried beans, soap, and infant milk formula. Contracts to restore Iraq's crumbling infrastructure were being blocked by the UN committee empowered to veto foreign investments. One-third of the country's oil revenues went to pay for the UN's operations in Iraq, including weapons inspections. With the main industries mothballed, dwindling dinars were left to circulate with greater than normal intensity deep inside the murky corridors of the bazaar.

A spider's web of powerlines slung across an alleyway marked the entrance to Souq Al-Safafir, the Bazaar of the Bronze Beaters, where Midhat al-Abbas, a carpet dealer recommended by a colleague, took my arm and plunged us into a teeming labyrinth of alleys and nooks rent by shafts of light and buzzing with dust, flies, hawkers, goldsmiths, beverage boys, confectioners, tailors and sidewalk backgammon champs. The watery light, and the snorkelling sound of smokers on their *shisha* water pipes, added to the submarine air of the covered bazaar.

In the clutter of brass pots and treadle sewing machines, bearers pushing rattling handcarts had right of way, the onus of avoiding collisions on the unencumbered. Pots of syrup and rosewater boiled in cauldrons as the sweetmakers prepared *halwa* and pastries swimming in honey and pistachio nuts for the breaking of the fast that evening. Sweet aromas battled gusts of hashish, cumin, Lysol, mint and sandalwood for control of the air. I felt as overwhelmed as Prince Husayn in *The Arabian Nights' Entertainments*, who upon beholding the Baghdad souk, exclaims, 'If in one street only there be such wealth and jewels so rare, Allah Almighty and none save He knoweth what may be the riches in all this city.'[11] The weapons inspectors no doubt felt the same.

Midhat had been selling carpets and collectibles in this cavernous place for almost twenty years. He walked with his hands clasped behind his back, a stakeholder swinging his worry beads as he stepped instinctively across the central drainage ditch in the lane running down to the river between Shuhada (Martyrs') and Ahrar (Freedom Fighters') bridges. Under vaulted ceilings, past yellowing tiled shopfronts and old mosaics of dancing girls, he stopped briefly here and there to contribute a stream of phlegmatic Arabic to a heated argument, or press cheeks with a relative or friend. Waiting under a decadent arch where the beehives had been scraped from the ceiling, beside a fountain in a marble niche with a chiselled Koranic inscription, stood a blind man in a tassled black *abbaya* (cloak), *disdasha* (long tunic) and white *a'gal* (headscarf) held firmly in place by black cords. A falcon's beak protruded from beneath the a'gal, and the skin of his neck fell in pastry folds into a collarless white shirt as he sipped rose-coloured tea from a gold-rimmed cruet with undissolved sugar swirling thickly on the bottom. Amid the clanging coppersmiths, roistering moneychangers and the muezzin's call, he heard everything and said little, keeping the tip of his scarf pinched in the corner of his mouth. Leaning into his robes, Midhat shared a quiet confidence before exchanging four firm cheek presses with him and leading me on again towards our destination, a Baghdad institution — the weekly carpet auctions.

In 1959, a young man from a village called Awja, about one hundred and fifty kilometres north of Baghdad, rented a small flat in the Al-Shibli building just off Al-Rashid Street, and moved in with a group of friends. At twenty, Saddam Hussein smouldered with indignation at the autocratic methods of Iraq's then military ruler, General Abdul Karim Kassem, who had overthrown the

British-installed monarchy the previous year. In their flat, Saddam and his associates hatched a bold scheme to end Kassem's tyranny. Carefully observing the comings and goings on Al-Rashid, they timed the movements of the prime minister's motorcade which regularly passed along the city's main street. On the appointed day they struck, unleasing a fusillade of bullets in a failed bid to assassinate Kassem. The prime minister's driver and an aide were killed, and one of the assassins was seriously injured. With a bullet wound in one leg, Saddam limped back to the flat, where his co-conspirators regrouped and argued among themselves about what to do next. The consensus — to stay in the apartment and lay low — seemed suicidal to Saddam, who claims to have swam the Tigris to escape, but more likely rode a donkey to Syria after obtaining treatment for his leg and changing into Bedouin dress. His instinct for action and survival had passed its first major test. As he had anticipated, most of the others were caught, but Saddam made it safely into exile.

Born into bitter poverty, Saddam had joined the socialist, pan-Arabist Ba'ath (Renewal) Party while still of school age, rising rapidly through its ranks due to his energy, organisational skills and violence. A student of the law, he excelled in breaking it, and was known to fellow students as Abu Mussaddess ('He of the Gun'). One day he turned up for an exam armed with a pistol and accompanied by four bodyguards. Of course, he passed.[12] When the Ba'athists seized power in a 1968 CIA-backed coup, he returned from exile as vice-president, and waited eleven years before confronting his own leader, General Ahmad Hassan al-Bakr, with his weapon of choice, a hand gun, and an ultimatum to stand aside, which al-Bakr promptly did. After that it was one war after another: with Iran, with the Kurdish minority and Shia majority, with Kuwait, Saudi Arabia, and finally, with the world in Operation Desert Storm. Not once did he achieve a decisive victory, but challenges to his leadership — and there were many — were deflected by the sophisticated and deadly police state he erected to preserve his own life and rule. Protected by the use of at least eight men who were his double, he never slept two successive nights in the same bed and ensured that all his movements were secret and unpredictable. The president wore a sidearm at all times and on one occasion he is said to have personally dragged a dissenting minister out of a Cabinet meeting and shot him dead. Early on, the Ba'athists had accelerated the development of Iraq's physical infrastructure, but the terror soon began to eat away at the fabric of society. The violence and Orwellian cult of personality which surrounded the leader had so traumatised ordinary Iraqis that one poor man made the headlines by claiming to have seen Saddam's face on the moon. Having once taken refuge in the bazaar, Saddam knew its potential for harbouring dangerous types, and his spy network watched it closely. Forty-two merchants had died in a single purge, accused of corruption, but most of them also happened to be Shias.

Reaching the Tigris, Midhat and I came upon several men furiously beating some big old rugs and laying them out on the stone levee bank to be shampooed and dried before selling. Oil wealth had been a disguised curse for Iraq's once estimable carpet industry. European carpet historians believe the origins of weaving may go back to ancient Assyria, part of which is in modern Iraq. Historians believe pastoral wool growing had its origins in the area around 9000 BC, and wool appears in the export inventories of Babylon as early as 1800 BC. At their height, cities like Ctesiphon, Babylon and Baghdad held huge stocks of the finest carpets in the world, and their designs live on in the carpets of today. But with the discovery of black gold, Iraqis felt they no longer needed to toil in the fields or at the loom, and went in search of jobs and modern amenities in the cities.

Now with sanctions destroying the modern economy, and with nothing else to fall back on, Iraqis were selling their possessions to survive. The auction houses did a brisk trade in carpets, among other things. In a two-storey warehouse nearby, a crowd of rug jackals had gathered to inspect the potential pickings from a mixed inventory of Persian, Caucasian and Turkmen origins. On a raised platform, the chief auctioneer sat dressed like a gangster in a red shirt, black tie, and pinstripe suit. In one hand he held a microphone and cigarette, in the other a mallet-sized gavel, which he would slam down intermittently, interrupting the mellifluous stream of Arabic superlatives with which he described his stock. On a separate podium, attendants held up lots and mugged for my camera. Watching over the entire scene from above was a hand-knotted portrait of Saddam Hussein. Like all artists and artisans, Iraqi weavers had been roped in to help construct his personality cult. Their carpets documented every stage of Saddam's turbulent rule, featuring scenes from the wars with Iran, Kuwait and the West, and were usually rolled out to mark great occasions like the dictator's sixty-third birthday.[13] Saddam had established weaving schools to reacquaint his people with a long-neglected skill, using the traditional crafts for his own cunning designs.

With both hands buried deep in the pockets of his 'alpine'-design cardigan, Midhat followed the bidding with a poker face, occasionally taking a cup of thick, aromatic coffee from one of the young boys whose tiny bodies were best suited to carrying trays of hot beverages through the crowded bazaar. Afraid at first that a simple nod or misplaced look might commit us to an expensive purchase, I mimicked Midhat's taciturn demeanour. At the major European and American auction houses, prices were approaching an all-time high. In July 1999 at Christie's in London, Sheikh Saud of Qatar paid £1 596 500 for a seven-by-four-metre sixteenth-century Safavid Persian medallion carpet — a world record price for an Oriental carpet at auction. The slightest whiff of recession, of course, would have the big Western auction houses drowning in red ink, but neither bombs nor sanctions could scare Baghdad's irrepressible auctioneers. There were no paddles, no mysterious telephone bidders from the Gulf states. If you wanted a rug you just stood there, stuck up your hand, and walked off with an outrageous bargain. The collapse of the dinar had instilled confidence, not fear. Dealers provoked hilarious bidding wars, certain that with the currency so weak they could never get burnt. Rugs here were not snapped up; they were rescued, taken in, saved. It was an orphan market, and dollar for dollar, the best value carpet buying I had ever seen. As lot followed lot stately Tabrizes, enormous Kermans and marathon runners from Hamadan were thrown down. On the rare occasions when bidding broke the $100 mark, gasps of suspense and excitement would ripple across the room. No bid was too small, and nothing was passed in. It was an unequal contest: a carpet reprise of the Gulf War. But search as I might, nothing surpassed the beauty of the Van Dyke waiting for me, I was sure, in the small shop on Sa'adoun Street. Midhat, however, had chosen his mark, and when a large Iranian Bijar kilim in exciting shades of burnt orange and apricot was held aloft, he raised four fingers and stole it for forty thousand dinars, about $25.

Al-Rashid Street buzzed at *Iftar*, the breaking of the fast. The crowds pouring out of Al Haida Khana Mosque mobbed the hawkers selling dates, who lined its honey-coloured brick and layered mosaic walls. Finding Hussain at the nearby multi-storey car park, I headed back across the Tigris to the offices of Dr Khuder Ahmed ad-Dulemi, editor of *The Baghdad Observer*. Dr Khuder was not a journalist by training, but what he lacked in expertise he made up for with aggression, and throughout the latest crisis the *Observer*'s lively coverage of the antics of the 'strayed dog Butler' and his 'spies' had been essential reading. Ushered into his office I found Dr Khuder at his desk chatting with a friend, a heavy-set man whose leather jacket creaked as he leant over to shake hands.

From a television set in the corner an evil, frog-like voice announced, 'This ... is CNN.'

'Allow me to introduce you to a very famous man of Iraq,' said Dr Khuder, jumping up to offer me a chair. 'Meet Abdul al-Sahdi. The Sheikh with One Million Camels!'

Sheikhs, almost by definition, are interesting. The leather jacket suggested this one was of the wastrel variety, an underemployed groovy Arab prince who owned a fleet of Harley Davidson motorcycles. He was probably president of the Baghdad chapter of the Hell's Angels. Above our heads, Saddam Hussein, the real power in the land, looked down patronisingly from a framed portrait. But one million camels was quite a herd, even for a politically neutered sheikh.

'They call it Operation Desert *Fox!*' said Dr Khuder, spitting on 'fox', a filthy, filthy word. 'But I call it Villains in the Arabian Desert.'

'*Ya' Allah!*' seconded the sheikh, Arabic for 'God help me'.

'They keep talking EYE-rack,' he continued. 'What is EYE-rack? Even when they speak the name of my country it is only to insult me.'

'You Western media! Bad language you are using!' said Dr Khuder, waving a handful of imported magazines at me, then quoting from them. '"*Saddam Hussein must behave.*" What? Is Saddam Hussein a naughty boy to behave? "*Saddam Hussein weasled out.*" They are calling our Saddam a weasel?'

'What is weasel?' asked the sheikh, smoothing his worn, lumpy face as if it was a bedspread.

'An American animal. Like ferret,' the doctor said, determined to stay on track. 'Now! Every country has got army. But Saddam Hussein, has he got army? No. He got "terror arsenal", "world's most sinister weapons". My God, my journalist friend. This is *all* propaganda. Can you imagine, the two of us, sitting here, you and I, having this talk, when suddenly the door is open and these so-called inspectors, these foreign agents, Mossad spy operatives, come into my office, open my drawers? It is very irritating for us. We are not a rug state.'

'Rug state?' I asked, intrigued.

'RuhUUG state,' Dr Khuder enunciated.

'I'm sorry, I don't understand.'

'RU–OH–GUH state!' said Dr Khuder, rightly becoming exasperated.

'Ohhhhh, of course, I see. *Rogue* state.'

'Exactly!' said Dr Khuder, relieved. 'We are not alone. France. Russia. China. Kofi Annan. My God! Even the Pope. All are against this policy. United States is isolated.'

'Back in London, if I went now, I would raise hell on this policy at Hyde Park Speakers' Corner,' said the sheikh, cracking his knuckles.

What a life this sheikh must have, I thought. Park Lane ... Mayfair ... Speakers' Corner? What would a sheikh be doing on a Hyde Park soapbox?

'I was regular there,' he continued, 'during my wrestling days.'

'Mr al-Sahdi was a champion wrestler. He fought in Britain and even World Championship Wrestling USA,' said the doctor. 'His fighting name was The Sheikh with One Million Camels!'

'Also Lion of Babylon,' the sheikh added.

The downsizing of the sheikh to three-ring jester did disappoint me. This whole war with its cartoonish leaders and their respective cheersquads seemed about as convincing as televised professional wrestling. Snatching the remote control, Dr Khuder killed CNN. In his grey woollen vest, white shirt and blue tie he looked every bit the scholar he was, having spent eight years at the School of Oriental and African Studies in London, where he had met the sheikh, who at the time was bouncing off British turnbuckles and arguing the toss on international diplomacy at Hyde Park. Then came the Gulf War and Iraqis like them found it difficult to stay on. Back in Iraq the hard times had begun, with no million camels to fall back on.

'I'm losing weight,' the sheikh complained, looking like a punching bag with the stuffing knocked out.

Dr Khuder was doing slightly better, although due to sanctions his staff had been cut back and the newspaper reduced to a four-page triweekly. The job of an Iraqi newspaper editor must be on par with facing a firing squad, and he kept casting nervous glances at the telephone, as if You-Know-Who might call. Saddam was known to be a voracious reader, spending three hours a day studying the Iraqi press and getting a daily briefing on foreign media reports.

'No, I have never had a phone call from the President of Iraq about any story in the *Observer*,' the doctor said, when I asked him about the pressure. 'When the President of Iraq has an opinion, he will comment on it in a very friendly way. Many times I have come close to him during meetings. He is keen to see his people assume the honour and dignity they deserve.'

The sheikh had spent a quarter of a century in Britain and the United States but, unable to get a visa renewal, he'd left behind his British wife and sixteen-year-old daughter, hoping to return. Seven years later his application was still pending and he had taken an Iraqi wife.

'This is British hospitality?' he said, raising a hand that questioned and condemned. To an Arab the offence was unimaginable, heinous and personal: the sin of inhospitality. Iraqis felt trapped and frustrated by their own culture. Here they were engaged in conversation with a Westerner, the citizen of a country which was part of the grand anti-Iraq conspiracy. They were hospitable despite themselves, all the while wanting to throttle me. This must have doubly frustrated the sheikh, because he knew exactly how to do it. They carried this dilemma like an injury, a sense of impotence which went against the Arab grain and fuelled their defiance.

'Seven thousand inspections are plenty enough!' cried Dr Khuder. 'They could inspect the whole of Russia, Europe and America with such inspections. And they find nothing! So why continue? I will tell you why: to gather more information to give to Israel, or to prepare better maps for targeting their bombs against us, like this latest escapade. Now we are decided. They will inspect us no more! Those days are finished! The Americans are nothing! Mark my words, we will defeat them!'

Returning to the Al-Safafir Market I found Midhat's shutters pulled down, along with those of almost every other shop in the souk. With my vision of a thriving late-night scene shattered, I moped around in the gloomy alleyways until I came upon a shaft of light spilling from a small bric-a-brac store at the end of a cobbled cul-de-sac. Seated outside the shop was a small plump man with liquid, expectant eyes. He resembled a harp seal dressed in a waistcoat and fob watch, waiting for someone to throw him a fish. The shop, which according to his card specialised in 'fancy articles', was about two metres square and cluttered like a madman's attic with inlaid ivory boxes, porcelain Chinamen, aqua enamel vases, busts of Jesus Christ and brass door knockers. On the wall was a portrait of the Queen of Sheba in a racy toga with one breast exposed. There were tiffin carriers from India, a century-old date-stamped samovar, clocks, nautical lanterns, lamps and pots, all hanging on hooks attached to the ceiling beams. Hikmat al-Okaili claimed to be eighty, a descendant of camel-trading Bedouin from the Arabian Peninsula who had come to Baghdad a hundred and fifty years before. His father had started the shop and had bought most of the inventory cheaply during World War I. With this capital, Hikmat had bartered a livelihood for more than fifty years.

'Look at this, my dear,' he said, picking up a copper bowl, kissing it and touching it to his forehead before handing it to me. 'This two hundred years old from the family of the Prophet. See the inscription. Heals sick people.'

As he replaced the holy bowl in its glass cabinet a tall, steel-grey Englishman accompanied by a young ponytailed Arab woman sauntered into the shop. I recognised them from a news conference given the previous evening by Iraq's pugnacious deputy prime minister, Tariq Aziz. The news conference had been crowded with coiffed television reporters accompanied by obedient Arab fixers. One of the fixers was under strict orders to defend a camera position.

'I don't allow anybody to stand here. I fight with them,' he was insisting eagerly to his British boss, who had so many bulging pockets on his commando-style reporter's vest that he resembled a human battery pack. Even the Iraqi officials got into the act of making sure that reporters from the main networks got prime positions. 'Jeremy! Jeremy! Over here,' they cooed. 'Yoo-hoo, Jane! I've got your seat for you.'

The fellow who had just arrived in Hikmat's shop was one of the television reporters. His upper body was dressed in a stylish woollen suit jacket with collar and tie, but from the waist down he wore only tight-fitting blue jeans and runners. This schizophrenic dress style reflected the fact that TV news journalists were always in a hurry, and ever-ready for the next piece to camera, shot from the waist up. Julian was returning to London after covering the bombing, and the nerve-thin Arab girl, with her coloured hair, hiking boots and neck pen, was his assistant. They were hunting for Christmas presents and — presuming that their time was more valuable than anybody else's — commandeered the shop and its owner's attention. Julian was like a honey bee with a taste for small silver boxes. He would pick them up, point at them, finger them and show them to his assistant, buzzing on to the next one to escape Hikmat's Venus flytrap entreaties. When, however, the vendor produced two silver eggs and a marvellous coffee pot engraved with birds in a garden, the buzzing bee was captivated. But the price of $600 stung him.

'No, no. You'll have to do better than that,' he shrieked, adding pointedly to his sidekick, 'I say, why don't we go back to the shop where we bought all those *nice* things?'

'Two hundred!' said the ponytail.

Hikmat looked at her balefully.

'Madam,' he scolded, 'this Esfahan silver. My heart goes tick a tick a tick.'

Then suddenly he was foisting the coffee pot on her and pushing her out the door, as if she was a grenade about to explode.

'Five hundred. Okay! Take it!' he was saying, conceding defeat on his own terms. It was Saddam's foreign policy writ small, the diplomacy of the souk Arab. But to Hikmat's Saddam, the foreigners played George Bush and Margaret Thatcher.

'Now look, old boy,' said Julian with a rehearsed spiel. 'I'm quite interested in your silver eggs, so long as the price is negotiable.'

'*Ya' Aini* [Oh my eyes]. Mistaaar! I don't want you to leave my shop with empty hands,' Hikmat wailed, catching a glass candlestick as it fell from a shelf without shifting his gaze from his customers. The Arab woman had already grabbed the eggs and was weighing them in her hands.

'Madam. Mistaaar, he know me! That is old pieces. That is fifty per cent silver from Iraqi Jewish peoples.'

Iraq's well-established and prosperous Jewish community had long since left the souk, and indeed the country. In the late 1940s, the Zionist movement organised a series of 'rescue operations' to relocate Jews to the new state of Israel from Muslim countries including Yemen, Algeria, Libya, Egypt and Morocco. Codenamed 'Babylon', the operation in Iraq harvested some one hundred and twenty thousand Jews, or about 90 per cent of the community. In March 1950, after negotiations with an undercover Zionist agent, Iraq gave its Jews one year to sell up and leave, confiscating their passports to prevent them ever returning.[14] Picking up the coffee pot and shining it on his paunch like Aladdin's lamp, Hikmat persisted. 'This is 95 per cent silver, Jewish! I give you three pieces, four hundred dollars.'

'That's quite all right, I'll survive,' said Julian, blowing his pressure tactics somewhat by saying he had a flight to catch. There were no flights in or out of Baghdad, except the ones dropping bombs.

'Mistaaar, he knows me. He will come back,' Hikmat assured me, shooing away a beggar who had come to the door. Five minutes later, as prophesied, Julian and his helper returned. Hikmat, now in a fever, began wrapping the pot and eggs.

'No, no, no,' said Julian, rubbing irritably at his buttoned-down collar.

Outside I could hear the shutters on the few remaining open shops being pulled down. Julian and his partner had taken the pieces and were conversing between themselves in secret French.

Julian (holding the pot): It's a nice little jewel of a thing.
Assistant (holding the eggs): For God's sake, this is worse than one of your pieces to camera. Make up your mind what you want!

But Julian couldn't help himself. Taking up a magnifying glass he inspected a Yemeni silver filigree brush, allegedly inset with a black stone from Mecca. Cigarette in mouth, the ponytail squinted, picked up the silver pot and took it outside into the fading light.

'It's covered in yellow spots,' she said.

'No, madam, no. Not like that,' Hikmat protested, grappling with her for his precious pot.

Then, without warning, the two of them exploded in thick, elongated, and quite possibly obscene Arabic.

'*Off* they go,' said Julian in a sing-song.

As a long ash fell from the woman's cigarette, the wail of a muezzin taunted the deserted bazaar, and Hikmat returned inside, swapping places with Julian who went out to huddle with his fixer. Having conferred, they marched back into the shop and recommenced hostilities.

'Three hundred for both,' the Arab girl said, referring to the pot and the eggs.

'Madam,' said Hikmat, 'you cut my heart.'

'We'll cut your heart and eat it,' Julian replied. I swear that is exactly what he said. 'Three hundred. My final offer.'

'Mistaaar. If you have a piece for that price, I will buy from you,' Hikmat responded.

Fed up with the machinations of the wily trader, Julian produced three crisp hundred dollar notes, planted them in Hikmat's palm, and marched the girl out the door. When they had gone the old man began closing up for the day.

'My child, she wait for me. My daughter, she wait for me,' he said.

I asked if three hundred was enough.

'It's enough. Enough for today,' he replied, confiding that the pot had been on the shelf for about ten years and the eggs were from his father's time. Then, taking a small silver box and wrapping it in a scarf, he headed off into the night.

21

Babylon

*Therefore its name is called Babel, because there
the Lord confused the language of all the earth*

— GENESIS 11:9

One of the world's first great cities grew up on a marshy
stretch of the Euphrates River on the western side of the
Mesopotamian plain, about a hundred kilometres south of modern
Baghdad. Its inhabitants called it Bab-Ilu, meaning 'of the gods'.
The Hebrews called it Babel. We call it Babylon.

Here, in the fertile lands between the Tigris and Euphrates,
tradition tells us the Garden of Eden was located. The Book of
Genesis relates that it was Nimrod the Hunter, a descendant of
Noah, who began construction of the city in the aftermath of the
Great Flood, which submerged all the lands between the two rivers
and beached the Ark on the side of Mount Ararat, eight hundred
kilometres to the north. After the flood the Mesopotamians rebuilt.

'They had brick for stone, and they had asphalt for mortar,' the
Bible says, referring to the Babylonians' use of natural deposits of
asphalt which bubbled to the surface as oil and, mixed with sand
and gravel, congealed in the hot sun. They used it to build highways
as well, but the bitumen road on which Hussain and I now sped
south, accompanied by Salar, was of more recent vintage. It slid past

willow groves, police checkpoints and low-slung whitewashed buildings. Beside it boys thrashed donkeys and powerline towers loomed over the salt marshes like giant steel centurions. There was no sign marking the 33rd parallel of latitude, but when we came to a mobile surface-to-air missile-launcher parked by the road I guessed we were near it. The launcher was raised at a sharp angle, ready to fire at American and British warplanes which flew scores of sorties every day, patrolling the Southern No-Fly Zone almost directly overhead.

In August 1992 President Bush, acting without the approval of the United Nations Security Council, banned Iraqi aircraft flying south of the 33rd parallel or north of the 36th and ordered his air force to patrol the 'air exclusion zone'. The idea was to protect Shia Muslims in the south and Kurds in the north from Saddam's predations. In the days after Operation Desert Fox the cat and mouse game involving American and British pilots and Iraqi air defences had intensified. Iraqi gunners could expect instant national celebrity if they brought a plane down. It was even dangerous to stand close to mobile launchers like the one we had seen, because laser-guided missiles fired by American and British pilots were constantly destroying them. But unlike the Gulf War, the Shias and Kurds had not revolted during 'Desert Fox'. They still blamed Bush for encouraging them to revolt in 1991, only to stand by and watch as Saddam's Republican Guard slaughtered tens, possibly hundreds of thousands, of people. All too late, Bush realised that if Saddam was overthrown, Iran might exploit the disorder to seize Shia-majority southern Iraq.

The Kurds — tough, Sunni Muslim mountain-dwellers whose language was similar to Persian — also had bitter memories of the Bush Administration. Early in his presidency on 16 March 1988 Iraqi Air Force planes bombarded the Kurdish-majority city of Halabja with mustard gas and nerve agents. The gas, which witnesses said smelt like burnt onions, killed an estimated five thousand people, mainly civilians, some of whom died laughing and dancing in the hysterical spasms induced by the chemical weapons.[15]

Apart from Iran, Iraq is the only country with a Shia Muslim majority. Two-thirds of Iraqis are Shias, half the population of Baghdad likewise, and the sect's holiest places, such as Kerbala where the Prophet's grandson Hussain is buried, are in Iraq. But whereas Iranian Muslims are Persians, Iraq's leaders see their land as an Arab country and throughout history have doubted the loyalty of Iraqi Shias. This ancient mistrust made a democratic Iraq almost impossible to envisage. In a speech to his troops departing for the Iran frontline, Saddam reminded them of certain historical 'facts', claiming that the Shias had contributed to the conquest of Babylon by Persia's Cyrus the Great in the sixth century BC, more than eleven hundred years before Islam was established. 'They have co-operated with the Jews to destroy Babylon and co-operated with them to harm Iraq and the Arab nation,' he said.[16]

Almost two thousand years before Christ, the first great city of Babylon began rising beside the Euphrates. As well as being an important military and administrative centre, it became a wellspring of religious and artistic inquiry, and it was here that astrology was invented. In 1760 BC the statesman Hamurabi developed and codified one of the world's first legal systems. Babylon was also one of the first major weaving centres.

'All the classical world knew and admired Babylonian carpets,' wrote Arthur Urbane Dilley, although there is some debate as to whether Babylonian weavings were carpets or tapestries. Whatever they were, Pliny praised them in his *Natural History*, Nero bought them for use as table covers, and the Hebrews used them as tabernacle embellishments as recorded in the Old Testament.[17]

The city's fortunes waxed and waned, but in 605 BC the great warrior-king Nebuchadnezzar II began massive public works to revive its former glory, extending the city across to the west bank of the Euphrates and constructing the great stone terraces known as the Hanging Gardens of Babylon. The Babylonian historian and priest Berosus, writing in the third century BC, described how Nebuchadnezzar had 'built lofty stone terraces, made a vista as if of mountains, and planted all sorts of trees' because his wife Amytis was pining for the mountains of her native Media.[18] Orchards, grape vines, and fig and olive trees graced the city, whose grandeur was capped by the famous Ziggurat of Etemenaki, more commonly known as the Tower of Babel, which rose almost ninety metres above the plain. Rebuilding the fortifications, palaces and canals of the world's largest city, covering an area of about a thousand hectares, required a vast labour force which was provided when Nebuchadnezzar sacked Jerusalem and shipped his Jewish captives to Babylon, where they would remain for almost fifty years until freed by Cyrus the Great in 538 BC. The Persians appropriated the city's arts, including carpet weaving. Alexander the Great intended making Babylon his capital, but weakened by his long expedition to Afghanistan and India, his return was marked by tragedy when he died there in 323 BC, aged thirty-three.

Having turned down my request to talk to the soldiers manning the mobile SAM launcher, Salar had insisted we drive directly to Babylon because 'only Babylon is mentioned in your program'. The gates of the great city stood before us now, conveniently situated across a car park. It was over a decade since I had beheld the majesty of the famed Ishtar Gate, named in honour of the Babylonian goddess of fertility, love and war. Clad in glazed tiles of ultramarine, its wondrous procession of bulls and fanciful creatures guarded the city and its presiding deity, Marduk. It was an amazing sight, especially given that I had never been to Iraq. The entire Ishtar Gate stands in the Pergamon Museum in Berlin.

In June 1887 a German archaeologist, Robert Koldewey, visited Babylon and 'saw a number of fragments of enamelled brick reliefs, of which I took several with me to Berlin'.[19]

Twelve years later Koldewey returned with a well-funded expedition. Over the next thirteen years, he would excavate the city's major features including its main ceremonial entrance, the Ishtar Gate; its principal temple, the Esagila, dedicated to Marduk; and the great processional way, trodden by such giants as kings Nebuchadnezzar and Darius, and Alexander. The twelve-metre high Ishtar Gate and processional way which linked it to the temple were decorated with colourful glazed ceramic tiles featuring lions, winged bulls, and the horned, fork-tongued walking serpents called *sirrush*, which boasted the front legs of a cheetah and the hind legs of a raptorial bird with powerful claws and great horny scales.[20]

Herodotus claimed the walls of Babylon were fifty-six miles long, eighty feet thick and over three hundred feet high. Although the city had never been lost, it was completely buried by centuries of Mesopotamian mud. With war clouds gathering in Europe, and Iraq a possible battlefield, Koldewey found a convenient excuse to remove a huge section of the ruins, including the entire Ishtar Gate, to Berlin.

'We were cramped for space,' he later wrote of the sprawling site, 'and could not spread out the pieces.'[21]

So moribund was Iraq after hundreds of years under Ottoman rule that its treasures were fair game for bespectacled European looters. Iraq has repeatedly demanded that museums in Britain and Germany return these important artefacts, but to no avail. In 2001, Britain signed the 1972 UNESCO convention on cultural property, but Germany remained outside it.[22]

In place of the Ishtar Gate built for King Nebuchadnezzar II's city over two thousand years before stood a shoddy replica guarded by a gnarled, stubbly old man, who looked as if he'd been there since the Germans stole the original gate. The replica's colours were garish, the sirrush unbalanced and unglazed. Marduk had lost his protectors. Apart from Salar, the gatekeeper and me, there was not another living soul in the place.

Starting our walk up the kilometre-and-a-half-long Street of Processions, we passed the new Ishtar Gate and headed uphill to the main palace. Our arrival was a melancholy affair. The reconstructed edifice, with its crenellated towers, was somehow flimsy, like something you might expect to see on a Hollywood movie lot. The walls of the palace rose some twenty metres high, most of it a cheap restoration built on the original shoulder-high foundations. Even here, Saddam's cult was inescapable. Every new brick laid during the Iran–Iraq War was stamped with the words: 'Built in the era of the victorious Saddam Hussein, the great defender of Iraq and its glory'. Saddam often compared himself to Nebuchadnezzar, especially in the late king's antipathy towards the Persians, and at Babylon a billboard depicted the two men and posters proclaimed: 'From Nebuchadnezzar to Saddam Hussein, Babylon invokes its glories on the path of jihad and glorious development'. But both the Hanging Gardens and the Tower of Babel had defied the efforts of archaeologists to positively identify them, despite Saddam's offer of a million-dollar prize to anyone who could restore life to the gardens.

After Alexander's death, the city had fallen into decay, local villagers carrying off the bricks to build themselves new homes. On the walls of the old city, large animal reliefs were visible, but the Lion of Babylon — carved from a single block of basalt, on which Ishtar rode — had been locked away. Near the main palace stood the artificial mound that some scholars believe is the ruin of the Tower of Babel. The original tower, as recorded in the Old Testament and recreated by the sixteenth-century Flemish artist Pieter Bruegel the Elder, was a seven-storey ziggurat, with a sloping ramp spiralling around it to the top. The marvellous structure was a credit to human organisation and endeavour, but God didn't like it.

And the Lord said, 'Indeed the people are one and they all have one language ... now nothing that they propose to do will be withheld from them ... Come, let Us go down and there confuse their language, that they may not understand one another's speech.' So the Lord scattered them abroad from there over the face of all the earth, and they ceased from building the city.[23]

From Gilgamesh — hero of the Sumerian epic who sought immortality in vain — to Alexander, the curse of Babylon was reserved for the arrogant. Even Berlin was destroyed, but the Ishtar Gate survived.

On the Mediterranean island of Patmos you can enter the cave where John the Apostle sweated out the prophecy that became the Book of Revelation. John saw the Euphrates dry up, and unclean spirits leaping like frogs from the mouths of dragons, the beast, and the false prophet all gathered at the place called Armageddon, and Babylon drank from the cup of God's wrath, and every island fell away, and the mountains were not found.[24] Carried by an angel to a wilderness, John met a woman sitting on a scarlet beast, the Great Harlot with whom all the kings of the earth had fornicated, and on whose forehead was written:

MYSTERY,
BABYLON THE GREAT,
THE MOTHER OF HARLOTS AND OF THE
ABOMINATIONS OF THE EARTH

A golden hour settled on the plain near sunset and the date palm groves seemed to sigh as we left Babylon. Not far from the old city's gates, we turned off the road and, at my request, made our way into a village called Qaddassiya to conduct a random sample of local opinion. The rains having failed, the farmers of the area had moved their plots closer to the Euphrates, an old survival technique. As we entered the village, we encountered the local civil militia, gathered in a circle of chairs with Kalashnikovs resting on their knees. The wholly unexpected arrival of a foreigner brought them immediately to their feet, and blood-thickened voices filled the air.

'By our souls, and by our blood, we will sacrifice ourselves to Saddam Hussein,' they cried, raising their guns.

The average age of Saddam's true believers must have been sixty. They were farmers by day, and seemed to believe an American-led invasion was imminent.

'We are not going to move. You will not shake us. We love our president,' they repeated, then confounded me by extending an invitation to dinner. But it had been a long day, and pleading a pressing commitment in the capital, we returned to Baghdad.

Back at the Al-Rashid Hotel, the Christmas tree in the foyer glowed quiet and bright, and the mosaic of George Bush's face which covered the floor of the entrance got another unavoidable trampling. It was the morning of my departure from Iraq, and before having my luggage sealed for the roadtrip to the Jordanian border, I returned to Sa'adoun Street. There, I was greatly relieved to find the Van Dyke where I had left it, unsold on top of the pile in the carpet shop. It remained perfect from any angle, a lost sheep that had strayed far from Bukhara and was about to embark on another migration. Plunging into negotiations, I was having difficulty reaching my target price of $100. No matter how much I pleaded, cajoled, threatened or charmed, the merchant stubbornly refused my demands for a 30 per cent discount. You would have thought it was a government-run hard currency 'free' shop, not a private carpet store. The best buy of my inglorious career as a collector was about to slip from my grasp.

With my life in carpets flashing before me, and the vendor folding up Van Dyke's hanky, I was seized by a vision of a tall, oddly dressed Englishman juggling a pair of silver eggs. Taking a crisp hundred dollar note, I slapped it hard into the merchant's palm, seized the Van Dyke and hurried off down Sa'adoun Street, too afraid to look behind in case he was giving chase. But as Hussain fired up the Chevy, I sneaked a glance across my shoulder and saw the merchant leaning on his doorway. He was smiling.

At the Information Ministry, Elham showed up with one of her sons, apparently hoping the display would warrant a substantial bonus, and Salar slipped me the latest copy of *The Baghdad Observer*. It was a nice gesture, or so I thought.

'Use it as an envelope,' he whispered, meaning that I should conceal a big tip inside the newspaper and return it to him.

As an official of the ministry sealed my bags, I perused the main noticeboard where statements and advisories were pinned, just to make sure I wasn't missing anything. A small notice caught my eye. Headed 'List of items not allowed to be taken out with departures', it was an inventory of things which it was illegal to export from Iraq. At number seventeen, my eyes froze.

Carpets, whether locally manufactured or foreign made, except for those which have been bought and paid for in hard currency from free shops or have been imported by the beneficiary in accordance with documents approved by the Foreign Ministry.

PART SIX

TAJIKISTAN

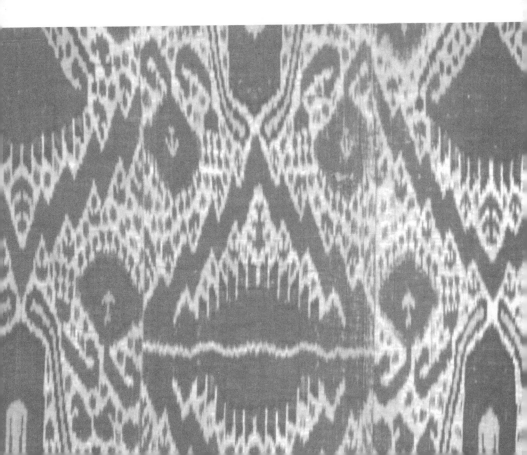

22

Tragic Tajiks

'Welcome to the New World Order,' said the aid official, parting the curtains in his overheated office and finding no view, only the leaden clouds that had grounded my flight, enforcing an extended stay in the Tajikistan capital, Dushanbe.

'Fifty thousand dead in a civil war,' Gerard Viguie continued. 'Half the country a restricted area. A network of industrial graveyards. Social fabric damaged. Soviet safety net gone. Food deficit. No free market. State monopoly and mafia control.'

He could have added 'landlocked and bankrupt', but the French director of the World Food Program's Dushanbe office was just warming up. Tajikistan, formerly the Tajik Soviet Socialist Republic, was Big Brother's orphan child, yet to find foster parents. Once it was the Old Silk Road equivalent of Singapore, the place through which all bartered things flowed. Now, as my guidebook described it, Tajikistan was 'a curiously incomplete country, much less than the sum of its parts'.[1]

It was April 1999, and people still recalled with horror that terrible day, 9 September 1991, when Tajikistan gained its independence.

'When the Soviet Union collapsed it was as if somebody blew a whistle and everybody stopped doing whatever they were doing. They're still waiting for the whistle to blow again,' said Gerard, burrowing into a pile of reports about food insecurity. The standard of living, a report just in said, was 'extremely low'. The annual per capita income had not yet passed three figures. There was rampant inflation and a lot of cotton, a useful commodity if you could succeed in transporting it. A seriously ill Dushanbe resident probably stood more chance of surviving by lying on the pavement outside the hospital than by going inside. Cartographers had barely noticed Tajikistan's appearance on the world map, and already people were discussing its imminent disappearance.

My intended destination, Afghanistan, may have been at war for twenty years, but Tajikistan had been suffering Moscow's torture for most of the twentieth century. In Stalin's cunning design of co-dependency, a pen might be made in Estonia and the ink cartridges in the Urals; bullet casings in Ukraine, the gunpowder in Georgia. A factory in Siberia made right-footed shoes, and only right-footed ones; the left-footed shoes were made somewhere in the western Soviet Union.[2] Stalin had played similar tricks with the borders of the constituent republics. As a result, most Tajiks found themselves living in Uzbekistan and large concentrations of Uzbeks were to be found in Tajikistan. Now, warlords and Islamists had infiltrated the Tajik government, bringing it into conflict with its Central Asian neighbours.

The good news was that after seven decades cloaked in the shroud of communism Tajikistan was a democracy with deep entrepreneurial roots. The Tajiks were descended from the Sogdians, whose city of Penjikent, some eighty kilometres from Samarkand, was the seventh-century equivalent of Wall Street. The bad news was that Penjikent was now in ruins, and at their very first presidential elections the Tajiks had voted for the leader of the old Communist Party. The branching route to reform was potholed and littered with dead ends. According to the complimentary newspapers pinned up Soviet-style on the public noticeboards, President Emomali Rahmonov had called 'an urgent meeting' to discuss ways of preventing a renegade army commander from neighbouring Uzbekistan, Colonel Mahmud

Khudaiberdiyev, from entering the capital. Rahmonov's control over the country was so patchy that he was laughingly referred to as the 'Mayor of Dushanbe'. Neighbouring countries had begun laying minefields and blowing up roads leading to the troubled republic.

Central Asia was awash with oil and gas. Proven oil reserves stood at up to thirty billion barrels, almost 3 per cent of the world total, and there were the trillions of cubic feet of natural gas, amounting to 7 per cent of global reserves.[3] But the poor Tajiks had virtually none. There were supposedly some gem deposits, but Tajik engineers had decided instead to focus on hydro-electric power, melting snow from the high Pamirs to run turbines. All this, while in the capital most residents could not get running water, let alone electricity. What chance of success did any of these grand schemes have?

The Tajiks were accustomed to coming last since Soviet times, when their per capita income was the lowest of all the SSRs. Now, a third of the republic's gross domestic product was drug-related. Helpfully corrupt bureaucrats were facilitating the transport of heroin from Afghanistan through neighbouring countries to feed the voracious appetites of addicts in Russia and Europe. Tajik diplomats had been caught carrying large amounts of narcotics in their diplomatic bags. A report by the Brussels-based International Crisis Group found that the drug trade was 'at the centre of a contest over the very essence of political order in at least Tajikistan and parts of Kyrgyzstan'.[4] Perhaps that explained the almost narcotic state of nostalgia for the Soviet past, when Moscow provided half the state budget as a cash subsidy and you at least got paid for doing nothing.

'The Soviet Union was the good old days,' said Gerard, closing his too-depressing books. 'Now the streets are full of unemployed ballerinas, concert pianists and pilots. Farmers are fighting to remain collectivised. Landslides are a job creation project.'

On Rudaki Prospekt, as Gerard had said, tutuless ballerinas pirouetted along the city's main boulevard, pianists busked on battery-operated organs at street corners, and pilots drove trolley buses. The main street also boasted 'Univermag', a sordid godown of smuggled household junk, and near it were more private businesses selling cheese, wurst and other delicacies imported from Europe, but past their use-by date. In a private art gallery they were selling — selling! — busts of Lenin. Picking one up, I was shocked by its deceptive lightness. There was also a carpet bearing the knotted image of Leonid Brezhnev. What were the artists trying to say?

The vodka, of course, was cheap and plentiful, not bad quality either. Eighty-five per cent Muslim-majority Tajikistan raised a collective 80 per cent proof toast to Russia's greatest invention and drank to forget the hungry years of freedom. Among the biggest tipplers were the country's statisticians. Experts trained in the art of national self-delusion, they had miraculously produced an unemployment rate of 2.4 per cent. Surely that was the *employment* rate?

The Hotel Tajikistan embodied the unique ennui of the socialist service establishment. Finding the particular restaurant serving your particular meal on a particular day was a treasureless hunt. Breakfast was in the basement bar, sometimes. Requiring a coupon, it consisted of yoghurt and sour *blinchikis* served on a genuine imitation snakeskin tablecloth. Dinner was on the ground floor near the lobby bar; I never found lunch. The horsemeat sausages were vile, the waiters refused to put meals on the room bill and were plagued by a mysterious lack of change, and one morning no one seemed to know where the coffee had gone. Yet there was something remarkably homely about the place, a sort of 'We're not trying anymore' bonhomie. The floor lady happily listened to my execrable Russian, handled my laundry and made endless samovars of *chai*. The hotel's rooms had balconies overlooking the snowcapped mountains to the south or, like mine, looked across Lenin Park, in which stood a statue of Vladimir Ilyich, eyes fixed on a future nobody else could see.

Beneath his gaze, flowing past the pastel-coloured, neo-classical buildings, was a confluence of Oriental and European bloodlines. The country's six million citizens were two-thirds Tajik, who spoke a dialect of Persian; one-quarter Turkic-speaking Uzbek; and the rest Russian, who had emigrated during Soviet rule. Old silver beards, dressed in turbans and bright Central Asian longcoats, stood out in the crowd at Barakat Market, the city's main bazaar. Trolley buses rattled past, their long insect-like antennae kissing the sparking gauze that hung above the streets, reviving fond memories of Omar Sharif's heart attack in *Doctor Zhivago*. The street signs were in Russian too, even though only a minority spoke Russian and the official script was Arabic. Hammer-and-sickle motifs had been left on public buildings, no doubt in the hope that all would be forgiven and that the communists would return.

One building of almost vibrating significance was the Hajji Yakoub Mosque and madrassa. Its turquoise tiles and golden domes commemorated a mullah who had fled to Afghanistan to escape persecution during the Soviet years. In 1989 there had been only one hundred and sixty mosques in all Central Asia. Four years later there were ten thousand and the number of madrassas had grown tenfold.[5] The teething problems of new nations had led many to conclude that Islam rather than tourism was the answer, and there were envious murmurs about the new freedoms the Afghans were enjoying under the Taliban. Since the militia's victories just across the border in northern Afghanistan, Muslim guerillas with Central Asian ambitions had been able to set up training camps at Hairatan, within a few hours' drive of cradles of Islamic civilisation like Samarkand and Bukhara.

'From Hairatan they can see the lights of Termez,' the Afghan ambassador in Delhi, Masood Khalili, had told me. 'They're dreaming of Central Asia. It's a golden opportunity to follow the white flag to Bukhara and the Ferghana Valley. Then they will take out their Islamometers and bad luck for anybody who fails.'

With one-third of its Cabinet in the hands of the Islamists, the Tajik government was doing little to prevent Muslim rebels fighting the regimes in neighbouring countries, such as the Islamic Movement of Uzbekistan, from operating on its soil. Tajikistan was so poor that it could not guard its borders, nor provide a modicum of security within them. Warlords like Rahman Sanginov, popularly known as 'Hitler', still controlled large swathes of territory, which they ran as personal fiefs, preying on travellers and kidnapping foreigners for ransom.[6]

It may have been difficult to buy a loaf of bread, but stealing one was easy. The gun was a 'coping mechanism'. In an unbroken chain of despotism the Tajiks had first come under the Imperial Tsars, then the Communist Tsars, and now the Crime Tsars. On a busy street a police car flashed down a late-model Mercedes sedan without number plates. As the policeman approached the vehicle the driver stepped out, a burly, heavily accessorised man in a polo-neck sweater and suit who reeked of crime. Smiling widely, the two men fell into a fond bear hug. There was no longer an official curfew in Dushanbe, yet only fools and suicidals stayed out after dark. Armed men roamed the streets in stolen cars looking for fair game. Even my local contact, Ahmed Muslim, a former mujahideen commander and now military attaché at the Afghan Embassy, had been held up several times.

With his billiard-bald head warmed by a Lenin cap, his French woollen overcoat and his Japanese car, Mr Muslim seemed quite cosmopolitan for a man who had been a guerilla fighter since his teens. Powerfully built, he had risen to command the three thousand-strong Seventh Regiment of the National Guard under Ahmad Shah Massoud, and later was in charge of Massoud's personal security. He had twice been wounded in action and his troops were the last to leave Kabul ahead of the victorous Taliban in September 1996. His speciality was anti-personnel and anti-tank mines, of which he claimed personally to have laid more than a thousand. Mr Muslim was liaising with Massoud's people in Afghanistan to arrange for a chopper to fly me into the small pocket of land in northern Afghanistan still under Massoud's control, but the weather remained obstinately stormy, too rough to risk one of the four ageing Russian helicopters which now made up Massoud's 'air force'. To pacify me, he offered a city tour, just like the good old Intourist days. We would experience the jewel in the crown of Dushanbe's pulsating nightlife, and an evening of rare cultural richness, by dining at The Elite Restaurant and Bar, Tajikistan's finest.

Needing to be back at the hotel by nightfall, we left at three in the afternoon. Cruising Dushanbe's dejected streets, Mr Muslim's hi-tech tape deck provided a form of aural Prozac. The ex-guerilla found solace in the songs of 1970s California rockers The Eagles. 'Take It Easy' and 'Tequila Sunrise' had him gently tapping his fingers on the steering wheel, and singing choruses — 'Such a lovely place, such a lovely place'. Cat Stevens's vocals on 'Lady D'Arbanville', however, appeared to unsettle Mr Muslim, who punched the stop button just as the singer began to growl, 'Though in your grave you lie'. After that he nervously kept one eye trained on the rearview mirror. The maps in the glove compartment listed mausoleums, glaciers, places of scenic beauty, and a section of road east of Dushanbe marked with the warning sign 'Danger! Roadmines between Komsomolabad and Rusan'. Mr Muslim had taken a personal interest in that one, circling it on the map.

In the bloody free-for-all that followed the Soviet Union's collapse, Islamic rebels and regional clan leaders in Tajikistan vied for power. Replete with vast armouries looted from Soviet Army bases, they fought over land, factories and cars, even chasing the Russians out of Dushanbe for a time, before a peace deal was signed in 1997. Even then some rebels kept fighting. The Tajik government had asked its old comrades in Moscow for twenty-five thousand troops to stabilise the situation. Unsatisfied merely with stabilising, the Russians had embarked on 'saving' the republic from all-pervasive Islamic terror. Unveiling his 'Eternal Bearhug' policy, Boris Yeltsin said the Afghan–Tajik border was, 'in effect, Russia's'.[7] By the mid-1990s Moscow was once again providing more than half the Tajik government's budget,[8] but had to pay big bonuses to encourage its troops to serve in Tajikistan. Given the perilous state of food security, and the complaints of its soldiers about the lack of nightlife, the Russians had further widened their role to include the running of restaurants.

The Elite was owned and operated by the 201st Motorised Rifle Division of the Russian Army. As we arrived another customer was leaving, chased out by a Russian soldier wielding a rifle butt. Feeling our way in the murkiness, past quadrilateral shoulders and décolletage, we reached one of the tables arranged around the dance floor. Shot glasses were placed prominently before us, but as an Islamic freedom fighter Mr Muslim felt more comfortable with beer. As the strobe light cranked up, the action began. Peroxide blondes in sequined ball gowns carried decorated war heroes onto the dance floor. These men of iron slumped like beached bull walruses across their partner's shoulders but the girls could take it, guiding them through the waltzes and polkas and wiping the occasional string of spittle off their gowns. It was difficult, but extremely necessary, to hide our awe and admiration. Everyone was heavily armed and in the deathly light of the nightclub even a convivial look might be misconstrued. We drank on after sunset, minding our own business.

Emboldened by this adventure I was tempted to admire another highlight of Dushanbe's nightlife, the International Casino, whose golden façade and flashing lights beckoned from the building opposite the Hotel Tajikistan. The recently established casino was a joint venture between a militia commander and Turkish investors. In a paternal moment, Mr Muslim had warned me of a local superstition.

'The Tajiks believe that anyone who even looks at that building will lose all their money,' he said.

The gambling Turks were no mere foreign investors; they were cultural ambassadors, sent to revive ancient links. The word Turk comes from *Tu'kiu*, the name given to the nomadic tribes on China's western periphery, who in the sixth century founded an empire stretching from Mongolia to the Black Sea. Now the Tajiks were getting Turkish blowback, with Ankara pushing joint ventures and cultural ties. Turkish airlines served the region, Turkish television was beamed in by satellite, Islamic missionaries from Turkey were building schools and providing social services, and Turkish theme parks were being opened. Nobody had told the Turks that most Tajiks spoke Persian.

It was after midnight when I made my dash to the casino, to be welcomed into the arms of post-Marxian Mammon by salmon-coloured carpets, cheesy Muzak and bull-necked bouncers packing heat. Under incandescent lights and security cameras young women in black miniskirts, waistcoats and collapsing stilettos thrust out their breasts, as if by order. The dealers were all Turkish, governed by pitboss Mehmet from Izmir, whose hip-hugging slacks, psychedelic cummerbund and green velour jacket set the tone. Mehmet had taken a Russian girl, Yelena, under his wing.

'You look tired, Yelena,' he told her, affecting a cheery concern.

'That's because I haven't had a day off for three months,' came her bloodless reply.

'She's a really nice kid,' he explained.

At the tables, stiff-backed Russians, confused Tajiks and worldly Turks defied the local taboos, shepherding herds of plastic chips — a throwback to their nomadic pastoralist days — towards the dealers. The casino's designers had installed searchlights at strategic points around the gaming room which blinded the gamblers and allowed the dealers to get away with murder. One minute, a happy Tajik man next to me at the roulette wheel was celebrating a windfall; the next, he was gone without trace. The croupier denied all knowledge of anyone fitting his description, even though the missing Tajik was the only person I had seen smiling all night.

Mehmet, who was fresh from a gambling cruise out of Kusadasi, took a shine to me and, taking the absent Tajik's chair, shared a few trade secrets.

'I heartily recommend number fifteen and number forty-one,' he said. 'Take both together.'

But when he pointed to the numbered plastic tags swinging from the waitresses' hips, I realised he was not talking about roulette. After exchanging e-mail addresses with him — turkish.pitboss@yahoo.com — I returned to the hotel, sharing a ride in a groaning lift with several heavily inebriated Russian soldiers. Overpowering me with garlic and vodka-laced breath, they insisted on shoving plates of boiled chicken in my face. Two floors of the hotel were occupied by the 201st Motorised Rifle Division and the soldiers alighted on the second. On my floor, the seventh, unsavoury characters conducted furtive conversations with underage girls. The *babushka* handed me my key with a leer and offered not tea but vodka. Once Rottweilers of the public morality in Soviet times, even the floor ladies had been bought off by the new free market degradation.

Unable to sleep I turned to my guidebook, which reported 'nasty incidents that have occurred in elevators and corridors, specifically in the Hotel Tajikistan. Do not advertise the fact that you are a foreigner, and keep your door locked at all times.'[9] How had I missed this advice before? Alarmed, I went to the door, peeking through the crack at the gloomy corridor. Surly, leather-jacketed men were lurking outside several rooms and the babushka had left her post. The book was right. It was a jungle out there. Locking the door, I read on.

If you do have to go out at night, order a taxi and arrange to be picked up at your hotel. Don't try to flag down a car on the road as it's unlikely that anyone with decent intentions will stop. On our night of arrival, not knowing any better, we approached a battered old Lada stopped at a traffic light, only to speedily retreat when we saw that the driver was absorbed in trying to jam a cartridge into the revolver in his hands ... Seek advice from the US Embassy in Dushanbe about the security situation before travelling outside the capital.

Being unable to sleep had its advantages. I was alert and ready when the crack of automatic weapons fire lacerated the street below. The shooting had come from just outside the casino, but by the time I reached the balcony there remained only the slushing sound of car tyres passing in the rain. Next morning several bullet holes in the plate glass windows of the hotel lobby confirmed that it had been no backfiring car. But a failed coup? A heist perpetrated on the gambling den? Muslim lads in high spirits celebrating the arrival of the latest trainload of vodka? It was just Tajikistan. I would never know.

23

A Warlord's Holiday

'It is commander's helicopter!' said the mechanic, throwing a coil of solder and another worn-out part onto the grass beside the runway of Dushanbe's combined military and civilian airport. They were forming a pile, these parts, and the majority of the engine's grease must have been on his hands. Like an evil mosquito with a long-barrelled machine gun protruding beneath the cockpit, the decrepit Soviet-built Mi-17 chopper squatted among the rotting hulks of disused aircraft like a sinister prop from a *Mad Max* film, a scrofulous insect shedding its skin. Inside, heavy drapes and two enormous red velvet-covered chairs recalled a funeral parlour. The ground crew had washed the aircraft — in aviation fuel — which spilled generously over the fuselage when a bowser truck decoupled prematurely. Pinned to the rear bulkhead was a red and blue Baluchi prayer rug, beneath which an elderly Tajik woman was blubbering a stream of Koranic incantations. A liquor cabinet — installed by General Dostum before the chopper was captured by Massoud's forces — was empty. As a heaving starter motor cajoled spluttering engines and drooping rotor blades, the shuddering behemoth clawed its way into the air and flung us towards Afghanistan.

It was the beginning of Islam's most important festival, the three day *Eid al-Adha*, or Feast of Sacrifice. I had been invited to spend the holiday with Ahmad Shah Massoud at his refuge in the remote

Hindu Kush, where he was holding out against the numerically superior forces of the Taliban. The general was waiting for me at his military headquarters at Taloqan in north-eastern Takhar province, from where we would fly on to the alpine retreat of Farkhar, on the upper reaches of the Taloqan River. As the chopper rode the bumpy thermals we crossed the immense valley of the Darya-ye Panj, a tributary of the Amu Darya which formed the border and writhed through a lichen-coloured landscape awaiting the annual thaw and deluge from the Pamirs. Moving along a valley on the Afghan side, the chopper flew low under Taliban radar, hugging the rolling hills until the pine tops of Taloqan came into view, and the pilot put us down on a football field among a scattering tribe of wild children.

Massoud had been fighting for a quarter of a century now, beginning with 'two dozen men, seventeen rifles and a hundred and fifty dollars in cash' and ending pretty much back where he started in the mountainous north-east of Afghanistan. One of the few mujahideen commanders who refused the comfortable option of exile after the Soviet invasion, he had stubbornly stood his ground on his home turf in the Panjshir Valley until the Russians had gone, and the legend of the 'Lion of Panjshir' was born. The name had a special resonance for the people of Panjshir, which means 'five lions', named after a group of favourite sons who are still honoured for their remarkable labours under Sultan Mahmud of Ghazni a thousand years ago. Massoud's capture of Kabul in 1992 was his crowning achievement, and by 1996 *Asiaweek* magazine was listing him among its '50 Most Powerful People in Asia'.

'An analytical, rational thinker renowned for his personal courage and commitment to Afghan independence,' his entry read. 'Occasionally tends to underestimate the strength of his enemies.'[10]

Certainly, he had underestimated the Taliban, who, on 26 September 1996, had chased him out of Kabul and into the hills.

'If he gives the order [to evacuate Kabul] one hour later, he doesn't get out alive,' The Gopher had told me in Islamabad, spilling cookie crumbs in excitement as he recalled the moment.

In April 1999, outnumbered two to one, Massoud was regrouping and waiting for cracks to appear in the Taliban's unity. The holiday at Farkhar, where former king Zahir Shah once hunted deer and trout, would be a time for planning, rest and reflection before the long and bloody summer ahead.

Kabul might be Afghanistan's largest city and Kandahar its de facto capital, but provincial Taloqan held Afghanistan's seat at the United Nations. Women in billowing, ghost-like chaderi strained to remain upright and unspattered as jeeps carrying heavily armed militiamen fishtailed through the spring slush, en route to the frontline only twenty-five kilometres away. Apart from food and cheap Kunduzi rugs, there was little to buy except small Greek and Buddhist artefacts dug up from the nearby ruins of Ai Khanoum, in antiquity the world's easternmost Greek city. A small statue sold for less than a jar of coffee, if you didn't mind trafficking in stolen antiquities. Massoud's compound — a collection of buildings with blasted windows located in a former market garden — had changed hands several times, with the Taliban having occupied it the previous year.

It had been seven years since I had sat at Massoud's feet in Charikar, as he prepared for the successful campaign to capture Kabul. He was barely forty then and everything was ahead of him. Now, nearer fifty, he was wise with failures. The jihad — once a simple question of faith — had become a moral and military quagmire, drained of meaning. When he walked away from Kabul, Massoud had walked away from his own legend, but his charisma was perennial.

Flanked by his lieutenants and walking tightrope-style along a low paddy wall towards me, he cut a striking figure, his wiry frame draped in a military-green pullover and spotless new camouflage fatigues, the pants tucked into gaiters above black polished boots. The vicissitudes of war had sculpted his body and his light, catlike steps displayed the agility of a much younger man. His trademark pakhool, the brown woollen pancake cap, was pushed back on his head, framing high cheekbones and a hooked nose. Silver streaked a straggling beard and crow's feet clawed at his piercing, almond-shaped eyes. It was the face of a hawk but with warm eyes and a disarming smile which flashed briefly as he shook hands, picked out a handful of sidekicks to travel with him, and boarded the chopper. As the aircraft rose he sat on a sidebench with the rest of us, looking mortified, and I thought for a moment that he shared my fear of flying. In fact, his sister had died of an illness the night before in Panjshir. He was thinking of her, with long, crooked fingers supporting his chin. Still, he was sticking to his schedule. The chopper swooped south-east across a wide gravel riverbed, a mere speck against the majesty of the Hindu Kush. Seated beside me on a pile of supplies was a teenage boy with a greenish, airsick complexion, holding a walkie-talkie. From behind us, rising over the din of the engines, came the gobbling sounds of several fattened turkeys destined for the commander's Eid dinner table. As the rotor-blades yawed in the thin alpine air, a river spilling like liquid silver over polished stones came into view beside a Renoir-print meadow framed by chocolate-box alps. The aircraft was supposed to drop us at Farkhar before proceeding up the steep-walled river valley on a resupply run. But, putting down with a thud, the pilot was unable to persuade the machine to take off again. One of the engines had seized, and Massoud's air force had just been reduced by a quarter.

Farkhar was like a militia summer camp. In the crisp air boys walked barefoot, shouldering strings of freshly caught trout, and teams of new recruits played volleyball between the barracks and the river. No sooner had we landed than Massoud plunged into a holiday mood, abandoning his uniform in favour of a loose-fitting salwar kameez and, taking off his hat, allowing a nest of wild hair to tumble free. Tucked up on the sofa in his quarters he shared sweets and green tea, chatting with comrades in a large, bright living room heated by a wood stove. For the next few days the warlord rested, reading from a library containing biographies of De Gaulle, Caesar, the Prophet Mohammed, Churchill, Mao and Guevara. He caught up on sleep, inspected nearby training camps, ensured that his guests were fed, and amused them with stories of his exploits. It was all very pleasant. Other Afghan warlords always made you slightly uncomfortable. Najibullah, Dostum and Malik were transparent killers, Hekmatyar's fastidious cleanliness and cool good manners were sinister, and the Taliban leaders spoke a language only they understood. Massoud, however, always came across as human — ruthless perhaps, but no more than was necessary in a war. Yet it had been many years since fortune had favoured him.

As we spoke in snatches over several days he dredged the past, panning for the golden lesson; the 'Lion' had been in many tight corners before, but had always broken out and defeated — or at least survived — his enemies. There was the failed coup against the Taraki government in 1978, when his first small army was obliterated, reduced from five hundred to fifteen, and forced to survive on mulberries in a remote corner of the Panjshir. Or the time the Russians took the Panjshir and he vowed to fight to the death with a handful of close lieutenants. And more recently his travails against the Taliban. Only two years before, twenty thousand of them had attacked from four directions and the entire town of Najrab at the gates to the Panjshir defected, forcing him back to Taloqan, then to Farkhar and finally into the hills.

'I'll never forget that morning,' he said. 'All my areas had fallen. My walkie-talkie, which is always choked with calls, fell silent. We were up to our necks in worry. I was trying to appear calm, making jokes. But nobody would laugh.'

At Farkhar, however, there was no sense of despair or panic. Massoud's confidence was that of a professional soldier at ease with the shifting fortunes of a long war. Within hours of our arrival in Farkhar he was rested and ready for business. A delegation of bearded, bead-counting elders and commanders arrived to pay their respects, and hear of the new United Front Massoud was cobbling together to replace his old Northern Alliance. Permitted to sit in on the meeting, I heard their reports on the situation in their areas, and Massoud's military forecasts. Some of the elders looked weary, their minds elsewhere as they chewed toothlessly on sweetbreads and cake. But they were mostly Tajiks, and the deliberations were infused with an unstated, clannish sense of common purpose. Massoud heard their reports with hooded eyes, exuding authority, fingertips poised on his thick lips. When they had said their piece he pushed a chunky gold watch back up his wrist, clasped his hands and leant forward.

'The Taliban are suffering serious defections,' he began, speaking over the hiss of the wood stove. 'The expected summer offensive by them may be delayed. This is good for us. We have more time to prepare.'

The elders listened in silence, their eyes settling on the schematic Afghan rugs covering the floor. In the course of a quarter-century, Massoud had become one of them; he was no longer the young 'Lion', but more of a grey eminence. In the beginning he had jousted in buzkashi and contested fiercely on the soccer field to earn the respect and comradeship of his men. But he hadn't ventured on to the sports field for several years now. There were strains between him and the political father figure of his Jami'at-e Islami (Islamic Society), Burhannudin Rabbani, and several of his top commanders had defected to the Taliban. Which of his men, I wondered, would betray him?

'There are ten to fifteen brothers I can rely on,' he told me after the delegation left, a lone gunman remaining to guard the door. 'Qanooni and Abdur Rahman are real stalwarts.'

It was a cool night, and around the camp people were preparing their meals and tuning in to Persian-language broadcasts of Radio Tehran. After dusk the generators started up, providing power to the radio hut where Taliban messages were intercepted. After dinner the generators were switched off, and only the flickering kerosene lamps and the soothing sound of the river remained.

Next morning I found Massoud under a spreading birch tree, reading a French magazine. His French language skills, acquired at the Kabul Lycée Istiqlal, had attracted a steady stream of visits by Paris-based correspondents, who embellished his image as a latter-day Che Guevara. During his four years in Kabul, Massoud had turned his force into a conventional army. Now he was returning to his guerilla roots.

'I'm not relying on a frontline anymore,' he told me, calling for a pencil and pad to illustrate the point. 'We have a definite line, but we're not depending on it. Around here we have twenty bases, with each village responsible for its own security. This is the same way I did it with the Russians. It's a resistance war. How many years will the Taliban keep fighting like this?'

It was a defensive posture, heavily reliant on minefields and employing psychological operations to engineer defections from the other side. As he explained the military nuances, sketching with quick, rapid strokes, he became energised and would occasionally bang his fist on the wooden arm of his chair to stress important points. This student of engineering who never graduated suffered the pangs of a creative man trapped in a destructive war of life. Yet he was good at war, and war seemed to like him.

The need to survive had tempered Massoud's early Islamic radicalism, and he now relied indirectly on support from his previous arch-enemies, the Russians. The United Front now billed itself as the only force capable of keeping the Taliban out of Central Asia.

Massoud claimed to be financing his war with the sale of emeralds from mines in the Panjshir and of lapis lazuli from the six-thousand-year-old mines in mountainous Badakhshan. The emeralds alone fetched $1 million a month and were sold through a Polish trading company. But Tajikistan was allowing Massoud the use of the Kulyob airbase, and Iran — which would back anyone opposed to the Shia-baiting Taliban — was providing cash and uniforms. Russia and Ukraine provided aircraft and weapons. 'Sometimes you accept the help of the devil,' Massoud's Dushanbe-based spokesman, Amrullah Saleh, had told me when asked about the Russian aid, 'but we do not get a single bullet without paying for it.'

On Eid morning hundreds of men and boys gathered on the maidan at Farkhar, dropping their weapons, walking sticks and prostheses onto the grass and spreading out their shawls and long coats to kneel in prayer. The introductory speaker was an official from Massoud's Jami'at who worked at the radio station in Taloqan. He said the year just past had been hard for the mujahideen.

'It has been full of war against the enemy,' he commented. 'Thousands of people have been killed or wounded.'

Following him came a *maulvi* who told the story of Ibrahim — Abraham to Christians and Jews — who proved his loyalty to God by preparing to sacrifice his only son, Isaac. Moved by such devotion, God placed a ram in Isaac's place on the altar of sacrifice. With the Eid prayers about to begin, a murmur rippled through the congregation as Massoud, wrapped in a brown woollen coat, hurried down from his lodge and knelt in the front row. The mullah resumed his sermon, which included a pointed reference to the need to bury corpses with their heads pointing towards Mecca. Breaking into a melodic prayer, his voice was carried on a stiff breeze into the snowcapped peaks, and the congregation bowed as one with their foreheads pressed to the earth. Between them and Mecca stood the crippled helicopter, which had stubbornly resisted all efforts to shift it.

After prayers Massoud was swamped by men of all ages, who kissed his hands and cheeks. On the riverbank, big knives were being sharpened on stones for a sacrifice. Soon they were slicing through the matted fleece of four goats, which were lined up facing west under the trees. The animals bridled briefly when their throats were opened, then relaxed with glazed stares as their magenta life's blood escaped beneath a carpet of pine needles.

24

Children of Adam and Eve

The hilltop was bare and a blustery wind snapped at the irregulars' ragged uniforms. It abducted the bleating of a passing shepherd's flock, hijacked the crack of small arms fire and carried off the occasional, echoing boom of something larger. Metal shards of exploded rockets and shells the same lead grey colour as the sky littered the peak where Abdul Wahdood, rifle in hand, watched his childhood ebb away.

In a greasy, heavily patched plaid jacket and rubber gumboots, the round-faced boy peered towards the Taliban tanks and troops occupying the hilltop opposite, across the deep green floor of the Bangi Valley far below. He buried his chin in a muffler, fending off both the wind and my persistent question — 'How old are you?' — until reinforcements arrived in the form of an older brother. Abdul was twenty, the brother said, even though his unformed features suggested he was about fourteen. If I didn't believe him, I could ask the kid himself. Go on Abdul, tell the foreigner how old you are!

'These young men are crazy,' Ahmed Muslim had told me in Dushanbe when I'd asked about the boy soldiers. 'They fear nothing. They are good fighters.'

But Adbul Wahdood feared plenty. He felt trapped equally by his too-clever brother and the nosy outsider. His eyes darted left and right, desperate for a way out. Had he been to school? No. How long had he been fighting? A year. What was his salary? Fifteen lakh *Afghanis*, about $30 a month. What was the average life expectancy of an Afghan boy-man? He didn't know, and I didn't ask him.

It was forty-six years.

Wild red tulips flanked the road to the frontline, luring the unwary into unmarked minefields along the likely route of the Taliban's advance. Massoud's forces were positioned along the hilltops on either side, happy to oblige any Talib who courted death by driving towards Taloqan. Both sides were waiting for the other to move, and the frontline was holding at the Bangi bridge across the Taloqan River. The settlements in the valley — including Chenzai, population forty thousand, situated directly below Abdul's position — were ghost towns, their inhabitants having moved away: the Tajiks to Taloqan, the Pashtuns to Kunduz. Leaving the car, we climbed steeply on foot up the mountain, observing the Taliban mortars as they fell impotently against the cliffs and into the ravines, raising clouds of dust and smoke. Yet the vast open spaces could induce a fatal complacency. The experienced gunners on both sides killed and maimed with remarkable frequency.

As we reached the top of the hill, a clutch of illiterate, lice-ridden boys and the hardbitten men who governed them asked for *baksheesh* in return for allowing themselves to be photographed. They wore an eclectic range of uniforms — Chinese runners, Russian Army coats, Central Asian brocaded skullcaps, and hammer-and-sickle belt buckles — and cradled Chinese-made AK-56s, with their familiar banana-shaped magazines, like teddy bears.

Far away, on the shores of Lake Geneva, a vociferous debate was raging over the plight of three hundred thousand children, some as young as seven, involved in at least thirty conflicts around the world. The issue dividing delegates to the United Nations-sponsored conference was not whether child soldiering was morally acceptable — all agreed it was not — but the precise age at which a boy became a man for military purposes. The 1990 Convention on the

Rights of the Child had set fifteen as the minimum age for combatants, and signatories were negotiating to raise the age limit to eighteen. Yet some countries were strongly opposing the move to raise the threshold. The opposition was not coming from Afghan warlords or states which sponsored terrorism or despotic banana republics. It was coming from the United States, which had about three thousand seventeen-year-olds serving in its armed forces, and from Britain, which liked to induct its youngsters even earlier. In fact, about half the world's armies were recruiting soldiers under eighteen, sometimes through compulsory conscription.[11]

For Adbul Wahdood the outcome of the deliberations in Geneva was the only academic thing about his life. His Uzbek father had been killed by the Taliban when they occupied Taloqan the previous year. The Uzbeks and other northern minorities believed they would be massacred if the Pashtuns returned. When mothers like Abdul's sent their sons to war they did not weep, but pushed them out of the nest with demands for revenge. Hate was essential to save their way of life. Sometimes it seemed hate *was* their way of life.

Directing the shelling of Taliban positions throughout the Eid holiday was Commander Wali Mohammed, a forty-one-year-old Tajik from Warsaj, who formerly belonged to Najibullah's pro-communist army. The Koran forbade fighting on religious holidays, but even the holy book made exceptions. Likewise, at the end of the jihad against the communists all mujahideen factions had accepted former communists and pro-Russian fighters like Wali Mohammed into their ranks, according to ethnicity. The new ethnic jihad against fellow Muslim Afghans was too important to split hairs over ideology. Wali Mohammed had a dozen tanks positioned on the nearby hilltops, and when they scored a direct hit on a Taliban position his troops cheered, watching through field glasses as three enemy bodies were dragged from a burning bunker. Should the Taliban take the Bangi bridge, then Commander Wali and his men would fall back, burying their weapons and discarding their uniforms if necessary, to blend in with civilians in

Taloqan, or retreat to the hills around Farkhar. Chasing them would be more children from the other side: undergraduates from the Pakistani madrassas like Akora Khattak. It was a short, brutal life, sustained by pulao served from steel slop-buckets.

The Pakistan government had been denying its involvement in the Afghan civil war like an alcoholic denies his dependence on drink. But in the mountains behind Farkhar was living proof that Pakistanis were up to their necks in the fighting. At a spartan prison in Lejdeh, an isolated settlement deep in the Hindu Kush, Massoud was holding scores of them captured by his forces. At my request he had scrawled a handwritten chit giving me permission to visit the remote prisoner-of-war camp, and one afternoon I was despatched in a jeep along a pitted road above the snowline. Arriving after dark, I followed the ghostly light of a guard's kerosene lantern through barracks where more than a hundred Pakistanis huddled under blankets, unaccustomed to such cold. They ranged in age from seventeen to thirty-seven and came from as far away as Karachi. It was estimated that up to half of all Taliban fighters engaged in major offensives were Pakistanis. Officers of Pakistan's army were also alleged to be directing battlefronts and logistics. They were meant to provide Pakistan with what it called 'strategic depth'. Afghanistan would provide a safe haven, should India ever invade Pakistan.

The prison commandant Syed Rahmatullah, a former judge in Kabul, allowed me to select prisoners at random from the cells. They were brought to a carpeted, low-ceilinged common room for a chat over green tea and sweets.

'The mullahs told me the Russians were still in Afghanistan and that it was our religious duty to evict them from a friendly Muslim nation,' said one of the prisoners. Mohammed was a twenty-five-year-old physician from Pakistan's leading medical institute, the Aga Khan hospital in Karachi. He had been captured while serving as a medic. 'Now I feel that what I was told about the situation in Afghanistan was wrong.'

The sentiment was supported by Abdul Jalil, a priest from Quetta, who had been told that all Afghanistan was under the Taliban's control. He had gone to Mazar-e Sharif in May 1997, having been invited to 'witness the implementation of Shari'a law'. Instead, he was captured by the anti-Taliban forces, and had spent the past two years in jail. But for him, theology mattered more than honesty.

'The Taliban lied to me. But they *have* brought Islamic law in some places,' he said, wide-eyed with worry that our meeting was some kind of trap.

Such subtleties were lost on the younger inmates like Fayez Ahmed, a seventeen-year-old from Rahimyar Khan in Pakistan's Punjab province. His downy cheeks could barely muster the mandatory beard of a Talib, but he made up for that with pure sectarian hatred.

'There is a verse in the Holy Koran which says, "Kill those who are not believers." Only when everyone converts to Islam will there be peace,' he said, rocking back and forth on his haunches, his wire-rimmed glasses dominating a mousy face. For Fayez, Christians and even minority Shia Muslims were kaffirs, infidels.

'Their books are not in the correct manner,' he said. 'They must die. There is no end to jihad. It will go on until Doomsday.'

The prison at Lejdeh was open to inspections by the International Committee of the Red Cross, and prisoners were allowed mailing rights and visits from relatives who risked crossing the frontline to get there. Massoud's forces had at various times been accused of torturing captives at other prisons by pulling out their fingernails, but the prisoners at Lejdeh were clearly being well looked after. By day they tended vegetable gardens beneath the towering peaks, overseen by armed guards. At Eid, Massoud's men had given them a cow, which they slaughtered facing Mecca. Some of them had been held prisoner for more than three years. Nine captives had been released in prisoner exchanges, although Massoud officials admitted to demanding ransom for important prisoners.

According to the warders at Lejdeh, most of the inmates were Punjabis, Sindhis or Baluchis.

Fayez Ahmed, who had received permission from his Muslim cleric father to join the Taliban, needed an interpreter in order to understand his Pashtun commander on the frontline. His brief, unsuccessful career as a soldier had ended in July 1997 with his capture at Charikar, north of Kabul.

'I was fighting well,' he told me, overcoming his earlier-stated contempt for any non-Muslim. 'I made the right decision, no mistake. When I'm released I will continue my Islamic studies, and when I finish my education I will do holy war. What our teachers tell me, I will do.'

As he spoke, the whole room watched him. Some older prisoners looked cross, as if his boldness might harm their chances of release, but others admired or were amused by the singlemindedness of youth. So tragically bleak was his attitude that I found myself trying to talk sense into him. Why should Christians and Muslims ever need to fight each other? Were we not both people of the book? And here in Afghanistan he was fighting fellow Muslims, not infidels. But my efforts proved fruitless. The beacon of jihad had illuminated his lacklustre life.

Warden Rahmatullah led the way out, his swinging lantern casting a wavering light on the cold stone walls. Pausing on the gravel road outside the prison, he embraced me warmly.

'We are all the children of Adam and Eve,' he said, bidding me farewell from that dark and troubling place.

Back in Islamabad a barrage of e-mails from another young man awaited me. Rasoul was undergoing rites of passage of a very different kind, trapped in a maze of suspicious 'protection officers', numbered forms, missing birth certificates and disappearing faxes. Although UN officials accepted that he was justified in fearing for his life, their safe houses were all full and the *chowkidars*, who controlled access to embassies, were demanding baksheesh before he could collect his forms. Much as he wanted asylum, he kept trying to return to Afghanistan to see his mother.

He had managed to secure an interview with the United Nations High Commissioner for Refugees. The official conducting the interview was a woman, who smoked throughout the meeting. From his note it was impossible to tell which he found more off-putting: the fact that the official was a woman, or that a woman should smoke. Apart from that, the interview had gone well and his case had been referred to the Australian High Commission, which had given him more forms to fill in and ordered that he undergo a full medical examination. The officially accredited doctor had examined Rasoul, taking x-rays and several blood tests.

The x-rays revealed that he was a tuberculosis carrier.

PART SEVEN

KASHMIR

25

Fire on the Lake

Mr Marvellous perched on the prow of his *shikara*, digging the water with brief stabs of his paddle, a garden sprouting in the boat behind him. Along the hull, the painted promotion read: 'Mr Marvellous Daily Frish Flower in My boat, seeds, balbs, plants'. I was his first customer that morning on Kashmir's Dal Lake, which made me lucky as far as Mr Marvellous was concerned. He would sell me the black rose, the crocus, the wild tulip and the blue poppy, but not the lotus. The lotus he would give free, so long as I would buy the daisies — fifty only — because I was lucky and he was Marvellous.

The plonk of a different paddle, this one heart-shaped, had woken me before dawn when another gondola nudged a path through the reeds towards my rented houseboat. It was midsummer and droplets of water rolled like mercury across the spreading lotus pads as we glided towards the floating market, a corner of the lake where gardeners came early to sell their produce in lavishly photogenic surroundings. The boatman Lassa had brought a breakfast of cloudy green *kawa* and tandoor bread with local honey, had puffed the bolsters, and taken down the sunshade to allow an unimpeded view of sunrise over the Himalayas. My job was to lay back and float, and listen to the plonk and dribble of his paddle as we headed unwittingly towards Mr Marvellous's ambush.

Over one thousand years old, the grandly named Srinagar — a corruption of Suryanagar, or city of the sun — had not impressed the authors of the British *Gazetteer*, who called it 'a striking picture of wretchedness and decay ... a confused mass of ill-favoured buildings, forming a complicated labyrinth of narrow and dirty, lanes badly paved'.[1] Yet the colonialists had overlooked the thrusting ambition of Srinagar's steeply pitched roofs and twisting canals to be a wooden Venice of the East. In the summer of 1998 normalcy was returning to the Kashmiri summer capital after ten years of violence between Muslim separatists and Indian security forces. Charred ruins still scarred the timber heart of the old city, but the commercial hub along Residency Road bustled with activity and one hopeful entrepreneur was even renovating the former maharajah's palace. Converted to a hotel, the palace was attracting visitors for the first time in years. On Fridays thousands of families were once again enjoying lakeside picnics, strolling in the enormous monumental gardens built centuries before by Moghul kings and fed by mountain streams. During the peak of separatist violence, the militants had banned golf, thrown acid in the faces of unveiled women, and forced cinema halls, video libraries, liquor stores and beauty salons to close. Now women had thrown off their veils to reveal faces of austere beauty, and at the golf course, sten gun-wielding soldiers helped retrieve balls from the rough.

India's only Muslim-majority state remained one of the most heavily militarised places on earth, a maze of sand-bagged bunkers, machine gun nests and checkpoints set up by Indian paramilitary forces to maintain order. Its combination of beauty, eccentricity and fear could still startle, like the electric blue kingfishers that explode into the air from beneath the lake's waters when you least expect it. On a typical day automatic gunfire would ring out in the street. Within minutes, dark-skinned paramilitary troops from all over India would pour into the area, ordering the pale-skinned Kashmiris to line up for identity parades outside their brick and exposed timber frame houses. The troops were jumpy, sometimes hysterical, and an air of menace prevailed. Yet like the curfew, the violence was sporadic, and after a few youths were hauled off, never to see their families again, the soldiers became calmer, shop shutters rose again, and life muddled on, as shallow and dirty as Dal Lake.

However, at Naseem Bagh, 'the garden of gentle zephyrs', life floated like the man-made islands formed of reeds and earth which dotted the lake. Dwarfed by a grove of enormous, four hundred year-old *chinar* trees planted by order of the Emperor Akbar, a line of barges clung to the shore. Confined to port by a sea of lotus and water hyacinth, they were hopelessly caught, like Kashmir itself, in memories of their Shangri-La days. At Clermont Houseboats fourteen guestbooks chronicled the glory years. Gulam Nabi Butt, a man of anxious disposition with a forehead as high and noble as the chinars, read and re-read the entries that never ceased reaffirming a standard of hospitality and service that in the opinion of his guests made Butt's the best hotel in the world. For added convenience Mr Butt had indexed in the back of each register the names of the VVIPs (Very, Very Important People) who had stayed. Framed portraits of politicians and millionaires, artists and ambassadors lined the office walls, a throwback to the days when bookings were essential. In this very garden, the late George Harrison and Ravi Shankar entertained friends at impromptu concerts, undisturbed by Beatlemania. 'My wife and I were overwhelmed by it all. Good wishes for the future,' the young Englishman's entry for 11 October 1966 read. Entries for the previous year seemed to overlook the war that had taken place that year in Kashmir between the armies of India and Pakistan. Was it some kind of *Death in Venice* conspiracy of silence, or were the guests too blissful in their quaint floating cottages to notice? The entries for the summer of 1989 betray no hint of what was about to go wrong; in fact, the celebration of the Clermont experience was at its peak. But on 20 April 1990 the looming tragedy received its first, oblique reference. As usual it was a restful and well-looked-after stay, wrote Edward Desmond, a correspondent based in New Delhi, 'even under these difficult conditions'. Three weeks later, David Housego of the *Financial Times* expanded: 'It was sad to arrive in such times, and at the height of the season, to find all the boats deserted. This has never happened in the history of Clermont.' By 13 May, the new guest profile — all journalists covering the conflict, all unsettled by the macabre juxtaposition of beauty and horror — was firmly established. 'Coming to Kashmir in times of such dismaying strife obviously tempers one's reaction to a place of such vivid beauty,' wrote James Clad of *The Far Eastern Economic Review*.

Over the following decade, the guestbook entries would chart the deepening chaos, confusion and despair.

Typically, India's indefatigable bureaucracy had recorded every aspect of the insurgency in meticulous detail. Of the 20 506 people killed in the period since 1988 in separatist violence, 9416 were militants, and 7463 were Muslims. The dead included 372 bureaucrats, 151 politicians and 1819 security personnel, as well as foreign tourists, journalists and members of religious minorities. Tourist arrivals, which had been seven hundred thousand a year before the rebellion, had fallen to nine thousand in 1994. In return, three hundred and fifty thousand Indian troops had moved in. There were a thousand empty houseboats, seven thousand under-employed gondola rowers, and the Aquatic Tourist Traders' Association regularly protested against declining business by assembling armadas of shikaras.

The statuesque Mr Butt had a few figures of his own. He hadn't turned a profit now in twelve years and his houseboats — which require constant maintenance to prevent them sinking — had been reduced in number from nine to four. It was all he could do to keep his staff on, and the far reaches of his raffish Edwardian garden had gone slowly to seed.

'People say, "Look at Gulam! He's smiling, he's pulling on okay",' Mr Butt said, fussing about me as Ramazan the bearer carried my bags across the creaking, rug-covered floorboards. 'But you know, when a houseboat sinks, it sinks very slowly.'

Kashmiris are distinctive in the way many of India's people are, with their own language, cuisine, dress and architecture, a fact Mr Butt never ceased to point out. Hinduism came first, followed by Buddhism, and then in the fourteenth century most Kashmiris voluntarily adopted a form of Islam heavily influenced by mystic Sufism. Their syncretic culture became known as *Kashmiriyat*. The territory repeatedly changed hands and shape, waxing and waning with the fortunes of conquerors and deal-doers. The Afghans took it from the Moghuls, then lost it to the Sikhs who surrendered it to the British who sold it to one Mr Gulab Singh of Jammu, who later added Ladakh to his realm. By then, the princely state of Jammu & Kashmir comprised four distinct regions: Hindu-dominated Jammu, Buddhist Ladakh, and the Muslim-majority Valley and Northern Areas bordering Afghanistan. The Kashmiris enjoyed profitable relations with the British, who revelled in an atmosphere of Moghulian luxury each summer when they flocked to the Valley to escape the insufferable heat of the plains. Forbidden by law from buying land, they persuaded the locals to build floating cottages similar to Oxford barges, which they gave dotty names like 'Buckingham Palace'. It was an English couple who persuaded Mr Butt's father to build his first houseboat at Naseem Bagh.

When the British left in 1947, the two new nations of India and Pakistan both wanted strategically important Kashmir, and, as troops from both sides descended, the muddling Hindu maharajah Hari Singh signed his Muslim-majority kingdom over to India. A brief war followed, leaving India with two-thirds, Pakistan with one-third, and the Kashmiris with a promised plebiscite on self-determination that never eventuated because both sides refused to withdraw their troops. In the coming decades India and Pakistan would fight several small, civilised wars over Kashmir. In the late 1980s, Muslim separatists inspired by the Afghan jihad contested elections and lost.

Blaming electoral fraud by the Indian authorities for their defeat, they began crossing over to Pakistan-occupied Kashmir to get the weapons and training they needed in their freedom struggle. At first the Kashmiris fought for independence, but groups demanding accession to Pakistan got the lion's share of the weapons, and soon eclipsed other shades of opinion. As in Afghanistan, fighting between the different rebel groups often took precedence over the war against India, and had divided the clergy. The mullahs of Hazratbal, based at the pristine, lakeside mosque where they kept a hair from the Prophet's beard, wanted to join Pakistan. At the Friday Mosque, a Saracenic structure of Gothic arches and wooden steeples, the architecture spoke of the uniqueness of Kashmir. The ten metre-high ceiling was supported by 392 pillars, each formed by a single deodar tree. Not surprisingly, the head priest there thought Kashmiris should stand on their own feet, and supported independence.

We were harvesting memories that morning as Lassa paddled me back from the floating market, past the boats of women who made a meagre living harvesting lake weed. The shikara's v-shaped trail of ripples snared thoughts of Salahuddin, a failed candidate at the rigged elections and now leader of the strongest guerilla group, the Hizbul mujahideen. The Hizbul was a joint venture between Pakistan's Inter-Services Intelligence agency and Qazi Hussain's Jama'at-e Islami, launched in 1989 to demand accession to Pakistan, rather than independence. At its peak in the early 1990s, it had run passenger bus services taking thousands of Kashmiri boys to the border for military training.[2] Had I imagined our meeting in the apple orchard? All that hopping from car to car, rickshaw to rickshaw, and the incessant backtracking designed to disorientate me so badly that I couldn't tell the authorities where Salahuddin was hiding. Finally a hike of several kilometres to a clearing where a picnic table and chairs awaited, and forty different kinds of apples for tasting. 'There are more militant groups than apple varieties,' he chortled, more like a cheerful cook in a British working man's cap than an armed priest. It must have been in 1992 in what Salahuddin liked to call the 'liberated area', just as he liked to call himself Syed Salahuddin when his real name was Mohammed Yousef Shah. His men called him Pir Sahib, a religious title for a military commander. Around us, they prowled the orchard with AK-47s as we chatted about the jihad, Salahuddin clearly enjoying the chance to flaunt his presence just thirty kilometres north of Srinagar. Born in Badgam in the Valley, he made much of the variety and sweetness of the apples his boys had provided. A true son of Kashmir, he kept a piece of fruit pressed against his nostril, sweetening the Kashmiri air he breathed as he threatened to continue the jihad until the last Indian soldier had left.

From the outset the fighting was vicious. Muslim separatists targeted the minority Hindu and Sikh communities in the Valley, committing sporadic massacres as a warning to them to flee. The assassination of civil servants, whose ranks were dominated by Hindu Brahmins, spread panic among the *pandits* and sent at least a hundred thousand of them into exile in other parts of India.[3] The Indian forces met terror with terror, and Kashmir descended into a vortex of torture, murder, arson and rape that left no family unscathed. Yet because it was a Kashmiri war, the social niceties still mattered. Once, driving on the Jammu–Srinagar road with a group of colleagues, our car strayed into a firefight near an army camp outside Anantnag. We had entered the Valley through the Jawahar tunnel that burrows kilometres under the Pir Panjal Range, and whose entrance is marked by a sign that reads: 'Go slow and let your life be as long as this tunnel'. Hearing the gunfire, we abandoned the vehicle and ran for cover to a sand-bagged bunker, where a pukka Indian Army man blocked our entry, insisting we should sign the guestbook. After an anxious delay amid staccato bursts of automatic rifle fire, he produced a neat ledger. In the column marked 'Reason for Visit' somebody had written: 'To save life'. As we waited inside for the battle to be decided, a bearer came ducking bullets and carrying a tray of tea cooked the Indian way, with the tea, milk and sugar boiled furiously together with cardamom. At one point he seemed to be contemplating taking refreshments over to the rebels, but thought better of it and returned to the kitchen.

When they weren't being too savage or too civilised, the antagonists were merely ridiculous. Muslim boys staged armed mutinies for the cameras in the rear gardens of their family homes, while Indian paramilitaries were so disinterested in the cause that their guns had to be chained to them in case they sold them. (The government claimed it was to prevent the guns being snatched from dead soldiers by militants.) It was not until the night they shot a Sufi that I realised how dead awful everything really was. He was one of those wandering Muslim mystics known as *dervishes*, renowned for their whirling dances, and had been seen roaming near the airport after curfew one night. A paramilitary officer said troops in two different bunkers opened fire, killing the Sufi, then blamed each other. His body was left laying in the middle of the airport road dressed in a heavy woollen cloak, or *pheran*, with a neat bullet hole in his forehead. When the shooting began, the officer said, the dervish first began to laugh, then raised his arms and waved them in the air. He died dancing.

As the insurgency got uglier and the original Kashmiri freedom fighters fell in battle, they were replaced by hardened jihadis from the international brigades that had fought in Afghanistan, some of which were funded by Osama bin Laden. Sometimes whole groups like the Al-Badr and Tehrik-e Jihad comprised foreign fighters, including Punjabi, Arab, Filipino and African students. Others, like the Pakistan-based Harakat ul-Ansar, took to kidnapping tourists, beheading at least one of them. Salahuddin no longer ventured into the Valley. Under the patronage of Pakistani intelligence he became corpulent to the point of immobility, content to issue occasional statements from the safety of Islamabad.

'The twelve million people of the state . . . have burnt their boats,' he said in one famous pronouncement. 'There is no point of return or retreating from the path they have chosen after due thought.'[4]

The path many Kashmiri Muslims had chosen 'after due thought' led, strangely enough, to India. If customers could not come to them, they would go to their customers. The smashed pod of Kashmiri enterprise spread its seeds from Ladakh to Kerala, Calcutta to Goa. Wherever tourists gathered you would find them with their painted boxes, shawls and carpets. Complacent local traders might doze in their shops, but the hungry Kashmiris were out spruiking on the broken pavements, snaring the unwary with their 'What your country?', 'No need buying', and 'Just one minute look see'. But a few — too old, stubborn or incredulous to leave — stayed on in the Valley.

At seventy-two, Gulam Rasull Khan still came every day to the offices of Gulam Mohidin & Sons, purveyors of Oriental carpets, furnishings and antiques, located in a prime position opposite the Maharajah's polo ground on the corner of Residency Road in Srinagar. Equipped with a neatly knotted tie and hawkish eyes that could spot a bargain at a hundred metres, he was the grandson of Abdul Gani Khan, the pioneer of Kashmir's papier-mâché and furniture export industries. It was Gani Khan who made the walnut screens and timber arches that welcomed Queen Mary to India for the Delhi Durbar in 1911. But it was another Englishwoman — a tourist holidaying in the Valley — who really changed his life, and his name.

'She liked the mohair pheran he was wearing and he explained that, in Kashmir, white was the colour of dignity. So she said, "Why not choose a dignified name?" So she thought for a little while, and then said, "Gani Khan . . . Gani Khan . . . Ganymede?" And my grandfather liked it, so that became his new name,' said Mr Khan.

It was said at one time that half of London was furnished by Ganymede. He had certificates from all the viceroys and commanders-in-chief, and bedroom suites were flown out of Srinagar by the planeload. Amazed by the power of his marketing, other traders were quick to adopt memorable names, and houseboat owners followed. Henceforth, visitors could spar with Suffering Moses over the price of papier-mâché boxes, authorise Honest Injun to obtain a length of twill, or commission Cheerful Chippendale to produce a walnut dresser.

In Mr Khan's ground-floor offices human antiques scratched away at bulky ledgers, the only evidence of technological change being a Bakelite telephone with a dial. Directing a bearer to bring tea, Mr Khan handed me his card, featuring a company crest and the words 'Est. 1874'. The telex address was 'Carpets'.

'Ganymede was not familiar with carpets. It was my uncle who adopted me and put me into this business,' he said, stirring his tea. 'Together these two families built up a massive collection of arts, crafts and curios. We had pink jades, porcelains and parchment paintings, bronze Buddhas and brocades that Chinese traders used to bring here from Kashgar. Unfortunately, all of it was lost in the fire.'

Srinagar's shambolic clutter of wooden houses capped with iron witches hats is a pyromaniac's delight. Harvested from the thick forests that blanket the steep hills, local hardwoods are cheap and plentiful, but also highly flammable. Winters are often so cold that Dal Lake freezes over. Charcoal is the main heating fuel, often used in small wicker baskets placed under people's pherans as personal warmers, or 'winter wives' as the Kashmiris call them. But a spark from a *kangri*, or for that matter a stray bullet, can set a building aflame. In 1936 a blaze ripped through the Khan family's original premises in a wooden building near Third Bridge, one of seven bridges that cross the Jhelum River in Srinagar.

'Everything went in that disastrous fire,' said Mr Khan with a sniffle. 'Luckily my uncle was insured.'

As they sifted through the wreckage an unexpected sympathiser arrived to commiserate. It was Maharajah Hari Singh, who at that time was building the grand palace overlooking Dal Lake and needed furniture and carpets to fill its many rooms.

'My uncle became the consulting art expert to the Maharajah, who trusted his taste implicitly,' Mr Khan went on, dreamily twirling the dials of a date stamp. 'We moved to this location and began building up another fantastic collection of exquisite pieces including many rare curios. You can see one of the vast carpets we got handmade up there at the palace hotel. Then the export business started. We had buyers coming to enjoy Kashmir and do a little business. We sold to Harrods and Bloomingdales — carpets, crewel work, chain-stitched items. We had forty-five looms in the city and a hundred outside. Later, my uncle, God rest his soul, consented to my request to train girls as weavers. The Muslim majority here wouldn't allow their daughters or wives to go out, so we gave them looms and they were able to work at home at their own pace. It was a sensation! Soon these girls were weaving their wedding rugs to be given as dowries when they married. I had a book about that. But it was lost in the Second Disastrous Fire.'

Times are bad when people begin enumerating their catastrophes. Mr Khan's family history seemed to parallel that of his century: World War I — Great Rug Fire I; World War II — Great Rug Fire II. With India and Pakistan having both tested nuclear weapons I feared for what might come next.

'You know, my dear,' said Mr Khan, 'we lost eleven hundred rugs in the fire in 1983; Persian and Kashmiri pieces of high quality. Ming porcelain, antique *jamavar* shawls, old bronze Buddhas melted. The Chinese parchment paintings burnt, all gone, all finished. All of them registered with the Department of Antiquities. I subsequently went to China and when I told them about the scrolls they cried. Now you don't see Chinese people crying at the drop of a hat. This time, alas, we were not insured. We had tried, of course, but the insurance companies sent experts from Delhi, and they couldn't agree on the valuation, so cover was declined. When that second fire happened, I couldn't even cry. Crying never saved anything. I just said, "God is Great. He will help us."'

The narrow staircase to the first-floor showroom creaked underfoot as the spry Mr Khan led the way past a bright red soda-acid fire extinguisher tendentiously mounted on the wall. Entering the gallery, the dry odour of ashes accosted my nostrils. There lay hundreds of carpet remnants selvedged and trimmed to remove the charring and flashmarks. Richly coloured borders hinted at Caucasian dragon designs, Jaipur Moghul hunting scenes and Persian palmettes of radiating petals. On the wall, a framed newspaper clipping from *The Current* dated 22 June 1953 recorded the gift of a carpet in the 'Amli' design copied from old shawls to Queen Elizabeth II on the occasion of her coronation. The cream-ground carpet had been made by children.

'With their nimble little fingers they work on the cross threads as if they were playing the harp,' the reporter marvelled.

'Not much left now,' said Mr Khan, with a bizarre chirpiness. 'We no longer supply the big American stores. A lot of people have jumped into floor coverings since we started. Naturally, it affects the business. But we're still making carpets based on these old designs. Fine silk, very valuable, woven here in Srinagar. Then came this Islamic uprising, but you know the strange thing is that the militancy has helped us a lot. For the past ten years it's been dangerous for people to leave their homes. There was nothing to do. No cinema halls, no golf courses. Only weaving, or reproducing those miniature Moghul paintings. Production has reached record levels.'

It wasn't quite true. At the factory near Third Bridge, under sagging ceilings, a handful of weavers worked several heavy-beamed looms, but most were dormant. A portrait of Mr Khan's uncle, a suited Anglophile with a fat cigar, stared down from one wall, a reminder of more prosperous times. At a draftsman's table a lone *talim* scribbled 'scripts', the coded instructions that guided the weavers row by row through the designs. The shorthand script of circles, strokes and dots was written with quills on peach-coloured paper, preferred because it was gentler to the weaver's eyes. Khurshid Ahmed, the scriptwriter, was translating the 'Laila and Majnu' design based on the Persian version of 'Romeo and Juliet', in which thwarted lovers drown themselves in a lake. In the all but moribund workshop, the thrumming of the metal comb used to beat down the rows echoed from a far corner. A weaver with a straggling beard and the bug-eyed stare of a veteran carpet-maker called out the instructions to a younger man beside him. They earned less than $50 a month and it would take them a year to finish the piece they were working on. The old firm was on its last legs, whittled away by the insurgency, intense competition from the looms of Mirzapur and Amritsar, improved education, migration of Kashmiri labour to other parts of India, and the reduction in the child labour force.

Asked about Gulam Rasull's sunny account of the business environment, the foreman snorted.

'That's just Gulam,' he said. 'That man is an incurable optimist — honest to the core — but a bit deluded. It's how he's survived these difficult years.'

26

The Pashmina 'Conspiracy'

'India is not a soft state!' declared the governor, a momentary shrillness disturbing the musty grandeur of Raj Bhavan as Girish Saxena directed the bearer in the soup-stained uniform to proffer tea and fish fingers for the last time. 'If the other side thinks so, then they are in for a surprise. India can absorb all punishments and such things as they would like to dish out to us. Kashmir is part of India! It's part of the secular, pluralistic, democratic nation we're trying to build here. It's a thread in the fabric of the India of our dreams.'

For ten years I had been scaling the hill above Cheshmashahi Gardens, enduring the layered security and stiff formality of the attendants surrounding New Delhi's man in Jammu & Kashmir. It wasn't just for the spectacular view from the verandah overlooking Dal Lake, a mystical waterscape trailing off in shaggy mists framed by poplars and willows. Gary, as he preferred to be called, might not have been out much — since the insurgency started it was life-threatening to do so — but as a former head of India's external intelligence organisation, the Research and Analysis Wing, he could at least mix in a few astute observations with the usual barrage of indignant diatribes that Indian officialdom reserves for Kashmir. He had even been to Pakistan once — although the Pakistanis never knew about it — and was very much in the loop of India's response to the Muslim separatist insurgency.

'Our grip has, if anything, become firmer,' he declared, stabbing a piece of fish with a forklet. 'Fundamentalism is on the retreat. The old spirit is coming back. People are coming to us with information. They don't want this militancy.'

India might not be a soft state, but Kashmir certainly was. Its *pashm*, or wool combed from high-altitude quadrupeds, had been renowned for centuries, and even as the governor spoke, a foreign hand was actively spinning a woolly conspiracy right under the old spook's nose. A mysterious Englishwoman had been seen scouting the ravines of Ladakh above five thousand metres on ponyback. She was looking for hairy goats.

In the settled agricultural lands of India people had never needed carpets. They had neither the flocks to produce wool nor a climate that required insulation against cold. But the Moghul conquest of Delhi in the sixteenth century introduced a wave of outside influences, from the Turkic and Persian languages, to carpet weaving. Early weavings made by Persian and Turkmen masters strictly followed classical designs, but a survey by the Moghuls reported that workshops established by Akbar the Great were producing work so good it transcended the sources of their inspiration. At their peak, Moghul weavers produced the most finely knotted carpets ever made, but traversing Kashmir in the seventeenth century the French traveller François Bernier recorded the ascendancy of a different product of the loom:

> In poetry and sciences they [the Kashmiris] are not inferior to the Persians. They are also very active and industrious. The workmanship and beauty of their palekys, bedsteads, trunks, inkstands, boxes, spoons, and various other things are quite remarkable ... But what may be considered peculiar to Kachemire, and the staple commodity, that which particularly promotes the trade of the country and fills it with wealth, is the prodigious quantity of shawls which they manufacture, and which gives occupation even to little children.[5]

Kashmiri shawls are woven from two main types of wool — *pashmina* and *shahtoosh*. Pashmina is combed from the Changra mountain goat herded by semi-nomadic Gujjar and Bakerwal shepherds in Ladakh. Like silk, it can be woven at more than two thousand knots to the square inch, and was used by Moghul weavers in their 'Mille Fleurs' carpets, as well as shawls. Shahtoosh, which means 'King of Wool', is even finer, and comes from the breast hair of the Tibetan antelope *Pantholops hodgsoni*, which runs wild in Ladakh at altitudes of six thousand metres and is commonly known as the chiru. To survive the severe cold in the alpine regions where it lives, the chiru evolved wool of an extremely high micron count. Shahtoosh spun into a shawl is so warm that a pigeon's egg wrapped in it will hatch without any other source of heat. These shawls, either plain or intricately embroidered in dazzling colours to form jamavars, have for centuries been highly sought after, particularly by the former Persian court. In Kashmir, one of the most popular designs was the *boteh*, the Persian word for leaf. This pear-shaped symbol spread like a virus after arriving in Europe on a Kashmiri shawl in 1800. Experts have argued ever since over its meaning and origins. It has been compared to the curling top of a cypress tree, a pine cone, foetus, sperm, almond, tear drop, magnified carpet mite and a flea. Kashmiris say it represents a bend in the Jhelum River above Srinagar, while some Zoroastrians see in it a tongue of their sacred flame. It is considered lucky and without doubt brought good fortune to the Scottish town of Paisley, which achieved wealth and fame on the basis of copying what became a hippie emblem.

The British, who were more interested in building strategic railways than in developing local handicrafts, nevertheless recognised the quality of the materials and workmanship of Kashmir, so much so that when they ceded control of the Valley to Gulab Singh in 1846, they demanded in return an annual tribute in perpetuity of 'one horse, twelve perfect shawl goats of approved breed (six males and six females), and three pair of Cashmere shawls'.[6] The Raj, however, saw a decline in the standard of carpet weaving, which no longer enjoyed the patronage of the Moghul court. Only in the final years of the Raj did the new mass markets in the West — which required only the suggestion of Oriental splendour, not its substance — revive output, if not quality. By the early 1960s some two million Indians were working as spinners, dyers, merchants, carpenters and weavers in the carpet industry, and it was estimated that one person in twenty depended on the trade. The city of Mirzapur boasted the world's largest assembly of looms, with sixty thousand weavers toiling night and day to fill export orders. The desperate chase for a share of a fickle market resulted in a stylistic hotchpotch which included such horrors as the 'hand-carved Chinese rug'. This derived its design not from the careful placement of knots of different colours, but by taking a monotone, long pile rug and literally carving a few floral borders into it with shears. Examples can still be found selling by the roadside near Mirzapur on the road between Varanasi and Allahabad.

In Kashmir, market forces and do-gooders were destroying the quality that the security forces couldn't kill. When Donna Karan started wearing shahtoosh, thousands of endangered antelopes began trembling on their hoofs. The ideally clad chiru could survive temperatures of $-40°C$, but not the greed that top dollar engenders. It took at least three dead chirus to make a shawl. Kashmiris insist the wool was traditionally harvested from thorn bushes the antelopes brushed against in the dry alpine desert. But with a single scarf selling for up to $15000,[7] open season was declared on the chiru. Helped by the easy availability of semi-automatic weapons brought in to fight the insurgency, hunting had never been so easy. Numbers of chirus in the wild plummeted disastrously to about sixty thousand, and experts estimated that *Pantholops hodgsoni* would be extinct within twenty years. The United Nations Convention on International Trade in Endangered Species banned the sale of chiru

In happier times, a street vendor hawks his wares in Kandahar, circa 1976. Founded by Alexander the Great, Kandahar became the first capital of a united Afghanistan in the eighteenth century. Later Kabul would replace it, but although ruined by decades of war, Kandahar remains key to control of the south.

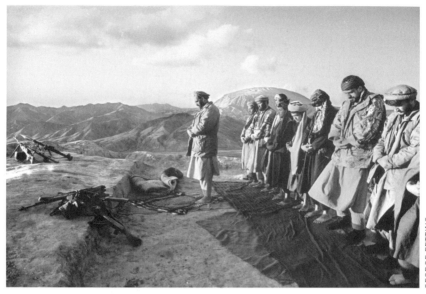

GEORGE FETTING

'In a golden light, they stood erect facing west towards Mecca with hands by their sides, then, cupping their hands to their faces, bore witness, uttering the *takbir* — "*Allahu Akbar*", God is great.' Afghan mujahideen fighters of the United Front (Northern Alliance), Chenzai, Takhar province, 1999.

GEORGE FETTING

Afghan boy soldiers, Chenzai, Takhar province. Earning $30 a month and fed on buckets of mutton rice, they grow old before their time in the daily brutality of war. All sides in the Afghan conflict rely heavily on teenaged gunmen, and half the world's armies, including those of the United States and Britain, recruit soldiers under the age of eighteen.

'Putting down with a thud, the pilot was unable to persuade the machine to take off again. One of the engines had seized, and Massoud's air force had just been reduced by a quarter.' Farkhar, Takhar province, north-eastern Afghanistan.

In April 1999, the Afghan opposition commander Ahmad Shah Massoud was fighting with his back against the walls of the Hindu Kush. The ethnic Pashtun Taliban religious army had pushed his forces into a small pocket of territory in the north-east, where the ethnic Tajik commander still enjoyed hero status.

On the banks of the Tigris River in Baghdad, carpets are washed before sale at the city's regular rug auctions. Economic decline caused by sanctions and government restrictions has stifled the ancient trade, producing artificially low prices in a closed market.

The 'five-dollar carpet', a knotted replica of the American five-dollar note complete with portrait of Abraham Lincoln, is the prized exhibit of this Tehran rug dealer. The lifting of the US ban on imports from Iran, including carpets, has not yet led to a hoped-for resurgence in exports from the world's largest carpet-producing nation.

The Saracenic Gothic architecture of the Jama Masjid (Friday Mosque) in the Kashmir summer capital, Srinagar. Like the city's largest mosque, Kashmiri culture, or *Kashmiriyat*, is a syncretic mix of influences. Hinduism was widespread in the Kashmir Valley until the valley's belated conversion to Islam in the fourteenth century, and Buddhism and Shia Islam prevail in the alpine desert of Ladakh.

KHALED MANSOUR

'The great nomad exodus from the Reg was in full swing, the broad valleys dotted with tents. Strings of camels, donkeys and people marched across the barren expanse, whipped by *shaitans*, literally devils, the small whirlwinds that suck up earth and spew it into the air.' Zabol province, southern Afghanistan, May 2000.

CHRISTOPHER KREMMER

At the turn of the century, the worst drought in living memory ravaged Afghanistan, exacerbating the torment already inflicted by twenty years of war. With their flocks decimated and winter pastures withering for the third year running, the nomad families were settling on the outskirts of towns and cities. These Pashtun children looked like being the last generation in their family to experience the nomad life.

A displaced woman from northern Afghanistan spins wool by hand in a camp on the outskirts of Kandahar. Carded, spun and dyed, the wool is woven on handlooms to produce the country's main manufactured export, carpets. In the top-heavy structure of the industry, the majority of profits accrue to dealers and middlemen, not weavers.

'The beauty of Isfahan,' wrote the English traveller-aesthete Robert Byron, 'steals on the mind unawares ... and before you know how, Isfahan has become indelible, has insinuated its images into that gallery of places which everyone privately treasures.' Naghshe Jahan square, Esfahan, Iran.

In midsummer, a young Iranian takes refuge in a teahouse under the Si o Se Bridge, Esfahan. The waters of the Zãyandéh River flow between the bridge's thirty-three arches, cooling patrons on the hottest day, just as the smoker's waterpipe cools the smoke from his apple-flavoured tobacco.

products in more than one hundred and thirty signatory countries, including India. Semi-autonomous Jammu & Kashmir refused to join the boycott, but with no market for their wares, tens of thousands of weavers still lost their jobs, and government promises of compensation failed to materialise. Dark rumours swept Srinagar that Indian intelligence agencies had engineered the ban to punish Kashmiris for their freedom struggle.[8]

With their homeland transformed into a killing field, and their industries under siege from environmentalists and social activists, Kashmiris needed a lifeline. It came in the form of silk. According to a Chinese legend, the delicate fibre was discovered when a princess accidentally dropped a silkworm's cocoon into her hot cup of tea. Plucking it from the cup she found the cocoon had unravelled in a web of glossy threads, and to this day cocoons are boiled to extract their fibres. Because it was usually more expensive than wool, silk tended to be used sparingly in carpets, as in the magenta-coloured silk highlights that enliven Turkmen guls. This was partly for religious reasons: the Prophet Mohammed abhorred silk garments as effete, and some Muslims still refuse to pray on silk carpets, considering the fibre somehow corrupting. But by the time the caliphate moved to Baghdad in the eighth century, silk had become an emblem of power and luxury, which it remains to this day. Despite possessing the world's finest wool, Kashmir now produces more silk carpets than woollen ones. Production on an industrial scale in China and India means silk is now cheaper than wool and this, combined with strong demand for its perceived luxury, means up to 80 per cent of output from many Kashmiri carpet workshops is now knotted in silk. Silk carpets are less durable than woollen ones, and purists regard them as the province of idle knot-counters with more money than taste.

In a quiet neighbourhood of Srinagar, the Englishwoman who had been seen poking about in the mountains of Ladakh was on a secret mission to stem the tide of mediocrity. Jenny Housego was no stranger to mountains, goats or carpets. A textile historian and designer, her interest was stimulated in the 1960s with a stint at the Victoria and Albert Museum in London during the reign of the late carpet empress Dr May Hamilton Beattie, and she had carried the passion with her ever since. During six years in Iran before the revolution she had 'discovered' the Shahsavan tribe, trekking into their summer pastures on Mount Sabalan and writing a book, *Tribal Rugs*, which put their weavings on the international carpet map and, for a time, sent prices soaring.[9] By the early 1990s she had moved to India, dabbling in cotton flatweave *dhurries* and soft furnishings, travelling frequently to Kashmir with her husband David and their family. It was on one such holiday in 1994 that her son Alex was kidnapped and held hostage by Muslim militants. Luckily, he was later released unharmed, and his undaunted mother returned to the Valley.

At her apartment in an exclusive quarter of New Delhi the floors were decked in tribal carpets and kilims. I had come hoping to talk about carpets, but instead was sucked into the whirlpool of Jenny's latest obsession.

'The whole Kashmiri shawl needs to be re-thought,' she said, searching for something amid the ordered chaos of samples bearing the name of her Kashmir Loom Company. 'Where are our brochures?' she demanded of Asaf Ali, one of her partners in the new venture, who dug out one of the pamphlets and handed it to her. It was a glossy job targeting the exclusive end of the European and North American markets, with images of handwoven shawls that shimmered in a mixture of pashmina and pure gold thread. The fleece was brought from Ladakh across the Himalayas through Zoji La Pass and into the Valley, where it was spun by women using the ancient Chakra wheel in their own homes. This delicate yarn was then woven on traditional handlooms in the rustic Shia neighbourhood of Srinagar where Asaf Ali lived. The company controlled every aspect of the process, from goat to shawl. Only the dyeing — which in any case was limited by their preference for natural colours — was outsourced to Amritsar. All the best dye-works of Srinagar had been torched during the insurgency. These new shawls would rely on subtle variations in texture, rather than colour, to achieve their designs.

Like militants, the principals of the Kashmir Loom Company were all sworn to secrecy. With the mills of Amritsar and Nepal churning out tens of thousands of shawls a day in pashmina-silk mix, and stealing designs like a squirrel hoards acorns, only a handful of trusted people could know of the pashmina experiment. They were terrified the bootleggers might get hold of the idea and destroy their market.

The restless Mrs Housego was packing for a trip to the Valley, after which she was due to launch her new range in Paris, where in a previous life she had graduated from the École des Hautes Études en Sciences Sociales. So absorbed had she become in the intricacies of traditional textiles that her life had begun to mimic them, with multiple personalities functioning at multiple levels. She could sit for hours in a mud-brick loom shed with Kashmiri weavers talking about their lives and techniques in fluent Urdu one day, and be wowing a Parisian fashion house the next. As we chatted, jumbo jewellery swung from her ears and she was constantly losing her train of thought.

'Now where was I?' she said, picking up the thread. 'Oh yes of course. No. We are not making rugs — or at least not yet. Who can tell? But we *are* making shawls, stoles and scarves by the traditional method, but with a very contemporary twist. It's smashing to be back in the world of wool!'

Asaf Ali, who had been trying vainly to draw her attention to some important detail of her program, finally succeeding by dropping the paperwork directly in front of her. Signing with a flourish, she resumed talking, editing, cancelling, ordering and explaining her new designs. She was enslaved to the loom.

'Most of my carpets are packed away in London. We never see them. But this shawl venture is not about collecting — we're *developing* a collection. Big difference. It's taken years, but we think we're getting there.'

By the time I reached Srinagar to inspect the venture first-hand, Jenny had gone off to France, but Asaf Ali and his brother Hamid were there to show me around. Their family had originated in Iran and were followers of Sayyid Ali Hamadani, a fourteenth-century Persian missionary who practically introduced the mellow Islam which took root in the Valley. Like every Kashmiri family, the Alis had been blighted by the conflict. They lost their stepbrother in a bomb blast in Srinagar in 1993, a tragedy which severely traumatised their father, who for a time lost his memory.

As he led the way down to the workshop Asaf looked beat, and admitted that the Kashmir Loom Company had taken over his life. But one passion had spawned others and he too was working on a wild variety of new designs and ideas, including beautiful, heavily embroidered jamavars which took up to ten years to complete; in the entire Valley there were probably only four or five families still making them. The eccentric Englishwoman's enthusiasm appeared to have infected everyone.

'It's strange isn't it?' Asaf said, bending to enter one of the workshops supplying his firm. 'Our family came as immigrants from Persia, where the Safavid Shahs used gold and silver thread in their rugs. Now, centuries later, we're doing the same thing here in shawls.'

In the dim light of the weavers' room, a young man sat on a hard wooden bench hunched over a loom, flicking the shuttle between a gossamer web of warps in a meditative silence.

Later that day, Jenny called from somewhere deep in the French countryside. The intricate handiwork of the people of war-torn Srinagar was dazzling the salons of Paris.

'We've lost something in our own culture, and we're looking for it in another,' Jenny said, struggling to explain the obsession. Then, abruptly changing the subject, she asked: 'Are you doing any carpet shopping?'

I said I might be.

'Well my dear,' she cautioned, 'just make sure you avoid those ghastly silk pastiches of old designs!'

27

An Afghan in Delhi

India has its own compass. The point labelled 'North' on ours reads 'Violence' on theirs. Just as Europe's historical memory is indelibly stained by the Mongol invasion, so India's is scarred by Mahmud of Ghazni, the 'Breaker of Idols' as he called himself, who in the eleventh century was the first in a long line of Muslim invaders from the north. These men conquered and pillaged, and some of them eventually settled in India and ruled as emperors. The Afghans were still coming, some as jihadi volunteers fighting to conquer Kashmir, others as refugees.

It was seven summers since Tariq Ahmed and his family had fled Kabul, and still they had no place to call home. With the Taliban still in power they could not return to Kabul. The student militia had driven a stake through the heart of the carpet business and would prevent Tariq's five daughters from continuing their education and stop his wife working. Although Western countries had an insatiable appetite for Oriental rugs, they were less interested in Oriental refugees. So, after the American missile strikes on Afghanistan in 1998, Tariq had left Nazreen and their daughters in Peshawar and travelled overland through south-west Afghanistan back to his hometown of Herat. From there he crossed into Iran, continuing on to Tehran, buying and borrowing rugs along the way. When he had assembled a large bundle of nice pieces, he consigned them to a freighter sailing for India, and consigned himself to a passenger plane headed in the same direction.

Suddenly, unexpectedly, Tariq Ahmed was in Delhi, hobbling across Alipore Road in a sky blue baseball cap and a beard towards my house. In a city where everything is coated in a patina of dust and grime, he sat on the edge of my sofa, trying not to soil anything. Searching the bags at his feet he came up with a bundle which he presented to my wife. It was a small carpet. Everyone blushed: Tariq with guilt at the modesty of the gift, my wife and me at accepting such a gift from a struggling refugee. Perhaps we also feared the reciprocal obligations it might impose.

'It's a small world,' Tariq said, crossing his legs one way, then the other, and looking extremely uncomfortable.

'I know,' I replied. 'Imagine ... in Kabul all those years ago, then Peshawar, and now we meet here in Delhi. Incredible!'

Three meetings in a decade weren't much of a basis for a friendship, and our conversation had a tendency to disappear into deep holes. Tariq was living in Bhogal, a suburb of New Delhi where most of the city's struggling Afghan émigrés lived, patronising the handful of Afghan bakeries and butcher shops around Lajpat Nagar that sold nan and good fatty goat meat. Unable to lower himself to sell door to door, he had fallen into the hands of the Kashmiri mafia, who controlled the capital's carpet trade. The Kashmiris were experts at paying a pittance for old rugs from rootless Afghans, and then selling them at obscene prices to naïve foreigners. Tariq described a dog-eat-dog existence in which getting the Kashmiris to pay for the pieces they'd taken on consignment was a lengthy and debilitating process.

Thinking that he might be missing home, I grabbed my photo album and together we trawled happily through pictures of Afghanistan. Then I turned a page and two men beamed at us. The tall, thin one was handing a cheque to the short, moustachioed one, who was pretending to be on the phone. Our first transaction! Afghan photolab processing had marred the picture but, like us, the image had survived, even if it was bathed in a strange, sulphurous blue light.

'I look so young,' Tariq said, as if he'd seen a ghost.

It was true. Life had hardened both of us.

'Can I take this?' he asked, saying he knew a shop with a colour photocopier which could make a decent reproduction.

Around the house lay evidence of my chequered history as a carpet collector. Soon Tariq was down on all fours, starting with the big red filpai in the living room and moving on from there. For years I had been putting off making an inventory, but now seemed the ideal time.

'Be cruel,' I told him, inviting on-the-spot appraisal of the entire collection. 'I want the truth. We've known each other long enough for that.'

Back in his natural element, Tariq was running his hands over the nap of each piece, flipping them like a pastry chef and scratching their backs. It was like old times, except now they were *my* rugs he was scrutinising. We had lived together, these carpets and me. It was like a marriage: I knew all their flaws, and saw reflected in them my own. They would never let me forget the times I had been ignorant, cowardly, niggardly, deceitful, jealous, greedy and pigheaded. There was little evidence here of finer qualities or of great successes. My rugs mocked me like a harsh wife. But Tariq was kind.

'You cannot any longer find carpets of that quality in Afghanistan,' he said, patting his trousers where he'd been kneeling on the 'wedding' rugs, and advising me to remove the new fringes I'd commissioned for them.

There was, of course, a certain amount of re-classifying. My Kurdish kilim became Turkmen. Saryks became Chubashes. Qashqais became Caucasians. It was an inexact science and we argued inconclusively as to the exact provenance of most of them. At one point I caught him concealing a smirk at a Chicken Street horror in which the dyes had run.

'You got it from Abdul Razzaque, right?'

Then, casting a sceptical eye over a Habib special, he suppressed a laugh.

'You paid three hundred for this?' he said, incredulous. 'I could have got it for you cheaper.'

When he told me exactly how much cheaper, I was mortified, and vowed revenge on Habib when I next travelled to Pakistan. A mountain of perhaps forty carpets had now formed on the living room floor and, apart from a few glimmers of hope, I could sense an almost personal regret in Tariq about all the disasters he could have saved me from. He felt bad for me, bad for my rugs, but didn't want to say anything depressing. So all right, they *were* a bit scrappy. Yes, I *had* cut corners now and then. But tell me, I asked, which is the best of them?

Pouting, he circled the pile, dragging out a piece here and there. Then his face brightened.

'This one! Definitely the best,' he declared, fondling it affectionately like a lost dog come home.

It was the Baluchi Cowdani prayer rug he had sold me a decade before in Kabul.

'You couldn't possibly remember that,' I gasped.

'Why not? It is the highest quality,' he said, nuzzling it. Then his eyes lit up at the sight of a curio on the bookshelf. It was the baz-o-band he had given me all those years ago in Kabul with a wish not to forget him.

'You remember how we planned to visit Bamiyan?' I asked him.

'*Insh'allah*, we will,' he said.

That year Tariq became a regular visitor to our home, performing useful services as a rug doctor. My wife would return to find us out on the lawn, pulling carpets back and forth face-down on the grass — Afghan 'dry-cleaning' — which released clouds of dust from the pile. Carpets that had once graced the floor now occupied the roof terrace, sun-ripening for months on end. Rugs dried out from air-conditioning were shampooed, creepers were stretched, and a small filpai with bold gulli guls had its drunken, wavering borders amputated, Taliban-style. He would give me tips on how to beat the carpet dealers; how the coded tags usually found on the back of a rug told a dealer how much he had paid for a piece; how, on average, a dealer would sell a rug for three times what he paid for it, unless he had a pressing bill to pay himself and needed to liquidate some stock. Tax time, and the days of the month when telephone and power bills fell due, were good times to buy.

On weekends, Tariq would arrive at our door with bags of fat-tailed goat meat, hard rice and freshly baked nan, and would spend hours happily mincing around in the kitchen, producing feasts of pulao and the delicious *mantu* dumplings and aushak 'ravioli'. In the Persian manner, he would always ask permission to leave and it was always granted reluctantly, for Tariq brought with him the entire culture of his wounded, magnificent nation. With our carpets, food and green tea we created a little Afghanistan of the days before the war, a refuge from brash, overheated and, in his case, unwelcoming Delhi. The Indian poet Rabindranath Tagore had written stories for children about the honest Afghan 'Kabuli-wallah'. But by the time Tariq arrived, Delhi's sixty thousand Afghan refugees were being lumped with separatist Kashmiris and scheming Pakistanis as unreliable Muslims.[10] As the main source of Afghan carpets in the city they were still known and liked in rug circles, but not at the Foreigners' Regional Registration Office, which by the end of the 1990s began refusing visa renewals. If they stayed they did so illegally, unable to venture outside their neighbourhood for fear of harassment by bribe-seeking police.

The only hope for change was if relations between India and Pakistan improved. One day, I returned home to find Tariq waiting. He had heard that the Indian prime minister was to visit Lahore to make peace with Pakistan. Certain that I would visit Lahore on this historic occasion, he had come bearing gifts which he wanted me to deliver to his family. There were neon marker pens sandwiched inside copies of the Bollywood fanzine *Filmfare*; CDs; bottles of body lotion; lip-guard, face-wash and *kajal*, the mascara worn by women and Talibs; cheap digital thermometers; tubes of Krack for cracked feet; a steam iron; American-produced Afghan videos; a variety of embroidered, mainly synthetic fabrics; rheumatic painkillers; toothpaste; photos; toy dolls; several kilograms of silver and white metal bangles; boxes; rings; earrings; mail. And two capsules of something called Virilon. Packaged in a box featuring the tantric temples of Khajuraho, it claimed to be an Ayurvedic preparation which 'ignites sexual urge, prolongs coital duration, and adds to natural virility'. It was best taken with warm milk half an hour before retiring, a kind of cross between Viagra and Horlicks. No side effects had been reported 'so far'. Finally, Tariq pulled out a wad of crisp currency notes and counted out $3000, enough to support his family for another six months. What sacrifice would he not make for them?

'Since I was cut from the reedbed, I have made this crying sound,' wrote the poet Rumi, after being forced to flee his beloved Balkh ahead of the invading Mongols. 'Anyone apart from someone he loves understands what I say. Anyone pulled from a source longs to go back.'[11]

Tariq's failure to find asylum in the West meant he was still within reach of home. But success had marooned my other Afghan refugee friend, Rasoul, on the other side of the world. To our mutual surprise, his being diagnosed as a tuberculosis carrier had been a positive sign. Reaching the medical examination meant that he was on the way to being accepted as a refugee. Tuberculosis was easily treated with a course of antibiotics and to gain asylum he had simply to sign an agreement that he would undergo the treatment once he arrived in his country of domicile. He had been issued a visa and was headed for Whyalla, an isolated town in South Australia which billed itself as the 'cuttlefish capital of the world'. Good fishing had not made up for the chronic unemployment it had suffered since the steelworks there cut back production. Rasoul was going there because his contacts in the church had kindly offered to support him in the difficult first few months. He would be departing Pakistan before we could meet, leaving behind his brothers in Attock and his mother and sisters in Mazar. Talking to him over the phone from Delhi, I warned him about the lack of jobs and the scarceness of interesting things to do in Whyalla.

'Then it is not so different to Mazar,' he replied, a young man brimming with energy for a new adventure. But who could fathom his destiny, or Tariq's? The odyssey was moulding them in the image of man as the Prophet Mohammed wanted him: 'a choice, a struggle, a constant becoming'.

'He is an infinite migration, a migration within himself, from clay to God,' said the late Iranian intellectual Ali Shari'ati. 'He is a migrant within his own soul.'[12]

28

The Good Shepherds

The goats that produce pashmina prefer the high country. They are happiest fossicking for tender green shoots that sprout briefly in the cool, lofty crags of the Himalayas while their patient shepherds wait in the valley below. When the snowbound passes open in early summer, the Gujjars and Bakerwals drive their herds from the Kashmir Valley into Ladakh, and from May until October spend a lot of time hanging around while their flocks forage. To pass time they smoke, mend their clothes and sandals, and sometimes take on minor construction work repairing the trails and small bridges that are constantly swept away by avalanches, landslides and blizzards at altitudes above four thousand metres. A few of them are paid retainers by Indian Army intelligence to report any unusual activities in the sensitive area north of India's National Highway 1A along the Line of Control (LOC) which divides Kashmir between India and Pakistan.

In early May 1999 two shepherds grazing their goats around Banju, in the mountains north-east of Kargil town, noticed a group of strangers traversing the rugged terrain.[13] Dressed in black salwar kameez, the men appeared to be neither soldiers nor mountaineers. An army reconnaissance patrol sent to investigate activity in the Turtok district three days later did not return. Other patrols had confirmed that hundreds of unidentified armed men had crossed the LOC from Pakistani-controlled territory, and had occupied a string of Indian Army posts routinely vacated during the winter. By 12 May, Headquarters Northern Command had placed all troops in Jammu & Kashmir on high alert and in the last week of May thirty thousand Indian soldiers swarmed into the ravines, six hundred and fifty kilometres north of New Delhi.

Pakistan's secret military operation in Kargil was already well underway in February 1999, when the Indian prime minister, Atal Behari Vajpayee, took a bus to Lahore in search of a historic peace deal. The Pakistani leader, Nawaz Sharif, had feted his guest with Moghulian extravagance by hosting a state banquet in the Diwan-e Am, or Hall of Public Audience, at the sixteenth-century Lahore Fort. All the while, Sharif knew the explosive impact the Kargil offensive would have on relations when the military operation was revealed. From their positions nine kilometres into Indian territory, the intruders — consisting of a mixture of mountain warfare experts from Pakistan's Northern Light Infantry and jihadi volunteers — could disrupt the army convoys which resupplied Indian troops occupying the Siachen Glacier. The strategy of using irregular forces had a history as old as Pakistan itself. In 1947, as the Kashmir Valley slipped from Pakistan's grasp, it had dispatched some five thousand Pashtun tribesmen in a desperate bid to seize Srinagar. The Pashtuns would have made it had they not delayed themselves in looting, rape and murder along the way. They had seized Kargil on that occasion, but were forced to surrender it again. Now, at Kargil, the jihadis provided cover, allowing Pakistan to claim its forces were not involved. If they could hold the ridges until snow blocked the mountain passes again in October, they would have established a new de facto border, and both Sharif and his army chief, General Pervez Musharraf, would be hailed as national heroes. Stabbed in the back at Lahore and having lost his parliamentary majority, Vajpayee was preparing to fight an election. Instead, he would have to fight a war.

'This is not an infiltration, but a kind of invasion aimed at altering our borders,' he said in a televised address to the nation in his capacity of caretaker prime minister. 'We must hope, my countrymen, that even now reason will prevail, that those within Pakistan who see the folly of aggression will have their way.'

At Clermont Houseboats on the shores of Dal Lake, the trill of water fowl and wheeling of kite hawks overhead had been replaced by the whir of helicopter gunships en route to the battlefield of the fourth India–Pakistan war. Having anticipated his busiest season in years, Gulam Nabi Butt was instead plunged into despair over the new terrors on the horizon.

'God forbid we should have to beg,' he said, drawing a line through the latest cancelled booking. '*Al'hum duli'lah*, thank God, we still have our homes to go to.'

The atmosphere at the houseboats was funereal as I awaited permission to visit the frontline. An uninterrupted convoy of army trucks kept me awake at night, farting and gnashing their gears on the road to Kargil through Naseem Bagh. Each evening the bearer Ramazan would arrive at the porch, shuffling off his *chapplis* to lay the table for dinner, which on the eve of my departure consisted of hard, dark duck and boiled lotus roots served on a silver platter. Repairing to the porch for coffee, I counted cool gusts off the lake as they began to outnumber the warm ones. Somewhere out there someone was fishing, throwing a net weighted with chains that clanked in the dark.

The army bus to Kargil next morning barrelled towards Sonamarg, an old serai town whose name means 'Meadow of Gold', where for centuries wool arriving from Ladakh had been traded for salt, tea, and other staples. Behind the town, the steeply rising peaks were clad in thick, green forests of cedar and pine, and long fingers of ice reached down from the Kohlahoi Glacier into the ravines. Beyond it, the crumbling road tracked higher towards Zoji La Pass which crossed the Himalayas at three and a half thousand metres above sea level, and was the scene of the world's highest-ever tank battle, when India used tanks to stave off Pakistan's troops at the time of independence. It was not a highway to war; the highway *was* the war. Every aspect of the operation to retake the heights originated along a road so narrow that the diesel-spewing military traffic could only move in one direction at a time.

Ten years after economic reform policies were introduced, it is still impossible to buy a decent light-fitting in India. Much as this may annoy the middle class, it is of no consequence to the nation. The nation of India is not interested in light-fittings; it hankers after achievements and challenges as big as Bollywood cinema. Slow to stir, the Indian Army behemoth was beginning to lumber with the slow but orderly transport of troops, weapons, and hundreds of truckloads of pack mules from the Valley to the Brigade and Division Headquarters in Ladakh. For long stretches the road was flanked by truck lots, tented billets, ammunition dumps, camps for inducted personnel undergoing orientation, and field hospitals. Amid the ringing of bells and lighting of oil lamps, tented Hindu temples served a constant torrent of troops praying on their way in, or giving thanks on their way out. Armed priests dressed in camouflage tied holy strings on the wrists of their fellow soldiers, and blessed their guns by applying red *tikka* to the barrels. They saw themselves as incarnations of Arjuna at the battle of Kurukshetra, on the eve of which Lord Krishna counselled the reluctant warrior on his moral duty to take up arms against his family's enemies. Unlike their Muslim opponents in the mountains above, the Indian troops belonged to many faiths, and apart from *mandirs*, the tent cities boasted *gurdwaras* for Sikhs, chapels for Christians and temples for Zoroastrians. Yet far from being a weakness, the diversity in the Indian ranks was a strength. There was no point having Marathas and Jats in the same unit if they couldn't speak the same language or drink from the same cup, so units were organised along ethnic, regional, religious and even caste lines, and competed to be the best. Vast and unwieldy, yet committed to its democratic secular Constitution, India squatted like a multicultural elephant, blocking the path to uniformity so fervently desired by Islam's new Saladins.

Zigzagging the switchbacks towards Zoji La, the bus driver exhibited a wreckless nonchalance, preferring to chat to his passengers than watch the precarious, unsealed road. With thousand-metre drops and no safety-fencing, every bend became a heart-thumping flirtation with the abyss. About one hundred kilometres east of Srinagar, we crossed the pass and descended into the awesomely barren wastes of Ladakh. Burnt-out hulks of vehicles littered the roadside near the town of Matayan, whose mainly Muslim population had fled from Pakistani shelling which had destroyed and damaged numerous buildings. Further along the road Indian gunners worked doggedly to repay the favour, ramming 155mm shells into the breaches of artillery guns, the barrels of which were tilted at insane angles to clear the surrounding mountains. With mind-numbing repetitiveness, the six-man crews loaded and armed their guns, shut the breaches, covered their ears and fired three rounds every fourteen seconds. It was costing a thousand dollars a shell, and every time they fired the barrels belched fire and Hell's choir ricocheted off the canyon walls. A ground burst from an incoming shell about a hundred metres from the road indicated they would have to change position before the Pakistanis registered the guns as a target.

'Don't worry,' said an officer on board the bus, when he saw me flinch. 'Getting hit is purely a matter of chance.'

Not since the Punic Wars in 218 BC, when the Carthaginian general Hannibal crossed the Alps in winter with sixty thousand troops, nine thousand cavalry and thirty-seven elephants, had there been such an awe-inspiring battlefield.[14] The glaciated, avalanche-prone rock pinnacles soaring up to six thousand metres above sea level demanded the skills of a mountaineer and the bloodymindedness of a soldier. Ascending to engage their enemy, the Indians often required pitons and rope. Enjoying conventional military superiority over its opponent, India's most obvious response would have been simply to attack elsewhere, occupying a larger tract of Pakistani territory or perhaps even a city like Lahore. But keen to avoid international intervention, New Delhi decided to limit the war to the single existing front, effectively ruling out a combat role for its stronger navy. Its fighter planes could barely manoeuvre within the confines of the mountains, and the rotor blades of its helicopters lost traction in air unthickened by oxygen. In the first week alone, the Indian Air Force lost four aircraft, three shot down and one lost due to engine failure. Restoring national honour at Kargil was up to the army.

Trailing like ants across the face of the Himalayas were tens of thousands of Indian *jawans* marching up and down the ridge lines in single file. Their standard kit comprised an olive green windcheater and woollen scarf, trousers tucked into boots, netted helmet and ammo pouches, a service-issue rifle and equally standard moustache. The enemy were better equipped and had the initiative, having secretly occupied an eight hundred square kilometre tract of territory with excellent planning and logistics. Numbering about seventeen hundred with two regular soldiers for every jihadi, they had acclimatised at training camps beneath the world's second-highest mountain, K2, for several months before crossing the LOC, unarmed and wearing salwar kameez over their cold weather gear so as not to attract attention.

'To move and fight at these heights requires at least 4000 calories a day, which is over half a ton of rations for 600 men,' wrote Lieutenant-Colonel (Ret.) Brian Cloughley, an authority on the Pakistan military. 'They have excellent (and very expensive) cold-weather clothing, a generous supply of ammunition, and lots of food. The food has to be cooked and snow melted to provide water, requiring almost the same weight in fuel blocks. It is difficult to supply ammunition at high altitude because of its bulk and density ... a band of guerillas could not arrange such demanding logistics without co-operation by Pakistani authorities.'[15]

As soon as the intruders had reached the abandoned Indian bunkers, porters began funnelling in machine guns, grenade-launchers, rocket-propelled grenades, mortars, anti-aircraft guns, Stinger missiles, night vision goggles, gas masks and even new snowmobiles. In April General Musharraf — a former commando — flew in personally to give the 'boys' a pep talk.

India's largest military operation in almost thirty years commenced at an extreme disadvantage. Not only did the enemy hold the heights, but India's forces by and large had lacked the time to properly acclimatise. At such extreme elevation it was exhausting for them to take even a few steps, and a significant proportion of deaths in the first days of the campaign were due to pulmonary oedema, in which fluid collects in the lungs, hindering absorption of oxygen in the thin alpine air and causing asphixiation. Cerebral oedemas were even more deadly. Compared to the infiltrators' thermal suits and sleds, the Indian Army could not even provide proper snowboots. There were not enough woollen — let alone bulletproof — vests to go around; their heads were protected by World War II-vintage steel helmets, not modern kevlar; on patrol in the heights they ate stale *puris* and smoked *bidis* to kill their hunger; their wages were laughable. But the Indians had one key advantage over their Muslim opponents: the daily army ration of sixty millilitres of Lord Nelson rum.

Sitting on a mound by the road near Pandrass, Major Suresh Kumar had taken off his boots and was inspecting his blisters. The hardbitten soldier from Ranikhet belonged to the Garhwal regiment which had spent several nights blasting bunkers above five thousand metres and would later receive a citation from the army chief for its work. But after nineteen years of service, Major Kumar cared more for his uniform than any medals his superiors might stick on it.

'The uniform is giving me the motivation. If any person is coming on our land, ultimately it's up to me to send him back to wherever he belongs,' he said, referring to the war as 'the office'.

A typical day at the office began at 8.30 p.m. with a four-hour climb in darkness to the summit of the objective to be taken.

'When we approach the bunkers, the intruders open up, but the angle is so steep their fire goes over our heads. When we get to within fifty metres or so, we open up with light machine guns, maybe destroy the bunkers with a rocket-launcher, then crawl up and lob grenades. If we come across any live Pakistanis we kill them and keep moving forward. Even if they're injured we kill them.'

Ladakh's peculiar geography means that in winter the prevailing winds sweep across the Tibetan plateau, chilling them before they reach the ice-blue headwaters of the Indus River. Eighty kilometres east of Sonamarg on the outskirts of Dras, a signpost reads: 'Second coldest inhabited place in the world. Minus 60°C, Jan. 5, 1995'. The twelve hundred residents had fled, and the cluster of ramshackle shops, many damaged by shelling, was populated mainly by the hungry stray dogs that had been left behind. All that was there for the soldiers, who drifted in from the mountains, was a single army telephone point where long queues of jawans formed to make calls to their relatives in far-flung parts of India.

Beyond the eastern end of the potholed main street, a vast swelling mound towered a thousand metres over the highway. Although the mountains had for centuries been held as sacred by Hindus, and since independence had been considered strategically vital by India, most of them had not been given names. Tololing was an exception, and its name would go down in history as the place where the Indians turned back the tide of armed Islam. Twelve days earlier, Pakistani-backed forces had been on top of it, directing artillery fire onto the national highway in clear view below them, cutting India's military jugular. According to local folklore some of the intruders had become so cocky they ventured down into Dras to do their shopping, mixing undetected among the Muslim-majority residents.

On the slopes of Tololing, a sprinkling of tents and crude wooden structures now marked the base camp of the 2nd

Rajputana Rifles. In early June a detachment of troops from the camp had sprinkled holy water on their regimental flag and begun the arduous ascent, moving mainly at night under enemy fire. It took more than a fortnight to inch their way up to within sight of the Pakistani position, where they paused to direct Indian artillery fire onto the occupied peak, a relentless bombardment that lasted almost twenty hours. At 8 p.m. on 20 June the shelling ceased, creating an eerie silence in which a Hindi song from a jawan's radio could be heard drifting up from the valley far below. Among the Indians was a twenty-three-year-old lieutenant, Parveen Tomar, the youngest of eleven men sent to Kargil from a Rajput family in the Baghpat district of Uttar Pradesh. Not all of them would survive. Springing from their footholds that night, the Indians attacked, raining mortars, grenades and automatic weapons fire on the bunkers. In the first wave several men were shot dead or lost their legs to land mines, and, with his company commander killed, the willowy Parveen, who had been in the army only six months, found himself leading the assault. Clawing his way to the summit beneath a shower of bullets he saw one of his comrades swept hundreds of metres to his death by a boulder rolled down by the defenders. Hearing the Indians approaching, the intruders began calling out a chorus of 'Allahu Akbar', and the Indians reciprocated with epithets and airbursts fired from rocket-launchers. It was death or glory at 2.30 in the morning at five thousand metres. Then they were on top of each other, the battlefield shrunk to twenty metres square. Those who survived had no idea how. It was Parveen who had raised the Indian tricolour on the summit as the mournful moan of conch shells drifted through the ravines to announce the taking of Tololing. Thirty Indians had been killed or injured in the assault, but their gallantry paved the way for further Indian successes as peak after peak fell to them. Now the sacred mountains were 'strewn with the mutilated, unclaimed bodies of soldiers. They are lacerated by artillery fire and by aerial bombardments. They echo with cries of war, or hatred, and of the pain of the dying and the wounded; and, increasingly, of the pitiful calls of the terrified intruders who are confronted with the mounting certainty of death for a futile cause, in a lonely, glacial world, far from the warmth and comforting presence of family or friend.'[16] Most of the mountains may have been nameless, but for the soldiers defending them, they all had the same name: India.

As we walked in the lee of the mountain, Parveen was never far from tears of pride and mourning. He felt the ground beneath his feet had been somehow sanctified by what he and his fellow soldiers had done. The bond the experience had forged between them was eternal, and yet twenty-two of his comrades were dead. He was a hero, but only luck had spared him. He hated his enemy but empathised with them. He had defeated them but he respected them, perhaps even loved them. He felt alone and ashamed to be alive, yet also proud. He was a mess of emotions.

'There were just bullets flying everywhere, people being killed. It was just luck whether you lived or died. No skill. Just fate. One of my boys had blood on his bayonet,' he said, with an awkward blend of bravado and self-pity.

Inspecting the vacated bunkers at the summit the Indians found several days' worth of rations, but no kerosene left for cooking. A couple of prayer mats and gas masks were scattered around, and there was a field telephone with wires leading back towards Pakistan. Winding the phone's magneto, one of the Indians shouted into the receiver, 'We're coming to get you!' Cold and hungry, they lit a fire with a tin of ghee they found, warming themselves and brewing tea and sugar in a metal helmet belonging to one of the nine Pakistanis they had just killed. Victory was as sweet as the tea.

As Parveen and his men celebrated their unit citation, the nation was celebrating with them. For the first time in their history, Indians had experienced the drama of war in their living rooms, via blanket coverage by private television stations. The faces of those killed stared out from newspaper pages every day, and in an unprecedented move, the army allowed the bodies of its dead to be sent home for last rites. The televised ceremonies galvanised a national spirit muffled by decades of grinding insurgencies and dysfunctional politics. 'Kargil knit the country together as never before,' the report of India's official inquiry into the war stated.[17]

But for the diminishing numbers of Pakistani soldiers falling back across the alpine ridges, the bitterness of defeat was suffered alone. According to their own government, they were never there, and after initially accepting the return of three bodies early in June Pakistan subsequently refused to take delivery of any more corpses, leaving it to Indian Army maulvis to bury them with full Islamic rites on the battlefield.[18] Transcripts of an intercepted conversation between a Pakistan-based commander, Afzal, and his field commander, Karim, captured their desperation:

> Karim: Their army has reached very near us. We need more men. Our water and ammunition is also running low.
> Afzal: Remember Allah's name.
> Karim: I'll worry about Allah later! Right now I need reinforcements![19]

Told they were liberating Muslims, the Pakistanis must have been dumbfounded when confronted by Muslim Indian soldiers determined to kill them. Hearing cries of 'Allahu Akbar' one night, intruders holding a peak near Khalubar reportedly ran from their positions to help the presumed reinforcements reach the summit. Only when it was too late did they realise that the words 'God is Great' came from the Muslim company of India's 22 Grenadiers.[20] As India's 'Operation Vijay' intensified, supply lines linking the intruders to their main sources of food, cooking fuel and ammunition began to break down. The snow which provided their drinking water had become contaminated with the cordite from exploded ordnance.

We reached Kargil, two hundred kilometres east of Srinagar, after nightfall, gladdened by the sight of familiar faces at the Hotel

Siachen. On a star-speckled night, at the junction of the Suru and Wakka rivers, with the odd Pakistani shell falling on the town, it was the centre of the world's attention. In Washington, Pakistan's prime minister, Nawaz Sharif, had agreed to an American suggestion that he withdraw his forces. Determined to maintain the jihadi fiction, Sharif couched the withdrawal as a request to the 'freedom fighters' who, he said, had achieved a great victory by internationalising the Kashmir issue. The unpalatable fact was that Pakistan had been routed, and its ill-conceived adventure had ended in a shameful and humiliating defeat.

The following morning, the Shia majority of Kargil residents came out onto the streets in greater numbers than they had in several months. Some weeks earlier the most bizarre event of the entire war had occurred in the town, when the Shias had made their annual Moharram procession, lacerating themselves as they walked through streets being bombarded by their fellow Muslims from across the LOC. Of course, the Muslims in Pakistan were mainly Sunnis, and the Shia minority there lived in fear of sectarian violence, which was being fanned by fundamentalist jihadi culture.

Although fought on only one front, Kargil was the first regular war on the subcontinent since 1971, the fourth between India and Pakistan, and the first since the two nations acquired nuclear weapons. Like all future conflicts between them, it took place under the shadow of mass destruction. India's official losses were 474 army officers and men killed, and more than a thousand injured. It was a measure of the viciousness of the fighting that only two prisoners — a downed Indian pilot, and a member of Pakistan's 5th Northern Light Infantry — were captured.

In India and Pakistan, analysis of the aftermath of the conflict in the two countries reflected the disparity in their fortunes. Writing in Pakistan's influential *Friday Times*, Najam Sethi summed up the national ennui, claiming that,

After 50 years, Pakistan is unable to agree upon who we are as a nation, where we belong, what we believe in . . . Are we Pakistanis first and Punjabis, Sindhis, Baluchis, Pathans or Mohajirs afterwards? Or vice versa? Do we belong to South Asia or West Asia? Are we Muslims in a modern Muslim state? Are we supposed to be like Saudi Arabia and Iran, which are orthodox Islamic states, or like Jordan, Egypt, Syria and Algeria, which are liberal Muslim states? If none of these fit the bill, then what?[21]

Sethi was arrested the day after the article appeared, and spent thirty days in detention for daring to analyse the affairs of the nation. The following month, another columnist, Dr Iffat S. Malik, challenged the hoary old issue of Kashmir where the freedom struggle, she said, had become 'corrupted'. 'It is no longer viewed as a purely Kashmiri fight against Indian oppression.'[22]

Although many Indian writers had criticised the handling and expense of the war, the consensus when the guns fell silent was that India's secular democracy had been vindicated.

'All fundamentalist creeds preach an identical message of exclusion and hatred,' wrote K. P. S. Gill, a former director-general of Punjab police and a counter-insurgency guru. 'These malignant doctrines, and not Islam, motivate what the fanatics in Pakistan and their supporters elsewhere call the jihad in Kashmir. The mullahs of Pakistan have reduced the teachings of one of the great religions of the world to a travesty, brainwashing young men — many of them mere children — to commit murder, and to die, in wayward wars of aggression on foreign soil. But this blasphemous creed offends against all religion.'[23]

On 15 August, Atal Behari Vajpayee took the salute on the ramparts of Shah Jahan's fort in Delhi on the annual celebration of India's Independence Day. The following month he would win a third term as prime minister. A month later Nawaz Sharif was toppled in a military coup, and General Pervez Musharraf took control of the country.

As winter approached in the mountains around Kargil, the shepherds who saved India were returning to their pastures in the Kashmir Valley. But the war in high places would scar them as well. When they returned to Ladakh the following year, the once-pristine landscape was laced with unexploded land mines and ordnance. The Muslim militants were back again, reverting to their former strategy of infiltration and hit-and-run attacks, rather than trying to hold territory.

The good shepherds were their first target.

PART EIGHT

THE DESERT OF HELL

29

The Gypsy Kilim

'The Kuchi are on the move!' said Terence Barker, draining the last precious cupful from the water cooler outside the database mapping room as he returned to his office. 'The drought forced them out of their winter grazing areas in the Reg earlier than usual this year. You'd better hurry up and get down there.'

The rambling double-storey residence where he worked in a leafy suburb of Islamabad was a triumph of function over form. There were two rubber plants in the stairwell, but otherwise barely a hint of decoration. The lights were fluorescent; maps of Afghanistan provided wallpaper. The building badly needed a paint job and the off-road vehicles parked in the driveway were dust-clotted. But Terence, whose business card described him as 'Program Manager — Livestock Development for Food Security in Afghanistan (UN Food & Agricultural Organisation)' — had more pressing concerns. Not only were the Kuchi nomads moving earlier, they were moving faster as well, chased out of Registan, the 'Country of Sand', in the year 2000 by the worst drought in sixty years. By May they would be moving north-east, driving their flocks along the grassy tracts between the Arghastan and Tarnak rivers, avoiding the Kabul–Kandahar highway as they headed for the high meadows around Lake Nawar — war permitting. The middle-aged British agronomist with the sweep of grey hair was attempting to keep track of their migration, and those of other nomads, by maintaining radio contact with his sub-offices across the region. There was also a western migration from Farah to Ghor and an eastern movement through the Khyber Pass and Kabul Gorge, all the way to Maidan Shahr, Paghman and Panjshir. But on a jacaranda-lined street, where wealthy Pakistanis walked their dogs every afternoon, it was the move to Mukkur that was occupying minds. Herd sizes were dwindling, grass cover was sparse and lambing rates were down. About the only thing that wasn't falling was the rain.

'It's odd,' said Terence, making coffee. 'They live mainly in the desert, yet their economy depends on rain. They occupy this strange niche which somehow supports about five per cent of Afghanistan's population. That's about a million people migrating to some degree or another. But this drought, combined with the war — it's killing.'

Nomads have long coped with the vagaries of man and nature. In the nineteenth century British agents reported that feuds with land-owning tribes had forced the Kuchi — whose name means 'to travel' — to move in large groups of up to ten thousand people. One agent wrote: 'They proceed with the caution of a military body in an enemy's country, move by regular marches, with advance and rear guards, occupy positions favourable for defence, and post pickets and sentries round their camps.'[1]

The Pashto-speaking nomads, also known as *powindahs*, had been encouraged by Afghan kings to spread into the central highlands as a means of putting pressure on the despised Shia Muslim Hazaras. But during the Soviet occupation — when the nomads found their traditional routes strewn with land mines — they had to stay put in their winter domiciles, placing strain on available resources and causing tensions with sedentary communities, with whom they were forced to spend the summers as well. After the Russian withdrawal the fighting between the mujahideen factions continued to make life difficult and it was dangerous for the gypsies to cross frontlines, with the result that many abandoned the annual journey to Hazarajat.[2] When the Taliban came on the scene, individual Talibs tried to coerce nomad women — who are uninhibited and do not cover their faces — into the chaderi.[3] But soon, realising the nomads' potential as fellow Pashto-speakers desperate for land, the Taliban actually flew some Kuchi into Bamiyan in the Central Highlands, arming them to fight off the local Hazaras.

'It was a political gesture rather than an effective grazing technique,' my agronomist friend said.

Terence Barker was a bit of a nomad himself: born in England, raised in Kenya, and on the road with the FAO for many years. Now politics had restricted even his peripatetic ways. After the cruise missile strikes on Afghanistan the UN had barred its British and American employees from entering the country on security grounds, making a farce of job descriptions like Barker's. A lot of frustrated refugee professionals were hanging around Islamabad and Peshawar, and several career-minded types had even taken out Irish, New Zealand or Australian citizenship in order to get around the rules. I empathised with their frustrated wanderlust. For years the fighting had prevented me reaching long-dreamt-of places in Afghanistan's Central Highlands, like Bamiyan with its enormous Buddha statues, the listing Minaret of Jam and the ethereal blue lakes of Band-e Amir.

'If only I'd been a Kuchi,' lamented Terence. 'Their sheep are their passport.'

Charts and rosters plotted the agronomist's efforts to continue his work by extension. A small carpet woven with the words 'Happy New Year 1998' and the emblem of the FAO hung from the wall, a memento from a carpet workshop he had established in Kandahar to provide employment for nomads who had lost their flocks. But because weaving was not a strong tradition among the Pashtuns, Turkmen weavers had to be engaged to teach them rug-making techniques.

'It was only in the refugee camps that the Pashtuns started to weave,' said Terence. 'They were basically farmers, and even the Kuchi generally didn't need to make carpets. They were doing quite well enough selling their sheep and agricultural produce. They own a quarter of the country's livestock, can you believe it? They used to operate as loan sharks for the settled tribes; you know, if somebody defaulted, they knew where they lived. By the way, if you get there don't forget to look for the women's jewellery. The anklets and ornaments and old coins they sew into their clothing are a good guide to how well they're doing. Some of those coins have been around since Bactrian times! But be discreet. The women are unveiled, so they tend to attract cameras and don't always welcome it. And be wary of approaching their camps. They have huge dogs that will savage a stranger.'

Marooned far from the nomad action, Terence took solace from the extensive statistics his survey teams had gathered about the gypsies. To begin with, being a nomad was not a cut-and-dried identity. Despite the Kuchi's low social status their numbers tended to swell during extended periods of good weather, as others joined them. As far back as the 1870s agent Major Henry George Raverty reported that the Sulaiman Khel and Aka Khel clans had reverted to nomadism.[4] Among the Afghans there was none of the false glorification of the nomadic lifestyle so prevalent in the West. People were willing to adopt or abandon it, according to their practical needs. If the latest drought continued, Terence expected, thousands of drifters would settle permanently on the outskirts of towns and cities. His surveys showed that 95 per cent of the nomads complained of inadequate access to education for their children, eclipsing their other concerns about the lack of medical and veterinary facilities, land mines, or problems with other tribes.

'We've discovered something truly remarkable about the Kuchi,' Terence said as he escorted me downstairs from his office. 'When we asked active Kuchi whether they would like to give up nomadism, only one in every hundred said they wanted to settle down. Can you imagine? A 99 per cent job satisfaction rating! Show me a city anywhere with that kind of contentment.'

Driving across Islamabad, I wondered what Terence's survey method might reveal if applied to the Pakistan capital. It was May 2000, and the country had been under military rule for six months. The Constitution was suspended and the gleaming National Assembly building at the end of Jinnah Avenue remained locked and deserted. Crude missiles had been fired at the US Embassy and United Nations offices by unknown forces, the elected prime minister was in jail, and the Opposition leader was in exile.

Discontent was brewing just beneath the placid surface of military rule, especially at Caravan Carpits.

'*Bismillah*! You have brought the life back to Pakistan!' cried Habib, shuffling his loose-limbed frame off the floor of the shop and grabbing me in a wrestling hold. He looked well in a newly laundered salwar kameez with an embroidered breastplate. A recent haircut had redefined his sideburns and given renewed prominence to his big jaw and aquiline nose. But like Islamabad's appearance of good order, his fresh look was deceptive.

'Business is nowhere, but taxes are increasing,' he said, wincing with gas. 'Three people cannot meet in the street, or army will stop it. No voices on the loudspeakers. This is army! Believe me, slowly, slowly, people is sick of Pakistan. Their heart is full of Pakistan.'

To my surprise, Habib had been following the drought in Afghanistan and the plight of the Kuchi.

'The sheeps are dying, maybe people also. Before, a sheep costs eighteen hundred rupees. Now one-fifty.'

I was curious to know why, as Terence had said, the Pashtuns didn't weave. Habib denied it.

'Who is saying like this? Of course Pashtuns make the car-pit. The Kuchi are making the car-pit.'

'Really? But I was told . . .'

'Believe me. BELIEVE ME. True is true. Habib is gypsy Pashtun from Sulaiman Khel peoples. Habib is KOOCHEEEE!'

Unravelling Habib's true identity was like peeling an onion. First he had revealed himself as an Afghan. Then the issue of his sexuality had been opened up by the hijras incident. Now he was claiming to be a desert nomad. Life was simpler when Habib was just Habib. But then he told me his 'true is true' story.

'My grandfather Abdul Samad was totally tribal. Totally. In the winters, our family would move from Logar to Jalalabad area. My father, Hajji Haider Gul, was also tribal for, maybe, thirty years. He cannot read a book, no writing, nothing. Still he is uneducated. Actually, he was selling the sheep wools, but slowly, slowly, he saw people making car-pits, and my father said, "Oh, they are making car-pits from this sheep wools. Must be a good benefit in it." So he watched them making, washing, cleaning, cutting and then taking to Kabul, in the city. The famous city. And people is buying the car-pits. And he says, "Why I only want to make the business selling the sheep wools and the camel wools?" So then he took the car-pits from the village and he make a good profit.

'After we make money in this business, then we got the land. My grandfather's time, we don't got any land. Of course, that time we were nomadic peoples, so we owned all of the land, all of the world, and we own nothing. But then we got the land in Raikoshi, and we grow some things, but main business of car-pits is still making. In that time, prices is very high in Kabul, more than Peshawar. Kabul people are rich people. So my father and brother go to Peshawar, buy old Afghan and Irani pieces and giving to the smugglers with the horse to go above the mountains into Afghanistan. So this was a good business. After that we moved to

Kabul, and then to Pakistan in the war time. Still always we are moving. Even now my brother is gone to Azerbaijan to find the car-pits! Can you believe it? This car-pit business is dangerous, definitely.'

Sitting on the floor with one arm flopping over his knee, Habib basked in my shock and amazement. A professional sceptic himself, he would go to great lengths to surprise and convince others about things, and took enormous pleasure in succeeding. Determined to prove that Pashtuns could weave, he led me into the godown to show me some kilims, once so undervalued that dealers would throw them in for free with a deal or use them to wrap the carpets they sold. Without knots or pile, their angular designs were obtained simply by changing the colour of the wefts, creating vertical slits in the body of the rug where the colour changes. These slits, which may or may not be sewn up, give them their other name, slitweaves. Because there are no knots, and therefore less work involved, kilims tend to be cheaper than carpets, although good examples have become more sought after by collectors in recent years. They are lighter and easier to transport, but older pieces are harder to find because flatweaves are not as durable as pile rugs.

Habib's kilims were crisp, uncluttered pieces which glowed with sunburnt colours. The designs were bold, usually with three large diamonds framed by a variety of *waziri* and other more obscure guls arranged in borders formed by crenellated cartouches. They were rustic, brash and whimsical, with a desert palette of ochre and apricot woven in odd, oblong sizes, reflecting the nomads' small portable looms. Unlike the rugs upstairs, which Habib used to roll like cigars, his kilims were folded and stacked.

'It was made by Kuchi people during summer near Nawar Lake,' he said, unfolding the first piece. 'There is a market in Mukkur where they are selling these pieces, genuine tribal pieces. Before, people think the city car-pit is highest quality. But when he knows tribal work, the colours, he is crazy for that. In two hundred years, people will still make city car-pits, but tribal car-pit will be gone, gone, gone. Who got it, got it. Who left, left.'

Much as I loved him, Habib's big talk could be irritating. In the back of my mind was Tariq's assessment that the rugs I'd bought at Caravan Carpits were vastly overpriced. A strange, angry iconoclasm had begun to infect my mood. Picking one of the Mukkuri kilims out of the pile and looking at it with obvious disgust, I made an offer one-fifth of the asking price. Habib had said often enough that he regarded very low offers as an insult. He looked at me goggle-eyed with disbelief.

'Im-possible,' he said, frowning and scratching his backside. But while his jaw remained set, his eyes betrayed a kind of terror. He sensed I had been talking to another dealer.

The bargaining session went on all afternoon. Lying that I had seen the selfsame piece for a tenth of the price in Peshawar, I wore away at him with niggardly increments and diversionary tactics.

'So *these* are Kuchi weavings. My friend Abdul *gives* these away,' I said, inventing both Abdul and his generosity.

Selecting cheaper, obviously inferior new pieces from the pile, I compared them favourably with the desired kilim, hoping that the tactic would force the price down. Habib's claims about provenance, age, quality and money-back guarantees were brushed aside. Taking out a notebook, I checked off an imaginary list of prices. His eyes flashed uncertainly once more. Finally, when Habib's weariness and confusion became transparent, I hit him hard with the lowest blow of all.

'Habib, I thought we were friends,' I said mournfully. 'Whenever I come to Islamabad I always visit you. *Always.* Now this — I mean, really! Is it worth so much to you? This one tiny, little kilim?'

Much to my relief it wasn't, and he handed over the Mukkuri for a song. Pashtuns are not entirely averse to compromise; they just take longer to accept the need for it.

Now it was Habib's turn to be sulky. As he bundled the Mukkuri, tying it expertly with twine to form a carry bag and handle, I told him I was planning a return visit to Afghanistan to find the Kuchi. As usual, he was against the trip.

'Why you want to put your luck in the trouble?' he said, frowning. 'One time success is too good for you.'

'It's your country,' I said. 'Don't you want to go home? You must really have gypsy blood in your veins!'

'You know, Mr Gentlemens,' he began, adopting a languid, superior tone. 'Kuchi is Kuchi. These people don't think much about what I have, what I don't have. Everything is getting from sheep, like milk, ghee, wool. They have good informations about where is the good grass, how is the weather. All the details, you know? This is his job, that's why he knows. Sometimes, they may be fighting with the landowners. If they eat grass the landowner doesn't mind it, but if they eat the wheat, then there is problem. Maybe they make a small battle. Big countries are fighting, so if uneducated people fight, it's also reasonable.'

The kilim was tied, the money paid.

'Kuchi life is too dirty,' Habib continued, screwing up his face. 'All your body is too dirty. You cannot keep your dress clean. Im-possible. They smell bad. Tribal means no education, only sheep. It's totally mountain, mountain, mountain. The water always is too far away. Before, all the world was tribal, but now people is getting educated, modern life is becoming Punjabi. Not *all* your life you must survive in the Kuchi way. For a few days I like to go to the river, to the mountains area, to make a picnic. When you go for a holiday, you also are like a gypsy.'

Habib handed me the nomadic weaving and, for no particular reason, began thinking aloud about his son.

'Actually I want to get him a school, you know, good knowledge. This is my dream.'

'But what about your business? Who will carry on?' I asked.

'No question. My son will be in this car-pit business,' he replied. 'This is also like tribal life. If I don't have sheep or camel, I do have car-pit! This is my grandfather's business; also I must have. We are thinking like this. So yes, my son will be in the car-pits. But he will be educated, and he will bargain better with customers like you.'

30

Death of the Nomads

Mike Sackett took a handful of grain from a hessian bag, tossed a few kernels into his mouth and chewed them. 'If they were hungry enough, I guess they'd eat it,' he said. Wiping the residue from his hands, he added: 'Starvation's not the issue. If the Afghans can't live normally in their villages they'll all move to Pakistan, and then we'll really have a problem. I suppose we've just got to find wheat that sticks.'

It was all very embarrassing. The hard red wheat in the warehouse was stacked high in bulging sacks marked 'Gift of the USA', ready for shipment to drought-stricken areas. It could save lives, this grain. Afghan villagers could mill it, mix it with water and make it into nan. But the American wheat wouldn't stick to the inner walls of the Afghan tandoors. The World Food Program (WFP) staff had tried mixing it in every conceivable consistency, but the doughy cakes kept falling off the oven walls and into the fire. They'd tried teaching people how to mix the wheat into gruel, but the illiterate villagers couldn't deal with it. For thousands of years they had survived on nan. They needed only nan. What the world was giving them was a problem, not a solution to their simplest need.

The director of WFP's Afghan project was having a bad aid day. Earlier, he'd been told that our trip across Pakistan's Baluchistan province to the Afghan border was off because his local office had failed to get the required clearances to cross the tribal areas. We had two big white Land Cruisers with Codan radios, coolers full of soft drinks, and maps and interpreters. But the government offices that issued the passes were on *chooti*. A less committed official would have packed up and returned to Islamabad, happy to have reclaimed his weekend. But Sackett was bloodyminded enough not only to work in a bureaucratic environment, but to circumvent it where necessary. When other Brits had been banned from entering Afghanistan, he had kept working on his other, Australian passport. Now he consulted his oracle, a troll-like Afghan, Abdul Bari, to whom all important decisions were referred. Bari was a settled Kuchi with an intimate knowledge of southern Afghanistan, a survivor who could balance the often conflicting agendas of the Taliban, Pakistan, the WFP and the UN.

Soon our jeeps were bouncing along the pitted backroads towards Pishin, avoiding the checkpoint on the main road where tribal area permits were scrutinised. Rejoining the main road to the border, we shadowed the rail line past Fort Abdullah and climbed towards Khojak Pass, the gateway through which British troops invaded Afghanistan after occupying Baluchistan's provincial capital, Quetta, in the nineteenth century. Cresting the pass we saw it, hundreds of metres below us: the Reg, sprawling with cruel majesty to the far horizon. A patch of measles on the Registan Desert floor identified Chaman, the last Pakistani town before the border. It was a daunting view, God's own warning to the fainthearted, backed up by map names such as Dasht-e Margo (Desert of Death), Sar-o Tar (Empty Desolation) and Dasht-e Jehanum (Desert of Hell). In early summer the stone bluffs of the mountains radiated heat, and hundreds of piquets, built by the British to defend the Raj from a feared Russian invasion, dotted the ridges. But beyond the mountains there was nothing, multiplied by heat, multiplied by nothing.

Nomadism exists where mountains meet deserts. When summer scorched the winter grasslands of the Reg, the Kuchi would migrate onto the cool highland pastures, returning to the desert when winter snows buried the mountains. Initially a matter of survival, nomadism had slowly permeated the culture of the region. With its imagery of migration and desert, Islam resonated strongly within nomadic communities. As a child, the Prophet had travelled with his uncle, Abu Talib, across the Arabian Peninsula. The Islamic calendar took as its starting point the beginning of Mohammed's Heijira from Mecca to Medina. The book of his inspired revelations, the Koran, is imbued with the mystic human journey through life, in which 'we are all returning'. So, along with their sheep, horses, cats, dogs, goats and camels, the Kuchi carried Islam out of the desert before summer each year, in search of better grass.

In 1878 Major Raverty wrote:

All their wants and requirements are supplied by their flocks and herds. The wool and hair furnish them with the materials for their kijzdas *or black hair tents ... their* gilims *or felt carpets, their sacks and bags, and other articles. From their milk they make butter, cheese, and* kurut, *which constitutes their food, save when making a feast or entertaining a guest, when a sheep or lamb is killed. A few copper cooking and other utensils, some clothes, and bedding constitute the remainder of their household goods; consequently they can move about with facility and celerity.*[5]

The Khojak Pass, where we now stood buffeted by rising thermals off the Reg, had long been part of the nomad superhighway into the Indus Valley. While the majority of Kuchi were pastoralists, some of the more enterprising facilitated the Silk Road trade, moving deep into India on their summer migrations. With the coming of the Raj they were required to deposit their weapons at armouries on the Indus, but could travel on the new trains to Bengal, Karachi or Bombay carrying carpets, embroidered skullcaps, pistachio and *chilgohza* nuts, dried fruits from Kandahar, lapis lazuli, jade, turquoise, Russian gold coins and even Venetian ducats. On their return from India they would take oranges, muslin, tea, coffee, glass, crockery and guns. As elsewhere on the Silk Road, the goods moved by relay, not a marathon. Returning to the Reg in winters, the southern nomads would meet up with those who had spent the summer north of the Amu Darya in places like Samarkand and Bukhara. Items exchanged with them were carried out and sold the following summer. The partition of India largely curbed this practice, although smuggling across the India–Pakistan border continues, exceeding the official trade. When Tariq Ahmed had come bearing rugs to Delhi, and loaded me down with small commodities to carry back to Peshawar for him, we were, in our own small way, continuing a tradition.

At Chaman, the car was submerged in a deluge of humanity, squeezing between the narrow gateposts into Afghanistan. In the bustle of moneychangers and bearers, the lone border guard on duty seemed quite overwhelmed, reduced to watching the human tide pouring past. Afghans, and especially Pashtuns, were entering Pakistan freely, without formalities. The soft border made Afghanistan a virtual province of Pakistan, or vice versa, depending on your point of view. The Afghan Immigration office was unsignposted, and occupied a mud-brick shack buried in the smugglers' bazaar in the town of Spin Boldak, where the task of inspecting our passports seemed to give a plodding, turban-wearing Talib an instant migraine. The office was plastered with posters of crossed Kalashnikovs spanning the globe and slogans urging Islamic revolution, but outside the shack, smuggling was the main game. Everyone was on the make, shifting barrowloads of fax machines, food processors, guns, cars and opium — all heading for Pakistan duty-free if the right palms were greased.

Extracting ourselves from Spin Boldak's chaotic commerce, we were soon truck surfing across the shimmering plain towards Kandahar, then leaving the highway after a few kilometres, headed north-east on the fragmented backroad to Arghastan. Fine bulldust exploded in clouds from the tyres of the lead truck and huge vicious dogs snapped at our tyres as we headed into a landscape of thornbushes and ravines, the jeep listing like a top-heavy ship on a rolling sea. Standing at regular intervals in the denuded fields were scarecrows — not stuffed effigies but live human beings warding off birds from their withered crops in the blazing sun. Families were fleeing the desert on foot and headed for Spin Boldak, confronting us with our first dilemma. The survey team's job was to examine the extent of the drought in Kandahar and Zabol provinces, but all around us were individuals in pressing need. At one point two men stumbled onto the road, a son supporting his ailing father. They were Kuchi walking towards town in search of medical treatment. Both of them had blood-red eyes and clotted voices, and when we gave the old man a mouthful of water he plunged into a coughing fit which brought him to his knees. As we drove on, carcasses of dead livestock became a common sight. Even camels, which can live for two weeks without water, had expired. Tortoises emerging in thousands from their burrows, as they did every spring, were the only living things in this desert of death. Puffy white clouds taunted them from a rainless sky.

The area's main water source, the Arghastan River, had run dry, and on its exposed bed some fifty local *spin-zhiri*, or 'white beards', squatted. They were in the throes of an emergency meeting to decide whether to evacuate their families and remaining livestock to Kandahar or Chaman. No bread had been baked in the villages for six months, 90 per cent of the livestock had died, and the people were surviving on boiled alfalfa. Approaching us, one of the men held out a letter sent on behalf of two hundred families to the Taliban's district administration. They had received no reply. The elder had a deeply furrowed, burnished face, with a jutting brow that shaded his eyes like sunglasses. Like all of them, his fingers kneaded worry beads.

'What is your opinion?' he asked our team leader. 'Will you give us food, or should we leave this place?'

Mike's carefully worded reply quickly dimmed the hope that had briefly lit many eyes on our arrival. The last thing he wanted was another flood of refugees, but the situation was too critical to string people along.

'We're here to look at the situation,' he said. 'When we return to Pakistan we'll recommend that food aid be sent here. But I can't guarantee it will come soon enough or be sufficient to feed everyone. You have to decide for yourselves whether to stay or leave.'

Following the dry riverbed we continued east through Maruf district, getting reports of Kuchi movements along the way. Some nomad families had crossed the area the previous day in trucks supplied by the Taliban to rescue them from the inferno of the Reg. As the shadows cast by the hills started to lengthen, Abdul Bari and our driver Ahmed stopped for *namaz*, facing the setting sun and kneeling on a woollen mat. It was after dark when we reached the district headquarters located in a mud-brick fort with anti-aircraft guns occupying the turrets. It had been a strange, disturbing day, a passage through Hell unscathed. But if there were pangs of conscience they were silenced by the enjoyment of a simple evening meal and light banter about what to do with the snorers in our party.

Next morning we had our second encounter with the Kuchi. Some of the nomads trucked out of the Reg by the Taliban had been dumped on the outskirts of Maruf, where they were sheltering in tents made of patchwork, not the traditional black goat hair. The only man in the camp, Gula Bagh, said his flock had been reduced to a fifth of its original size and now consisted of about fifty sheep, not enough to support the four families in his group. They were waiting for another lift to Ghazni, where they hoped to meet other members of their clan and decide what to do next. He had ten Pakistani rupees, so I gave him some money and took a few photographs, which neither Gula Bagh nor the colourfully dressed nomad women with unveiled faces objected to.

But as I was taking the shots, a carload of Talibs appeared from the district headquarters, remonstrating with me until I stopped.

As we turned north into Zabol province the situation became increasingly desperate, with people streaming down hillsides to meet our cars. Time and again the brief light of hope died out in their faces as the survey team explained its limited mandate. The orchards and nut groves, which had once been Afghanistan's pride, were dying. It would take at least seven years before new trees bore fruit, and nobody was planting. In Abu Khala a woman broke into our meeting with the village elders. Addressing us directly and angrily she said that they were hungry and demanded that we give food, not talk. An old man in a torn vest, who had been sitting on the ground eating the petals of a wild rose, stood up to speak.

'My beard is white, but I have never lived through anything like this drought,' he said. 'It is affecting everyone, the settled and the free. Wells thirty metres deep have dried up. What are we to do?'

A hot, sulphurous wind carried Mike Sackett's stock reply away, the truth as harsh as the weather.

Hitching a ride with us to the next village, a local Taliban member pointed to the hills behind Abu Khala and said that one of the cruise missiles fired at the bin Laden training camps had landed there, hundreds of kilometres off target. The militia had sent a team of technicians who had dismantled the missile and taken the pieces away for further study.

'Our homes have become the road of the snake,' he said, reminding me of Tariq's identical comment on the Soviet invasion years before. Now everything was upside down. The settled were abandoning their villages, nomads were settling, and fiery snakes slithered across the sky.

The great nomad exodus from the Reg was in full swing, the broad valleys dotted with tents. Strings of camels, donkeys and people marched across the barren expanse, whipped by *shaitans*, literally devils, the small whirlwinds that suck up the earth and spew it into the air. Small children covered in amulets to ward off the evil eye walked alongside the adults. Only infants rode, being tied to the donkeys' backs on a cushion of quilts beside cheap aluminium cooking pots. The women traipsed unfettered, their temples and chins tattooed. They wore plastic slippers and were draped in flowing, brilliantly coloured dupattas and skirts with coins sewn into them. Young girls collected strands of wool left on thornbushes by passing sheep, and the boys collected kindling or shot birds with their ever-present sling-shots, making a game of this serious business of survival. Fathers entertained their families by playing small stringed *rebobs* as they walked at the head of the line, usually with a camel or two.

While the survey team was busy in a village meeting, Bari and I walked back to a tent we had spotted in the middle of a wide valley halfway between Maruf and Shinkay. Challenged by a large dog on the perimeter, we waited until the slavering animal was secured and we could approach. Three men sat on a quilt laid out on the bare earth in front of the patchwork tent. A blackened kettle simmered on a small fire, boiling water taken from the inner tubes of truck tyres. The men were part of a larger group of about fifty Kuchi, belonging to the Sulaiman Khel clan of Ghilzai Pashtuns, and were headed for Mukkur. Their combined flock of seven hundred sheep had been reduced to about fifty. There was only one large sheep in the camp, one horse and one camel.

'The camel is dying,' said Hainday, a flat-nosed elder, explaining that they had wintered in Sourawakh and left before the festival of Eid. They had received no help from the Taliban, had nothing left to sell and could not remain in Spin Boldak because they could not repay loans taken there to buy food. Once moneylenders themselves, the Kuchi were now in hock. There seemed little else but habit drawing them towards Lake Nawar, like whales beaching themselves in the shallows of remembered oceans. Without flocks to graze there was nothing for people to do there. When I asked Hainday where they had spent the previous night, he pointed to a mountain at the end of the valley. Spread out, and with their animals sick, they were making very slow time.

Of the fifty people, only the mullah who belonged to the family could read. His son, Abdul Qayoom, said he intended to look for labouring work in Ghazni and, if he got it, would settle there.

'Last year was also bad,' he said, 'but two years of drought in a row is too much. We're broke. I don't see what choice we have.'

Around the camp a pack of young boys played games and seemed clever and healthy, with bright smiles and glowing skin, their leathery bare feet untroubled by the thorns and stones. The fittest had survived. They were lively miniatures of their fathers, with ample turbans and little walking sticks. From the tent a baby cried, and looking inside I saw a lone woman draped in a bright red veil. She was suckling an infant and was seated on the loose, sandy dirt that kept blowing in under the open side of the tent. A pile of mattresses occupied a corner of the shelter. There was no sign of weavings. In silence, she turned her face resolutely away from me.

Leaving the camp, Bari shook his head in dismay. 'This will be the time the Kuchi settle,' he said with foreboding. 'It was at a time like this that my grandfather gave up the nomadic life.'

We spent our second night at Shinkay, which seemed more like an ammunition dump than a village. The building occupied by the local Taliban leaders bristled with guns and ordnance, and artillery shells leant against the walls. In Islamabad, The Gopher had given me a bleak preview of what to expect from the Taliban administration.

'We've met them a number of times,' he said, plying me with his latest batch of freshly baked cookies. 'Regrettably, I've come to the conclusion that they're hopeless. We've given them all kinds of talking points — nice-as-pie ones, business-as-usual ones, mean-as-hell ones — but no matter what, the result is always the same. They just sit there, staring at you with their fourteenth-century faces.'

In *The Adventures of Hajji Baba of Ispahan*, Hajji makes the same point somewhat differently. 'Of what use is a beard,' he asks, 'when an empty sconce is tied to the end of it? About as much as a handle is to a basket without dates.'[6]

According to an old Afghan saying, when the emir is tired, there is no rain, and in Shinkay there was little evidence of a functioning administration. Almost four years after seizing Kabul, the Taliban controlled all but one of the country's thirty provinces, but were bogged down in the war against Massoud and the Shia Hazaras. They made few demands on the people, but gave little in return. At a clinic built as an aid project there was no medicine, equipment or doctors. In fact, it was being used as a caravanserai.

Having covered a little over three hundred kilometres, we set off the following day for Qalat. With savage but unintended irony, the survey was due to end with a banquet luncheon hosted there by the governor of Zabol province, before we headed down the highway to Kandahar.

As the famous hill fortress of the Ghilzai Pashtuns loomed in the distance, I was leafing through Nancy Hatch Dupree's account of Qalat's glorious history.

Nineteenth-century travellers approached the land of the Ghilzai between Kalat-e Ghilzai and Ghazni with fear and trepidation, for the 'much dreaded' Ghilzai Pashtun were a large, fiercely independent, aggressively valiant Afghan tribe whose daring exploits fill the pages of Afghan history. Their finest hour came early in the 18th century when their leader, Mir Wais Hotak, declared independence from Persian rule and his son, Mahmud, then seized the throne of Persia in 1722.[7]

The Hotak clan, to which the Taliban leader Mullah Mohammed Omar belonged, had revived the tradition of defiance, of which Qalat Fort was a great symbol. A miraculous spring gushed forth at the summit of the hill, and the mullahs in the area were revered in

Afghanistan as Sayyids, descendants of the Prophet who had the power to cast spells. Their charms, written in musk and rosewater on slips of paper, were folded and placed in small silver boxes to be worn on the person. Although the Sayyids' influence was declining, Afghans still believed their charms could cure disease, protect soldiers, induce romantic love and bring misfortune to enemies. Inhaling the smoke of a burning magic chit could relieve pain but not, apparently, bring rain.[8]

The governor of Zabol had been called away to the frontline and could not meet us. His deputy was Mullah Gul Agha, a hirsute young doomacrat who resembled a Muppet, with mournful eyes and shoulder-length black hair protruding from under his turban. The prospect of a free meal had attracted a dozen or so other men who appeared to have no role in the administration but were friends of the deputy governor. As usual we had to shake hands with everyone in the room, including several children who had followed us in from the street, and who found this protocol a great lark. The Afghans scrutinised us with head-tilting curiosity, as if we were a species of exotic animal they had never encountered. Whispering among themselves, and pushing chunky gold watches back up their forearms, the Talibs listened to Bari translate Mike's report. He told them that half the livestock in the worst-hit districts was already dead and that a shortage of drinking water was looming. He advised them to dig wells.

'We're in touch with Kandahar, but they're too busy to help,' said Mullah Gul who, judging by his expression, desperately longed to be elsewhere.

Mike took a very deep breath. It was going to take more than a free lunch to buy his silence. 'I think you need to help yourself,' he said.

The deputy governor was unfazed. 'It's up to the UN to feed the people.'

Sackett looked at him with a doubtful expression. 'We can't feed everyone,' he said. 'That's the government's job.'

The other Afghans followed the exchange like spectators at a tennis match, stroking their beards with dull comprehension. The food eventually came; generous servings of chicken and mutton in gravy, vegetables, yoghurt and piles of nan. Mullah Gul's digestion was disturbed by the telephone which kept ringing in his lap. He spoke furtively into the receiver, casting suspicious glances at us.

As in Iraq, the UN was hitting with one hand and helping with the other. Twelve million Afghans were officially classified as drought-affected, four million severely, yet the country remained under sanctions for refusing to hand over Osama bin Laden. The country's bank accounts and other assets abroad were frozen and its airline was prohibited from leaving Afghan airspace. The UN Security Council resolutions even applied personally to Mullah Omar, whose job description was given in the sanctions documentation as 'Leader of the Faithful'.

When the meal was over and the conversation resumed I asked Mullah Gul if there wasn't a contradiction between, on the one hand, the Taliban defying international opinion about women's issues, minority rights and the export of terrorism and, on the other, their desire for the international community to singlehandedly fund and conduct drought-relief operations.

As Bari explained the question to the mullah, the young Talib looked to the ceiling for Allah's patience.

'It's not the Taliban who have problems with other countries,' he said. 'It's other countries that have problems with the Taliban.'

31

A Prayer for Bad Roads

And towards God is the journeying

— THE KORAN

Take any map and you'll see an eerie pattern of railways converging on Afghanistan from five different countries, but falling short. In Pakistan the lines struggle through the tortuous Khyber and Khojak passes, only to peter out at the border. Tajik railways skirt the Amu Darya without ever crossing it, and the lines from Uzbekistan and Turkmenistan give up the ghost just a few kilometres after entering Afghan territory. Iran's train lines reach out towards Herat and the south-western province of Nimroz, but in not one case do these railways make a significant penetration into Afghanistan. It is not a problem of gauges. There is simply no internal rail system with which to connect. The rulers in Kabul never sat securely enough in their chairs to carry through such projects during the golden age of rail. Foreign aid built roads, but unlike a train line, a road cannot be prised up in sections and carted off — a real possibility in such a turbulent and unruly land where central government employees risk being murdered or kidnapped for ransom if they venture into the provinces. Not surprisingly, the mail comes late, mostly not at all, and electricity, telephone and education services are rudimentary. The roads are bad.

Turning south on to the main Kabul Highway, we struck our first decent stretch of tarmac in three days and the mood in our truck lifted. Good food and comfortable beds awaited us in Kandahar, a hundred and thirty kilometres away, and everyone was keenly anticipating the chance to relax a little. Young Ahmed had driven well on the backroads, handling the bulky Land Cruiser with skill. In most parts of Asia, when you hire a car, you get a driver as well, whether you want one or not. Years as a frightened, frustrated and reluctant passenger had led me to conclude that older drivers were better than younger ones. Their longevity, for one thing, indicated a degree of luck, if not skill and caution. But Ahmed's faultless performance overcame my prejudices.

When it came to roads, bad ones were always preferable to good ones, a conviction responsible for the small prayer I always said at the start of any road journey:

Oh Allah, the Compassionate, the Merciful,
Let the road be bad,
For if it is good, the speeding driver
will surely kill us all.

The Kabul–Kandahar highway, built with American aid in the 1950s, was in superbly poor condition, pitted and broken for long stretches. The huge craters caused by tanks and land mines restricted Ahmed to a sedate pace. Here and there, however, the original concrete macadam reappeared and on one such section the vehicle carrying Mike and the others suddenly overtook us on our left, as cars should in Afghanistan. Bari, who was seated in the back behind me, leant forward, scanning the road ahead, his fingers sinking into the backrest of my seat with deepening tension.

'Ahmed is not a driver,' he told me with a frozen smile. 'No, actually he's a pilot.'

'Really?' I said, looking at Ahmed, who could not have been more than twenty-five.

Laughing at the joke, the driver accelerated to catch up with the other vehicle, singing along to the Pet Shop Boys' cover version of 'Where the Streets Have No Name', which was blasting from the tape deck. Bari remained craning forward, second-guessing the intentions of every oncoming vehicle.

We were whipping along at eighty kilometres an hour when a yellow and white taxi suddenly appeared in our path, overtaking a truck coming towards us. Turning to Ahmed, I saw that he was singing dreamily with a smile on his lips and a faraway look in his eyes. His startled double-take came about a second too late, as the huge weight of the Land Cruiser ploughed into the taxi with the sickening sound of shearing metal. As the front of our car rose above the taxi's bonnet, the horrified faces of its passengers looked up at us. We slid off, crashed down again and were heading off the road down a gentle embankment when Ahmed's reflexes kicked in. Turning hard left to stay on the highway, the Land Cruiser began sliding sideways. I could feel the vehicle's weight shifting above its centre of gravity, and for a fleeting moment it balanced on its own fulcrum, all the while sliding forward with an unstoppable momentum. Suddenly, we had all the time in the world; time to realise that, without doubt, we were going to roll the car; time to hope — but not enough to pray — that our guardian angels would protect us; and time to know that there was nothing anyone could do to influence the outcome. When the driver's-side wheels lifted off the road, something I had feared for a decade began to unfold. And Afghanistan was the last place on earth in which I wanted it to happen.

As the car landed on my side with an enormous impact, I heard a sound like a bomb going off and the windscreen instantly froze, then sprayed me with glass chips. Suddenly we were upside down, as if in some amusement park ride, only to come smashing down again, on Ahmed's side. While the tonnes of metal were airborne the cabin had become weightless and clipboards, water bottles and cassettes flew around amid the terrible noise. But now the car was deathly quiet, apart from the settling sounds of debris. Hanging awkwardly in my seatbelt, I blinked the grit from my eyes and felt a bump on my head, which was wet. The only immediate pain I could feel was the seatbelt buckle pinching me under the weight of my hip. My call to the others elicited a wave of groans from Bari and the driver, both of whom were still stunned.

In over a dozen trips to Afghanistan it was the first time I could recall having worn a seatbelt, or even being driven in a car that had them. The wet patch on my head was water, not blood, having spilled from a flying plastic bottle. Extracting ourselves from the wreck, we hobbled around a bit, then argued with the offending taxi driver, who blamed us for getting in his way. His impudence seemed somehow reassuring. Miraculously, nobody had been killed or seriously injured. Peering through the open window of the taxi, I saw that the driver's seat cover was a small, very lucky carpet.

In Kandahar, prayers for rain were being held at the mosques. On the outskirts of town, in a wasteland of bricks and tarpaulin tents, were some of the twenty thousand nomads trucked out of the Reg by the Taliban. They were living among chickens and bulldust twisters in gaps between war-damaged buildings. Women with all the coins ripped off their dresses complained about the weather, dead flocks and lack of money. The babies balanced on their hips were irritable from birth, tormented by the heat and dust. One old woman dressed in rags was spinning a handheld spindle, deftly whorling teased wool collected around her wrist into a ball which hung rotating in front of her like a hypnotist's watch. The incessant clatter of beseeching voices, hot sun and spinning wool made me woozy, and I took refuge in a nomad's tent, sitting down on a ragged, dog-chewed remnant of a Mukkuri kilim like the one I'd bought from Habib.

The owner of the tent, Mirza Khan, gave me tea. He was one of the Kuchi rescued from the Reg, but his father had died of thirst, along with most of their five hundred sheep. There was no room in the Taliban trucks and choppers for the few animals that survived, so they'd abandoned them in the desert.

'Year by year the desert is getting closer,' he said. 'It no longer has any grass. The whole country is becoming a desert.'

I wanted to know what it would take to get the nomads back on their feet, and there ensued a spontaneous open-air jirga in which the issue was thrashed out in minute detail by a large group of men. After a torrid argument, they agreed that a hundred healthy fat-tailed sheep were required to support one family. The sheep should be at least two years old and would cost about a hundred and fifty thousand *caldar* for the flock, or about $3000.

Later that night at the UN guesthouse there was interest in the figures I had collected, but not much optimism. Three thousand dollars, the aid workers said, would be better spent feeding those at risk of starvation. If it was going to cost the Kuchi that much to get moving again they would probably have to settle, even if it meant depending on handouts. Disgusted, I retired early but got little sleep. The walls of the guesthouse radiated heat and I lay awake troubled by fate. In Central Asia, the war against the nomads had been won long ago. In the Middle East, most of Jordan's quarter of a million Bedouin had packed up their tents for good, harassed by drought and lured into government settlement programs.[9] In Iran, similar programs were reducing nomad numbers by tens of thousands every year. And in Afghanistan, nature itself had turned against the wanderers. Even a 99 per cent approval rating couldn't save a nomad culture based on the 'hereditary, ritualistic, symbolic and mystical act' of migration.[10]

The following morning the mountains around Kandahar rose out of a sea of dust as I made my way to the bazaar to hire a taxi for the border. My bones and muscles ached, and a stabbing pain shot up my vertebrae as I got into a yellow and white car identical to the one we had destroyed the previous day. The all-pervasive dust had got into my lungs and clogged my sinuses, my lips were a cluster of scabs, and I was taking antibiotics for severe diarrhoea. Sharing the hired car was Ahmed Hashimi, a student who was making a day-trip to Chaman or maybe Quetta, he wasn't sure. Passing the Taliban checkpoint on the airport road, yet another driver — this one a rat-faced youth who steered with his nose on the wheel — blew the dust out of a cassette and shoved it into the tape deck.

'You like Indian music?' Hashimi shouted into my ear from the back seat over the distorted sound coming from the speakers. Keen to practise his English, Hashimi placed his head between the front seats and relentlessly bombarded me with banal questions. Worse still, as we got up to speed I realised that I was still shaky from the previous day's accident, and was rattled by the approach of oncoming vehicles. My nervousness greatly amused Hashimi, whose beaming face kept appearing over my shoulder.

'This man is a good driver. You should not to worry,' he said. When I asked how he knew the driver was good, he replied: 'I don't know.'

It was all so irritating.

Afghanistan has over twenty thousand kilometres of highway, eighteen thousand of them unpaved. Along the road to Pakistan old men with shovels stood around piles of gravel and barrels of boiling tar, an air of despair surrounding their efforts to maintain the road. The tanks that had torn it up now lay dead beside it, unable to rust in the pitiless dry air. The faces of the road gang members were ravaged and seemed besieged; whether by war or nature I could not tell. All travelling the same highway. All on their own Heijiras. All in need of a prayer for bad roads. Beyond the road gang, a large carbuncle lay camouflaged in the middle of the road, which we hit so hard that my head struck the roof, and the car came to a sudden halt. We had run aground in the middle of the desert, engine oil gushing from a smashed crankcase.

'No problem,' Hashimi said, as the driver reached into the glovebox for the Afghan driver's panacea, a tube of some kind of glue or plastic metal. Diving under the car, he began trying to stem the flow, but the crack was too big and he emerged defeated, covered in coagulated grease and glue. Like a mad black devil, he proceeded to frighten passing drivers by waving them down and demanding more glue, in the process collecting a large number of half-used, dried-up tubes. From the beginning I had hated everything about this driver: his sparse, clumpy beard, his rodent features, his dull leer, and his nose on the wheel. My hand was lifting, drawn up by the power of a psychotic urge to batter him, when suddenly a loud voice rent the sky above the stranded car.

'Leave him to me!' cried the voice of the Almighty. 'For he is a driver, and they are a stiff-necked people.'

So I heeded the word of the Lord and let the driver be.

We stood there in the wilderness for quite some time, the passing cars all too full to take us to Chaman. There was a miserable argument with the driver over money and we were constantly enveloped in clouds of fine, choking dust thrown up by the cars and mini-vans which plied the road like skiffs on a rolling sea. A twister lashed us with small stones before staggering off into the endless, brutal Reg, the sand blast making my eyes weep.

Hashimi, who throughout the ordeal had maintained an admirable good humour, looked at me with a gentle smile.

'Why are you angry?' he asked.

In my frustration, it seemed like a stupid question, yet the answer lodged hard in my throat before spilling out.

'Because ...' I said, choking on the words, 'because I don't know when I will see Afghanistan again.'

Even the dust seemed precious to me then.

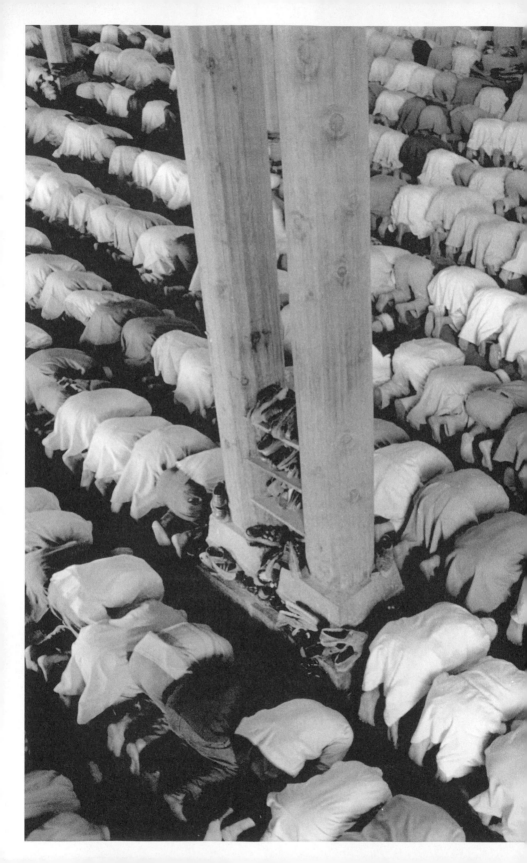

PART NINE

ESFAHAN

32

Carpet Nation

Somewhere on the road from Kandahar I had decided that I needed a holiday — preferably a long holiday. Quetta, the capital of Pakistan's Baluchistan province, was not the obvious choice, but from there I could at least consider my options.

Beyond the reach of the monsoon, the sprawling, dun-coloured city of over a million people lay in a bowl of saw-toothed mountains at eighteen hundred metres above sea level. One of the hottest places on earth, it had recorded temperatures above 55°C. Alexander the Great almost died of thirst leading his weary followers towards Persia along Baluchistan's Arabian Sea coast, surrounded by water but not a drop to drink. The mountains are as cruel as the sea, floating and gloating above Quetta, dusting themselves in snow while the great flat-bottomed valley shimmers with heat. People in the provincial capital complained that it had got hotter since the nuclear blasts in the Chaghai Hills west of the city two years before. The words of a long-forgotten Arab poet who once visited the region lingered like radiation from the blasts.

> *Oh Allah, seeing thou hast created Baluchistan,*
> *What need was there of conceiving Hell?*[1]

Under normal circumstances I might have purchased twenty metres of fine muslin cotton and wrapped it around my head to beat the heat, as the Baluchis do, but there was trouble in Quetta. Resentment against the authorities had simmered for over a quarter of a century since the brutal suppression of a Baluchi separatist movement. A *bandh* called by tribal leaders had shut down most shops in the city. The tribal leaders were protesting against moves by the military government to crack down on smuggling from neighbouring Afghanistan. Smuggling was the khans' main source of income, and several bomb blasts outside key government offices in recent days were seen as a warning to the administration to back off.

Cursed with a strategic location, Baluchistan had long been a centre of intrigue, with the perpetual warring of the tribes complicated by the arrival of outsiders, from the Aryans and Alexander the Great, to the Russians and British. Although vast, Baluchistan was home to only eight million of Pakistan's one hundred and forty million people, and the khans now preferred the amenities of Quetta to the scorching deserts. Recently, the province had become an important source of new recruits for the Taliban.

Flattened by an earthquake which killed twenty thousand people in 1935, Quetta was now a utilitarian frontier town clustered around Zarghoon Road, with only a few colonial edifices like the Army Staff College and the occasional avenue of old pines to recall its grand history. In vacant lots not rebuilt since the tremblor, Kuchi families had pitched their tents, having sold off their flocks and possessions, unable to return to the Reg. About the only traders defying the general strike were the rug merchants, whose location in the basement of Gul Market provided cover. The arcade bulged with new Kuchi stock, but I needed to conserve cash for my vacation.

Checking into the Hotel Serena, built by the Aga Khan as a refuge for the sensitive soul, I plunged into the holiday mood. The hotel boasted many arbours irrigated by gurgling watercourses in homage to the Baluchi village. The exterior walls were daubed with tan stucco and, inside, tribal textiles occupied spotlit niches. On a tranquil evening, soothed by a cascading rivulet and a cool night breeze, I unfolded a map titled 'Caspian Region: Promise and Peril', filched from a borrowed copy of *National Geographic,* and traced a route with my thumb to the west of Quetta. Older maps than mine showed Baluchistan as an eastern province of Persia, stretching from Kerman to the Indus River. However, the deserts, mountains and saltpans of the Baluchis were now split between Pakistan and Iran. Before leaving Delhi I had obtained a one-week transit visa, enough to travel overland from the Pakistan border to Tehran if I hurried. Alternatively, if I could get the visa extended, a more leisurely pilgrimage to Iran, the quintessential carpet nation, might be possible.

Ever since explorers first recorded their travels to Persia, carpets have been making an impression. Chinese and Arab travellers of the eighth and ninth centuries found rugs being knotted in the southern province of Fars, and today Iran is the world's largest exporter of oriental carpets, commanding a third of the $3 billion a year trade. With twenty distinct carpet regions and some four thousand different rug types, carpets employ more people than oil and are the country's second biggest export. The Persian knot, along with the Turkish, is used in the vast majority of the world's handmade rugs, and when the late Shah was on tour the very throne of Persia itself was little more than a carpet, folded up until only one man could sit on it.[2] In the words of one author: 'No other country can boast the same range of master workshop, workshop, village and nomadic rugs, and none even comes close to the diversity of Persian design.'[3] As if to flaunt Iran's status as the world's only carpet superpower, its weavers in the year 2001 produced a phenomenal five thousand square metre, twenty-two tonne, patchwork carpet. Commissioned for the Grand Mosque of Sultan Qaboos in Oman, it had taken five hundred weavers three years to tie the estimated 1.7 billion knots needed to realise the design in forty-two separate pieces which were to be sewn together on delivery.[4]

Many believe that the world's oldest carpet, the 'Pazyryk', was made in Persia and then taken to southern Siberia where it was found. The medallion-design 'Ardebil' carpet, woven in 946 AD by Maqsud of Kashan, and considered the acme of technical perfection, was found in a mosque in the north-west Persian town bearing its name, while the 'Hunting' carpet, considered the finest with its intricately realised portrait of a mounted chase in pure silk, was also made in Persia.[5] The American rug enthusiast Arthur Urbane Dilley spoke for the majority when he wrote that Iran 'is the hearth of our reverie ... which ever was the centre of the life of weaving'.

On the mountainous Iranian plateau, nomadic pastoralism was a sensible alternative to sedentary agriculture. But under the patronage of shahs Tahmasp and Abbas in the sixteenth century, the workshops in Persia's cities ushered in the golden age of classical carpet production. Sheep with the finest wool were bred on special farms, and vegetable plantations grew the plants needed for making dyes. The Shah's habit of gifting fine carpets to other monarchs created a sensation among the European nobility, and by the end of the seventeenth century high demand was placing a strain on Persia's production standards. After Shah Abbas's death in 1629, support for weaving waned, and the 'decline of Persian carpet weaving mirrored the downfall of the nation as a whole'.[6] It would be more than two centuries before Western interest in Persian carpets was spectacularly revived at the Vienna World Exhibition in 1873.

The appeal was direct and immediate. Each one of these carpets, individually created through long hours of work, seemed to speak a language all its own, yet one that was common to them all ... Some spirit, the spirit of its creator, had entered through the deft and skilful hand that knotted it, and this spirit seemed to give an answer to the questions that sprang up in the Western mind ... How poor the ordinary machine-made carpet seemed in contrast. The machine constructed by European genius turned carpets out automatically and without inspiration to perform their function, identical one with another, in huge series, perfect and impersonal . . . Now, like an epidemic, practically the whole of the bourgeoisie was possessed with the desire to furnish its rooms with the knotted carpet of the Orient.[7]

At Quetta railway station a gleaming black steam engine waited on a plinth, destination nowhere, while a flatulent diesel loco snorted and wheezed, ready for the long journey to Iran. The day before at the booking office, the ticketing staff had taken their seats at an elevated counter staring down on all who came before them like High Court judges. No would-be passenger dared approach the bench until the clock struck nine. Their Lordships had been known to make examples of the impatient.

'We are under military rule now, after all,' said a man seated next to me, a fly on his lapel lazily crossing its legs.

On the stroke of nine all this carefully cultivated order collapsed. Elbowing my way forward through the mêlée, I encountered a major domo type clenching a cigarette holder between his teeth, who suggested I take the Chilten Express — there was no other train to the border. It departed once a week provided there were sufficient passengers to operate the service.

'Will there be enough passengers on Saturday?' I asked.

'In due course we will inform you,' he replied in a censorious tone. 'At Taftan border you will buy another ticket for Iran side. The journey will take nineteen hours, subject to conditions, and train will depart at 11.45 hours on Saturday morning subject to passenger numbers being adequate. After buying your ticket, you must reserve your seat. This is your ticket. Seat and compartment will be intimated tomorrow.'

Military motivations, not profit, had persuaded the British to build the railway, which would have helped in the event of war against Russia. On the platform at Quetta, Pakistani police sporting moustaches, stubble, grey flannel kurtas, leather sandals and berets roamed like wolves stalking sheep. Before our departure they conducted several sweeps of the compartments, taking particular interest in foreigners' passports. As the bogies creaked and we got underway, I realised that amid all the checking and explaining, I had neglected to buy provisions for the journey. Leaving the compartment, I headed off to check the dining car but got no further than the end of the carriage. The doors at either end were locked. As it transpired, there was no dining car.

The desolation beyond the rail line was unrelieved apart from a few camel trains, which at times outpaced the diesel one. Returning to the six-berth compartment, I found a family of Hazara Afghans had suddenly appeared from nowhere and were unwrapping a variety of food items — chicken, flat bread, fruit and cold cans of cola — and setting them out on the green leatherette bench seats. It was going to be a long journey, unless I could cadge some of that food. I was hungry, and tried to look it. The Hazara man, Sher Mohammed, was a dead-ringer for Genghis Khan and his square-faced little girl had impish eyes, big sunburnt cheeks and a knot tied on top of her head. They had wedged themselves between piles of nylon bags and bales containing rice which they were taking to Iran to exchange for cans of Pepsi, which could then be sold in Pakistan. Emerging from under the bales, Sher's son Abbas introduced himself, and handed me a boiled egg. When I had eaten that, his father shoved a flatbread sandwich full of chicken into my hand, urging me, 'Don't be shy!' Sitting with his legs tucked up under him like a khan after eating his fill, he entertained himself by having a post-prandial chat with his daughter. He was asking her whether she was Pakistani or Afghani, to which she replied resolutely, 'Afghani!' Taking a deep breath, he repeatedly explained that upon reaching the Iranian border it was important she should answer 'Pakistani'. Smiling mischievously, the girl continued crying 'Afghani! Afghani! Afghani!' all the way to Iran.

As the train's tempo picked up, the bogie beneath us unleashed a deafening rattle and sand began flying into the compartment. With none of the windows or doors closing properly, and the little girl beginning to cough, we entered a long tunnel. Emerging after what seemed like minutes, Sher's glasses were coated in so much dust that I could barely see his eyes. As he stood up to switch on a light, an avalanche of dust fell from his kurta, plunging his daughter into another raking fit. He stood there for a while, flicking the malfunctioning light switch, muttering 'Pakistan, Pakistan' and sighing heavily.

In the middle of the night I awoke to find the train had stopped. It was four o'clock and there was a damp patch of saliva on my knee where the sleeping girl had dribbled. Lifting her head and resettling her gently, I wandered out into the corridor. By night, the desert was cool. Beyond the train's headlight, an endless chain of ghostly telegraph poles seemed to bob up and down under their wires until disappearing into the wilderness. The crunching footsteps of an engineer approaching to check something underneath the carriage punctuated the silence. When I asked him where we were, he replied, 'Chaghai.' Somewhere in the range north of the line was Pakistan's nuclear test range. It had taken fifteen hours to cover about three hundred kilometres, still only halfway to the border, and we were obviously going to be late. Without the help of the alternator, the train's corridor lights slowly began to fade and it was soon pitch black. After a while, two long groans of siren could be heard coming from the direction of the engine, and a shudder ran through the old metal joints of the train. For a moment it felt like an earth tremor — or worse — but when a second shudder followed I realised we were moving again.

Just after noon the next day the Chilten Express ground to a halt in a siding at Taftan, and I joined the stampede to the Immigration window. Waiting for our passports to be stamped, I recognised a young Westerner I had seen while getting my visa at the Iranian

Embassy in New Delhi. Andre was a Slovak backpacker who looked striking in a red bandanna and a cowry shell necklace he had bought in Goa. He had travelled overland through Iran to India, knew the ropes, and was now returning the way he'd come.

'Why are you hanging around?' he asked, knowing better. 'It takes ten minutes to cross the border on foot, but it's five hours if you stay with the train. The Customs checking is terrible.'

Collecting my backpack and leaving my copy of Salman Rushdie's *Imaginary Homelands* on the train, I hurried to catch up with Andre's economical stride as he marched through the last dust-baked village in Pakistan towards a gleaming new building on the border. Inside the Iranian Immigration office, everything seemed so spotlessly clean that when I spotted a refrigerated water cooler I was unable to resist taking several draughts, something I would never have done in Pakistan. Posters displayed dress standards for women and framed photographs formed a political triptych: smiling President Khatami and dour supreme leader Ayatollah Khamenei flanking the overcast visage of the late father of the Islamic Republic, Ayatollah Khomeini.

Emerging from Immigration we found ourselves in a large car park under a burning sun, the same sun that had fried my brain a thousand times in India, Pakistan and Afghanistan. Yet everything seemed different here: the buildings were better constructed, the roads smoother, the people more efficient. It was like crossing a civilisational watershed, as if this arid outpost had more in common with distant Europe than it did with the Pakistani village adjacent to it. Suddenly, the stamp in my passport seemed a valuable thing, a *laissez passer* granting the freedom of the republic for one week. Excited, I resolved immediately to seek its extension at Zahedan, the capital of Iran's Sistan-va-Baluchestan province.

The Islamic revolution of 1979, and the seizing of American diplomats who were held hostage for 444 days by radical students, bumped Iran off the tourist map. War with neighbouring Iraq raged through most of the 1980s. Only when it ended, and the Soviet Union pulled its troops out of neighbouring Afghanistan and subsequently collapsed, did Iran get some badly needed breathing space. Two decades after the overthrow of the Shah, Tehran still had not re-established diplomatic relations with Washington, but the 1997 presidential elections heralded a new openness. Mohammed Khatami, a descendant of the Prophet and the son and grandson of ayatollahs, emerged as the leading spokesman for a new Islamic liberalism. Khatami argued that Iran suffered from a 'historical ailment' resulting from centuries of despotic rule 'which has shaped our temperament to become irreconcilable with freedom'.

> *We Muslims once had a dominant civilization and were shaping human history in a way that we are no longer capable of today. We want to regain our place in history and, if possible, build a future that is different from our present and even our past, without rejecting those who are different from us, and without ignoring scientific thought and the practical achievement of humanity.*[8]

Khatami's winning smile and promise to expand individual freedom, strengthen the rule of law, and rein in the extra-Constitutional activities of revolutionary remnants won him 70 per cent of the popular vote. On the first anniversary of his election, he addressed students at Tehran University, once a hotbed of Islamic revolution, but now a seedbed of reform. When eventually the adulation died down, he told those gathered: 'The future of religion is that it has to cope with freedom; otherwise it has no future.' Most cheered, but a small group struck up the old revolutionary chant 'Death to America!', prompting reformist students to counter with the cry 'Death to Monopoly!'. 'For a moment Khatami stood quietly, the late afternoon sun filtering in golden shafts onto the speaker's platform. Then he uttered a remark that silenced everyone. "I prefer," said the President of Iran, "to talk about life, not death." '[9]

As the elections proved, Iranian democracy was a reality, but so was hardline clerical reaction against it. Khatami's popularity divided the religious leadership and provoked a reaction from conservatives, who were fighting reform tooth-and-nail in the courts and on the streets. The laws of the Islamic state were loaded in favour of the status quo. Non-Muslims were free to adopt Islam, but Muslims were prohibited by law from changing their religion. Iranian intellectuals like Abdul Karim Soroosh argued that without freedom of religion, democracy was meaningless. 'First, in order to be a true believer,' Soroosh said, 'one must be free. To become a believer under pressure or coercion isn't true belief. This basic freedom is also the basis of democracy.'[10]

Catching up with my new travelling partner I felt a rush of freedom myself, but I was not as free as Slovak Andre, who had cast off all the chains that bind us in this world. At the Immigration post he had advised me not to change money — the taxi drivers gave better rates, he said — but now, as we trudged towards a small cluster of private taxis, he advised me there was no need to change money at all.

'You still have some *rials* from your last trip?' I asked, perplexed.

'No. I have none,' he replied.

'Then why don't you change some money?'

'I don't have any.'

'What, no dollars? No rupees? Nothing?'

'You don't need money in Iran!' he exclaimed. 'I have crossed this entire country and I'm telling you, the hospitality is amazing. People invited me into their homes. They fed and clothed me. I was like a son to them. So I realised that in Iran you can forget money. Come with me. I will show you the *real* Iran.'

Ignoring the assembled taxi drivers, Andre trooped off to the nearest crossing, where he proceeded to flag down a pickup truck driven by some Revolutionary Guards. Hopping into the back he called me to join him and, without thinking too much, I scurried over and leapt in the back too. Soon we were hurtling across the desert at obscene speed on the wide, flat highway — too late to pray for a bad road or avert panic. I had read somewhere that seventeen thousand people died in Iran every year in car accidents — one every forty minutes — which is more than the number of fatal heart attacks. Convinced I would be the first to die simultaneously from both, I banged on the rear glass window of the cab and made frantic 'slow down' motions. Seeing my plight, one of the guards climbed halfway out of the cabin, twisting to face me with his hair whipped by the wind. Cupping his hands to prevent his words flying away, he said in clear English, 'If you drive normally in Iran you will never reach your destination. Here, driving safely is dangerous,' then slipped back inside to join in the laughter with his friends.

At the Mirjave crossroads the guards dumped us at a checkpoint. Shouldering his backpack, Andre began to walk, but a policeman's whistle called him back. After a while, an off-duty guard with a locally made Paykan sedan arrived and quoted an exorbitant price for the eighty-kilometre ride to Zahedan. We ignored him, but whenever any other passing driver showed interest in giving us a lift, the policeman shooed them away. The guard, meanwhile, sat in his car a short distance away, whistling tunes. After an hour of this, I suggested to Andre that we accept the soldier's kind offer of a ride.

'But this is madness,' he said, offended. 'He is asking for more than I spent during my entire visit to India. It's impossible. I will never pay it.'

Of course, Andre couldn't pay it. He didn't have any money. So I paid, and discovered the secret of travelling impecuniously.

The owner of the car was called Nematullah, a proud type who spoke no English. As we drove along, he allowed me to interrogate him. When I said 'USA' he made a fist and punched downwards.

'U–S–A *haram!*' he cried.

'Israel?'

'Israel *haram!*' he roared, punching down harder.

Iraq was also evil, as were Britain, Pakistan, Egypt, Turkey, Jordan and Saudi Arabia. He liked India, France and China, but when I mentioned Afghanistan he grimaced, struggling for the right word, and came up with 'Amazon'. Afghans, he felt, belonged in the jungle, a commonly held view in Iran. Indeed, talking to Nematullah was an excellent primer in the many enmities of Iranian foreign policy.

Since the time of Darius, absolutist rulers have governed Iran. Before the revolution, twentieth-century shahs were an odd combination of social modernisers and political despots who abandoned the Islamic calendar and established close relations with Israel. In the 1930s Reza Shah enforced Western dress, and ordered soldiers to shoot anyone who disagreed. His son, Mohammed Reza, broke the power of feudal lords and distributed land to the poor, but outlawed political parties, shut down the *majlis*, or parliament, and built up a huge secret police network to spy on, torture and kill anyone who opposed him. To keep Iran out of the Soviet orbit and protect Western investments in its oil industry, Western liberal democracies colluded with the tyrannical shahs. The CIA played an active role in the 1953 coup d'état that deposed a nationalist government that had tried to nationalise the oilfields. When Dwight D. Eisenhower visited Tehran in 1959, his limousine was driven from the airport down what was then called Eisenhower Avenue, but is now Azadi (Freedom) Street, over 'several miles of carpets'.[11] This welcome, like much that the Shah did, was self-consciously historical, recalling the *pah-endaz* ceremony in which the Shah's feet were never supposed to touch uncovered ground.[12] When the caliph Haroun al-Rashid walked from Baghdad to Mecca, a distance of well over a thousand kilometres, the entire route was spread with carpets and other costly cloths.

The Shah's intolerance of dissent, love of extravagance, and assaults on the powerful clergy inevitably prompted a reaction against the monarchy. By undermining the nationalists and leftists, the CIA and the Shah gave the clergy its opportunity to lead the opposition. As in Afghanistan, the medieval clerics would partly have the West to thank for their victory, but would feel no debt of gratitude. A few years after the Shah's extravagant celebrations at Persepolis marking the 2500th anniversary of the Persian monarchy, the 'whole imperial court crumbled; the army, into which billions of dollars had been poured, disintegrated; [and] the so-called elites either disappeared or found their way into the new state of affairs'.[13] Some two million people, including leftists, wealthy families with connections to the monarchy, artists, and ethnic and religious minorities fled the country. In a few cases, they exported themselves inside rolled-up rugs.[14]

As a member of the Sepah-e Pasdaran, or Revolutionary Guard, Nematullah took all of this very personally. He kept pointing at the sky, making exploding noises and saying 'Ar-mair-ee-KAH!' I guessed he was referring to the 1988 shooting down of an Iran Air passenger plane by a US warship cruising the Persian Gulf in which 290 people died. No compensation had ever been paid, but restitution of a kind was about to take place. As Nematullah's whining Paykan rattled into Zahedan he began rubbing his thumb and forefinger together and patting his pocket, and eventually took out his wallet, showed me a ten thousand rial note and jabbed me in the chest. Furious when I explained that I had no rials and Andre had no money at all, he began driving in an angry fashion, hurling the Paykan into the dusty back alleys of Zahedan, grabbing spivs by the scruff of their necks and demanding to know where the blackmarket moneychangers were. When he found one, I handed over three crisp hundred dollar notes, and received in return a bale of rials, the first money I had ever seen featuring images of demonstrators, in this case the suit-with-no-tie students whose seedy look became the emblem of revolutionary chic. Dumping us with a scowl at the inter-city bus station, Nematullah drove off to enjoy his earnings, while I gave Andre some money and bid him a fond farewell, fervently hoping never to see him again.

At Zahedan's grandly named — nothing else was grand about it — office of the Administration of Emigrants and Foreign Followers' Affairs, the staff were plunged into hysterics by my request for a visa extension. Had I not arrived only that day? I could 'come back in five days' or 'try again in Kerman', a seven-hour bus ride away. As Kerman was the first great carpet city on my route, I chose the latter option.

At one time, Kerman carpets dominated the American market in oriental rugs, and the town's woollen portraits of US presidents, replete with the Stars and Stripes and the presidential seal, were much loved. Perhaps the foreign affairs office there would be more obliging. Sucking on a sour cherry juice sachet, I gazed out of the bus window at a passing panorama of desert, barren mountains and nomad women dressed in floral prints herding sheep through the sage bush. At several points, the bus was forced to stop at Customs checkpoints set up to prevent smuggling of untaxed imports and illicit narcotics. A flood of cheap heroin from neighbouring Afghanistan was weakening the fibre of Iranian society, even though most of the drugs were destined for Europe. While the Customs police tended to give male passengers little more than a cursory glance, the billowing chador could conceal many secrets and the women were without fail herded off for body searches conducted by female police behind screened enclosures. Despite these elaborate precautions, the authorities were losing the battle against the aggressive, well-armed drug traffickers. Rather than attempting to sneak past police posts, the Afghanistan-based drug lords would attack them with rockets, grenades and machine guns. Three thousand police had died fighting them.[15] If police captured a ring member, the ring would simply kidnap some civilians and hold them hostage until their people were released. In a recent case in Kerman a group of foreigners had been abducted from their hotel rooms, and Western embassies in Tehran were advising their citizens not to visit the city.

Kerman, a man from Zahedan told me, was a city of pimps, and arriving at the bus station the contrast between young Kerman Man, slouching in blue jeans that revealed every bump and lump of his anatomy, and Kerman Woman, in her black shroud, was stark. The only elegant figures to be seen were the mullahs, whose grey cloaks, black capes and neatly trimmed beards lent some dignity to the place. In the Bazar-e Vakil, a three-kilometre-long labyrinth that ran from Tohid Square to the main mosque, chests of Ceylon tea stacked in the arcades recalled the days when Kerman was a Silk Road city trading turquoises from the surrounding mountains for imported commodities. The Persians are tea drinkers and in a subterranean vaulted brick grotto which once served as a bathhouse, the golden brown liquor was served from long-handled pots, neither too weak nor too strong, with lump sugar broken from tall hard cones placed in the mouth. Reclining on fine kilims stuffed to make bolsters and smoking apple-flavoured tobacco in their bubbling *qalians*, the Kermanis still had control of at least one precious commodity: time. Carpets had proven less reliable.

Persian merchants first began to exploit the Western taste for exotic floor coverings on a commercial scale under the stable reign of the Qajar kings (1787–1925). In the 1870s, the British–Swiss firm Ziegler and Co. opened an office in Tabriz to manage their trade in cloth, opium and dried fruits to Europe, but soon diversified into carpets and wool, opening branches across the country. It was a Ziegler's man who found the Ardebil.[16] As supplies of old rugs quickly evaporated, new production came to the fore, influenced by the taste of Western customers for lighter shades and softer colours. Dealers in London and New York would mail cartoons — rug jargon for 'designs' — to their agents in Kerman. Before long, demand outstripped supply and the Persian weavers were forced to cut corners to keep up. Their solution, introduced in the nineteenth century, was the *jufti* knot that allowed weavers to make rugs twice as fast by tying their knots across four warp strands instead of two.

However, carpets produced this way had half the life of others, and when synthetic dyes were introduced the corruption of Persian carpet quality was complete. The jufti crisis was only overcome by the formation of the Tabriz cartel, which protected its market by strict quality control. The appetite of a fast-modernising West for reminders of a more ornate past had almost killed the object of their desire, and by the turn of the twentieth century the Shah had banned the use of aniline dyes. Given the nature of the illicit substance concerned, it was easy to apprehend offenders, whose stained right hands were cut off as a warning to others.[17]

By the 1920s, rug making had become Kerman's principal industry, with 90 per cent of production sent to the United States. Then came the Great Depression, and, one by one, the American firms 'gathered in their carpets, closed their dye houses, their designing rooms, their godowns and their offices, and withdrew'.[18] Under the nationalist policies of the Pahlavi dynasty, restoring health to the carpet industry was a priority, and the last Shah's wife, the Empress Farah, had done creditable work in reviving traditional crafts. However, by then it was too late for Kerman, which had gained a reputation for polychromatic floor coverings, or commercial goods, 'much corrupted by attempts to meet Western tastes'.[19]

Prior to World War II the United States Senate had instructed American consuls in Islamic countries to report on carpet-making activities, such was the importance of the industry. Before the revolution in 1979, Iran had been the United States' main source of oriental carpets, supplying some 40 per cent of the US market. However, Tehran's breaking-off of diplomatic relations with Washington hit the industry hard, and Iran gradually slipped to fourth place behind China, India and Pakistan.[20] In 1987 Washington banned all imports from Iran, ostensibly in retaliation for its attacks on shipping in the Gulf, costing Iran half a billion dollars annually in lost oil exports and a further $55 million in carpet sales. A similar ban had been imposed after the revolution but was lifted when the war with Iraq began, presumably to allow the Iranians to buy more weapons.

Between Kerman and Tehran lay a thousand kilometres of almost unrelieved desert. The road plunged north-west along the southern boundary of two largely unexplored deserts, the Dasht-e Lut (Desert of Emptiness) and Dasht-e Kavir (Desert of Salt). In Kerman, the Aliens' Bureau had refused to extend my visa, suggesting I try Yazd instead. The uncertainty was bothersome. It was Monday, and without a renewal by Thursday — which in Iran is the end of the working week — I would have no option but to rush through to Tehran and get an extension there, or worse, leave the country. As I boarded the bus for Yazd the air cooled and it began to rain. These long road journeys were not the burden they might seem. The buses were clean and modern, and seated high above the road with the arid landscape framed by a large window I found myself mesmerised by the passing panorama. Between mountain passes the desert stretched itself like a tawny cat, and birds flocked to the clay brick towers farmers had built to obtain their precious droppings. Low, dark clouds hugged the plateau as we approached Yazd, one of the oldest, hottest places on earth, but alighting from the bus, a gust of cool air sodden with the joy of rain saturated my senses.

The similarity between the Persian words for water and blue — ab and abi — indicates their intimate association, and Yazd's array of blue-tiled mosques and public buildings creates the illusion of a lake in the desert. Marco Polo called it a 'good and noble city', while Robert Byron spoke of the cold colours and lucid designs of its mosques. Square vented wind towers called badgirs dotted the skyline, capturing and cooling breezes to naturally ventilate homes. The soaring blue-tiled minarets of the Friday Mosque dominated the old quarter, where the alleys were barely car-wide and locals used coded door knocks to ensure that a member of their own sex met them at the door. In a small atelier beside the jail where

Alexander the Great had imprisoned his opponents, tilemakers continued their work in the painstaking traditional manner, chiselling floral designs and setting them on a cement base. Houses huddled around their central courtyards and step wells descended ten metres. The older houses still boasted *khasinair* baths, with fire chambers heating the water from beneath. Climbing onto a rooftop I found clear views over the mud-brick domes, badgirs and minarets to the Shir Kuh mountains, over four thousand metres high, where the city's inhabitants rode snow sleds in the bitterly cold winters. As in Kerman, the communal bathhouses of Yazd had been converted into restaurants.

Returning to my $5-a-night hotel near Behesti Square after dinner, I found the night concierge glued to a television courtroom drama. It was, in fact, a real-life courtroom drama, the trial of a man accused of the attempted assassination of Saeed Hajjarian, an important advisor to President Khatami who was partially paralysed by a bullet left lodged in his spine. The accused, a former soldier from Yazd, claimed he was acting under orders of unnamed superiors, widely believed to be hardliners opposed to reform. The next report was about another trial in Shiraz in which thirteen Jews were charged with spying for Israel. The Jews, who according to their own lawyer were religious fundamentalists who had admitted to the charges, were paraded in grey prison uniforms. Iran's courts had become a coliseum where liberals and conservatives waged their battles through gladiators and pawns. The concierge was actually a student who used the quiet nights to cram for his exams. Turning from the television, he looked at me with a tired expression.

'Iran is like medieval Europe. We need a reformation to divorce religion from politics,' he said.

When the news ended, a graphic of a loom appeared in a corner of the screen. On the loom was a carpet on which one gul sparkled then enlarged to form the station logo of Iran's national broadcaster.

Of all the many distinctive characteristics of its people, the Islamic Republic had made Shia Islam the pre-eminent gul in a nation of unequals. Ninety-three per cent of Iranians are Shias, but the sect accounts for only one in ten of the one billion Muslims worldwide. Surrounded by Sunni-dominated countries, Iran's religious and political establishment is imbued with a sense of siege and a missionary obligation to preserve the sect. But keeping the flame of a unique faith alive was the national mission long before Islam. 'Iran' means land of the Aryans, the fair-skinned raiders who swept across the plateau from what is now southern Russia around 1800 BC, with a second wave six hundred years later. Unlike the Arabs, a people different in race, language and religion who came to Islam as pagans, the Persians already had a rich religious history based on the teachings of Zoroaster. The Friday Mosque at Yazd is built on the ruins of a fire temple, but although Mohammed's god was fanatically substituted for Zoroaster's, 'there persisted in the souls of his Persian worshippers a rich and subtle mysticism which was unknown to the Arab conqueror. Indeed the special quality of the Persian character turned Iran from orthodox Mohammedanism to the Shiite heresy.'[21]

Yazd was the world's leading centre of the faith founded by a man who was said to have been born laughing at Balkh in the seventh century BC. Setting off in search of rectitude and compassion, he converted Vishtaspa, the King of Balkh, and also attracted Hindu and Greek followers. Zoroaster knew physics, astronomy and gemology, cured a blind man with herbs, and even fought a holy war against the Turkmen enemies of Vishtaspa. He taught that after death, the human soul would be weighed on scales that measured its good deeds against its evil ones.[22] As his beliefs found new adherents from Persia, he incorporated aspects of their previous faith, Mithraism, which included a god of light who came to earth via a miraculous birth and was resurrected after death. By the time of Zoroaster's death the foundations of the new religion were well established. These included the conviction that life is a battle between good and evil, and that a day would come when each soul would be assigned to Heaven or Hell for eternity; Sunday was the Sabbath, and what we know as 25 December was observed as a religious festival. The three wise men from the East who followed the star to Bethlehem and gave gold, frankincense and myrrh to the infant Jesus were probably Zoroastrian *magi*, and it is reasonable to believe that as Christianity expanded it absorbed many of the rituals and beliefs first conceived by Zoroaster.

When the retired British carpet dealer Arthur Cecil Edwards visited Iran in 1948 he found that the 'bill of a Zoroastrian banker of Yezd [*sic*] is accepted as sound paper from one end of the country to the other'.[23] But although Zoroastrians are universally respected as honest and industrious, and their religion is recognised along with Islam, Christianity and Judaism as one of the Islamic Republic's four official faiths, the law of the land discriminates against the minorities. Non-Muslims are not permitted to marry Muslims unless they convert to Islam. The penalty for fornication out of wedlock for Muslims is a hundred lashes, but if the man involved is not Muslim, the penalty is death.[24] For all that, the reform era was good news for the Zoroastrians, who for the first time in decades were garlanding their homes with lights to openly celebrate the harvest festival.

Near Markar Square I entered a cream brick compound inside which a garden of tall pines formed a small oasis in front of a convent-like building with a wide verandah. Fire had been central to Aryan rituals long before Zoroaster, spreading not just to Persia but to India, where it remained important in Brahminical rites as well. Inside the reception hall of the Atéshkade of Yazd, a thick glass window allowed non-Zoroastrians to view the massive brass urn in which heavy blocks of wood blazed in the sanctum sanctorum where the faithful gathered. The heat of the flames radiated through the thick glass, warming my face as I strained to get a better view of the inner chamber. A large brass bell hung on a heavy chain, and several holes in the ceiling released the smoke. In the shadows I could make out somebody moving around inside behind the urn. A complicated inscription beside the window declared that this same fire had burnt continuously 'not withstanding many wars and difficulties' in various places for almost fifteen hundred years. According to the inscription, a special priest designated as a *hirboo* kept the fire blazing by adding a piece of dry, long-burning wood such as almond and apricot several times a day. It was hard to imagine managing such an awesome responsibility for so long. The Zoroastrians were only human, after all. Hadn't anyone nodded off? If they had, and the embers had died, the temptation to cover the whole thing up would have been enormous. I was told later that the constant need for wood to feed the voracious flame kept the Atéshkade in perpetual penury, and accounted for the lack of trees around Yazd.

For all its historic and architectural splendours, Yazd — like Zahedan and Kerman before it — failed to provide the desperately desired visa extension, the lack of which was threatening to deny me quality time in Esfahan. For a carpet pilgrim, forgoing the capital of the Safavid shahs would be akin to a Hindu never dunking in the Ganga, or a Muslim never visiting Mecca, for as an old Persian saying puts it, '*Esfahan nesf-e jahan*': Esfahan is half the world.

On the road to the former royal capital Robert Byron passed me heading in the opposite direction towards Yazd. It was 1933, and the traffic on the road was smaller and slower, but judging by his diary, nothing much apart from the spellings had changed. 'The desert between Isfahan and Yezd seemed broader, blacker, and bleaker than any, despite the warm spring sun,' the Englishman observed. 'Its only relief was the ventilation mounds in the *kanatas*, strung out like bowler hats in rows of ten and twenty miles, and enormously magnified by the clear shimmering air.'[25]

The bowler hat vents of the underground channels, which moved water from distant bores across the desert without substantial loss due to evaporation, were still visible, and the air still shimmered. In Na'in, a town of baked-sand houses exactly halfway between the Pakistani and Turkish borders, our bus driver paused for tea. For centuries Na'in's reputation had been based on making the finest *abas*, cloaks traditionally worn by Persian men, but around the time of Byron's visit the industry was in rapid decline because of the laws making Western dress compulsory. With few other options available to them, the weavers of Na'in began turning out rugs which 'in terms of technical perfection often surpassed the greatest Safavid carpets'. Kerman had done the same thing when its famous shawls were eclipsed by those of Kashmir, prompting Arthur Cecil Edwards to observe: 'The Persian people, when other activities fail them, turn to carpet weaving.'[26]

In the dusty main street, gleaming showrooms stuck out like gold teeth, displaying large, intricate carpets with a profusion of curvilinear designs, scrolls, escutcheons and arabesques, along with the 'vase' symbol, believed to have originated in Sumeria as a representation of a water goddess. Spectacular, maze-like medallions radiated from these masterful creations, but Na'in's genius was somehow cold, almost stultifying. The weavers had concentrated on design and high knot counts to the almost total exclusion of colour and most of their work was wrought in dull monotones, giving a 'curiously bland overall appearance'.[27] I wished the bus had stopped somewhere else. Byron, perplexed by the apparently ageless perfection of the ruins of Persepolis, could have been writing about the carpets of Na'in when he complained, 'they are what the

French call *faux bons*. They have art, but not spontaneous art, and certainly not great art. Instead of mind or feeling, they exhale a soulless refinement . . .'[28]

Back on the bus, the new passengers from Na'in were mainly women who immediately discarded their long black cloaks, revealing well-tailored suits. I sensed that there was more to it than merely changing for a more comfortable bus ride. Esfahan was calling.

33

Teahouse of the Misfit Moon

The Safavid dynasty, cradle of the great age of Persian carpets, slowly dissolved in wine and other indulgences in the early eighteenth century, when Afghan tribesmen from Kandahar marauded into Esfahan and hastened its lingering death. It had taken a century since the death of Shah Abbas I for the rot to set in. The Afghans were mere litmus to the empire's corruption. The marauders, however, were soon swept away by another bandit, twenty-year-old Nadir Guli Beg, later to crown himself Nadir Shah, a Persian-born Turkmen who went on to conquer Delhi and seize the famous Peacock Throne — which had been dismembered by feuding tribes on their way home — and the Koh-i-Noor diamond before his death in 1747 at the hands of an assassin. His rule terminated not only the classical age of Persian weaving, but also the spectacular period of Moghul carpets. Persia's decline continued for the rest of the century with the capital moving to Mashhad, Shiraz, and finally Tehran.

Like a marauding Afghan, I stormed into Esfahan amid much chaos and enmity. On the outskirts of the city, a family of Afghan refugees had boarded the bus, led by a grandfatherly figure with the beard of a *magus*. The Iranians, whose hatred for the Afghans was legendary, coldly directed the noble elder to the very back of the bus, a place normally reserved for women. Afghans were seen at best as honest simpletons and a cheap source of labour for doing the menial jobs that Persians would rather not bother with. Iranian opinion towards their neighbours had been further embittered by the Taliban's murder of eight Iranian diplomats and a journalist in Mazar-e Sharif during their seizure of the city in August 1998. Across Iran, huge billboards presented those killed as martyrs, although the Taliban said they were spies.

It was Thursday just before midday and offices and shops were closing early for the Islamic weekend. With chances of obtaining my visa extension fading, I took a taxi from the outskirts of the city, but got lost searching for the Foreign Affairs office south of the Zāyandéh River, arriving only as a torrent of staff poured out through the main gate to begin their weekend. In the passport section a lone clerk was putting away some files in a lockable cabinet. As he saw me approaching, he froze with his key in the lock and cast a nervous glance at a wall clock.

'We're closed,' he said, but his words somehow lacked conviction. Hearing me out, he reluctantly disappeared into an adjoining office, returning with an elder whose grizzly demeanour suggested he would brook no nonsense.

'Do you have all the required documents?' the boss asked.

'Yes, I think so,' I said.

'And a spare page in your passport?'

'Yes. Here it is.'

'Then do it,' the boss ordered his assistant, and returned to his office.

Stamps were thumping, paper shuffling. I would have kissed the hand of the clerk, but it might have interfered with his work. Nowhere in the world, I told him, had I encountered such masterly efficiency, such supreme levels of courtesy and service — a credit to the Islamic Republic and, in particular, the Esfahan office of the Foreign Affairs department. A warm welcome awaited the entire staff should they honour me with a visit in my own country. The clerk returned my passport bearing the precious seven-day extension.

'That will be fifteen thousand rials,' he said.

Fifteen thousand rials was about two dollars. I didn't have it. The curse of Slovak Andre invaded the room. I must have given the sponging swine five times that, and now it had cost me Esfahan. Checking all my pockets three times, I placed their contents on the counter: nine thousand rials and a used sour cherry juice sachet.

'I don't suppose you take US dollars?' I asked.

He said they didn't, and trooped off to find his manager, who returned with arms swinging and head thrown back, carrying his weight like a sumo wrestler.

'I thought you said you had everything,' he said, somewhat exasperated. 'You don't have any rials?'

'No, well, I mean yes. But only nine thousand. I was ... I was robbed in Zahedan. You know those *bloody* Afghans ...'

My words trailed off. I just didn't have the heart to go on with the charade. The manager had already helped me once, and a fee was a fee. He stroked a worn face, staring at the wall clock. It was 12.15. The weekend was wasting away. With obvious disdain he prodded the rial notes on the counter to separate them. No magic had increased their number. He scratched his cheek, mumbled something to his offsider, and walked away.

'It's okay,' said the clerk.

'The beauty of Isfahan,' wrote Byron, 'steals on the mind unawares. You drive about, under avenues of white tree-trunks and canopies of shining twigs; past domes of turquoise and spring yellow in a sky of liquid violet-blue; along the river patched with twisting shoals, catching that blue in its muddy silver, and lined with feathery groves where the sap calls; across bridges of pale toffee brick, tier on tier of arches breaking into piled pavilions; overlooked by lilac mountains, by the Kuh-i-Sufi shaped like Punch's hump and by other ranges receding to a line of snowy surf; and before you know how, Isfahan has become indelible, has insinuated its images into that gallery of places which everyone privately treasures.'[29]

My weighty backpack felt light as air as I wandered down the broad, tree-lined boulevard of Chahar Bagh towards the Si o Se Bridge, named Thirty-Three after the number of its brick arches that leapfrog the Zãyandéh. In the calm waters, long-legged birds waded and couples and children paddled boats. Under the bridge, waiters hopped across stepping-stones carrying blue-glass qalians and cruets of rose-coloured tea. Protected from the sun, and with a breeze off the water cascading between the arches, the bridge teahouse was the coolest place in the garden city.

Heaven, says the Koran, is a garden. 'A gushing fountain shall be there, and raised soft couches with goblets placed before them; silken cushions ranged in order and carpets richly spread.'[30] In Iran, the sense of arriving in a garden paradise whenever you reach a city is heightened by the deserts you cross to get there. However, the oasis cities could not have survived without the deserts, which acted as impenetrable barriers to invasion by the Uzbeks and Turkmens, and it was for this reason that Shah Abbas made his capital in Esfahan, which became and remains to this day Iran's most elegant city. The Chahar Bagh, which bisects it with a corridor of trees, led me north across the river to the Abassi Hotel, a remarkable structure of ponderous classicism built onto the royal caravanserai where guests of the shahs had for centuries watered and rested themselves and their horses. It was this very caravanserai to which the eponymous hero in *The Adventures of Hajji Baba of Ispahan* returns after being kidnapped and forced to guide his Turkmen abductors on a raid to plunder the city.

In the Great Square known to the Persians as Naghshe Jahan (Design of the World), rainbows arced in the spray of the central fountain. Where the shahs once played polo between marble goalposts, which still stand at either end, a sprinkling of families picnicked and played football on the lawns. On the perimeter of the vast space, twice the size of Moscow's Red Square, rose the grand domes of the Imam and Sheikh Lotfullah mosques, set back slightly, as if not to impose on the important business of the people's relaxation.

'The domes and façades of Isfahan are waterfalls of blue, and their colours are both exciting and relaxing,' an admirer once observed. 'As the façade glitters in the sun, it is like a rug of sapphires and gold with here and there the harsher blue of diamonds.'[31] The Lotfullah, once the mosque where the women of the court worshipped, squatted like a peacock among pigeons, blushing blue in a futile attempt to fit in with the uniform line of arched shopfronts bordering the eastern side of the square. Gazing up at the light refracted through the grilles beneath its dome induced in one visitor 'the feeling of being submerged in a watery grotto'. Another commented that it was 'as though the Persians, always threatened by the invading sands of the desert and scorching under the hot sun, built this cool interior as a sanctuary where they could be reminded of the things most precious to them — water and the cool evening sky'.[32] The Imam Mosque, formerly the Shah Mosque, with its gargantuan doorway open to all, was 'so deep in the bazaars that it even serves as a thoroughfare for them'.[33] Sinuous calligraphy spilled across the mosque's glazed ultramarine tiles, lyrically proclaiming the hundred names of Allah, and honey-coloured bricks formed ridges framing the tiles. It recalled Rosita Forbes's eloquent description of the façades of Samarkand as 'sea and sand with sunshine caught between them'.[34] The tall, tottering palace of Ali Qapu resembled a drunk about to fall over. Climbing its tiled staircase, I emerged on the verandah of kings, with its eighteen tapering columns supporting an exquisitely detailed ceiling. Frescoes of courtesans decorated the rear walls, and in a private chamber upstairs wine-bottle motifs set the tone for carousing. Marco Polo found that the wily Esfahanis boiled their wine to make it sweet and therefore, they argued, permissible under

Islam. Most middle-class Iranians still ply guests with a glass or two of cherry-flavoured vodka in their homes.

From the pleasure podium of Ali Qapu, beyond the enchanted enclosure, the city spread itself towards the horizon. Ugly buildings are prohibited in Esfahan. They go to Tehran or stay in Mashhad. Planters vie with planners to outnumber buildings with trees. Attracting nightingales, blackbirds and orioles is considered as important as attracting people. Maples line the canals, reaching towards each other with branches linked. Beneath them, people meander, stroll and promenade. The Safavids' high standards generated a kind of architectural pole-vaulting competition in which beauty is the bar, and ever since the Persians have been imbuing the most mundane objects with design. Turquoise tiles ennoble even power stations.

In the meadow in the middle of Naghshe Jahan, as lovers strolled or rode in horse-drawn traps, I lay on my back picking four-leafed clovers and looking at the sky. There was an intimacy about its grandeur, like having someone famous in your family. The life of centuries past was more alive here than anywhere else, its physical dimensions unchanged. Even the brutal mountains, folded in light and shadows beyond the square, stood back in awe of it. At three o'clock, the tiled domes soaked up the sunshine, transforming its invisible colours to their own hue, and the gushing fountains ventilated the breeze and passed it on to grateful Esfahanis. But above all was the soaring sky, captured by this snare of arches.

Hanging from the doorways of the shops lining the square were carpets, all bait for the unwary, because if there was ever a knotted tourist trap it was here, where the intoxicating scenery could have made Slovak Andre loosen his purse strings. Laying on the pressure, the dealers had resorted to a variety of gimmicks to seduce customers: one offered Internet access; another gave 'lectures' on the history of rugs. One dealer had even been known to throw in free air tickets to Shiraz and Kish Island to clinch deals.

Darius Hamadani was a respected member of the syndicate which controlled the Esfahan carpet market, and came recommended by Tehran-based diplomats. At his Art of Persia gallery, situated just off the square, the diminutive, baby-faced Darius was busy in his office when I arrived and sent me upstairs to wait for him. The showroom was a light and airy functional affair in which everything — including the carpets — seemed new. Poking about the piles while I waited, I came across several unusual pieces like woven collages. They were elaborate Bakhtiari camel and donkey bags, woven in a mixture of carpet, soumak, and weft-wrapped kilim, known as *tacheh* or *khordjin*, which had been opened out for use as wall hangings or floor coverings. Thus altered, bags that once sold for $20 or $30 could fetch over a hundred. Appearing at the top of the stairs Darius's smiling face, framed by unruly curls, appeared as fresh and clean as his shop.

'You like these bags?' he asked, ordering an assistant to bring us drinks. 'You know, I was one of the first dealers in Iran to sell these open khordjin. I saw them first in Turkey.'

The drinks when they came were not the predictable tea or cola, but a Persian speciality, the cooling *sharbat-e sekenjebin* prepared from sugar, vinegar and water.

'The sour and the sweet are equally balanced,' Darius said, passing me a cruet, 'just like life's blessings and miseries.'

This charming, sophisticated man had read his *Hajji Baba*, and knew well that the business of selling carpets had as much to do with aura as substance. Like Hajji, he had spent long years in Turkey and returned home with a jaundiced view of the Turks and a conviction that Iran was the best country on earth. Yet he was clearly a man troubled by unsatisfied ambitions, and his frequent boasts betrayed his insecurities. As he spoke, he kept one eye trained on me to detect the slightest sign of doubt, ever ready to curtail or elaborate his stories.

Called away to the telephone, Darius made the most of another opportunity for grandstanding.

'Beniamino, darling. You won't believe what I've found,' he told his caller. 'That's right! The Varamin you wanted. It's a beautiful piece. Should I send it?'

As his telephone conversation escalated in a series of exaggerations, two touts I had noticed ambushing tourists in the square arrived with their quarry in tow. Covering the mouthpiece, Darius motioned impatiently to his assistants to attend to them. There were several foreign backpackers hanging around as well, one of whom said Darius had let him call home and send e-mails for free, and had even arranged cheap lodgings.

'Darius is a real human being. He's the man,' the backpacker said, but I couldn't overcome my own suspicion that, human being or not, Darius was just one hell of a salesman.

Returning after checking that his other customers were being looked after, Darius found me inspecting a Shahsavan mafrash that I had pulled from the stack.

'You have excellent taste,' he said with calculated flattery. 'I can see that you know rugs well. So for you I have something special, something for the *connoisseur du tapis*, no? A shipment of rare things is coming on Saturday. Come back then and I guarantee you will be impressed. If there is time you may also like to look at my prize pile, the private collection. Only because you are a man of the carpets.'

Agreeing to return, I wandered off to continue browsing the square. At Persepolis Carpets they were serving *falooda* with saffron ice cream, and I almost turned tail at the prospect of yet another scam. But before I could flee, a bespectacled young man placed a plastic cup in my hand.

'We're celebrating a purchase,' said Cyber Ali, nodding at a German tourist who was over by the desk.

'Ya, zat's right,' said the man, spooning falooda into his mouth with one hand, while signing a charge slip with the other.

The cheerful atmosphere of this impromptu purchase party was infectious. Stacked against a rustic brick wall was a lively and anarchic selection ranging from mechanical Tabriz rugs to wild tribal pieces. Hanging down from atop one pile was a Qashqai.

'In sheer variety of designs, clarity of colour and fineness of weave, they have seldom been surpassed,' Jenny Housego had written, referring to the rugs of Persia's most famous nomads in *Tribal Rugs*.[35] The Qashqai tribe's origins are lost to history, but their Turkic language, similar to Azerbaijani, led some to hypothesise that they had been chased out of the Caucasus by the Seljuks in the eleventh century, or by the Mongols a century later. Fifty thousand Qashqai families still made the annual migration, driving their sheep through rivers to wash their wool before shearing. It was the longest and best-known nomad trail in Persia, stretching about three hundred kilometres 'from their winter quarters near the Persian Gulf to the cooler summer pastures of the southern Zagros Mountains'.[36] Between a third and one half of Iran's population consisted of ethnic minorities including Azerbaijanis, Kurds, Arabs, Turkmens, Uzbeks, as well as Bakhtiari, Lurs, Qashqai and Baluchi nomads. At times, the power of the nomad confederations had challenged the sovereignty of the Persian state, which had responded by trying to obliterate nomad culture. In the 1930s Reza Shah ordered tribal leaders to halt all migrations and settle on agricultural lands. The land provided was infertile and thousands died, but the nomads outlasted the Shah, who abdicated in 1941 after siding with Nazi Germany. Reza Shah's successor in the Pahlavi dynasty, the last Shah, Mohammed Reza, resumed the offensive with a settlement policy based on incentives. By the late twentieth century, Iran was managing to settle about twenty four thousand nomads a year. Two million remained on the hoof.[37]

The Qashqai rug lay on the floor where Ali had unfolded it. It was no museum piece, just a good, honest rug off a crooked nomad loom. A zigzag central medallion was distinctly Caucasian and formed a corral in which stood a chestnut-coloured horse with white stockings, surrounded by fourteen abstract peacocks. Another fourteen birds, some of them dowdy peahens, fossicked in a rosy field which they had pecked threadbare in places. Without the horse — which might in fact have been a cow — the design resembled a psychedelic aviary. The main borders appeared to have been dyed in *kaveshk*, a wild weld mixed with a small quantity of madder for a sunburnt look, complemented in the minor borders by powder blue, oatmeal, lime and a notoriously fugitive pink, which might not run so long as I never washed it. It was all wool, knots, warps and wefts, and the curly, undyed fringes were so natural that I could have sworn the sheep itself was hiding beneath. Six fat Turkmen guls were left unfinished where the design collapsed in chaos, and numerous abrashes indicated that the wool had been dyed in small batches during an actual migration. It was a compact, one metre by one-and-a-half-metre party of a rug — exhausting to look at, let alone weave. But the maker was both indefatigable and literate, signing it 'Allah Hamazar' in Persian. The price for this entertainment was half what you might spend on a good dinner.

Looking up, I noticed that the shop had become a hive of activity with clutches of customers being attended to. The gallery was tastefully set up and while some staff sold, others were busy on the telephone or playing backgammon against a computer. Going over to the stacks, I read the folds of Turkmen, Baluchi and Luri rugs, until my eye paused on a strange floral piece in black and lemon with touches of celadon green, which Ali removed and unfolded.

'This is a Lilihan,' he said, pushing his spectacles back on his nose. 'It's from Chahar Mahal.'

Chahar Mahal was a predominantly Bakhtiari area where Armenian Christian settlers had established villages. The Armenians had been forcibly relocated from Jolfa, Yerevan and Kars in the sixteenth century, when Shah Abbas ethnically cleansed his disputed border areas. As many as two hundred and fifty thousand Armenians were forced out, with a third of them dying on the way to Esfahan and the Zagros foothills. Lilihan was one of the villages they established in the district of Kemereh, about ninety kilometres from Esfahan. Arthur Urbane Dilley had called their rugs 'much commercialised'. The Lilihan that Ali showed me had been worn so flat with age that flecks of its cotton base were visible. Dabbing it with a wet white handkerchief left a red tint, indicating that it had been 'painted', a cheap way of re-colouring bald patches, some of which had also been re-piled. A forest of spreading branches formed a paradise park, double-wefted in Turkish knots so that it could not be folded without cracking. Well within my means, and the foreign tourist export quota of twelve square metres of carpets duty-free, I bought both the rugs, and was duly rewarded with another cup of the delicious saffron ice confection and an invitation for a night on the town with Cyber Ali.

The somnolence of Naghshe Jahan on a hot summer's day surrenders after sunset as Esfahanis and visitors fill the square, marking out their territory with carpets and straw mats. Everywhere, flames sprout from portable stoves, here boiling water for tea, there cooking ten-course meals for extended families, and children chase themselves silly like fireflies. In preparation for a night under the stars, travellers roll out their bedding, a cheaper, more comfortable, and probably safer alternative to a hotel. The Man in the Moon had come down from his orbit, and, with his head cocked and face flushed, was peeking over the tops of the buildings lining the square, captivated by all the life of this world, and I pitied the misfit moon, the eternal outsider.

As we picked our way through the crowds, struggling to avoid stepping on people's hands or faces, Ali explained that he was a student who worked part-time to pay for his tuition and support his mother. His father had died several years before, making Ali head of the family of five, despite the fact that he was only twenty-two.

I was curious about his name. Cyber? Was it Persian?

'Like Cyrus, you mean?' he said, laughing. 'Actually, no. My friends gave me this name because I spend too much time surfing the web.'

At the end of the square, Ali led the way up a narrow staircase to an old *chaikhune* with a terrace overlooking the entire scene. Here couples courted, reclining on carpeted benches under an open sky, and took turns on the water pipe. The romance was traditional — no embracing in public — but there was much airy gesticulation with hands that speak and eyes that glisten; perhaps a couplet or two. The twin minarets of Imam Mosque were bearded with fairy lights, and the drunkard Ali Qapu leered at the chaste, spotlit dome of Lotfullah across the fountain. Between them, private pleasures and public order merged ineffably on the lawns.

'I have never encountered splendour of this kind before,' an astonished Byron had written in the 1930s, and the effect now was more or less the same.[38]

Around us, people played chess and backgammon, the former banned by the mullahs soon after the revolution, but now allowed. A newspaper left on a bench informed me that voting had taken place in parliamentary elections, and that reformers were leading in all carpet-weaving constituencies, including Shiraz, Ardebil and Tabriz. But affairs of the heart, not the nation or loom, were pre-occupying Ali, who sat transfixed by a ravishing beauty sitting opposite us with her sisters. He had started patting down his hair and rearranging his bookish wire-rimmed spectacles on the bridge of his nose.

'She is so beautiful. I would *die* for that woman,' he said to me, expanding in great detail on the subject. But he was rendered speechless when the girl revealed her own fluency in English by asking where I was from, and inviting us to join her group. Ali's ears were still glowing red with embarrassment when he noticed a suspicious-looking character a few tables down.

'You see that man,' he said, whispering behind his hand with a theatrical secrecy. 'He's a spy.'

'A spy?' I replied, alarmed. 'But I came on a holiday. I didn't think I needed a journalist's visa.'

'Not that kind of spy,' Ali continued. 'He's a carpet spy.'

'You must be kidding.'

'Not at all! The big dealers pay these people commissions to inform about foreigners who are in Esfahan. Right now he sees you are with me. But if you were alone he would approach you and ask what's your name, which country are you from, which hotel are you staying in, what places have you visited. He would make friends with you and would lead you to the carpet dealer who is paying him.'

'You mean a tout?'

'Higher than a tout. These guys are experts in their field. They'll stop at nothing.'

A vision flashed before me of the millionaire San Francisco art collector who falls to his death just after buying an Oriental rug in Robert McNeal's 1970s novel *Carpet of Death*.[39] Was I about to meet the same fate?

'So who's paying this guy?' I asked Ali, perturbed.

'I don't know. Maybe Darius. Have you been to Art of Persia?'

'Why yes, I did go there. Just before coming to your place.'

'See what I mean. He's put a tail on you!'

Traditionally, Esfahan was a conservative city where people observed the social niceties, but the establishment of several major educational institutions had attracted large numbers of students from all over central Iran, and given the former royal capital the character of a university town. As Cyber Ali led the way out of the square, dodging and doubling-back now and then to throw off Darius's spy, we found that the city outside had come alive. It was Thursday night and the fragrant air of Esfahan was edgy with the start of the weekend. Apart from the ubiquitous Paykans, the roads were thronged by Daewoos, Kias, Peugots and Nissans, evidence that twenty years after the revolution Iran's economy was opening up. People were piling into cars and restaurants, and youths cruised the tree-lined streets on motorcycles, arms linked like stunt teams. Taxis were communal and to get one you needed only to stand on a street corner and wait for a spare seat in a shared sedan going your way. Taking the front seat of one, Ali directed me to squeeze into the back beside two generously proportioned women in full chador. As the car moved seamlessly through the evening rush hour heading for a restaurant on Mir Street, Ali seemed to be chatting up the invisible women. In a freshly laundered collarless white shirt with his hair slicked down, he looked ready for anything at the start of the weekend.

'In Iran we have a lot of what we call *koongoshad*,' he said, a remark that elicited giggles from under the veils. 'It means "wide arse", you know, the kind of guy who believes in fate and just sits around drinking tea and waiting for life to happen to him. As you will see, I'm not like that.'

Leaping out of the cab carelessly he almost bowled over a petite young woman who appeared to be wearing a baseball cap under her headscarf.

'Hi there,' said Ali, turning one hundred and eighty degrees as he passed her.

To my surprise the girl, whom Ali later confessed he did not know, happily entertained this wolfish behaviour.

The Islamic revolution could claim a number of important achievements. Literacy had doubled, with three out of four Iranians now able to read and write. Iranian women, who had never been forced into the full veil, were now the best educated in the Muslim world, accounting for half of all university admissions, and one in three doctors. But I feared that the social restrictions the republic imposed had turned Iranians into a nation of sweaty palmed sex maniacs for whom, as the poet Ibn al-Sabuni put it, furtive love 'is more yielding and better keeps its promises'.

Dancing down a flight of stairs, Ali led the way into an Iranian version of a pizza parlour serving cola and funny food, where browbeaten fathers took their hormonal daughters to be cruised by equally hormonal young men.

'That's an old girlfriend of mine,' said Ali, pointing at a haughty looking young woman in a stylish suit and scarf. 'She doesn't acknowledge me anymore.'

Before the 1979 revolution most urban Iranian women had adopted European dress, but after it the *hejab*, or covering, was strictly imposed. In the privacy of their homes, Iranian women still wear whatever they like, but in public it is illegal for any female over the age of nine to reveal any part of her anatomy other than her face, toes and hands. No hair, shoulders or thighs are to be seen, and certainly no cleavage. The official legal penalty for disobeying the regulations is seventy-six lashes. Yet in Esfahan, home of the amazing shrinking chador, young women were pushing back their headscarves to reveal more hair, and the old body bag had been nipped and tucked to be more form fitting. Shapely legs clad in denim jeans flashed in the folds of mini-chadors, and in the relative privacy of restaurants and cafés, veils hung over the backs of chairs, allowing potential marriage partners to see one another. The sexes had breached the dam walls of segregation; our restaurant even had unisex toilets where, Cyber Ali claimed, he had just been cruised by two girls. Unlike Saudi Arabia, Iranian women were permitted to drive, but not to ride a bicycle. For men, trimmed beards were considered politically correct, but were not compulsory. Allergic to orthodoxy, Ali was completely clean-shaven.

'I shave to rebel,' he said, coming on to two statuesque young women at the next table, despite the presence of their dates and the persistent calls coming through on his 'handy'.

Cyber Ali's idea of rebellion was to make enough money to buy his way around regulations he didn't need. He claimed to have been active in the student movement until July 1997, when the biggest student protests since the revolution were brutally crushed. The protests started in Tehran after the closure of a reformist newspaper, but soon spread to most major cities, and became violent after police and right-wing vigilantes attacked demonstrators. Under pressure from elements in the military, which publicly threatened to stage a coup if the violence was not halted, President Khatami denounced the student leaders for their 'evil aims'[40] and televised trials showed the ringleaders admitting to contact with foreign powers. But even if organised opposition had been snuffed out, youth remained a powerful force for change. Two-thirds of Iran's population was under twenty-five, the result of the revolutionary baby boom of the 1980s, when mullahs exhorted Iranians to breed an Islamic generation, and the average number of pregnancies was six per woman. The population mushroomed, from thirty-four million to sixty-six million, before saner policies were introduced. Nowadays you can't even get a marriage licence without passing a family planning course, and contraceptives are free.

The noise in the basement restaurant reached a hysterical level as the chatter of excitable teens reverberated through the cheesy chamber, with its vile colour scheme and Iranian cover versions of Western pop classics. I longed for the classical Persian virtue of the teahouse, and its patient society. Several times I suggested to Ali we head back there, but he was a persistent suitor, preferring instead to strike up a conversation with the girls at the next table, who like all young Iranians were impatient for change. With the voting age set at fifteen, youth would decide Iran's future, but most of them weren't even born when the revolution happened. All they knew was 30 per cent unemployment, double that in their own age group. Those lucky enough to get a job earned less in real terms than people had before the revolution, and whatever they made was quickly eaten away by inflation. Iranian youth was educated and discontented. Their most popular music was produced by expatriate Iranians like Ebi Farsi, whose lyrics pilloried the clerical establishment from the comfort of 'Los Tehrangeles'.

'They had the matches and made a fire,' went the line of one song, referring to the mullahs. 'They sent youth to war, while washing their beards in rosewater.'

But with no direct experience of any other system, many young Iranians seemed to believe in little more than a pizza parlour parody of the West, picked up in snatches from satellite television. Some were even thinking the unthinkable.

'We want the Shah should come back,' said the girl who seemed to be Ali's newest prospect.

When we asked for the bill it came on a chit stamped 'Have a nice time'. Ali insisted on paying, not just for me but also for the adjoining table. A few weeks earlier he had sold $17 000 worth of carpets in a single day on a 10 per cent commission, or so he boasted as we left the restaurant followed by the stern gaze of Imam Khomeini.

The *basijis* were on the streets, right-wing elements in plain clothes waving Kalashnikovs about as they flagged down cars for unofficial identity checks. Named after the revolutionary fanatics who had volunteered as human mine-clearers during the Iran–Iraq War, they had no official function, but purported to enforce law and order during elections and emergencies. The reformist parliament was having difficulties reining in the revolutionary organisations set up to shadow the untrusted organs of the state: the basijis and the Ansar-e Hezbollah (Party of God) shadowed the students; the Revolutionary Guard shadowed the army; the unelected, cleric-dominated Council of Guardians shadowed the parliament; and the indirectly elected Supreme Leader shadowed, and was more powerful than, the elected president.

'In most of the world people are trying to keep hope alive, but these people want to keep fear alive,' said Ali, pointing at the basijis, who had access to armouries stored in friendly mosques.

Then suddenly, before we reached the intersection where the hardliners directed traffic, he disappeared into a shop, the windows of which ran with moisture, emerging with two long-stemmed gladioli, one for me, and one for his mother.

'I know it seems strange to a Westerner, for a man to buy another man a flower,' he said, 'but this is the Persian way.'

In the taxi heading home, Ali confessed that he wanted to study abroad. He was a fan of James Joyce and W. B. Yeats and was considering Ireland, but after some questioning confessed that there was an Irish girl behind his choice of both poetry and country. But even this worldly, thrusting young Persian had his doubts about exile.

'I love speaking English. It's more than just a language — it gives us freedom in the mind,' he said. 'But for a Persian, there is still nowhere like Persia. I'm wondering what happens if everyone leaves. I'm not a big person to change anything. But at least I can start with my children.'

They were profound thoughts for such a young man, and self-consciously qualified at the first traffic light.

'Anyway, if I can't go to the teahouse, I'll miss it,' he said.

34

The Gates of Paradise

Time had become sticky and elongated. It had only been a week since I'd left Kandahar, but Iran had already imprinted itself on my psyche, reassuring me that Muslim culture could survive war and social turmoil, and perhaps emerge strengthened. Unlike most of the countries that surrounded it, it was at peace, and although the society was in the grip of upheaval, it was intact.

Under the Safavid shahs, Esfahan had become a lightning rod for the arts, its painters, poets, jewellers, architects and weavers exalting the senses with an 'epicurean audacity of thought and speech' worthy of the great Persian poet Omar Khayyam.[41] Although the shahs were zealous Muslims, their appetite for art led them to patronise artisans and traders of many faiths, including Jews and Armenian Christians. Both communities had at various times excelled in commerce and the art of dyeing, and like minorities everywhere were respected for their thrift, hard work and skills, which in the case of the Armenians included brewing the sly grog enjoyed by Muslims to this day. Like the Jews before them, the Armenians had been active middlemen in the silk trade, withholding the secret of the Chinese technology from Europeans for centuries, and selling the finished product to European agents operating from ports on the Gulf. A number of the Armenians relocated from the border areas by Shah Abbas had settled south of the Zāyandéh River on the outskirts of the then capital, christening the area New Jolfa in honour of their original homeland and building one of the most important cathedrals in the Middle East. As Esfahan expanded to incorporate it, the Armenian quarter became a prosperous ghetto.

It was Friday, the Muslim Sabbath, and New Jolfa's deserted streets had the dreamy serenity of a normally busy thoroughfare on an off-day; business-minded or not, the Christian Armenians saw no reason to hustle if the rest of the population was on leave. An intermittent stream of customers was emerging late from a modern apartment block which rose from the old mud-brick lanes, trickling into cornerstores to buy flatbread and milk. As Ali and I passed, a man hosed down the shop's awning, splashing water onto the hot asphalt, evoking steamy recollections of both our childhoods.

The Armenians were weavers with centuries of experience, and some experts contended that they, not the Persians or Turkmens, had invented the hand-knotted carpet which later would become so closely identified with Islamic cultures. The German academic Volkmar Gantzhorn claims early carpets were not floor covers for nomad tents, but icons and tabernacle covers, crowded with cruciforms rather than crescents. Gantzhorn also claims that even Islamic garden carpets — based on a cruciform grid of water channels separating garden beds viewed from above — had Christian origins, and that Muslim prayer rugs began life not as direction finders for Mecca, but as the hanging covers of pulpits:

A critical study of the existing source material makes clear that the hypothesis which posits the origin of the knotted-pile carpet in the Turkmenian region, and its import to the West by Turkic people such as the Seljuks, is completely unfounded ... all the so-called 'Turkmenian tribal guls' known in the carpets of central Asia belong to a single design evolution, one which was dependent on the developments in central and West Armenia ... From there began the migration of designs into the regions where new production centres were being established as a result of emigration or enforced settlement of Armenian artisans there.[42]

Across a pretty courtyard from Vank Cathedral stood the Armenian Museum in which lay preserved fragments of seventeenth-century table carpets whose Christian symbolism was unmistakable. A seventeenth-century piece made by Armenian weavers in the Caucasus glowed in pomegranate red, Persian blue and gold, and was adorned with a spiky fisherman's knife symbol. Ali had his nose pressed to a glass display case holding a two hundred and fifty-year-old Josheghan featuring the 'Tree of Life' from a village near Shahr-e Kord, whose inhabitants were renowned for having held off the Mongols. But a Bakhtiari 'Four Seasons' design with pink and yellow roses arranged in panels brought out the dealer in him.

'I'm sure I can find something like this,' he muttered.

Instead, I drew his attention to one of the museum's most spectacular exhibits. Placed under a microscope was a human hair. Inscribed along its length by Bahram Hagopian in 1974 were the words: 'To know wisdom and instruction, to perceive the words of understanding'.

Whether due to their modest numbers, or the sense of insecurity that exists in a non-Muslim enclave, the Christians of New Jolfa were determined to keep a low profile. Their beautiful whitewashed church seemed too small to warrant the title 'cathedral', and squeezing inside with Ali, we found ourselves in a shoebox chapel so dominated by its altar that there was barely room for a hundred parishioners. A chandelier hung from a towering blue and gold dome atop pointed arches, the shape of which suggested Islamic influence. But whatever Vank Cathedral lacked in scale or purity of design, the strange, top-heavy chapel made up for it in its glorious detail. Rich carpets covered the altar floor, and murals depicting the suffering saints gleamed with dark agony. The higher walls were inflamed with frescoes of triumph and torment. Demons were pushing sinners into monsters' mouths with tongues of flame, while those rescued from the trapdoor of Hell waited in orderly lines to enter the Gates of Paradise. God the Father, Jesus, and the Holy Spirit — this trinity I could never quite understand — sat one on top of the other, radiant in hierarchy. The angels fluttered about on wings, while the saints were disembowelled and subjected to gory tortures, with their eyes gouged out, heads crushed in screw presses, and boiling oil poured into their rectums. It was Dante's *Divine Comedy* rendered on a grand scale in oils.

Craning his neck to take in the full horror of it, Ali looked slightly detached. But like most Iranians of his age, he was curious about other religions, if only because the state had made them illicit.

'What is it supposed to be?' he asked, a Muslim in the cathedral.

'It's Judgment Day,' I replied.

'Why of course! We have this in our religion also,' he exclaimed, happy for the similarity. 'So tell me. Where is Mohammed in this?'

Then it was as if all that terrible beauty, the whole weight of its ponderous architecture, its soaring dome and chandelier, its lurid murals and carpets, and the altar's grand fresco with its wooden cross and portraits of the saints, had been placed on top of my head. And I realised how offensive a good church could be. All this glorification of blood and punishment. All these righteous images of martyrdom. All this Christian jihad.

'Well?' insisted Ali. 'What happens to Mohammed on the Christian Judgment Day?'

'He goes to Hell,' I answered, hurrying out before the whole damned thing collapsed on me.

Awaiting me were the gritty delights of greater Tehran, population twelve million, where the mullahs are so unpopular that taxi drivers refuse to pick them up, and Islamic agitprop billboards jostle with ads for Paco Rabanne. I looked forward with anticipation to the

Carpet Museum, established by the Empress Farah, and nights of traditional Persian music at the Bagh-e Saba chaikhune on Shariati Avenue. There would be meetings with remarkable people, like Josephina Gabbai and Moses Baba, the last of the Jewish traders on Ferdosi Street, once home to a powerful carpet cartel, where I would find a 'five-dollar carpet', literally a woollen counterfeit of the Abraham Lincoln-adorned banknote. There would be afternoons at the Shah's summer palace at Saadabad in the Alborz foothills, whose gardens and villas were now open to the public, and mornings at the bank vault holding the most ostentatious collection of baubles ever assembled, including a crown so heavy with gold and diamonds that it would have broken the Shah's neck had he ever worn it. I would spend time too in rat-infested South Tehran, the cradle of Khomeini's revolt, where the poor still scavenge in garbage cans and sleep with their hands out, their lives unchanged by revolution. But leaving Esfahan was like undergoing a kind of surgery in which you leave your important parts behind. How many hearts had that great square stolen? How many lovers had it consigned to life's longings? How many carpet wars had been fought there? Who had won?

Darius Hamadani had given me the names of the leaders of the Esfahan carpet syndicate, whose offices were deep in the convoluted arcades of the bazaar that trails off behind the northern end of the square. Entering its cool galleries framed by repeating arches was like exploring the rib-cage of a snake, except for the motorcycles with kilim panniers that squeezed between the stalls, cart-pushers and slanting beams of light. Tabriz is Iran's largest carpet market, but Esfahan's Bazaar Farsh Ferosha (Bazaar of the Carpet Sellers) is one of its oldest. From the vaulted roof, a huge banner of Imam Khomeini hung down, twisting in the draught that whistled along the alleys. Such is the reputation for meanness of the Esfahani merchants that according to Edward Browne in *A Year Amongst the Persians* they would keep their cheese in a bottle, imparting flavour to their bread by rubbing it on the glass. However, when revolution became inevitable they, like business people across the country, sided with the clerics, bolstering them against the Leftists who were the other main faction in the uprising. The bazaaris preferred Shari'a law to the class justice of the looters.

When Arthur Cecil Edwards visited Esfahan in 1948, the blue-fisted dye-workers complained to him of the high cost of madder. Now, I was delighted to find the ancient art still being conducted inside the bazaar, although using contemporary materials. One of the stalwarts, Jaffar Sebghatullahy, welcomed my impromptu arrival, leading me through the long narrow passageway of his premises to show me his true colours. They were out the back, stored in plastic drums with markings like 'Acid Blue 113'. An assistant was pouring the powdery contents of one such drum into a huge vat, producing a navy liquid that flowed thickly through the clumps of wool on hooks lowered into the steaming vats at the push of a button. Jaffar, whose father was also a dyer, had rigged up the plant himself based on little more than a photo of a similar plant in Germany.

'This colour will never change. Leave it in the sun for a hundred years, it will remain the same,' said Jaffar, proud of what purists would regard as the problem. The wool — Merino imported from Australia — would be ready in an hour. They dyed three hundred kilograms a day at a cost of fifty cents a kilogram.

As I penetrated deeper into the labyrinthine marketplace, plate-glass shopfronts with fluorescent lighting and even computers started popping up. In the heart of the covered bazaar stood a gleaming branch of the Bank Melli Iran, elbowing for space between the old rug market's dusty storefronts. In a nearby courtyard vast quantities of carpets — mainly of the Na'in and Esfahan varieties — were being sorted, sold and shifted.

The apparent capitalist anarchy of the bazaar concealed the hidden power of the syndicate. In every city this powerful clique governed admission to the trade. It was the syndicate that checked the credentials of anyone proposing to sell carpets in the bazaar, and adjudicated disputes between the dealers, and between dealers and customers. In Esfahan, the procedures included urine tests to ensure that would-be dealers were not opium addicts. Most dealers concentrated on exports, selling to the passing trade on the side. The syndicate did not control prices, but it did keep an eye on quality in order to protect the reputation of Esfahani carpets. The head of the syndicate was elected, but the family who had controlled it since the time of the Shah were the Mohavedians.

At their spartan tile-floor premises in the Sarai Amin wholesale market, Mohsen Mohavedian, the son of patriarch Mohammed Rahim, held court with his mobile phone under a large wall carpet featuring dervishes, mosques and the Ali Qapu palace. The bazaar was buzzing with news about the recent bankruptcy of a German-based Iranian dealer with outstanding commitments to most of the one thousand or so members of the Esfahan syndicate.

'We've lost about two billion *tomans*,' he said, meaning twenty billion rials, or about $25 million. 'It's set off a chain reaction of defaults. Sorting out the disputes this will cause is going to be one big headache.'

There had already been instances of violence, no murders as yet, but several shirt-frontings by desperate dealers.

'That's about as violent as these *jang-e farsh* [carpet wars] get,' said Mohavedian Jr, much to the amusement of his acolytes.

Even the good news was bad. The lifting of the US embargo on the import of Persian carpets in March 2000 had not provided the boost expected by the Esfahani merchants.

'When the US banned Iranian carpets, we increased our exports to Europe, with the result that a huge surplus of Iranian rugs built up there. When the US lifted the embargo, the Europeans immediately dumped large quantities of Persian rugs on the American market. The prices are so low now that it's not worth us sending anything. We preferred the embargo. At least then there was a steady flow of smuggled pieces getting into the US, and if you got something through you felt a real sense of achievement. Overall, of course, the embargo hurt Iran. Commercial relations that had taken decades to develop dried up in a few years.'

Running one hand through his hair, and twining his worry beads around the other, Mohsen Mohavedian said he suspected a conspiracy.

'Maybe it's because some of the main carpet importers in America are Jews. They're not eager to work with Iran. There were no Americans at last year's carpet fair in Tehran. Now they go to India, Pakistan and China, just like Iranian designers went to those countries when they couldn't get work here after the revolution.'

Strange things were indeed happening in the market, but I doubted organised Jewry were to blame. The rise of clean Scandinavian lines in design and architecture meant classical Persian carpets with their tendrils and arabesques were losing favour in Europe. However, at Mohavedian & Sons, conspiracies ruled, some quite startling.

'It's all because of those damned nuclear bombs,' said one of the hangers-on lounging in the brightly lit office.

The walls of the bazaar were suddenly all ears. Nuclear weapons were a sensitive issue in any language. The United States had banned American companies from investing in Iran over Tehran's attempts to acquire them, and with a foreigner present, Mohsen called a halt to the discussion.

'Let's discuss that some other time,' he said.

However, his older friend refused to desist. 'No, I'm sick of it. Let the truth come out,' the bead-counting interjector said. 'All our troubles were caused by the Chinese. They gave us those blasted weapons. President Hashemi Rafsanjani took delivery of them, and in return promised to keep Iran's carpet exports low, so as not to compete with China's. And we're the ones who pay!'

Back at Art of Persia, Darius assured me the story of the nukes-for-carpets deal was nothing more than bazaar gossip.

'You spend too long in this business and your brain will turn to wool,' he warned me. 'Your entire life will be tied up in knots!'

The promised special shipment had yet to arrive, but he led me upstairs anyway to inspect his prize pile. Apart from the Shahsavan mafrash there were several unusual pieces, including a Kurdish Elephant's Foot and several confronting Caucasians. I would have liked the mafrash, but it cost too much, so I settled for one of Darius's Bakhtiari khordjin from the popular pile.

As I inspected his wares, looking out for signs of repair, bleeding or inconsistency, I noticed a tourist group had arrived, brought in by a member of Darius's spy network. They were standing in a group, aspirating in 'ahs' and 'ohs' as one of the staff unrolled a selection of cheap and nasty new pieces, cradling them like precious heirlooms and peppering his spiel with alluring but bogus tales of the ancient art of the carpet. Since tourists formed the bulk of local custom, and the average tourist was not willing to pay more than about $200 on a rug, the whole business had inevitably been dumbed down.

There was something terribly familiar to me about the sales pitch, as familiar as a religious ritual or a momentary *déjà vu*. Darius had been on the phone, but returned now, sidling up to me as he also looked on.

'Don't you just love those people?' he whispered in my ear, like a proud parent witnessing a child's rite of passage. 'The romance of carpets is alive for them.'

And I knew then that for us, somewhere in the web of materials, techniques, provenance and price, it had died.

'I know what you're thinking,' said Darius, reading me like the back of one of his Caucasians. 'You're wondering where it goes, that romance of the rugs? Don't look so afraid and worried.'

Slumping down on his prize pile-turned-bean bag, Darius took a cruet of tea from the tray of a bearer, and motioned to me to take the other. There was something distinctly evil about his languor.

He knew too much, the lost innocence replaced with a world-weary cynicism. Raising his tea in a parody of a toast, he began to explain.

'You are just like the good man who goes to what we Muslims call behesht, Paradise, and you Christians call Heaven,' he said, blowing on his drink to cool it. 'It's lovely in Heaven, of course, but a bit boring. So one day, the man goes wandering through all the big white puffy clouds, and eventually he comes to a huge doorway.

'"What's inside there?" he asks the giant who is standing guard outside the door.

'"It's Hell," the giant says, but when the man asks if he can take a peek inside, the giant says, "Sure!"

'So, the man goes inside, and when he see what Hell is all about, he cannot believe his eyes. Everywhere people are laughing and drinking, dancing and making love with the women, and the man realises that this is the real Paradise, and that Heaven is really Hell. So after he has stayed there and enjoyed the hospitality — which is really wonderful — he thanks the giant, and goes back to Heaven.

'For some time, this man is troubled. All night he dreams of his adventure, especially the beautiful, friendly women he met there and the men who only loved to drink and gamble all day. And day by day, these fond memories weigh more and more heavily on his mind, until one day he cannot tolerate the pressure any longer. So he asks the archangel Gabriel to arrange a meeting with God.

'When the appointed time for the meeting comes, and the man stands before the blinding light of the Almighty, he announces that he wants to leave Paradise. Allah, the Compassionate, the Merciful, is shocked by his request. Nobody has ever asked to leave Heaven before. God worries about setting a precedent, but after some time He decides that even the saints in Heaven must have free will. So after thinking about it for a long time, God calls the man before Him.

'"As you wish my son," He tells him. "With my blessings you shall go. But remember that once you leave Heaven, you can never return."

'Overjoyed with his freedom, the man rushes off to pack his belongings, saying goodbye to all the saints and angels — who really are nice people, but a little bit dull — and goes back to Hell.

'When he reaches the doorway to Hell, the giant seems surprised to see him.

'"You again?" says the giant. "What do you want?"

'"I want to go to Hell," says the man, which makes the giant laugh so much that he bends over, and can only say, "Be my guest."'

Darius too was laughing, so vigorously and for so long that I began to feel decidedly uncomfortable. Who was he really? A carpet dealer? Or Satan himself? Eventually, he regained his composure sufficiently to light a cigarette, and take his tale to its grim conclusion.

'Entering Hell,' said Darius, leaning forward, his face flushed with ominous excitement, 'our man is shocked to see that there is a big change there. No longer does he see beautiful women, and there is no music or laughter either. Just *filthy* rats running in dark corners, bats flying in his face, and cold, rattling skeletons hanging everywhere. Around his feet, small fires are burning, and his ears are full of the cries of agony of sick and starving people. The place is unrecognisable. So the man, who is really beginning to panic now, turns to the giant, and he says to him, "Please sir, tell me there is some mistake. Where is the happy place I saw before? Where is all the beauty, and the laughter, and the sweet music?" And the giant, who is weeping with laughter now, so much that he can barely speak, looks at the man and says to him, "You poor, poor fool! When you visited us last time, you came as a tourist. Now, you live here."'

EPILOGUE

In March 2001, Taliban fighters using tanks, rockets and dynamite obliterated the Buddhas of Bamiyan. The Taliban's supreme leader, Mullah Mohammed Omar, who condemned the statues in the name of Islam, defended his action, insisting that 'all we are breaking are stones'. The operation to erase what the Indian parliament called 'one of the greatest examples of human creativity' took several weeks because, as a senior Taliban official put it, the idols were 'tough'. Their destruction was condemned around the world by Muslims and non-Muslims alike.

On a crackling, frequently dying telephone line from Peshawar, Nancy Hatch Dupree sounded tired and desperately sad. Now seventy-three, the American aid worker and travel writer had been working to save the statues before most people knew they existed. But the world had woken up too late and all that remained was rubble, chunks of which began showing up for sale in the Pashtun tribal areas near Peshawar.[1]

'Destroying the Buddhas was so un-Afghan ... it has nothing to do with Islam,' Nancy said, her voice straining with incredulity. 'This policy is being orchestrated by outsiders. They want to erase the Afghan identity whose roots go back before Islam. Afghanistan is being wiped off the map.'

Certainly, the Bamiyan Buddhas had been removed from my map; the one marked 'Things to See'. Patience had played tricks on me as I'd waited for the day when Tariq Ahmed and I could go together to stand before their majesty at the heart of a peaceful Afghanistan. The idea that I might outlive them never occurred to me.

On 11 September 2001, the iconoclasts struck again, this time at the heart of America. Using hijacked commercial airliners as missiles, they destroyed New York's tallest buildings, the twin towers of the World Trade Centre, and cut a swathe through US military headquarters at the Pentagon in Washington DC. Some three thousand people died in the co-ordinated terrorist attacks on the two symbols of American military and economic power, while a fourth hijacked plane crashed into a field in Pennsylvania, killing all on board, after the passengers fought valiantly to prevent it being used as a missile against an unknown target. Authorities identified nineteen hijackers linked to Osama bin Laden's Al-Qa'ida network, and the United States promptly declared war on terror. The following month, US warplanes began a sustained campaign of bombing backed by the deployment of ground forces in Afghanistan, where bin Laden was still living under the protection of the Taliban.

Two days before the attacks on America, the 'Lion of Panjshir', Ahmad Shah Massoud, consented to an interview in the northern Afghan town of Khwaja Bahauddin with two Moroccans claiming to be journalists, but the interview had barely got underway when the television camera exploded, killing one of the Moroccans and Massoud. The leader of the greatest act of Muslim resistance in the twentieth century — the jihad against the Soviet invasion of Afghanistan — fell to Muslim assassins, one of them only twenty-two years old. A week later, Massoud's coffin was carried from his home village of Jangalak by thousands of weeping mourners and laid to rest on a bare hilltop near Saricha in the Panjshir Valley. He was forty-nine, and left behind a thirteen-year-old son, Ahmad.[2]

Deprived of their charismatic leader, Massoud's forces faced probable defeat in the civil war at the hands of the Taliban and its Arab and Pakistani supporters. But two months later, with the assistance of US air and ground forces, Massoud's United Front returned in triumph to Kabul, as the numerically superior Taliban abandoned the capital without a fight.

When I returned to Kabul in November 2001, the war was unfinished. Although Massoud never regained consciousness, and would never see Kabul again, portraits of him suddenly materialised across Afghanistan, especially in the capital. With his unmistakable features peering out from car windows and public buildings, his legend was put to work enhancing the legitimacy of the post-Taliban political order, and bolstering the position of his Jami'at-e Islami at the very heart of it. The departure of the Taliban was greeted with a mixture of celebration and anxiety. Women walked the streets alone and unmolested for the first time in a decade, but cautiously kept to their chaderi. Men rushed barbers' shops to shave off their beards, and music and posters of Hindi movie sirens proliferated. But the 'liberators' were the same forces that had helped destroy much of the city a few years earlier. Preparations for a huge international effort to rebuild Afghanistan were laced with uncertainty about whether the warring factions could settle their differences amicably and share power.

In December 2001, the Taliban abandoned its spiritual headquarters of Kandahar. However, despite the efforts of US special forces and Afghan tribal leaders, Osama bin Laden and Mullah Omar both remained at large. A summit of Afghan political leaders held in Bonn agreed to form an interim ruling council, which was given six months to establish a new administration and organise a loyal jirga, or grand council, to choose a new government, which would rule for two years and then hold general elections. A Pashtun tribal leader who had served in the former mujahideen government, Hamid Karzai, was sworn in as prime minister. His deputy defence minister was the Uzbek warlord Abdul Rashid Dostum, who had fought his way back to Mazar-e Sharif with the help of CIA advisors.

Starved of business for over twenty years, many dealers in Kabul's main surviving carpet bazaar on Chicken Street had given up the rug trade or were supplementing it with other wares. Second-hand leather jackets shipped in from Europe now draped shopfronts where carpets had once proudly hung. But with hopes running high for the return of peace, members of the far-flung Afghan diaspora were returning, from expatriate Afghans called to serve in the new government, to foreign well-wishers. Having failed to obtain asylum in the West, Tariq Ahmed was preparing to go home with his family and revive his business from scratch. Ghulam Rasoul Ahmadi was living in Australia, where he worked in a car plant, refereed volleyball matches and served as vice-president of an Afghan community association. But Rasoul, who had also become an Australian citizen, was attempting to head home. His family had decided it was time for him to get married, and his brother Yaqub had been charged with the task of finding him a bride and organising the celebrations in Mazar. He also expected to finally collect his degree from Balkh University. Zhala Najrabi was considering several proposals of marriage from suitors around the world.

In February 2001 Kuwait celebrated the tenth anniversary of its liberation from Iraqi occupation, but Saddam Hussein remained president of Iraq. In Tajikistan, the International Crisis Group described the situation as 'precarious'.[3] After twenty years of fighting as one of Ahmad Shah Massoud's most trusted lieutenants, Ahmed Muslim left Dushanbe and settled with his family in the Netherlands. India's war in Kargil was followed by continued failure in its efforts to improve relations with Pakistan, and intensified attacks in Kashmir by Pakistan-based separatist groups, who threw acid in the faces of unveiled women in Srinagar and continued to recruit young Kashmiri men for jihad. However, there were signs of the US-led war on terror putting Islamabad under pressure to scale back the Kashmiri operation.

In the year 2000, a French Savonnerie carpet sold for a world record price of $4 million.[4] Jenny Housego's Kashmir Loom Company was doing well, but Butt's Clermont Houseboats was barely afloat, and after a career spanning half a century, the incurably optimistic Gulam Rasull Khan retired from Gulam Mohidin & Sons of Srinagar in April 2001. Habib, man of a thousand faces and the world's most sedentary nomad, is still Habib. He can be found most days in his shop in Islamabad, 'breaking the leg of English' and harassed by tax-inspectors and hijras.

In August 2001, Mohammed Khatami was sworn-in for a second five-year term as Iran's president. In Esfahan, Cyber Ali's relentless social schedule continued between selling carpets and uncovering Darius's spy plots. As the twenty-first century began, Islam was one of the world's fastest growing religions, practised by more than one billion people. On current trends one in three of the world's population will be Muslim by 2025.[5]

In early 2002, former Afghan king Zahir Shah — crowned in 1933 and deposed in a coup in 1973 — was planning his return to Kabul to give his blessings to the new political system. The 'miracle' the late communist-backed president Mohammed Najibullah told me could never happen was on the verge of becoming a reality. Another miracle awaited. On 1 January 2002, newspapers around the world reported that the authorities in Kabul hoped to rebuild the Bamiyan Buddhas, and that several foreign countries had expressed interest in supporting the project.[6]

Notes

PART ONE

1 Sir Richard Burton (trans.), *The Arabian Nights' Entertainments*, Heritage Press, New York, 1955, p. 220

2 Henry S. Bradsher, *Afghan Communism and Soviet Intervention*, Oxford University Press, Karachi, 1999, p. 161

3 Zahiru'd-din Muhammad Babur Padshah Ghazi, *Babur-Nama*, Annette Susannah Beveridge (trans.), Munshiram Manoharlal Publishers, New Delhi, 1990, p. 202

4 Babur, *Babur-Nama*, p. 202

5 Robert Byron, *The Road to Oxiana*, Pan Books, London, 1981, p. 273

6 Bradsher, *Afghan Communism and Soviet Intervention*, p. 178

7 ibid., p. 336

8 Volkmar Gantzhorn, *Oriental Carpets*, Benedikt Taschen Verlag, Köln, 1998, p. 22 (originally published as the thesis 'The Christian Oriental Carpet')

9 Nancy Hatch Dupree, *An Historical Guide to Afghanistan*, Afghan Tourist Organisation, Kabul, 1977, p. 47

10 Benjamin Walker, *Foundations of Islam: The Making of a World Faith*, HarperCollins India, New Delhi, 1999, p. 119

11 ibid., p. 321

PART TWO

1 Walker, *Foundations of Islam*, p. 234

2 Manuel Komroff (ed.), *The Travels of Marco Polo (The Venetian)*, Horace Liveright, New York, 1926, p. 24

3 Kathleen Hopkirk, *Central Asia: A Traveller's Companion*, John Murray, London, 1993, p. 123

4 Jack Franses, *Tribal Rugs from Afghanistan and Turkestan*, handbook to exhibition at Franses of Piccadilly, Ditchling Press Ltd, London, September 1973, p. 5

5 J. M. A. Thompson (ed.) in introduction to A. A. Bogolyubov, *Carpets of Central Asia*, Crosby Press, Hampshire, 1973, p. 1

6 Charles W. Jacobsen, *Oriental Rugs: A Complete Guide*, Charles E. Tuttle Publishers, Tokyo, 1962, p. 96

7 Poem by Rabi'a Balkhi, translated by K. Habibi (1967) and quoted in Louis Dupree, *Afghanistan*, Princeton University Press, Princeton, New Jersey, 1978

8 Edward Allworth, *The Modern Uzbeks: From the Fourteenth Century to the Present; A Cultural History*, Hoover Institution Press, Stanford University, Stanford, 1990, p. 3

9 *Newsweek*, 17 March, 1980; G. Whitney Azoy, *Buzkashi: Game and Power in Afghanistan*, University of Pennsylvania Press, Philadelphia, 1982, p. 136

10 François Bourliere (ed.), *The Land and Wildlife of Eurasia*, Time Inc., New York, 1964, p. 83

11 'Following the hoofprints of Alexander the Great' by J. J. Fergusson, *The Independent*, London, 2 August 1997

12 'New dates for old clothes: India, Southeast Asia and the textile trade' John Guy, in *Hali*, No. 103 (March/April 1999)

13 Ahmed Rashid, *Taliban: Islam, Oil and the New Great Game in Central Asia*, I.B. Tauris Press, London, 2000, p. 56

14 James Morier, *The Adventures of Hajji Baba of Ispahan*, Oxford University Press, London, 1824 (reprinted 1963), p. 228

15 Byron, *The Road to Oxiana*, p. 89

16 Bruce Chatwin, preface to Byron, *The Road to Oxiana*, p. 10

17 Byron, *The Road to Oxiana*, p. 239

18 Gavin Hambly, *Cities of Mughal India*, G. P. Putnam's Sons, New York, 1968, p. 15

19 Jalal-ud-Din Balkhi, Coleman Barks (trans.) with John Moyne, *The Essential Rumi*, Penguin, Harmondsworth, 1999, pp. 112–13

20 Walker, *Foundations of Islam*, p. 304

21 Chatwin, preface to Byron, *The Road to Oxiana*, p. 14

22 Omar Khayyam, Edward Fitzgerald (trans.), *Rubaiyat of Omar Khayyam*, Atelie Honar, M. Salashoor, Tehran, p. 24

23 Babur, *Babur-Nama*, p. 564

24 Walker, *Foundations of Islam*, p. 92

25 N. J. Dawood (trans.), *The Koran*, Penguin Books, Harmondsworth, 1974, Ch. 33, Verse 49

26 *Holy Bible: The New King James Version*, Genesis, Ch. 3, Verse 16, Thomas Nelson Inc, 1982; published by India Bible Literature, Madras

27 Dawood (trans.), *The Koran*, Ch. 4, Verse 34

28 'Last Soviet Soldiers Leave Afghanistan' by Bill Keller, *The New York Times*, 16 February 1989

29 Walker, *Foundations of Islam*, p. 185

PART THREE

1 There is no Badshah Market, nor any Caravan Carpits company in Islamabad, these being devices invented at Habib's request to protect him from tax-inspectors

2 'Taliban head says Rabbani sabotaging UN peace efforts' by Rahimullah Yousufzai, *The News* (Pakistan), 2 February 1995

3 Mullah Omar later broke his ban on meeting foreigners, entertaining a Chinese delegation in late 2000

4 Rashid, *Taliban*, p. 24

5 Walker, *Foundations of Islam*, p. 280

6 Burton (trans.), *The Arabian Nights' Entertainments*, p. 75

7 Richard Ettinghausen, *Arab Painting*, Macmillan, London, 1977, p. 15

8 ibid., p. 12

9 Alastair Hull and Jose Luczyc-Wyhowska, *Kilim: The Complete Guide*, Thames & Hudson, London, 1993, p. 8

10 'In Defence of Khomeini' by Karen Armstrong, *The Australian Financial Review Weekend Review*, 20 October 2000

11 'Conversation with Terror', interview with Rahimullah Yousufzai, *Time* (Asia), 11 January 1999, Vol. 153, No. 1

12 Yossef Bodansky, *Bin Laden: The Man Who Declared War on America*, Prima Publishing, Rocklin, California, 1999, p. 10

13 'Afghan man survives wall ordeal', *BBC World Service* (website), 16 January 1999

14 Marquess Curzon of Kedleston, *A Viceroy's India: Leaves from Lord Curzon's Note-book*, Sidgwick & Jackson, London, 1984, p. 101

15 Burton (trans.), *The Arabian Nights' Entertainments*, p. 667

16 W. A. Hawley, *Oriental Rugs: Antique and Modern*, John Lane, London, 1913, quoted in Hull and Luczyc-Wyhowska, *Kilim: The Complete Guide*, pp. 35–38

17 *Hali*, Vol. 102, p. 118

18 Gordon Redford Walker, *Oriental Rugs: An Introduction*, Prion, London, 1999, p. 187

PART FOUR

1 'Deadly from land, air or sea, the 550mph smart missile that can think for itself — at least in theory' by Tim Radford, *The Guardian*, 18 December 1998

2 Walker, *Foundations of Islam*, p. 115

3 Walter B. Denny, *Sotheby's Guide to Oriental Carpets*, Simon & Schuster, New York, 1994, p. 11

4 Arthur Urbane Dilley, *Oriental Rugs and Carpets: A Comprehensive Study*, Seribner's, New York, 1931, p. 8

5 ibid., p. vii

6 Jacobsen, *Oriental Rugs: A Complete Guide*, p. 96

7 Nazneen Zafar, *A Practical Guide to Pakistani Rugs*, Liberty Books, Karachi, 1992, p. 56

8 'Restoring Antique Carpets' by Wasim Fatima, *The Nation* (Pakistan), 1 June 1994

9 'Pakistani carpets do not exist' by Zahrah Nasir, *Dawn* (Pakistan), 10 March 1995

10 Jacobsen, *Oriental Rugs: A Complete Guide*, p. 16

11 'Carpet industry to be shifted from Peshawar', Bureau report, *The News* (Pakistan), 19 August 1999

12 Julia Bailey, 'Early Caucasian carpets', in David Black (ed.), *The Atlas of Rugs & Carpets*, Tiger Books International, London, 1994, p. 74

13 'The promise of Pakistan' by John McCarry, *National Geographic*, October 1997

14 Edward W. Said, *Covering Islam*, Random House, New York, 1997, p. xv

15 Samuel P. Huntington, *The Clash of Civilizations and the Remaking of the World Order*, Simon & Schuster, New York, 1996, p. 111

16 Pamela Constable, 'Pakistan's Moral Majority', *The Washington Post*, 22 June 2000

17 Geoffrey Moorhouse, *To the Frontier*, Sceptre, London, 1988, p. 172

18 *BBC World Service* (website), 26 November 1998

PART FIVE

1 Komroff (ed.), *The Travels of Marco Polo (The Venetian)*, p. 30

2 Michael Rogers, *The Spread of Islam: The Making of the Past*, Elsevier-Phaidon, New York, 1976, p. 39

3 'A wartime city split in two: calm days, explosive nights' by Howard Schneider, *The Washington Post*, 18 December 1998

4 'Basic instincts guide hi-tech war', *The New York Times*, reprinted in *The Sydney Morning Herald*, 22 December 1998

5 'Arab with Designs on Apocalypse' by Tony Walker, *The Sydney Morning Herald*, 23 June 1990

6 Huntington, *The Clash of Civilizations*, p. 90

7 'U.S. policy on Hussein still unclear' by Tim Weiner, *The New York Times*, 3 January 1999

8 Richard Butler, *Saddam Defiant: The Threat of Weapons of Mass Destruction, and the Crisis of Global Security*, Weidenfeld & Nicholson, London, 2000, pp. 195–6

9 ibid., p. 223

10 'Iraqi–Iranian War Reflects Ancient Ethnic Rivalry, Baathist Struggle Against Islamic Fundamentalism' by Edward Cody, *The Washington Post*, 22 March 1982

11 Burton (trans.), *The Arabian Nights' Entertainments*, p. 220

12 'Moving Target' by Ross Dunn, *The Sydney Morning Herald*, 21 February 1998

13 Photo by Faleh Kheiber, Reuters, 3 April 2000

14 'How Israel Gathered Jews', review by Ronnay Gabbay of *Operation Babylon* by Shlomo Hillel, *The Sydney Morning Herald*, 11 June 1988

15 'The Deadly Legacy of Saddam's Chemical Attack' by Owen Boycott, *The Guardian*, February 26 1999

16 'Iraqi–Iranian War Reflects Ancient Ethnic Rivalry, Baathist Struggle Against Islamic Fundamentalism' by Edward Cody, *The Washington Post*, 12 March 1982

17 Dilley, *Oriental Rugs and Carpets*, p. 2

18 'Gardens Legend Still Flowers' by Graeme Hammond, *The Sunday Herald Sun*, 7 July 1996

19 Robert Koldewey, *The Excavations at Babylon*, Macmillan & Co., London, 1914, p. vi

20 ibid., p. 48

21 ibid., p. 30
22 'Digging for the Truth' by Helen Nicholson, *The Sydney Morning Herald*, 2 September 1995
23 Genesis 11:6-8, *Holy Bible: The New King James Version*
24 Genesis, Chps 16–17, *Holy Bible: The New King James Version*

PART SIX

1 John King, John Noble and Andrew Humphreys, *Central Asia*, Lonely Planet, Melbourne, 1996, p. 421
2 'The wagons of Azerbaijan' by Rod Curtis, *The Sydney Morning Herald*, 6 May 2000
3 'The war for black gold' by Shantanu Guha Ray, *Outlook* (India), 10 April 2000
4 'Fabled Silk Road now paved with narcotics' by Scott Petersen, *The Christian Science Monitor*, 8 January 2001
5 Huntington, *The Clash of Civilizations*, p. 96
6 International Crisis Group, *Central Asia: Fault Lines in the New Security Map*, Osh/Brussels, July 2001, p. 12
7 'The Empire Strikes Back', *The Economist*, 7 August 1993, p. 36
8 Huntington, *The Clash of Civilizations*, p. 271
9 King *et al.*, *Central Asia*, p. 429
10 '50 Most Powerful People in Asia', *Asiaweek*, 5 July 1996
11 *Voice of America*, 14 January 2000

PART SEVEN

1 *Gazetteer of Kashmir and Ladak, compiled under the Direction of the Quarter Master General in India in the Intelligence Branch* (1890), Manas Publications, Delhi, 1992, p. 772
2 'On the turning away' by Muzamil Jaleel, *The Indian Express*, 2 August 2000
3 Brian Cloughley, *Nuclear Risk-Reduction Measures in Kashmir*, The Stimson Center, Washington DC, 19 November 1998, p. 58
4 Manoj Joshi, *The Lost Rebellion: Kashmir in the Nineties*, Penguin Books India, New Delhi, 1999, p. 290
5 François Bernier, *Travels in the Mogul Empire A.D. 1656–1668*, (Constable's Oriental Miscellany of Original and Selected

Publications Vol. 1), Archibald Constable and Company, Westminster, 1891, pp. 402–3

6 Bernier, *Travels in the Mogul Empire*, p. 403

7 'Soft, Warm and Illegal Shahtooshes become an elegant fashion accessory at a grim price' by Nadya Labi, *Time*, 18 October 1999

8 'Wrapped in Controversy' by Sarah MacDonald, *Good Weekend* (Sydney), 9 December 2000, pp. 95–6

9 Andrew Middleton, *Rugs & Carpets: Techniques, Traditions & Designs*, Mitchell Beazley, London, 1996, p. 82

10 South Asia Human Rights Documentation Centre, 'Betrayed and Abandoned: Afghan refugees under UNHCR protection in New Delhi', New Delhi, November 1999

11 Balkhi, *The Essential Rumi*, p. 17

12 Ali Shariati, 'Anthropology: The Creation of Man and the Contradiction of God and Iblis, or Spirit and Clay', in Hamid Algar (trans.), *On the Sociology of Islam: Lectures by Ali Shariati*, Mizan Press, Berkeley, California, 1979, quoted in Said, *Covering Islam*, p. 67

13 The Kargil Review Committee, *From Surprise to Reckoning: The Kargil Review Committee Report*, Sage Publications, New Delhi, 1999, p. 98

14 ibid., p. 18

15 'Kashmir with a capital N' by Brian Cloughley, *The Canberra Times*, 5 July 1999

16 'Battle for the Mind: Nobody Can Be A Winner in Kargil' by K. P. S. Gill, *The Times of India*, 9 July 1999

17 The Kargil Review Committee, *From Surprise to Reckoning*, p. 20

18 'Pak Army disowns its dead soldiers', *The Times of India News Service*, 8 July 1999

19 'A Worsening War' by Praveen Swami, *Frontline* (India), 16 July 1999

20 'Muslim Grendiers surprise enemy' by Gaurav C. Sawant, *The Indian Express*, 10 July 1999

21 Edited version of a speech by Najam Sethi to the National Defence College, *The Friday Times* (Pakistan), 7 May 1999

22 'Kargil: one year on (Part II) — What went wrong' by Dr Iffat S. Malik, *The News* (Pakistan), 28 June 2000

23 'Battle for the Mind: Nobody Can Be A Winner in Kargil' by K. P. S. Gill, *The Times of India*, 9 July 1999

PART EIGHT

1 Major Henry George Raverty, *Notes on Afghanistan and Baluchistan* (1878), Abid Bokhari, Quetta, 1976, p. 496
2 United Nations Food and Agricultural Organisation, *Activities of Kuchi Survey Team*, Working Paper No 1/99, June 1999, p. 5
3 'Afghan Woman Appeals to Taliban to Ease Strictures' by Michael Battye, Reuters, 22 October 1996
4 Raverty, *Notes on Afghanistan and Baluchistan*, p. 497
5 ibid., p. 503
6 Morier, *The Adventures of Hajji Baba of Ispahan*, p. 404
7 Dupree, *An Historical Guide to Afghanistan*, p. 320
8 Sirdar Ikbal Ali Shah, *Afghanistan of the Afghans*, Octagon Press, London, 1982
9 'Jordan: kingdom in the middle' by Thomas J. Abercrombie, *National Geographic*, February 1984
10 Hull and Luczyc-Wyhowska, *Kilim: The Complete Guide*, p. 183

PART NINE

1 Dilley, *Oriental Rugs and Carpets*, p. 200
2 Morier, *The Adventures of Hajji Baba of Ispahan*, p. 148
3 Lee Allane, *Oriental Rugs: A Buyer's Guide*, Thames & Hudson, London, 1988, p. 95
4 *Oriental Rug Society of New South Wales Newsletter*, Vol. 21, No. 3
5 Arthur Cecil Edwards, *The Persian Carpet: A Survey of the Carpet Weaving Industry*, Duckworth, 1953, pp. 8–10
6 Middleton, *Rugs & Carpets*, p. 11
7 Reinhard G. Hubel, Katherine Watson (trans.), *The Book of Carpets*, Barrie & Jenkins, London, 1971, p. 9
8 Mohammed Khatami, *Islam, Liberty and Development*, Institute for Global Cultural Studies, Binghamton University, 1999, p. 14
9 'Iran: testing the waters of reform' by Fen Montaigne, *National Geographic*, July 1999
10 'Letter from Tehran: We Invite the Hostages to Return' by Robin Wright, *The New Yorker*, 8 November 1999
11 'Observer: A Few Words at the End' by Russell Baker, *The New York Times*, 25 December 1998

12 Morier, *The Adventures of Hajji Baba of Ispahan*, p. 145

13 Said, *Covering Islam*, p. 23

14 'Women lift veil on Iranian art' by Samantha Ellis, *The Sydney Morning Herald* (reprinted from *The Guardian*), 13 March 2001

15 '185 officers killed in encounters with drug smugglers', IRNA (Islamic Republic News Agency), 16 May 2000

16 Middleton, *Rugs & Carpets*, p. 10

17 Hubel, *The Book of Carpets*, p. 10

18 Edwards, *The Persian Carpet*, p. 202

19 Walker, *Oriental Rugs*, p. 68

20 'Gulf War embargo a factor in shifting market' by Nancy L. Ross, *The Washington Post*, 25 February 1988

21 P. Masson-Oursel and Louise Morin (contributors), 'Mythology of Ancient Persia', *New Larousse Encyclopedia of Mythology*, Hamlyn, Middlesex, 1959, p. 323

22 ibid., p. 312

23 Edwards, *The Persian Carpet*, p. 214

24 'Human Rights in Iran, Without Discrimination for All Human Beings (An Interview with the First Female Judge in Iran)', *Jameah*, 16 February 1998

25 Byron, *The Road to Oxiana*, p. 176

26 Edwards, *The Persian Carpet*, p. 314

27 Walker, *Oriental Rugs*, p. 61

28 Byron, *The Road to Oxiana*, p. 167

29 ibid., p. 172

30 Dawood (trans.), *The Koran*, Ch. 3, Verse 6

31 Frank MacShane, *Many Golden Ages: Ruins, Temples and Monuments of the Orient*, Charles E. Tuttle, Rutland, Virginia, 1962, p. 190

32 ibid.

33 Michael Rogers, *The Spread of Islam: The Making of the Past*, Oxford, 1976, p. 58

34 Kathleen Hopkirk, *Central Asia: A Traveller's Companion*, p. 166

35 Jenny Housego, *Tribal Rugs*, Scorpion, UK, 1991, p. 14

36 Hull and Luczyc-Wyhowska, *Kilim: The Complete Guide*, p. 217

37 IRNA, 9 November 2000

38 Byron, *The Road to Oxiana*, p. 175

39 Robert McNeal, *Carpet of Death*, Robert Hale, London, 1976

40 'Thousands heed call and march for Islam', *The Sydney Morning Herald* (reprinted from Reuters), 15 July 2000

41 Khayyam, *Rubaiyat of Omar Khayyam*, p. 7

42 Gantzhorn, *Oriental Carpets*, pp. 511–12

EPILOGUE

1. *Sunday Telegraph* (UK), 1 April 2001

2. 'Amid Wailing, Lion Laid to Rest' by Marcus Warren, *The Age* (reprinted from Reuters), 18 September 2001

3. International Crisis Group, *Central Asia: Faultlines in the New Security Map?*, Osh/Brussels, 4 July 2000, p. 7

4. 'Bag A Carpet' by Peter Fish, *The Sydney Morning Herald*, 21 February 2001

5. 'A Prophet of Doom' by William Rees-Mogg, *The Times* (London), 20 September 1999

6. 'Statues May Rise Again', *The Sydney Morning Herald* (reprinted from Reuters), 1 January 2002

Bibliography and Suggested Reading

Said K. Aburish, *Saddam Hussein: The Politics of Revenge*, Bloomsbury,
London, 2000

Ludwig W. Adamec, *Historical Dictionary of Afghanistan*,
The Scarecrow Press Inc., Methuen, New Jersey and
London, 1991

Hamid Algar, *On the Sociology of Islam: Lectures by Ali Shariati*,
Mizan Press, Berkeley, 1979

Lee Allane, *Oriental Rugs: A Buyer's Guide*, Thames & Hudson,
London, 1988

—— *Kilims: A Buyer's Guide*, Thames & Hudson, London, 1995

Edward Allworth, *Modern Uzbeks: From the Fourteenth Century to the
Present; A Cultural History*, Hoover Institution Press, Stanford
University, Stanford, 1990

G. Whitney Azoy, *Buzkashi: Game and Power in Afghanistan*,
University of Pennsylvania Press, Philadelphia, 1982

Zahiru'd-din Muhammad Babur Padshah Ghazi, *Babur-Nama*,
Annette Susannah Beveridge (trans.), Munshiram Manoharlal
Publishers, New Delhi, 1990

Jalal-ud-Din Balkhi, Coleman Barks (trans.) with John Moyne,
The Essential Rumi, Penguin, Harmondsworth, 1999

Nicholas Barnard, *Kilim*, Thames & Hudson, London, 1994

Major Henry Walter Bellew, *Races of Afghanistan*, Sang-e-meel
Publications, Lahore, 1999

Ian Bennett (ed.), *The Country Life Book of Rugs and Carpets of the World*, Quarto Books, London, 1977

Valerie Berinstain *et al.*, *Great Carpets of the World*, Vendome Press, New York, 1996

François Bernier, *Travels in the Mogul Empire A.D. 1665–1668* (Constable's Oriental Miscellany of Original and Selected Publications Vol. 1), Archibald Constable and Company, Westminster, 1891

David Black and Clive Loveless (eds.), *Rugs of the Wandering Baluchi*, David Black Oriental Carpets, London, 1976

David Black (ed.), *The Atlas of Rugs & Carpets*, Tiger Books International, London, 1994

Wilfrid Blunt, *Isfahan: Pearl of Persia*, Elek Books Limited, London, 1966

Yossef Bodansky, *Bin Laden: The Man Who Declared War on America*, Prima Publishing, Rocklin, California, 1999

A. A. Bogolyubov, *Carpets of Central Asia*, Crosby Press, Hampshire, 1973

Jeff W. Boucher, *Baluchi Woven Treasures*, self-published, Alexandria (USA), 1989

François Bourliere (ed.), *The Land and Wildlife of Eurasia*, Time Inc., New York, 1964

Wilhelm Bode and Ernst Kühnel, *Antique Rugs from the Near East*, E. Weyhe, New York, 1922

Clifford Edmund Bosworth (trans.), *The Book of Curious and Entertaining Information*, The University Press, Edinburgh, 1968

Henry S. Bradsher, *Afghan Communism and Soviet Intervention*, Oxford University Press, Karachi, 1999

Edward Granville Browne, *A Literary History of Persia*, T. Fisher Unwin, London, 1902

—— *A Year Amongst the Persians*, A & C Black Ltd, London, 1893

Wilfried Buchta, *Who Rules Iran? The Structure of Power in the Islamic Republic*, The Washington Institute for Near East Policy and the Konrad Adenauer Foundation, 2000

Sir Richard Burton (trans.), *The Arabian Nights' Entertainments*, Vols 1 & 2, Heritage Press, New York, 1955

Richard Butler, *Saddam Defiant: The Threat of Weapons of Mass Destruction, and the Crisis of Global Security*, Weidenfeld & Nicholson, London, 2000

Robert Byron, *The Road to Oxiana*, Pan Books, London, 1981

Bruce Chatwin, *What Am I Doing Here*, Pan Books, London, 1990

E. J. Chinnock (trans.), *The Anabasis of Alexander, Literally Translated with a Commentary from the Greek of Arrian*, The Nicomedian, Hodder & Stoughton, London, 1884

Brian Cloughley, *Nuclear Risk-Reduction Measures in Kashmir*, The Henry L. Stimson Center, Washington DC, 1998

Stephen Cohen, *The Pakistan Army*, Oxford University Press, Karachi, 1999

Marquess Curzon of Kedleston, *A Viceroy's India: Leaves from Lord Curzon's Note-book*, Sidgwick & Jackson, London, 1984

N. J. Dawood (trans.), *The Koran*, Penguin Books, Harmondsworth, 1974

Walter B. Denny, *Sotheby's Guide to Oriental Carpets*, Simon & Schuster, New York, 1994

Arthur Urbane Dilley, *Oriental Rugs and Carpets: A Comprehensive Study*, Scribner's, New York, 1931

Maud Diver, *The Judgment of the Sword*, John Murray, London, 1924

Louis Dupree, *Afghanistan*, Princeton University Press, Princeton, New Jersey, 1978

Nancy Hatch Dupree, *An Historical Guide to Afghanistan*, Afghan Tourist Organisation Publication, Kabul, 1977

Arthur Cecil Edwards, *The Persian Carpet: A Survey of the Carpet Weaving Industry*, Duckworth, London, 1953

Richard Ettinghausen, *Arab Painting*, Macmillan, London, 1977

Kurt Erdmann, *Seven Hundred Years of Oriental Rugs*, Faber & Faber, London, 1970

Jack Franses, *Tribal Rugs from Afghanistan and Turkestan*, handbook to exhibit at Franses of Piccadilly, Ditchling Press Ltd, London, 1973

E. Gans-Ruedin, *Antique Oriental Carpets from the Seventeenth to the Early 20th Century*, Thames & Hudson, London, 1975

Volkmar Gantzhorn, *Oriental Carpets*, Benedikt Taschen Verlag, Köln, 1998 (originally published as the thesis 'The Christian Oriental Carpet')

Roman Ghirshman, *Iran: From the Earliest Times to the Islamic Conquest*, Penguin, Harmondsworth, 1954

Paul Greenway and David St. Vincent, *Iran*, Lonely Planet, Australia, 1998

Hali magazine, London

Gavin Hambly, *Cities of Mughal India*, G. P. Putnam's Sons, New York, 1968

Janet Harvey, *Traditional Textiles of Central Asia*, Thames & Hudson, London, 1996

W. A. Hawley, *Oriental Rugs: Antique and Modern*, John Lane, London, 1913

Ann Hecht, *The Art of the Loom: Weaving, Spinning & Dyeing Across the World*, Rizzoli, New York, 1990

Holy Bible: The New King James Version, Thomas Nelson Inc, 1982; published by India Bible Literature, Madras

Kathleen Hopkirk, *Central Asia: A Traveller's Companion*, John Murray, London, 1993

Jenny Housego, *Tribal Rugs*, Scorpion, UK, 1991

Reinhard G. Hubel, *The Book of Carpets*, Katherine Watson (trans.), Barrie & Jenkins, London, 1971

Alastair Hull and Jose Luczyc-Wyhowska, *Kilim: The Complete Guide*, Thames & Hudson, London, 1993

Human Rights Commission of Pakistan, *State of Human Rights in 1999*, HRCP, Lahore, 2000

Samuel P. Huntington, *The Clash of Civilizations and the Remaking of the World Order*, Simon & Schuster, New York, 1996

International Crisis Group, *Central Asia: Fault Lines in the New Security Map?*, Osh/Brussels, 4 July 2000

Charles W. Jacobsen, *Oriental Rugs: A Complete Guide*, Charles E. Tuttle Publishers, Tokyo, 1962

Uwe Jourdan, *Oriental Rugs Vol. 5 — Turkoman*, Battenberg Verlag, Ausburg, 1989

Manoj Joshi, *The Lost Rebellion: Kashmir in the Nineties*, Penguin Books India, New Delhi, 1999

The Kargil Review Committee, *From Surprise to Reckoning: The Kargil Review Committee Report*, Sage Publications, New Delhi, 1999

Omar Khayyam, Edward Fitzgerald (trans.), *Rubaiyat of Omar Khayyam*, Atelie Honar, M. Salashoor, Tehran, no date

Maulana Wahiduddin Khan, *Islam and Peace*, Goodword Books, New Delhi, 1999

Mohammed Khatami, *Islam, Liberty and Development*, Institute for Global Cultural Studies, Binghamton University, 1999

John King, John Noble and Andrew Humphreys, *Central Asia*, Lonely Planet, Melbourne, 1996

Robert Koldewey, *The Excavations at Babylon*, Macmillan & Co., London, 1914

Manuel Komroff (ed.), *The Travels of Marco Polo (The Venetian)*, Horace Liveright, New York, 1926

Louise W. Mackie and Jon Thompson, *Turkmen*, The Textile Museum, Washington DC, 1980

Frank MacShane, *Many Golden Ages: Ruins, Temples and Monuments of the Orient*, Charles E. Tuttle, Rutland, Virginia, 1962

William Maley (ed.), *Fundamentalism Reborn?*, Hurst & Company, London, 1998

Robert McNeal, *Carpet of Death*, Robert Hale, London, 1976

Bruce M. Metzger and Michael Coogan, *The Oxford Companion to the Bible*, Oxford University Press, New York, 1993

Peter Marsden, *The Taliban: War, Religion and the New Order in Afghanistan*, Oxford University Press, Karachi, 1998

P. Masson-Oursel and Louise Morin (contributors), *New Larousse Encyclopedia of Mythology*, Hamlyn, Middlesex, 1959

Roland and Sabrina Michaud, *Afghanistan*, Vendome Press, New York, 1980

—— *Horsemen of Afghanistan*, Thames & Hudson, London, 1988

Andrew Middleton, *Rugs & Carpets: Techniques, Traditions & Designs*, Mitchell Beazley, London, 1996

Enza Milanesi, *The Carpet: An Illustrated Guide to the Rugs and Kilims of the World*, I.B. Tauris Press, New York, 1999

Geoffrey Moorhouse, *To the Frontier*, Sceptre, London, 1988

Oriental Rug Society of New South Wales Newsletter, Sydney

James Morier, *The Adventures of Hajji Baba of Ispahan*, Oxford University Press, London, 1824

Bernadotte Perrin (trans.), *Plutarch's Lives*, 11 Vols, William Heinemann, London, 1919

Major Henry George Raverty, *Notes on Afghanistan and Baluchistan* (1878), Abid Bokhari, Quetta, 1976

Saeed Rahnema and Sohrab Behdad, *Iran After the Revolution: Crisis of an Islamic State*, I.B. Tauris Press, London, 1995

Ahmed Rashid, *The Resurgence of Central Asia: Islam or Nationalism?*, Oxford University Press, Karachi, 1994

—— *Taliban: Islam, Oil and the New Great Game in Central Asia*, I.B. Tauris Press, London, 2000

David Talbot Rice, *Islamic Art*, Thames & Hudson, London, 1986

Captain J. A. Robinson, *Notes on Nomad Tribes of Eastern Afghanistan*, Nisa Traders, Quetta, 1980

Michael Rogers, *The Spread of Islam: The Making of the Past*, Elsevier-Phaidon, New York, 1976

Olivier Roy, *Islam and Resistance in Afghanistan*, Cambridge
     University Press, Cambridge, 1986
Salman Rushdie, *Imaginary Homelands: Essays and Criticism 1981–91*,
     Granta Books, London, 1992
Edward W. Said, *Orientalism*, Penguin, London, 1978
—— *Covering Islam*, Random House, New York, 1997
Idries Shah, *The Sufis*, Doubleday, New York, 1964
Sirdar Ikbal Ali Shah, *Afghanistan of the Afghans*, Octagon Press,
     London, 1982
Audrey Shalinsky, *Long Years of Exile*, University Press of America,
     New York, 1994
Desmond Stewart (ed.), *Turkey*, Time Inc., New York, 1965
Parvis Tanavoli, *The Tacheh of Chahar Mahal*, Yazssavol Publications,
     Tehran, 1998
Jon Thompson and Louise W. Mackie, *Turkmen Tribal Carpets and
     Traditions*, Washington, 1980
United Nations Food and Agricultural Organisation, Afghanistan,
     Preliminary Survey of Kuchi Nomads, 1998
Benjamin Walker, *Foundations of Islam: The Making of a World Faith*,
     HarperCollins India, New Delhi, 1999
Daniel S. Walker, *Oriental Rugs of the Hajji Babas*, Thames &
     Hudson, London, 1982
Gordon Redford Walker, *Oriental Rugs: An Introduction*, Prion,
     London, 1999
Nazneen Zafar, *A Practical Guide to Pakistani Rugs*, Liberty Books,
     Karachi, 1992

Glossary

abrash — change in tone or intensity of colour of a textile not
    relating to the design, caused by inconsistent colour of yarn used

Afghani — Afghan currency unit

Amu Darya — river which forms the northern border of
    Afghanistan, known to the ancient Greeks as the Oxus

arabesque — repetitive interlaced floral pattern

Arg — citadel

As'salaam aleikum — 'Peace be upon you', a common Islamic
    greeting

babushka — elderly Russian woman

baksheesh — tip

balay (Persian) — yes

bandh (subcontinent) — general strike

beg — Central Asian tribal leader

bidi (India) — rolled tobacco-leaf cigarette

boteh — ancient textile motif commercially known as 'Paisley'

brocading — weaving technique which produces a raised pattern
    on the surface of a flatwoven textile

buzkashi — Afghan equestrian game played with a headless goat or calf

caliph — supreme head of the Muslim community, combining
    political and religious authority

caravanserai — traditional inn for travellers

cartoon — textile design illustrated on paper

cartouche — panel on a textile containing inscription or motif *chaderi* — Afghan version of the *chador, burqa* or veil covering a woman's face and body

chai — tea

chaikhana (Afghanistan) or *chaikhune* (Iran) — teahouse

chapan — long coat

chappals or *chappli* (Kashmir) — sandals

charpoy — rope cot or bedstead

chooti (India and Pakistan) — holiday

chowk — crossroads

chowkidar (India and Pakistan) — caretaker or watchman

Dari — dialect of Persian spoken in Afghanistan

dervish or *qalandar* — wandering follower of Sufi Islam

dhurry, dhurries (pl.) — cotton flatweave rug

dragoman — guide/interpreter

dupatta — scarf covering a woman's hair

Eid ul-Fitr — feast which concludes fasting month of Ramadan

Eid al-Adha — Feast of Sacrifice, commemorating the sacrifice of Ibrahim

emir — ruler

falooda — milk-based dessert topping containing vermicelli and rose syrup

farsh (Persian) — knotted carpet

fatwa — ruling of religious jurist

filpai — literally 'Elephant's Foot', term used to describe *gulli gul* octagonal carpet design

flatweave — rug made without knotted pile, as in *kilim* and *soumaq*

gilam jam (colloq. Afghanistan) — 'carpet thief'

godown — storeroom or warehouse

gujjar — nomad pastoralist of northern India and Afghanistan

gul — literally 'flower' in Persian, refers to stylised flower heads or medallions of Turkmen weaving

gurdwara — Sikh temple

Hadith — code of conduct based on sayings attributed to the Prophet Mohammed, second only to the Koran *hafiz* — person who knows the Koran by heart

hajj, Hajji — the pilgrimage to Mecca, one who makes it

handle — the feel of a rug, especially relating to stiffness or flexibility

haram — impure to Muslims

hejab — code of modest dress for Muslim women

Heijira — Mohammed's flight from Mecca to Medina in 622 AD, first month of the Muslim calendar

hijra (Urdu, Pakistan) — hermaphrodite, transsexual

Imam — Muslim prayer leader

Insh'allah — God willing

jang — war

jamavar — woven woollen scarf heavily brocaded in silk or pashmina wool

jawan — Indian soldier

jihad, *jihadi* — striving to be a good Muslim or holy war to defend Islam, person who engages in these activities

jirga — tribal council or decision-making assembly

juval or *chuval* — bag woven by Turkmens for storing or transporting household goods

Kaaba — focal point of Muslim holy shrine at Mecca, which traditions say was built by Ibrahim

kaffir — infidel, one who does not subscribe to the Koran

kangri (Kashmir) — wicker basket containing a clay firepot, filled with charcoal and worn under a cloak, acts as a personal warmer

kawa (Kashmir) — green tea

khan — Pashtun tribal chief or landlord, now a common surname

khordjin — double saddlebags or paniers used on a donkey, camel or horse

kilim — rug without knotted pile

kohl — powdered antimony, precursor of mascara

Koran — the sacred book of Islam

Kuchi — Pashto-speaking nomadic pastoralist

kurta — man's overshirt

lashkar — tribal military force, now also denotes small, highly mobile military unit

madrassa — Islamic religious school

mafrash — box-shaped woven storage bag for bedding and clothing (some say a small Turkmen tent bag)

magus, magi (pl.) — hereditary priest of ancient Medes and Persians, three wise men of Bible story

maidan — open space in a town or village, usually a field or square

mandir — Hindu temple

masjid — mosque

masturbah — ledge, usually elevated and made of stone of a bazaar stall

maulava (Urdu, Pakistan) — master, teacher

maulvi — Muslim religious man

mazar — mausoleum

mihrab — prayer niche in mosque facing Mecca, carpet design imitating this

minaret — tower of mosque from which the call to prayer is announced

Moghul — Indian ruling dynasty founded by Babur, a Turk from Uzbekistan

mohajir — migrant or refugee for religious reasons, Muslims who left India at Partition

Moharram — commemoration of martyrdom of Hussain

muezzin — cleric who announces the call to prayer

mujahid, mujahideen (pl.) — religious warrior fighting holy war

mullah — man of religious knowledge

namaz — Muslim prayer

nan — unleavened bread

pakhool — woollen beret worn in many parts of Afghanistan and Pakistan

palmette — floral design with radiating lobes and petals

pandit — Kashmiri Hindu Brahmin

pashm, pashmina — fine soft wool from Himalayan mountain goat used in shawls and sometimes carpets

patka (Punjabi, Gurmukhi) — head scarf under turban

pheran (Kashmir) — woollen cloak

pulao — rice cooked with meat and vegetables

purdah — cover, curtain or screen used to separate women or men

puri (India) — fried bread

pashtunwali — code of traditional rights and obligations of the Pashtuns

qalian (Persian) — smoker's water pipe

qazi — judge or law officer in Islamic societies

qibla — direction of Mecca

Raj — British Empire in India

Ramazan (subcontinent) or *Ramadan* (Middle East) — Muslim month of fasting, ninth month of Muslim calendar

rebob — stringed musical instrument from Afghanistan

runner — long, narrow carpet or kilim used in halls and corridors

salwar kameez — flowing cotton pants and overshirt of same colour and material

samovar (Afghanistan) — vessel for making tea, teahouse

Sayyid — descendant of the Prophet Mohammed

selvedge — outer warps braided to strengthen sides of a rug

serai — resting place

shaheed — martyr fallen in combat

shamiana (Urdu, Pakistan) — large tent or open-sided structure for meeting or entertaining

Shari'a, Shari'at — Islamic jurisprudence based on the Koran, code based on it

Shia — Muslim sect which recognises Ali as Mohammed's successor

shikara (Kashmir) — gondola or canoe

shisha (Arabic) — smoker's water pipe

shuttle — stick holding weft thread

slit-weave — vertical slits which occur in kilims where colour changes

souk — market or bazaar

soumak — weaving technique in which wefts are wrapped around each warp

Sufism, Sufi — Islamic mystical and ascetic doctrine, person who follows it

Sunnah — Sunni Muslim legal code based on the Koran and Hadith

Sunni — Orthodox Muslim

Sura — Koranic verse

talib — religious student

Talib — member of the Taliban

Taliban — fundamentalist Islamic movement which governed most of Afghanistan from 1996 to 2001

talim — writer of coded 'script' containing knotting instructions for weavers

tandoor — oven

Tashakour (Persian) — 'Thank you'

tiffin (India) — food or light meal, especially one taken at midday

tikka or *tilak* — paste, usually of red lead or sandalwood, applied for ceremonial purposes to objects or the body, especially the forehead

tonga — horse-drawn carriage

torba — a small woven bag used by Turkmens to store personal effects

ulema — body comprising religious authorities

ummah — the global community of Muslims

wallah — salesman or service provider, as in carpet *wallah*, shikara *wallah*

warp — foundation of a carpet consisting of threads of yarn running vertically

weft — lengths of yarn running over and under the warp at right angles

yakhni — mutton served as stew, roast or pulao

zakat — tax in Islamic countries

Timeline

FEBRUARY 1979	Islamic revolution in Iran
JULY 1979	Saddam Hussein seizes presidency of Iraq
DECEMBER 1979	Soviet invasion of Afghanistan
SEPTEMBER 1980	Iraq invades Iran
MAY 1986	Mohammed Najibullah becomes president of Afghanistan
JULY 1988	Kashmir uprising begins
FEBRUARY 1989	Soviet Army withdraws from Afghanistan
AUGUST 1990	Iraq invades Kuwait
AUGUST 1991	Soviet Union collapses, end of Cold War
APRIL 1992	Mujahideen rebels seize Kabul
SEPTEMBER 1996	Taliban militia seize Kabul, execute Najibullah
MAY 1997	Taliban briefly occupy Mazar-e Sharif, driven out
MAY 1997	Mohammed Khatami elected president of Iran
MAY 1998	India and Pakistan test nuclear weapons
AUGUST 1998	Taliban capture Mazar-e Sharif; United States embassies in Africa bombed; US Tomahawk cruise missile attacks on Afghanistan
DECEMBER 1998	US–British Operation Desert Fox attacks on Iraq
MAY 1999	Indian and Pakistani forces fight ten-week war in Kashmir

NOVEMBER 1999	United Nations Security Council imposes sanctions on Afghanistan
APRIL 2001	Taliban militia destroy Buddhist monoliths in Bamiyan, Afghanistan
JUNE 2001	President Khatami re-elected in Iran
SEPTEMBER 2001	Ahmad Shah Massoud assassinated by Arab suicide bombers posing as journalists; hijacked airliners crash into the World Trade Centre and the Pentagon, murdering up to four thousand civilians
OCTOBER 2001	US-led coalition begins sustained bombing and invasion of Afghanistan to destroy Osama bin Laden's Al-Qa'ida network and remove the Taliban from power
NOVEMBER 2001	Taliban abandon Kabul, Mazar-e Sharif, Jalalabad, Herat, Taloqan and other main cities; replaced by United Front and tribal leaders
DECEMBER 2001	Taliban abandon Kandahar; Mullah Mohammed Omar and Osama bin Laden still at large; Afghan factions meeting in Germany agree to form an interim government and to allow an international peacekeeping force to provide security in Kabul
JANUARY 2002	Minister in Afghan interim ruling council says the new government intends rebuilding the Bamiyan Buddhas with foreign aid

Index

Picture Credits

About the Author

Born in Sydney, Australia, in 1958, Christopher Kremmer has spent the past decade exploring Asia and writing about it for print and broadcast media. His award-winning first book, *Stalking the Elephant Kings*, unearthed the skeletons of communist rule in South-East Asia.

PHOTO COURTESY OF CHRISTOPHER KREMMER